Ride, Boldly Ride

The publisher gratefully acknowledges the generous support of the Ahmanson Foundation Humanities Endowment Fund of the University of California Press Foundation.

Ride, Boldly Ride

The Evolution of the American Western

Mary Lea Bandy and
Kevin Stoehr

UNIVERSITY OF CALIFORNIA PRESS
Berkeley · Los Angeles · London

University of California Press, one of the most
distinguished university presses in the United States,
enriches lives around the world by advancing
scholarship in the humanities, social sciences, and
natural sciences. Its activities are supported by the UC
Press Foundation and by philanthropic contributions
from individuals and institutions. For more information, visit www.ucpress.edu.

University of California Press
Berkeley and Los Angeles, California
University of California Press, Ltd.
London, England

Library of Congress Cataloging-in-Publication Data

Bandy, Mary Lea.
    Ride, boldly ride : the evolution of the American
western / Mary Lea Bandy and Kevin Stoehr.
        p.   cm.
    Includes bibliographical references and index.
    ISBN 978-0-520-25866-2 (cloth : alk. paper)
    1. Western films—United States—History and
criticism.   I. Stoehr, Kevin, 1967–.   II. Title.
    PN1995.9.W4B255   2012
    791.436'278—dc23
                                                2012014955

Manufactured in the United States of America

20   19   18   17   16   15   14   13   12
10   9   8   7   6   5   4   3   2   1

In keeping with a commitment to support environmen-
tally responsible and sustainable printing practices, UC
Press has printed this book on Rolland Enviro100, a
100% postconsumer fiber paper that is FSC certified,
deinked, processed chlorine-free, and manufactured
with renewable biogas energy. It is acid-free and
EcoLogo certified.

Contents

Illustrations

Acknowledgments

Ride, Boldly Ride: The Evolution of the American Western grew out of a suggestion by Glenn Lowry, director of the Museum of Modern Art in New York. At the turn of the millennium, he asked the chiefs of the museum's six curatorial departments to contribute a book of studies about their respective collections. I eagerly grasped this opportunity to tell a story of the Western in American cinema, about cowboys and ranchers and new citizens of the West who were creating settlements in magnificent landscapes—never mind the occupation by tribes of Indians who were there first.

I am indebted to Charles Silver, director of the Film Study Center at the Museum of Modern Art, who helped me to discover much of the history of the art of cinema; to Film Department curator Laurence Kardish, an invaluable colleague, for his advice and support; to film curatorial assistant Jenny He, who had assisted in selecting film stills to accompany the text; to Katie Trainor, film collections manager, for her help with additional stills; and to Harriet Bee for her friendship and editorial advice. I give special thanks to Clint Eastwood for contributing the foreword to this book, and most of all to my husband, Gary, for his continual advice, support, and criticism. Finally, I am grateful for the many Hollywood filmmakers who have created one of America's richest forms of cinematic art.

—*Mary Lea Bandy*

I express my gratitude to Kenneth Loving, Loretta Stoehr, Mark Griffin, and Charles Silver for their support and encouragement. Thanks must be given to the late Bruce Ricker, too, for his help with various aspects of this project. I also give special thanks to Mary Francis, our editor at University of California Press, and Ellen Geiger, vice president and senior agent at the Frances Goldin Literary Agency, who have stood faithfully by this project since its inception.

—*Kevin Stoehr*

Foreword

Most filmmakers tend to be devoted to movie history. Any new motion picture with serious intentions provides an opportunity for a director to respond to cinematic traditions, whether reverentially or critically. For example, the first major Western in which I was featured, *A Fistful of Dollars,* was a remake of Akira Kurosawa's *Yojimbo,* which was in turn a playful parody of Kurosawa's own earlier samurai films. Like most members of the cinematic community, I have always taken pleasure in exploring connections and chains of influence like these.

I also recognize influences in my own work. I dedicated *Unforgiven* to a pair of filmmakers who had some effect on my early years of directing: Sergio Leone and Don Siegel. Growing up, I experienced many of the classic Western films by the likes of John Ford, Howard Hawks, William Wellman, and Anthony Mann—and watched quite a few of the not-so-great Westerns to boot. When a Western movie is done right, with the passionate commitment of everyone involved, it rises above mere entertainment or spectacle.

The genre has outlasted the critics who have predicted its demise ever since D. W. Griffith directed his one-reel "oaters." But the public's recognition of the Western movie as a genuine art form was a long time coming, and it helped that the right people lent a hand in making that acknowledgement clear. Mary Lea Bandy is one of those individuals, and I got to know her when the Museum of Modern Art began programming screenings and retrospectives of my films, starting in the early

1980s. Mary Lea also worked with Bruce Ricker in coproducing the documentary *Clint Eastwood: Out of the Shadows.*

Countless pages have been written about the Western film over the years. But often these books and essays, while dealing with plots and actors and directors, do not explain why these movies, or at least the best of them, belong to a genuine art form. *Ride, Boldly Ride* offers such an appreciation. Many of the films discussed here have a powerful effect on viewers, not only because of the acting performances and directorial styles, but also because their stories revolve around themes of violence and tragic loss, and because their images reveal the beauties and challenges of the natural landscape. In addition, the best Westerns offer a feeling of adventure and exhibit a visual tempo that is not unlike musical composition.

Mary Lea's book draws the reader's attention to some of the Western films that have been underappreciated or that do not neatly correspond with rigid definitions of the genre. While there is much that we can learn here about classics like *Stagecoach* and *Red River,* the book also pays tribute to such movies as *3 Bad Men, The Wind, The Big Trail, Ruggles of Red Gap, The Westerner, Northwest Passage, Jubal,* and *Comanche Station.* With movies like these, it is clear that the Western film has a broad and rich history, one in which I am proud to have played a role.

—*Clint Eastwood*

Introduction

[Anthony Mann on the Western]: Well, I think the reason why it's the most popular and long-lasting genre is that it gives you more freedom of action, in landscape, in passion. It's a primitive form. It's not governed by rule; you can do anything with it. It has the essential pictorial qualities; has the guts of any character you want; the violence of anything you need; the sweep of anything you feel; the joy of sheer exercise, of outdoorness. It is legend—and legend makes the very best cinema. It excites the imagination more—it's something audiences love. They don't have to say: "Oh, I know about that"; they just need to feel it and be with it, because legend is a concept of characters greater than life. It releases you from inhibitions, rules. . . . And this is what the Western does—it releases you, you can ride on the plains; you can capture the windswept skies; you can release your audiences and take them out to places which they never would have dreamt of. . . . And, more important—it releases the characters. They can be more primitive; they can be more Greek, like *Oedipus Rex* or *Antigone,* you see, because you are dealing again in a sweeping legend.[1]

[Kenneth Turan interviewing Clint Eastwood]: What is it about the Western that makes it so resilient?

[Eastwood]: I guess because of the simplicity of the times. Now everything's so complicated, so mired down in bureaucracy that people can't fathom a way of sorting it out. In the West, even though you could be killed, it seems more manageable, like a lone individual might be able to work things out some way. In our society today, the idea of one person making a difference one way or the other is remote.[2]

The cinematic tradition of the Western is a complex, collective memory and, on close viewing, no more nostalgic for the good old days than Jane Austen's novels are sweetly romantic. Aside from a sense of adventurous freedom, an emphasis on the natural landscape, and a fusion of history and myth, what retains our interest throughout these seemingly repetitive Western sagas is the westerner himself, a character dear to us for his psyche and his physique. The invader and defender of western territories required great strength, courage, endurance, quickness, and strategic intelligence. The Western protagonist might not talk quite as much or as wittily as Henry V or Cary Grant, but that is because he is listening and thinking and feeling. Like a detective, he relies heavily on his intuition but sometimes has to figure out what really is going on, distinguishing the truth from the lies. He has to contend with the rustler, the card shark, the thief, the murderer, and the gunfighter that the wealthier villain hires to do his dirty work. On top of all this, as if greedy villains are not enough of a challenge, there are the Indians who fight with ferocity and know the meaning of sacrifice.

The leading protagonist of the Western is pretty sure to be a man, but not a kindly, upright sort of guy. Heroic in a classical sense, he is a courageous, fit, and active type, eager for adventure or plagued by it, a personality formed by adversity and challenge, as wily and selfish as any of his Homeric or Virgilian predecessors who were teased by the Olympian gods. Cowpoke or gunfighter, he can ride like the wind and rope a horse or steer at a hundred yards. He is likely to be a "good bad man," the character conceived and formed in the second decade of the twentieth century by Broncho Billy Anderson, William S. Hart, and Harry Carey Sr. This character often has a revelation at some point in the plot and sees the errors of his ways, or is blinded by the goodness and purity of the heroine and, by the final reel, undoes the mischief he and his friends have caused. He can serve as easily as sheriff or hired gun, pursuer or pursued, until the real villains are unmasked.

The westerner's instincts, it has been made clear to us in many an opening scene, are superb: he knows what to do, which usually means going considerably beyond assumed limits. More important, his character is fixed before he encounters the challenges of the script, for no westerner grows up on the screen. Faced with evil and danger, he might wake up, give up, try to atone, or revise his commitment to the bad guys (or occasionally bad gals), but in his case the child is certainly father to the man. His disposition is a given, which is why we admire our cowboy hero. We know that he has grown up in this landscape before the story takes place: *we* are seeing it for the first time, but it is understood that our youthful or aging cowboy knows his way around every sagebrush and arroyo. He sleeps anytime and anywhere, with a saddle and horse blanket for bedding, rides as easily in the dark as at dawn, and can expertly spot smoke signals or just "git a feelin'" for trouble that will arise in the narrow rocky canyon ahead.

Essential to the figure of the westerner is his weapon. Whether he carries a six-shooter or a rifle, Colt or Winchester, every man of the West has mastered the use of a gun or has bought control of those who have. The knife and the bow and arrow are powerless to overcome such armaments, and native tribes have learned to trade and handle the West's most effective portable enforcer. Good guy or outlaw, the westerner is, or has been, a gunfighter. Killing and avoiding being killed are, or were, his principal activities—not just the climactic scenes or the denouement, but the stuff of everyday Western life. This was how the real Old West was settled, through violence, as raw frontier became territory, and then territory gained statehood, taking along with it various practices and prejudices that were transmitted into law. Justice and moral order were imposed and dispensed by strong, courageous men who used violence to fight violence.[3] To be an effective lawman, the Hollywood westerner must likewise have the cunning and skills of the warrior, and that is why he often is a southerner who learned his trade and honed his skills in the brutal training ground of the Civil War. As Robert Warshow tells us in his influential essay "Movie Chronicle: The Westerner" regarding this solitary, reposed figure and his willingness to use violence when needed: "There is no suggestion . . . that he [the westerner] draws the gun reluctantly. The Westerner could not fulfill himself if the moment did not finally come when he can shoot his enemy down. But because that moment is so thoroughly the expression of his being, it must be kept pure."[4]

The Western introduces the fixed character of its principal protagonist without necessarily filling us in on details of his past but instead following his actions and reactions to events and situations and landscapes. It is not so much that our hero always improves his moral character by enduring life-threatening crises as that we come to understand him better. He might be exhausted by the end, or wounded, or dead. He might have sought and achieved revenge, at no little price, and after it is all over he might be as bitter and alone as at the start. He wants to *survive*, not necessarily to triumph, and on his own terms. Cole Thornton, the gunfighter played by John Wayne in Howard Hawks's *El Dorado*, points out to James Caan's youthful character, Mississippi: "Ride, boldly ride? Well, it don't work out that way." Western life is too contradictory, too difficult to always have a happy ending, but some recognition and knowledge of the contradictions and difficulties might be gained. In the end, as in the mythical tales of the medieval knight, the story of the westerner is in many cases a story about a journey through landscape and reality toward the goal of self-knowledge. And along the way there is almost always a need to struggle for survival and to fight against others.

And what is the fight all about? In most instances, it is about control of the land, land for the white man's community to tame, nurture, and establish as homestead and town. It is about taking from the earth its riches, its gold and silver, its trees and beavers and buffalo—about making the land yield itself to human desire. And, as important as the land itself, there is the essential resource of water, along with the rights governing its usage. No matter how learned he might be in the ways of the West, no westerner can guarantee a supply of water. And water is also possibly the most elusive and treacherous element in the larger landscape. Rivers have to be crossed, and their rushing currents can destroy wagons as well as drown cattle, horses, and men; they might erupt in flash floods or dry up; riverbeds might cause animals to mire in mud or quicksand. Watering holes might disappear, become poisonous, or be ruined by users too stupid, careless, or vengeful to care about the consequences. Drought kills, but heavy rains, followed by a sudden burst of cold weather, can turn steers' hides to icy sheets and cause grass to become brittle and inedible. Deep snow might fall at the wrong time, preventing passage or freezing cattle, sometimes burying families beneath avalanches. The scarcity of water is as dangerous as an Indian war party, and the two often occur together to destroy, or at least impede, the white man's progress.

The Western hero helps to fight the good fight, but he is hardly ever a successful and settled landowner. Nor does he usually want to settle down before the credits fade. He is typically a loner, passing through, unwed and unencumbered by family and responsibility. On occasion, if he survives his troubles on the range or in the dusty streets of Dodge City or Tombstone, his gal will throw a rope around him and he will think about becoming respectable. This, at least, is the scenario established by Owen Wister's *The Virginian,* which set the character of the Western hero: a slightly less than good man, a southerner turned westerner, laconic and handsome, smarter and stronger and faster on the draw than everyone else, and pestered by an ornery cuss who tempts his best but weaker-willed friend to go over to the wrong side of the law.

The law, not incidentally, is the law of the land—not necessarily the federal law of the United States but the code of the newly created territory, imposed at will by settlers or often-corrupt sheriffs or judges and enforced by posses or vigilantes. We rarely see shelves full of law books in Western courts, which are usually set up temporarily in the saloon, the judge having suspended drinking during the trial. The Declaration of Independence may be the code of ethics behind this territorial will, but the Bible is the most visible text in Westerns, followed by the handbill. Absent a unified legal structure, justice and its dispensation are quick on the trigger. Thus the Virginian hangs his best friend, Steve, and two others for rustling—no trial, just hang 'em the next morning, and let a supporting character explain to the confused heroine, Molly, why this is what a man has to do.

Western screenplays derived from novels and short stories, including those published by popular presses, more often than from newspaper or journal accounts or historical records. It is not that filmmakers rejected history or realism, but that they were enticed by legend and therefore blended mythmaking with a manufactured sense of authenticity. The myth *is* the reality, as was famously proclaimed in John Ford's *The Man Who Shot Liberty Valance:* "When the legend becomes fact, print the legend." Scripts utilized actual events, people, and places, both to legitimize the fictional narrative in an historical framework and to give some pretense of remaining faithful to that history. Various films accomplished this pretense simply and efficiently by printing a specific place and date over the shot that follows the opening credits, such as "Texas, 1868," which introduces Ford's *The Searchers,* despite the fact that the film was shot mainly in Monument Valley on the border between Utah and Arizona.

And so, through Westerns, filmmakers reflected creatively on America's social and political history. Some, like Ford and William S. Hart in the first half of the century, earnestly mixed historical realism and patriotism, however populist in flavor. Filmmakers such as Fred Zinnemann (*High Noon*) and Arthur Penn (*Little Big Man, The Missouri Breaks*) later used Western themes metaphorically to represent current political or cultural preoccupations. The more intellectually challenging Westerns tended to interpret American history freely—especially the actions of its law keepers and its outlaws—so as to arrive at larger moral truths. Westerns have always managed to combine apparent "material" accuracy—a concern with specific facts about a given event or series of events, or at the very least a semblance of concern with such facts—with a kind of "discursive" accuracy that conveys the overall *meaning* and *significance* of such events.[5] This is not so much a difference between truth and myth as a distinction between the factual truths of history and the ways in which those "truths" have become conveyed in narrative form, especially in a form that has a meaningful impact on us. But whether it veers toward realism or symbolism, the Western film helps to tell a story, usually more than a merely superficial one, about what it means to be—and what it took to become—an *American*.

History is inevitably mixed with tragedy, and the story of America's westward expansionism is also the story of the frequent suffering and loss experienced by pioneering settlers, by townspeople attempting to build structured communities in the middle of the wilderness, and by those displaced natives who were forced to make way for the railroads and the civilization-builders. The narratives of several landmark Western films discussed at length in this book deal with tragic suffering and a sense of loss: Victor Sjöström's *The Wind,* Howard Hawks's *Red River,* John Ford's *The Searchers* and *The Man Who Shot Liberty Valance,* and Clint Eastwood's *The Outlaw Josey Wales* and *Unforgiven.* On the other hand, many of the great Western films have managed to maintain a balance between tragedy and comedy, and some Westerns tend toward being purely comical. The Western comedy should certainly not be overlooked as an essential component of the genre, and one enlightening example is *Ruggles of Red Gap* with Charles Laughton.

Several of the films selected for focused examination here have not been traditionally included or emphasized in other surveys of the Western. *The Wind* and *Ruggles of Red Gap,* for example, are almost always ignored, and yet they not only contain basic elements of the genre but also stretch and mold the parameters of the Western in intriguing and unique ways. Essential classics such as Ford's *Stagecoach* must, of course, be accorded their due as standard-setters. But not enough attention has previously been paid—beyond books that address Ford's entire body of work—to his silent feature Westerns *Straight Shooting* and *3 Bad Men.* These early but nonetheless impressive films are addressed here within the wider context of other silent Westerns, such as D. W. Griffith's pioneering Biograph Westerns, Thomas Ince's and Francis Ford's early trailblazers *The Invaders* and *Custer's Last Fight,* William Hart's *Hell's Hinges,* and James Cruze's *The Covered Wagon.*

At the time of the release of Ford's landmark Western *Stagecoach* in 1939, Hollywood was just beginning a renaissance of "A-Westerns" that filled the landscape of American cinema in a prominent fashion until the nation became fully engaged in World War II and war films began to predominate. These Westerns included, in addition to *Stagecoach,* Cecil B. DeMille's *Union Pacific,* Henry King's *Jesse James,* Michael Curtiz's trio of *Dodge City, Virginia City,* and *Santa Fe Trail,* Fritz Lang's *The Return of Frank James,* Wesley Ruggles's *Arizona,* and Raoul Walsh's *They Died with Their Boots On.* It was Walsh who directed one of the first big-budget A-Westerns of the 1930s, just after the end of the silent era: *The Big Trail,* an epic story of frontier survival and settlement that, along with Wesley Ruggles's *Cimarron,* harkened back to Cruze's *The Covered Wagon* and also anticipated such later prairie schooner sagas as Ford's *Wagon Master.* A detailed look at the 1939–1941 A-Western is offered here, including a focus on two underappreciated examples: William Wyler's *The Westerner* and King Vidor's *Northwest Passage.*

The immediate post–World War II era ushered in a series of visually and psychologically expressive Westerns that included Vidor's *Duel in the Sun,* Ford's *My Darling Clementine,* Walsh's *Pursued,* and Hawks's *Red River.* We pay special attention to the latter film within the wider context of Hawks's recurring collaborations with John Wayne. Postwar movies such as *Red River* led to the emergence of a kind of "super-Western" (to steal André Bazin's term), predominant in the 1950s. In these super-Westerns, conventional elements of the genre were fused with, or in some cases superseded by, themes and visual stylizations that were borrowed from other types of cinema, such as film noir. These movies—and especially those directed by Anthony Mann, Delmer Daves, and Budd Boetticher—tend to be psychologically complex and existentially charged, forging a path for the revisionist or even postmodern Westerns that were to follow in the 1960s and 1970s: Sam Peckinpah's *Ride the High Country* and *The Wild Bunch,* Robert Altman's *McCabe and Mrs. Miller,* and Penn's *Little Big Man*—to name but several.

In addition to exploring the mid-twentieth-century Western through a focus on selected movies by Mann, Daves, and Boetticher, we examine Ford's two later masterworks (*The Searchers* and *The Man Who Shot Liberty Valance*) in terms of their own profound ways of deepening and transforming the genre. Finally, we argue that Eastwood's Westerns serve as a fitting culmination of sorts, especially in their fusions of traditional and antitraditional elements and when appreciated in the wider context of the post-Fordian and post-Hawksian Western. This is especially true when one considers that Eastwood's major works either reflect or combine (always intriguingly so) two distinct modes of the genre, as a result of his earlier work with two influential filmmakers: the stylized, "operatic" Westerns of Sergio Leone and the character-oriented, narrative-driven Westerns of Don Siegel. Eastwood's masterpiece *Unforgiven,* most especially, blends the best aspects of the traditional *and* antitraditional Western.

Not surprisingly, the post-*Unforgiven* world of the movie oater is a world in which the distinction between the classical and postclassical conceptions of the Western has become antiquated. Works of this period range from the more conventional (e.g., Kevin Costner's *Open Range,* Ed Harris's *Appaloosa,* and Joel and Ethan Coens' remake of *True Grit*) to those that radically integrate genre elements (e.g., Jim Jarmusch's *Dead Man,* Paul Thomas Anderson's *There Will Be Blood,* and the Coen brothers' *No Country for Old Men*). The Western film has indeed become a kind of territory that is defined by borders and boundaries regularly crossed in dialectical fashion, a cinematic terrain in which the adventure of the genre includes the essential task of modifying and amplifying what has gone before. It is not that the traditional Western has been negated and thereby transcended by its ongoing transformations; rather, it has been integrated into a realm of highly creative and self-conscious reverence.

CHAPTER I

Diverse Perspectives in Silent Westerns

Landscape, Morality, and the Native American

The movie "oater" was born during the last decade of the nineteenth century, as the world of cinema was first emerging and around the time that the American West was closing its final frontiers. In the decades between the Civil War and World War I, by which time the territories of Arizona and New Mexico had been granted statehood, the nation could savor a nostalgia for a fading frontier while hearing news of the actual dangers of its concluding scenes. One could traverse the continent on the Southern Pacific in the 1880s, riding through territory not far from where the escaped Apache leader Geronimo was holed up in the Chiricahua Mountains. Or one could read of daring journeys, thanks to the new publication venture of inexpensive paperbacks known as dime novels, which had appeared as early as the 1860s in a series brought out by Erastus Beadle, appealing to a mass audience eager to enjoy adventures of outlaws and cowboys. Edward Judson, who wrote under the pen name Ned Buntline, was the best-known dime novelist. On the stage, a national celebration of the taming of the wilderness was initiated in the 1880s, in typical American style, as a form of highly successful commercial exploitation by some of those who had played key roles at historic moments. William "Buffalo Bill" Cody, a former chief scout for the U.S. Cavalry, famously launched the story of the Wild West as a form of live spectacle that included representations of Custer's Last Stand and appearances by Sitting Bull.

Live spectacle soon became filmed spectacle. American history and the American cinema were inevitably fused, especially when it came to depictions of the post–Civil War Old West. Among early film documentaries were Edison's 1894 recordings of reenacted scenes from Buffalo Bill's Wild West show, including quick glimpses of a Native American buffalo dance, a sharpshooting demonstration by Annie Oakley, and in the case of *Bucking Broncho,* a cowboy's horse-riding demonstration before a group of entertained spectators. In 1902 the popularity of the Western surged with a novel about a lonesome cowboy, *The Virginian,* by Owen Wister. It became an instant best seller, and this was followed in 1903 by Edwin S. Porter's movie *The Great Train Robbery.* Shot at Edison's New York studio and in New Jersey along the Lackawanna Railway, the eleven-minute-film created an illusion of reality. A violent robbery takes place aboard a seemingly moving train, an effect created by intercutting studio shots with matte shots of the passing landscape, the exteriors of the moving train, and later the escape and chase of the robbers. The shot of a gunman firing directly at the audience, the bright colors tinting the puffs of gun smoke, and the strongbox's explosion all added to the film's broad appeal.

The year 1904 witnessed the release of Biograph's *Cowboy Justice,* along with Edison shorts such as *Brush between Cowboys and Indians, Western Stage Coach Hold Up,* and *The Little Train Robbery,* a follow-up parody of the film company's earlier success. These early silent productions contained many of the elements that would be repeated throughout Western movies for decades to come: bold adventure, broad humor, impressive horse riding, outdoor-location shooting, and violent conflicts.[1] By 1909, the genre had come to dominate the American film market, and Western films were being produced in great numbers to satisfy public demand. In his informative book *Shooting Cowboys and Indians: Silent Western Films, American Culture, and the Birth of Hollywood,* Andrew Brodie Smith details the process by which early Western movie production in the silent era helped to establish cinema's white male hero, contributed strongly to the development of the American film industry, and led to the founding of that industry's future "headquarters" in Los Angeles.[2]

With increasing advances in film technology came new creative possibilities in depicting more complex storylines. Movie companies such as Biograph, Pathé, Essanay, Kalem, Bison, and Selig produced many of the genre's pioneering one-reelers and multireelers in the first two decades of the twentieth century. The best of these motion pictures, and most especially those made by D.W. Griffith for Biograph between 1908 and 1913, helped to establish the Western film as a specific form of visual and narrative *art*, at least for those who could see beyond the "mere" value of these films as recurring vehicles of public entertainment. Griffith regularly utilized cinematic techniques—such as dramatic camera angles and crosscutting between parallel scenes for purposes of suspense-building—that helped to advance the new art form.

Griffith's early Westerns, made between 1908 and 1909, were shot chiefly in New York and New Jersey and used the wooded river and lake country of the East Coast as a substitute for Western landscapes. The lush eastern countryside offered serene settings, in which the Native American is presented positively and not merely as some antagonistic "savage." As Scott Simmon has suggested in his book *The Invention of the Western Film,* the idyllic presentation of the landscape in these films echoes an appreciation of the Native Americans, who were connected more intimately to the natural world than the white settlers were. The presentation of a tranquil landscape echoes symbolically the idea of a general "natural harmony" that exists (or should exist) between humans and nature, as well as between various human beings, whether "red" or "white."[3]

The Biograph Company produced enough early movies about Native American life that their own promotional reviews and plot summaries, called *Biograph Bulletins,* began to refer to the narrative subject matter as a well-established category of film. The bulletin for Griffith's "East Coast Western" *The Mended Lute* (1909) leads off with the following statement: "Moving Picture Stories based on the life and customs of the American aboriginals have ever been attractive, and we conscientiously doubt if there has ever been a more intensely interesting subject matter presented than this Biograph production."[4] The bulletin for Griffith's *The Redman's View* (1909) begins with this declaration: "The subject of the Redman's persecution has been so often the theme of story that it would appear an extreme exposition of egotism to say that this production is unique and novel, but such is the case, for there was never before presented a more beautiful depiction of the trials of the early Indians than this."[5]

The Mended Lute focuses on the rituals and values of Native American life, with its plot centered on the rivalry between Standing Rock and Little Bear for the hand of Rising Moon. Standing Rock, Rising Moon's "rich" suitor, is favored by her father because of his potential dowry. The film ends with a ritual test of courage involving torture, in which Standing Rock binds Little Bear and slices his chest with a knife. Little Bear passes the test and earns the respect of Standing Rock, allowing Little Bear and Rising Moon to run off to a "land of happiness" (as the final title card reads). There is also effective use made of the natural landscape, particularly the impressive shots of canoes gliding down streams and rivers. The movie, subtitled *A Stirring Romance of the Dakotas,* was deemed a "master-piece" by the *Biograph Bulletin,* which also called the film a "combination of poetical romance and dramatic intensity."[6]

Griffith's *The Redman's View* shows a similar though predictably limited appreciation of indigenous life, expressed primitively by the very title of the movie. Here we are introduced to a young Indian couple in love, but when the white men (called "the Conquerors" in the title card) invade their lives, the young man is forced to make a choice between, on the one hand, staying with his beloved and protecting her and, on the other, caring for his father on their long trek after they have been banished from their home by the whites. Eventually the father dies and his body is placed on a pyre in ritual fashion. The young man returns to reclaim his girl from the white men who had taken her captive. Here the white men, not the "Injuns," are the disruptive savages.

The Redman's View expresses a tension between the initially idyllic, *seemingly* authentic view of native life and the subsequent threats against that life in the form of white civilization. As Armando José Prats observes in his book *Invisible Natives: Myth and Identity in the American Western,* it would *appear* that Griffith offers us an explicit contrast between two perspectives, each of which seems to possess its own independent integrity and historical truth: the opening scenes of Indian life, soon followed by a depiction of that existence as endangered and embattled by another culture. In reality, according to Prats, both views are actually subsumed under the "myth of conquest," so that any appearance of a distinct portrait and honest appreciation of the Native Americans, even by way of contrast, is mere illusion. As he tells us in reference to Griffith's film and its opening sequence:

> When *The Redman's View* produces its first shot of the conquerors, it transforms the significance of the opening scenes (the Indian idyll) to produce something like Parkman's image of an unsuspecting culture about to be crushed by empire's relentless march. Thus "the red man's view" designates not a scene from a culturally independent way of life but a *dialectical response* to history's intrusion in the ahistorical scene. The camera, it turns out, though it witnessed the opening idyll, never gave us the Indian's "view"

but rather the view *of* the Indian, and its presence in the village initiated the dialectical process whereby Conquest could be introduced only so that it might be thereafter condemned.[7]

The "redman's view" in the film's opening sequences is, in other words, defined by the overall narrative and its implicit ideology, one typical of the Western genre and its underlying mythos. The Indians, even when shown in their native setting before any signs of conflict arise, are inevitably the waiting victims of American expansionism and must confront enemies who are the necessary vehicles of Manifest Destiny. Any such perspective that pretends to depict native existence apart from the story of their gradual conquest is a false or at least derivative viewpoint, according to Prats's interpretation. And so the depiction of the Native American in certain scenes of these early silent films, especially those made by Griffith in his East Coast productions, is ultimately anti-idyllic in its overall framing of a people on the verge of conflict and eventual genocide—particularly in light of our retrospective historical knowledge and, of course, given the unfolding of the overall narrative.

The plots of some of Griffith's early silent Westerns present the relationship between the white man and the Native American in terms of this kind of tension and so with a degree of moral ambivalence. To take another example, in *The Broken Doll* (1910), the whites are presented as both kind and cruel to the natives, though in very different contexts. On the one hand, a white girl, at the suggestion of her mother, gives her beloved doll to a young Indian child who admires it, and the two girls hug and kiss. On the other hand, a small group of Indian men visits town, and one of them accidentally bumps into a drunken white man who has just stood up after sitting in front of the saloon. The white man shoots him dead on the main street, and the Indian's shocked friends bring his corpse back to their village of tents. Subsequently, they go on the warpath to avenge the man's unjust death. Meanwhile, the chief discovers his daughter's new doll and throws it away. The daughter runs to get the doll, finds its head broken off, and decides to give the doll a proper burial. She subsequently becomes aware of the impending attack by her tribe and runs off to warn her new friend and her family. The Indians travel to town to wage destruction, while the white girl's father goes to town ahead of them and warns the townspeople of the impending "invasion." They manage to scare off the Indians, later praising the young Indian girl for her warning once they have learned of her action. But when the white men fire on the attackers, the girl is accidentally shot.

She tries to stumble back home, but in a tragic and sympathetic ending, she dies near the doll that she had previously "put to rest."

This type of ambivalence in presenting the white man's relationship with the Native American is echoed in later multireel silent Westerns such as *The Invaders* (1912) and *The Covered Wagon* (1923). The former movie, produced by Thomas Ince, is a three-reel film that uses genuine Native American actors, a casting idea that was too seldom revisited in later Hollywood Westerns. The film depicts the battle between the United States Cavalry on one side and Sioux and Cheyenne warriors on the other, devoting substantial attention to details about the everyday lives of the Indians and not solely focusing on action fights or glimpses of cavalry existence. Francis Ford, older brother of director John Ford and a pioneering filmmaker in his own right, portrays the leading officer of the cavalry. It is more than probable that Ford, as with other Ince productions in which he acted, took a hand in the directing of the movie under Ince's supervision.

In the opening scene of *The Invaders,* Ford's character oversees the signing of a peace treaty between the government and the Sioux. The treaty expectedly turns out to be a temporary agreement of convenience for the expansionist whites, especially considering their plans to extend the railroad through the Indian territories, land that is supposed to remain off limits by virtue of the treaty. The initial scene presents a peaceful gathering of former enemies, a gathering that ends with an apparently happy handshake. And given the fact that the film presents the perspective of the Native American, focuses sympathetically on the heroic daughter of the Sioux chief and her love for a white man, and emphasizes the violent consequences of the railroad surveyors' treaty-breaking, the viewer is led to realize that it is the white "conquerors," not the "noble savages," who are the invaders of the film's title.[8]

Both sides of the conflict between red and white, even if subsumed by the wider myth of conquest, are also considered in James Cruze's *The Covered Wagon* (1923). This movie was wildly popular, making possible John Ford's production of his saga about building the transcontinental railroad, *The Iron Horse,* a year later, since it was now demonstrated that an historical epic about the labors and trials of American expansionism could win over audiences. Cruze's film ambitiously reconstructs the experience of a great migration of pioneers from the Missouri River to Oregon and anticipates later wagon train movies like Walsh's *The Big Trail* (1930) and Ford's *Wagon Master* (1950). Driving the story is the conflict between the settlers and the gold-seekers, for this tale is set in 1848, when gold was discovered in California. The travelers are split between their greed for land—in their Jeffersonian aim to establish an agriculturally self-sustaining territory—and their greed for the gold that would enable the creation of a potential urban environment based on trade and industry.

The treatment of Indians in *The Covered Wagon* is ambivalent, and the native perspective, as Prats has observed about such films, is defined by, dependent on, and thereby at least partially distorted by the overall story of American expansionism. An intertitle gives the Indian's point of view regarding the white man's plow: "With him he brings this monster that will bury the buffalo, uproot the forest and level the mountain." The natives are initially shown trying to earn money by helping to bring the wagon train, at ten dollars a wagon, across the river, but the pioneers refuse as they think the cost is too high. Once they have crossed the water, the villain of the film, Sam Woodhull (Alan Hale), confronts an Indian, calls him a "thieving savage," and shoots him dead. We find out a short time later from Woodhull, who barely survives an attack by the Pawnees, that the Indians have killed his own party. But then other men from the wagon train learn that this attack was an act of retribution provoked by Woodhull's earlier killing. One of the men reports that Woodhull must have done something "tricky" to provoke the attack, since the Indians had appeared harmless. So here we see the Indians as fierce aggressors, but only after being provoked by a villainous white troublemaker.

This kind of dual-edged appreciation for the perspective of the Native American is undercut to some degree by the overall sense of progress and historical necessity that is central to the underlying myth of civilization-building. However limited such an appreciation of Indian life may be, it is echoed by a few later silent Westerns of the 1920s. These include *The Vanishing American* (1925), directed by George B. Seitz and based on a novel by Zane Grey, and *Redskin* (1929), directed by Victor Schertzinger. Both movies starred Richard Dix, an athletic white actor whose rugged physical appearance and stoic facial expressions made him halfway credible (in the eyes of producers and audiences) in portraying an Indian. *The Vanishing American* depicts injustices suffered by Indians at the hands of a sadistic reservation agent. Dix's character eventually escapes from the cruel life of the reservation and later evolves into a hero on the battlefield in World War I. The film also starts off with a broad-ranging historical prologue that traces the history of past injustices suffered by "weaker" races and peoples. But this prologue winds up espousing a principle of Darwinist determinism—and so "the weak" must accept that they will simply perish in the end, a principle that undercuts the otherwise sympathetic subject matter.[9] In *Redskin,* Dix plays Wing Foot, who is taken away from his community as a young boy and forcibly educated in a government-run school for young Indians. He eventually comes to recognize that he will never really belong in the white community, and he returns to his reservation, only to face severe criticism from his father, among others. The movie is unique for being a late silent Western that focuses on Wing Foot's perspective throughout, but it ultimately advocates the idea that different peoples should remain separate. Moral ambivalence once again saturates the narrative.

The cinematic portrayal of the Native American changed over the years since Griffith's earliest Westerns, but so did the portrayal of the Western landscape, even within Griffith's own oeuvre. In early 1910, Griffith and his Biograph team, including chief cameraman G. W. "Billy" Bitzer, began wintering out West so as to shoot in sunnier climes when the weather hampered production back East. At that time the natural landscape depicted in these post-1910 films became more authentically Western, with vast empty desert places replacing northeastern lakes and forests. The move to capture a new type of setting that was closer to the reality of the American West may have also been, as Simmon suggests in *The Invention of the Western Film,* a response to the criticisms of some movie reviewers that the traditional silent Western film up until 1910 had become little more than an overworked cliché, with minimal innovation in terms of both narrative and setting. The move may have also been a reaction by American film companies to stiff competition with European movie companies who were making their own outdoor adventure movies. The American filmmakers may have sought a more indigenous setting that could not be easily imitated by the Europeans.[10] As Western film expert Edward Buscombe has observed:

> From the early days of the last century, Westerns have used landscape to ensure authenticity. Indeed, in the period before World War I, when American cinema was faced, for the only time in its history, with fierce foreign competition in its domestic market, the Rocky Mountains and the deserts of the southwest gave the American Western film a "unique selling point" as compared to the Westerns being made in Europe and the eastern United States by the French Pathé company. . . . Deserts particularly were favoured. Europe too had mountains (and would use them to considerable effect in the Westerns produced in both West and East Germany during the 1960s), but it had no deserts and canyons to rival the spectacular sights of Arizona and Utah

(even though Sergio Leone shot his Dollars trilogy in the arid country around Almeria in Spain).[11]

Simmon proposes convincingly that the move to a more authentic Western setting also presented creative challenges to silent filmmakers such as Griffith. The primary challenge was to "fill" or "master" the bleak empty desert places that had replaced lakesides and forest-framed clearings. The natural choice was to shape this kind of cinematic space, otherwise unpopulated, around highly charged action and dramatic conflict.[12] Action and conflict could easily be drawn from the actual history of the American West as presented by writers such as Francis Parkman (*France and England in North America*) and Theodore Roosevelt (*The Winning of the West*).[13] And so these kinds of scenes engendered a new narrative focus, one that was unlike the "East Coast Westerns" that Griffith and others made before 1911. The newer Westerns emphasized battles between cowboys and "Injuns" and, within white society, between heroes and villains. Such battles were typically waged over unclaimed land that was waiting to be conquered and controlled and cultivated, precisely the type of empty landscape that was the backdrop of these more action-packed Westerns shot in the Southwest, chiefly in California.

Griffith's Westerns subsequently adopted the view of the Indian as a figure of fierce savagery, the primitive enemy of white civilization and the chief obstacle (aside from nature itself) to American expansionism, as evident in his final Western for Biograph, *The Battle of Elderbush Gulch* (also known by the title *The Battle at Elderbush Gulch;* 1913). Its *Biograph Bulletin* states that this film is "unquestionably the greatest two reel picture ever produced,"[14] and it features such silent-era luminaries as Mae Marsh, Lillian Gish, Lionel Barrymore, Henry Walthall, and Harry Carey Sr. The film has plenty of action, including a rousing fight between Indians and townspeople, plus a good deal of engaging sentimentality. As Prats tells us, "Aside from its formal accomplishments and from whatever importance it may have had in the development of D. W. Griffith's career, *The Battle at Elderbush Gulch* merits close attention for the way in which it charts the direction of the Indian Western. Perhaps more than any other single silent short, it determines and develops the dominant perspective of the Myth of Conquest."[15]

Two young orphan girls are brought to live with their uncle at his ranch, but the ranch boss tells them that they cannot keep their two little puppy dogs. The older girl must retrieve the dogs, but she soon discovers that the animals have run away and are now in the possession of

FIGURE 1. Indians angrily mourn their murdered comrade in D.W. Griffith's *The Battle of Elderbush Gulch* (1913). Courtesy of the Museum of Modern Art.

two Indians who are returning to their village to enjoy, of all things, a dog-eating feast. Their uncle goes out in search of his niece and, seeing her in the presence of the Indians, shoots at them, killing the chieftain's son and prompting an Indian attack. In one suspenseful sequence, the older girl sneaks out a small trapdoor of the cabin during the violent fighting to rescue a baby who has been crying outside. She saves the baby and deposits it in the trunk below her bed. An endearing subsequent shot shows the two girls, the baby, and the two puppies all peering out of the trunk once the fighting has stopped. Gish's character is overjoyed to find that her baby has been saved.

In its demonization of the Native American and its focus on the violent conflict between the "savage" and the "civilized," *The Battle of Elderbush Gulch* echoes Thomas Ince's production *Custer's Last Fight* (1912) starring Francis Ford. The film shows us the Sioux and Cheyenne making hostile attacks in response to an encroaching white civilization. *Custer's Last Fight* makes clear that the Indians are to blame for the ensuing violence. Rain-in-the-Face seeks to ensure his reputation as

FIGURE 2. Lillian Gish's character (*center*) rejoices at the rescue of her child after a battle with Indians in *The Battle of Elderbush Gulch*. Courtesy of the Museum of Modern Art.

a Sioux warrior by attacking the whites. He boasts of killing two civilians, and as we soon learn, this inspires the Native Americans in the region to draw into "nations" to attack the whites. The leader of the Standing Rock Indian agency sends for someone to arrest Rain-in-the-Face, and orders are sent to Fort Abraham Lincoln, where George Armstrong Custer (Ford) is stationed. An order arrives from Washington for Sitting Bull, the leader of this region's Indian nations, to surrender to an escort. Sitting Bull defies this order, and so Custer and the Seventh Cavalry are ordered to join General Terry's army in defeating Sitting Bull. While the Indians attack in response to the encroachment of white civilization, we learn that it is Rain-in-the-Face's need to boast of killing whites that prompts the Indian attacks and the ensuing battle.

Moral complexity or ambivalence becomes inevitable in depicting a historical period in which violence against the enemy was sometimes initiated by an ever expanding white civilization, often in the name of Manifest Destiny, and sometimes initiated by the increasingly frustrated and decimated victims of that expansionism. The continent was not big enough, seemingly, for the whites to tolerate the existence of Indian peoples, nor was it large enough for the latter to tolerate a fast-growing nation. The only solution, as we can learn from the story of the Old West, lay in bloodshed and massacre. But a civilization or culture that is willing to vanquish and eliminate other peoples in acts of genocide undertaken for the sake of territorial expansion is never devoid of its own internal moral conflicts. And the Western genre has been dominated as much by tales of white frontiersmen warring against one another in the name of "good" and "evil" (usually in the form of gunslinging showdowns) as by confrontations with the "savage" warrior who is already native to the land.

HELL'S HINGES AND CONFLICTS BETWEEN WHITE WESTERNERS

Examples of early Griffith Westerns that were shot out West and that deal mainly with the morality of "white culture," with little or no reference to Native Americans, include *In the Days of '49* (1911) and *Under Burning Skies* (1912). In the first of these, subtitled *An Episode in the Times of Gold Fever,* a man named Bill (George Nichols) strikes gold and sends a message back home for his wife, Edith (Claire McDowell), to join him. Traveling by stagecoach, Edith meets a gambler called Handsome Jack (Dell Henderson), and they find themselves mutually attracted. But Jack discovers that she is married. Meanwhile, Bill awaits his wife's arrival. After meeting up with her husband again, Edith seems disappointed with Bill now that she has met Jack, who meets with her privately and tells her to join him soon so he can take her away. Bill soon realizes (as announced by title card): "My wife doesn't love me." The theme of conscience soon emerges, as it does in many of these early Western morality tales that focus almost solely on the internal tensions between members of frontier society. An intertitle proclaims: "Jack realizes the great wrong he is working." Jack eventually departs, having undergone a dramatic transformation of character, and he writes a letter to Edith telling her not to be a fool, to appreciate what she has, and to return to her husband.

In *Under Burning Skies,* a problematic romance and a sudden moral transformation once again become central themes. A rivalry breaks out over Emily (Blanche Sweet) between a sober good man (Christy Cabanne) and a drunken "bad guy" named Joe (Wilfred Lucas), both of whom desire her. Joe swears off alcohol and his immoral lifestyle for the sake of the girl, but only for a moment, since he quickly returns to his old ways. Griffith uses his trademark method of suspenseful cross-cutting as the men hunt for each other with their guns drawn. Emily is alerted to the impending gunfight, and she runs to put herself between the two men who have almost reached each other at the corner of a building. The good guy gets to marry the girl, and Joe goes to drown his sorrows in liquor. When Joe discovers that they have left town with their mule, he vows vengeance and follows them out into the desert, still inebriated. We then witness the couple dying of thirst, with Emily becoming faint and her new husband becoming delirious. Joe happens upon them, laughs vengefully, and taunts them with his canteen of water. He prepares to leave but ultimately changes his mind, revealing a lightning-quick reversal of character that borders on the ludicrous. But it is the type of personal metamorphosis that will later become a staple theme in the films of the Western actor and director William S. Hart, not to mention many later Westerns in general. The couple is saved and Joe (now "good") stumbles off into the desert, the rapid flux of human life having been played out against a fairly static landscape.

The focus on white westerners and their moral transformations is amplified by *Hell's Hinges* (1916), produced by Thomas Ince but almost certainly directed for the most part by its star, Hart, with some nominal credit given to Charles Swickard.[16] In many ways, the film revolves around the theme of passion and its capacity to change the character of an individual. Blaze Tracy (Hart) falls head over heels in love with Faith (Clara Williams), the devoted sister of the Reverend Bob Henley (Jack Standing). Blaze, at first presented as an antihero, "becomes good," like many a "good bad man" in Westerns, in this case because of Faith's example and Tracy's love for her.

As the symbolic embodiment of passion as well as *com*passion, the traditional cowboy hero may be compared with the medieval knight who undertakes self-transforming journeys and adventures, adhering to some code of chivalry. In many cases each gains a sense of moral self-improvement through his love of a beautiful maiden whom he wants to serve. This theme is certainly a hallmark of many of Hart's Westerns, including *Hell's Hinges*. Viewed in a far broader perspective, it is a theme illustrated throughout the literature of the later medieval period, as well as in the symbolic fiction of Romanticism. This theme is represented most famously, perhaps, in Dante's *La Vita Nuova*. Dante's love of his beloved Beatrice gives him a higher sense of purpose and a feeling of fulfillment, and the hero of *Hell's Hinges* follows a similar self-enlightening pathway to a significant degree.[17] As Charles Silver tells us in his book *The Western Film:* "William S. Hart was, more than anything, the reincarnation of the chivalrous spirit of the Middle Ages, and his films are visual hell-fire sermons, soul-saving morality plays."[18]

But the film also presents us with the negative effects of passion, and so the lesson here about the possible intersection between passion and virtue is a qualified one. Faith's brother becomes a moral degenerate through his spirited lust for the ladies, and most especially when he is in the presence of prostitutes and dance-hall girls while full of liquor. One early intertitle announces with irony: "His [the Reverend Henley's] Imagination. A mission appealing to his sense of romance." Here he has a brief daydream of beautiful women congregating around him while outside of a church, tempting his inner desires. After this dream, the corrupt pastor is then assigned to a mission on the prairie, as his superiors know that he is prone to fall for women in his parish and that he needs to be sent somewhere "safe" to redeem himself. The conjoined themes of temptation, sin, virtue, and spirituality emerge clearly.

The Reverend Henley and his sister, Faith, travel by stagecoach to his newly assigned township in the Old West. Shots of hillsides and barren countryside are interspersed with shots of Hell's Hinges, a violent town where men are shot in the street. The majority of townspeople are blatant sinners, but there are a handful of decent and religious people ("the petticoat league," as they are labeled by the others) in this "sin-ridden town." These believers await the arrival of their new preacher, and we witness the minister's first church meeting, which is held in a barn functioning as a church. The townies ride in to start trouble during the service, but Blaze Tracy, previously established as a fellow sinner who scoffs at morality and religion, rides to the rescue when he is told of what is going on. We recognize that he has seeds of virtue in his heart.

After we see the new minister's sister praying during the church service, the film cuts to the image of a large stone cross by the ocean, a symbol that (along with her name) expresses her deep spiritual conviction. Faith asks if there is anyone who will heed her call in the face of the ridiculing townspeople who are there to stir up trouble for the churchgoers and the new preacher. The corresponding intertitles are presented against a painted backdrop of radiant sunrays, with clouds and a tiny cross in the background. Blaze responds quickly to Faith's prayers, and we witness how her virtue and spirituality help to instill in

FIGURE 3. *Hell's Hinges* (1916): Blaze Tracy (William S. Hart, *right*) reacts to Faith Henley (Clara Williams, *center*, with hand outstretched) while her brother, the Reverend Bob Henley (Jack Standing, *to left of his sister*), and other townspeople look on. Courtesy of the Museum of Modern Art.

Blaze a desire for the same, leading to his gradual transformation. The obvious connection between virtue and faith can also be related to such religious-themed Westerns as James Edward Grant's *Angel and the Badman* (1947), with John Wayne and Gail Russell, as well as John Ford's *Wagon Master* and *3 Godfathers* (the latter based on a Peter Kyne story, whose other film versions include Ford's early silent *Marked Men* of 1919 and William Wyler's *Hell's Heroes* of 1930).

The members of the oppressed congregation go about building a real church. Meanwhile, villainous saloon owner Silk Miller (Alfred Hollingsworth), Blaze's former friend and someone who wants to make sure that religion and law never come to Hell's Hinges (as one intertitle informs us), asks one of the dance-hall girls to get the minister drunk and to sleep with him so that the townspeople will witness his sinfulness and lose faith in him. When a gathered crowd discovers Henley sleeping off his hangover the next morning with the dance-hall girl on his bunk, Silk tells his old friend: "He's like all the rest of 'em, Blaze; a low down hypocrite and liar. There ain't no such thing as real religion."

Blaze then compares the morally weak preacher with a steer that you cannot depend on if it breaks free and goes wild. The film thus draws a sharp distinction between "real religion"—that of Faith and the other churchgoers—and "false religion"—that of the Reverend Henley, who merely mouths the words but does not truly believe in them.

Soon the minister revels in his degeneracy, shoving a woman and drinking with the saloon patrons, part of the wild crowd. One of the saloon drinkers shouts, "To hell with the church! Let's burn her down!" They choose the parson, now intoxicated again, to strike the first match. The churchgoers fight to save their house of worship, the Reverend Henley is shot in the melee, and the barn is shown burning along with a wooden cross on the roof. Blaze sees the flames and smoke in the distance and rides to save Faith, who now holds her dead brother in her arms. Blaze goes to the saloon and shoots his pistol at the closed door where, in a fairly ridiculous cut, the door is instantly broken off its hinges by the bullet and the many saloon patrons exit with their hands up in surrender. Blaze shoots a ceiling lantern to the floor, and as the building begins to burn down, he allows the saloon patrons to leave. If the church is to be destroyed, this house of sin will be, too. We now witness a series of apocalyptic images of the town in flames and smoke, a symbol of the negative effects of fiery passion, while Blaze returns to fetch Faith. They depart, carrying away Henley's body.

There are remarkable landscape shots at the end—including a fiery sunrise and a majestic canyon—and these images symbolize the positive power of passion, that of genuine love conjoined with virtue. Blaze and Faith are shown at the grave of the minister with a primitive wooden cross visible on a nearby hillside. Blaze embraces his girl against a misty ravine and he tells her: "Over yonder hills is the future—both yours and mine. It's callin', and I reckon we'd better go." The final intertitle reads: "Whatever the future, theirs to share together." Like many a later Western film, *Hell's Hinges* demonstrates that the Western myth is often founded on a dialectical tension between tragic loss and optimistic faith.

The authentic look of Hart's Westerns, and the ethical awakening of his protagonists, set the stage for such Western classics as Hawks's *Red River*, Ford's *The Searchers*, and Eastwood's *The Outlaw Josey Wales*. While Hart did not share the folksy charm of silent Western star Harry Carey Sr., his quiet dignity and tight-lipped stoicism paved the road for Western actors such as Henry Fonda, Randolph Scott, and Eastwood. And Hart's appreciation of the variability of human nature, and of our opportunities for moral self-transformation, emphasizes one of the primary themes at the heart of the genre: the transience of life as played out against the seemingly eternal world of nature that lies beyond us.

FORD'S *STRAIGHT SHOOTING*

As the preeminent director of Western films in the twentieth century, John Ford had been influenced by the personal styles of William S. Hart and Harry Carey Sr. But his early artistry had been shaped most of all by D. W. Griffith and Ford's older brother Francis. When asked by Peter Bogdanovich, "Who were your early influences?" Ford replied:

> Well, my brother Frank [Francis]. He was a great cameraman—there's nothing they're doing today—all these things that are supposed to be so new—that he hadn't done; he was really a good artist. . . . Oh, D. W. Griffith influenced all of us. If it weren't for Griffith, we'd probably still be in the infantile phase of motion pictures. He started it all—he invented the close-up and a lot of things nobody had thought of doing before. Griffith was the one who made it an art—if you can call it an art—but at least he made it something worthwhile.[19]

John Ford's Western oeuvre illustrates through its unity-amid-diversity the three major strands of storytelling we have explored so far: the violent conflicts between reds and whites (*Stagecoach, Fort Apache,* and *The Searchers,* for example), the conflicts within white culture in the Old West (*Stagecoach, My Darling Clementine, Wagon Master,* and *Sergeant Rutledge,* for instance), and even the sympathetic portrayal of the Native American perspective in the face of an expansionist United States government (*Cheyenne Autumn*).

Ford directed *Straight Shooting* in 1917. An adventure comedy, the film reveals the young Ford's already mature sense of visual style and narrative drive, his skill at connecting to his audience both intimately and on a rousing grand scale, his rhythmic intertwining of comedy and sorrow, and, in close collaboration with Harry Carey Sr., his creation of a strong, independent, lonesome cowboy. Its assured rhythms and narrative pace, developed characters, depth of emotion, and superior location-shooting reveal a strong sensibility for and accomplished handling of the genre.

John Ford came to California in 1914, and he later claimed to have played a clansman in Griffith's *The Birth of a Nation* in 1915. Francis had been directing two-reelers and serials at Universal, and "Jack" (as he was then known) became his brother's chief assistant and occasional cameraman, actor, writer, and even stuntman. He subsequently directed nine films on his own between March and December of 1917. All but the first, *The Tornado,* were Westerns. With *The Soul Herder,* Ford teamed with Harry Carey Sr. and Hoot Gibson, and in August he directed his first feature-length Western, *Straight Shooting,* the third of twenty-five films he would make with Carey. Ford was then twenty-three years old.

Straight Shooting is a standard struggle between ranchers and farmers for control of water. By 1915, when Francis Ford made *Three Bad Men and a Girl,* Universal was turning out more than half a dozen Westerns each week. Carey was an experienced movie actor, first at Biograph where he often played a villain or decent-hearted outlaw, then at Universal starting in 1915. His career had stalled, as John Ford recalled to Bogdanovich:

> They needed somebody to direct a cheap picture of no consequence with Harry Carey, whose contract was running out. . . . I knew Harry very well and admired him; I told him this idea I had and he said, "That's good, let's make it." I said, "Well, we haven't a typewriter," and he said, "Oh, hell, we don't need that, we can make it up as we go along." These early Westerns weren't shoot-'em-ups, they were character stories. Carey was a great actor, and we didn't dress him up like the cowboys you see on TV—all dolled up. There were numerous Western stars around that time—Mix and Hart and Buck Jones—and they had several actors at Universal they were grooming to be Western leading men; now we knew we were going to be through anyway in a couple of weeks, and so we decided to kid them a little—not kid the Western—but the leading men—and make Carey sort of a bum, a saddle tramp, instead of a great bold gun-fighting hero. All this was fifty percent Carey and fifty percent me.[20]

John Ford and Carey usually coimagined their own stories and scripts for two-reelers shot quickly on location. With *Straight Shooting* they expanded the story to five reels, and despite some opposition at Universal, the picture was released complete.[21] Cheyenne Harry (Carey), as the Prairie Kid, agrees to do a hatchet job for the ranchers, until he sees the error of his ways and transforms himself, echoing Hart's character of Blaze Tracy in *Hell's Hinges.* Harry is the prototype of Ford's reluctant hero who is not afraid to kill when necessary, but who "wouldn't plug someone in the back." As developed by Ford and Carey, Cheyenne Harry reinvents the westerner, originally conceived in earlier literature such as Wister's *The Virginian* (1902), drawing on a similar ambiguity about who is right and who is wrong in settling the West. He is a gun for hire, leading an uncomplicated life and liking nothing better than to get drunk with his pals in the saloon.

From Cheyenne Harry's vantage point as an amused observer, he finds it as easy to keep on good terms with greedy ranchers and tough outlaws as to do so with young farmhands. He is not looking to settle down; he cherishes his freedom to sit by the river, hone his limited skills, and avoid getting caught. Too much involvement could lead to permanence, and he prefers to pass by. He is a loner and an outsider to the farmers' way of life, not unlike Gary Cooper's drifter Cole Harden in the first half of William Wyler's *The Westerner* (see chapter 5) and John Wayne's outlaw Quirt Evans at the outset of James Edward Grant's *Angel and the Badman*. And as Cheyenne Harry, exiting a cabin door, turns to look back and is shaded and enclosed within the frame of the door, we anticipate Ethan Edwards (John Wayne) in the famous final shot of Ford's *The Searchers* (see chapter 8).

Cheyenne Harry never seems in a hurry; he likes to pause and look about him, though he can ride fast when the plot calls on him to act decisively. It is this rhythm of stasis and action, of quietly touching or leisurely comic moments between sequences of hard riding and shooting, that makes *Straight Shooting* a signature Western for Ford, and that will distinguish his later films. The hard riding and gunplay climax in an exciting range war: men and horses race atop canyon cliffs, across rivers, and down hillsides at center screen and often straight at the camera. There is also much hard drinking in a comic sequence in the saloon, offset by moments of mourning, of realizing the price paid to tame the West.

Straight Shooting takes place in a once-endless cattle-grazing territory now divided by farmers' fences. Little sky appears above the high horizon as the hillsides fill the screen: we see riders on horseback in the foreground, the landscape dipping away from us in middle ground, then rising to a high horizon from which cattle and cowboys and outlaws can race down and toward each other (and us). Rather than relying solely on repeated cuts of men and horses racing left to right, chasing one another, Ford contains much of the action in the depth of the landscape, compressing movement in the frame. Thrilling and beautiful, it makes us relax and enjoy the excitement, for we are looking *through* space, *into* the landscape, not *at* a flat plane or backdrop supporting horizontal or diagonal movement.

Ford develops this sensibility for a contained, framed landscape as he experiments with location shooting in his three Westerns of the 1920s and 1930s: *The Iron Horse, 3 Bad Men,* and *Stagecoach*. Panoramic vistas were popular in the films of Hart, Fairbanks, and others in the second decade of the twentieth century as well as in James Cruze's *The Covered Wagon* of 1923, particularly in films where the story takes place in more than one territory. Ford, too, combines various locations to create his landscapes of the imagination, such as the fusion of hills and valleys and flat riverbed in *Straight Shooting,* but here he plays with depth rather than horizontality. In *Straight Shooting* we most often look *down* into the landscape, be it grazing land or the wooded riverside. In certain shots the landscape fills the screen entirely, as the men barely visible at the top ride down to the bottom and center of the screen. Black-Eyed Pete and his outlaw gang split their loot in the hidden Devil's Valley: his men ride single file through a narrow slit in rock walls that rise high before us, then down a steep dusty trail in the hillside, a swirling mass of men and horses, quickly ordered at bottom into a line as neat as a regiment.

We cut to the village of Smithfield, where Cheyenne Harry leaves his horse to get soaked in the rain so he can go and get soaked in liquor in the saloon. The ensuing scenes establish the characters of Harry, a good-time cowboy who can be bought by corrupt pals, of the cowardly sheriff who represents the occasional hypocrisy of Ford's law-and-order enforcers, and of the naive and kindhearted young kid, Sam Turner (Hoot Gibson), a type later represented in Ford's Westerns by Harry Carey Jr. and Ben Johnson (as in *Rio Grande* and *Wagon Master*). Cheyenne Harry signs on for a job not knowing precisely how evil the ranchers are; he is not thinking clearly, and he has yet to meet the heroine. The sequence in the saloon typifies what would become another Ford tradition, a change of pace by switching from action to satirical dialogue and gesture, a move that gives individuality to the characters while indulging the director's bent for broad comedy. Drinking is funny in *Straight Shooting, 3 Bad Men,* and *Stagecoach*: it endears the imbibers to us in that they are all "good bad men" who will perform heroically if not chivalrously to save a woman.

The death of a loved one often drives the plot of the early Western, and in *Straight Shooting* it is the murder of the heroine's brother, Ted, the only son of farmer Sweet Water Sims. Ted is shot while drawing water from the spring. Harry rides across the creek and comes upon the boy's burial. He witnesses the father's collapse and convincingly states his innocence: "I've done dirty things in my life—but I wouldn't plug someone in the back." He takes Sims home, entering through the doorway (a typical Fordian framing device) and shaking hands with Joan Sims (Molly Malone) as he thanks her for opening his eyes to the ranchers'

FIGURE 4: In John Ford's *Straight Shooting* (1917), Sweet Water Sims (George Berrell, *left*), his daughter, Joan (Molly Malone, *center*), and Sam Turner (Hoot Gibson, *standing*) mourn over the grave of Ted Sims. Courtesy of the Museum of Modern Art.

evil nature. He then walks out the door, away from us, remaining en-
grossed in thought as he rides across the creek, the sun dappling the
trees. He rides away as he had come.

Subtly handled, too, is Ford's tenderness toward the heroine, especially
in a scene that presages women's moments of reflection in his later films.
Joan's sorrow and sense of loss are quietly revealed when, alone in the
cabin, she removes Ted's plate from the table and holds it close to her as
she recalls all that just happened—just as Martha, in Ford's *The Searchers,*
will caress her beloved Ethan's coat before he leaves home once again
after having only recently returned (see chapter 8). We may also recall
that beautifully touching moment in Ford's *The Grapes of Wrath* (1940)
when Ma Joad (Jane Darwell) holds a pair of treasured earrings to her
ears in front of a broken mirror before discarding them along with other
"unnecessary" items as she is about to embark on her family's grueling
odyssey to California.

Once the villainous rancher Thunder Flint (Duke Lee) learns that
Harry will no longer side with him against the farmers, he wants him
killed straightaway and assigns the dirty work to Placer Fremont (Vester
Pegg), who had done in the Sims boy. Sam Turner overhears and rides off
and across the creek (in stunningly photographed shots) to warn Harry.
During the prolonged shootout sequence, Harry walks with care, his
long legs in cuffed jeans, swaying slightly from side to side as he glides
along ever so slightly pigeon-toed. John Wayne, who acted with Carey
in *Angel and the Badman* and *Red River,* would later adapt the older
star's outfit and walk—so unlike Carey's contemporaries Hart and Tom
Mix. Carey's outfit, like his character, seems simpler and more authentic
in its understatement.

The deaths of young Sims and his killer, Fremont, are the prelude to
Flint's launch of the range war between farmers and ranchers, the type
of conflict that will be echoed by such Westerns as Wyler's *The Westerner* (see chapter 5), Ford's *The Man Who Shot Liberty Valance* (see
chapter 8), and Kevin Costner's *Open Range* (2003). Farmers assemble
at the Sims home, and excitement grows as both sides gather support.
Flint's men take off through the trees and cut through a landscape that
fills the screen as they ride down and around the Sims farm. Harry,
whose morals are eccentric but effective, rides to the entrance of Devil's
Valley. Encountering men standing guard, Harry is escorted through the
rock slit to Black-Eyed Pete's hideout, where he asks for help in defending the farmers. The outlaws swarm and descend from the hillsides,
racing to reach the farm that has been surrounded by ranchers, who

quickly scatter in fear. The scenes are fast and exciting; the few extended moments of tension are subordinated to straightforward, cleverly edited sequences of rout and escape. Very little is repetitious and, by 1917, filmmakers like Ford relied on Griffith's parallel editing of climactic scenes in order to build suspense. Here shots of ranchers who surround and shoot at the cabin are intercut with shots of the farmers firing back while the outlaws ride to the rescue. This is reminiscent of the siege of the cabin in Griffith's *The Battle of Elderbush Gulch*.

Harry pledges to go straight and tells Black-Eyed Pete that it is time to say good-bye. Harry rolls a cigarette while looking out the door; he cannot decide what to do: "Me, a farmer? I belong on the range." He says he needs a day to think it over, goes to the woods, sits quietly, and seems to pray. When Sam comes along, Harry says that he is leaving Joan to Sam and bids him farewell. At sunset, his decision made, Joan finds Harry and he gives her his answer: it seems he will stay. According to Tag Gallagher in his book *John Ford: The Man and His Films*, the film originally ended with Harry sending Joan back to Sam, and he is "left facing the sun alone"; but the present happy ending was added on to the reissue of 1925.[22]

Straight Shooting, similar to Ford's later Westerns and most especially *My Darling Clementine*, never veers into action for the sake of action. It is leisurely and steadily paced and accented by pauses and reflections, yet also proves exciting in the climax of the range war. Ford learned much from his brother Francis and from Griffith, and he developed his own handling of a simple story, depiction of character, and cinematography in a spirit that was closer to the earlier Biograph films than to Griffith's contemporaneous epics *Intolerance* (1916) and *Hearts of the World* (1918). The early style of John Ford is distinct, however, and Gallagher suggests that "in place of Griffith's dramatic shaping, all events in *Straight Shooting* have equal value, and thus ignite a more active symbolism into land, light, water, and foliage."[23]

Ford demonstrates a grasp of rhythm and space that enables him to keep a steady beat, occasioning the viewer's observation of place and detail in order to imbue themes and character with varied meanings. Here an evocation of quiet intimacy receives equal screen time with, and has the same presence as, a shoot-'em-up range war. Other directors will observe the changing natural world in lyrically intimate ways: Satyajit Ray, Jean Renoir, Yasujiro Ozu, and Akira Kurosawa situate their characters in an inseparable relation with their landscapes. Ford uses outdoor space not merely for action settings but also to let his characters pause to feel, reflect, or remember, which Cheyenne Harry does best in sun-spangled woods by the river. Ford shows in *Straight Shooting* how well he understands the situating of the westerner in his particular space so as to give definition to issues of community, conflict, alienation, passage, and redemption. His pacing allows, too, for the depiction of the duality of human nature: for characters to be both wise and stubborn, both funny and brutal, both selfish and self-sacrificing—as we will also see in later Ford Westerns starring Henry Fonda, James Stewart, and John Wayne.

FORD'S FINAL SILENT WESTERN: *3 BAD MEN*

In the Western as epic, westerners are less interesting as individual personalities, serving instead as the supporting cast in stories of expansionism enacted by mid-nineteenth-century settlers in a tremendous, beauteous terrain. The frontier eventually reached the Pacific, having been pushed back by overland wagons, gold rushes, and land grants, as well as by the successful linking of nationwide telegraph and railroad systems. All of these stepping-stones in frontier development were prime subjects of Western epics in the second and third decades of the twentieth century. These films popularized, with sincerity and some historical accuracy, the advancement of the white man's culture and economy.

The success of *The Covered Wagon* spurred production throughout the 1920s of large-scale, costly adventures filmed in glorious locations. John Ford filmed a pair of these patriotic epics about nation-building. The first was *The Iron Horse* of 1924, which focused on the successful completion of the northern intercontinental railroad in the 1860s, culminating in a cinematic recreation of the hammering of the last spike at Promontory Point, Utah, on May 10, 1869, by Leland Stanford. Progress comes at a cost, and Ford is sympathetic to the hardships and deaths of settlers and native people; his deep sense of loss, key to his later Westerns, is already apparent. Ford's second epic Western was *3 Bad Men* of 1926, which tells the story of the Dakota Land Rush of 1876, when a vast territory was opened up to settlers.

Despite its initial blustery justification of westward expansion into the Dakota territory, its essential lack of sympathy for the displaced Sioux, and its lapse into melodrama, *3 Bad Men* is Ford's most meaningful Western of the 1920s. The film reveals greater complexity and grayer shades of meaning than *The Iron Horse*. The leisurely unfolding of the plot prior to the land rush allows Ford to establish character and the moral duality of the white man: his greed and his desire to build a community. By situating the wagon camp in the valley below the Grand Tetons, Ford creates a backdrop that is often more visually compelling than the staged drama played out before it. The three bad men emerge from this landscape: it is their world, and Ford gives them his time and attention.

Like the reluctant Western heroes of the second decade of the twentieth century portrayed by Hart and Carey, Tom Santschi's Bull Stanley is a big, rough, but understated man of greater strength of character and more subtle intelligence than we would initially expect. He listens and learns, though it is his deep response to the vulnerability and decency of a beautiful young southerner that makes him reset his course. His love for her is clear, as is his conviction that he could never marry her, for he is an outsider, an outlaw, and a man with a past. Having thought it through, Stanley makes his choice, not just for himself but for the three bad men: he and his pals will help and protect her, find her a husband, and defend her from evil even if they must sacrifice their own lives to do so.

At the opening of 3 Bad Men, it is made apparent that there is gold in the Dakota hills. It is 1876, and President Grant has issued a proclamation that will open the lands of the Sioux to the overflow of emigrants. 3 Bad Men begins with a civics lesson of sorts, its numerous introductory titles setting down the reason, or excuse, for the great land rush. And so the film shifts from the grandiose to the specific, introducing the handsome young fortune-seeker Dan O'Malley (George O'Brien), who rides casually along playing his harmonica while wagon after wagon arrives at the foot of bold, sharp-peaked mountains. Dan meets Lee Carleton (Olive Borden) and her father, who are bringing their thoroughbred horses from the South to participate in the land rush. Then three scruffily outfitted outlaws ride up, brilliantly lit by the sun and framed against the mountains, to observe the long line of wagons and cattle following the ridge above the river. Bull Stanley tells his pals, Mike Costigan (J. Farrell MacDonald) and Spade Allen (Frank Campeau), "It ain't gold I'm looking for, but it's a man just as yeller." The cast is complete as we encounter the man whom Bull is ultimately seeking: local sheriff Layne Hunter (Lou Tellegen), slick in his fancy duds and a wide-brimmed white hat.

In quick order, Ford establishes an ironic moral structure that will sustain his most fully realized Western feature to date: the bad guys are not all that threatening, and the upholder of the law is clearly corrupt, a precursor to such villainous lawmen as Judge Roy Bean (Walter Brennan)

FIGURE 5. Dan O'Malley (George O'Brien) plants a kiss on Lee Carleton (Olive Borden) in a romantic scene from John Ford's epic *3 Bad Men* (1926). Courtesy of the Museum of Modern Art.

in Wyler's *The Westerner,* Dad Longworth (Karl Malden) in Brando's *One-Eyed Jacks,* and Little Bill Daggett (Gene Hackman) in Eastwood's *Unforgiven.* The outlaw trio decides to steal the thoroughbreds, but Hunter's men beat them to the wagons. The three bad men ride swiftly to chase away Hunter's men who already have killed Lee's father. When

Stanley tries to comfort Lee, she weeps on his chest. Positioned before peaks blazing in the sun beneath bright clouds, Stanley becomes suddenly noble and stops his pals from taking the horses, echoing once again the theme of moral awakening through love that was embodied by the earlier discussed characters of Blaze Tracy in *Hell's Hinges* and Cheyenne Harry in *Straight Shooting*. Meanwhile, down in the new town of Custer, pretty young Millie (Priscilla Bonner) tells Hunter that a minister has arrived and they now can wed. He scoffs at her, and she realizes that her seducer has no intention of marrying her.

The film *3 Bad Men* can be viewed as a tragedy, with its comic scenes serving as cathartic interludes, for much of the film is concerned with loss, humiliation, unstoppable evil, and death. Its outlaw hero, Bull Stanley, is as melancholy as any classic gunfighter. The tragedy has not so much to do with the grander history of the land rush itself; the often uneasy melding of the fictional plot and the reality of history plagues many films and not only the Western. Sheriff Hunter is a cardboard villain, heavily made-up and literally dressed to kill, and his contempt for his girl and the townspeople is obvious. Whoever crosses him pays a heavy price. O'Brien, who had played the leading role in Ford's previous feature *The Iron Horse,* is handsome but stolid, nominally but secondarily the lead. The true heroes are Stanley and his sister, Millie, who is seduced by the real villain. The strengthening of Bull's character—the ways in which he expresses his love and his willing sacrifice, joined to his sorrowful realization that others will succeed in the new society of the West—reminds us of John Wayne's Tom Doniphon in Ford's later masterpiece *The Man Who Shot Liberty Valance* (see chapter 8).

Stanley's reach for moral regeneration begins when he stops his pals from taking the horses. That night Lee Carleton hires these three bad men, who admit they are available, as business is not what it used to be. She cannot pay them wages, just yet, but Stanley says that they will work for free. "Then you'll be *my* men?" she asks, and they take off their hats in gallant reply. Stanley is in love with her. When he learns that Hunter, who has vowed to get even with them, also intends to seduce Lee, he knows he must defend her honor while seeking the man with whom his sister left home. He is thoughtful as he polishes the bullets he has saved for such a purpose. Meanwhile his pals have gotten drunk, and a disgusted Stanley decides: "What our gal needs is a husband. We'll find a marryin' man—if we have to shoot him." His pals select a simpering, Chaplin-like dandy in the saloon, while Stanley finds the good-looking O'Malley, to whom Lee is already attracted.

The narrative shifts among scenes of the developing romance between Lee and O'Malley, the comic carousing of Stanley's pals, the villainous activities of Sheriff Hunter, the tragedy of the once innocent Millie, and the strengthening of Stanley's heroic attempts to protect Lee, find his sister, and defeat Hunter. The sheriff's viciousness knows no limits as he incites his men to send flaming wagons to crash into and burn the church full of women and children (shades of *Hell's Hinges*), and during the ensuing shootout Millie is fatally hit. The sheriff has told his men to sneak that night into the Dakota reservation, so as to be ahead when the rush begins. Stanley weeps over his dying sister and later carries her body at the head of a parade of settlers riding on horseback with torches.

Flames and smoke rise from the ruined church, and a burning cross stands vividly against the dark sky. The terror is palpable as Hunter incites the lawless, feckless townspeople, those who prefer the saloon to the arrival of religion and decency and who can be incited to commit destruction and murder. This sequence amplifies the evil of Hunter and his absolute rule over Custer. Nothing can stop the sheriff: he has caused the deaths of Lee's father, the old man Lucas, and Millie, not to mention his destruction of the church and attempt to murder the minister as well as the women and children trapped inside the building. And we are just halfway through the story!

Now dawns the day of the land rush, and we see people sweating, cursing, and fighting to get to the head of the line. Millie's brief funeral gives way to people hurrying about. Wagons move to their places amid clouds of dust, waiting for the dot of noon. The minister urges a family to keep their plow, for wealth is in the land. When the cannon is fired, the opening of the land rush is photographed in a high panning shot that gives full sweep to the broad scale of wagons and riders. Later we see the rush from under hoof, with horses leaping wildly over the cameras. Dust and chaos, carriages racing along, riders straining their horses, and a man riding a tall bicycle give way to wagons crashing in accident after accident.

The most fearful moments in Ford's films are often those involving children in danger, such as Bill's leap from the train in *Just Pals* (1920), the baby bounced around the desert in the arms of the 3 *Godfathers*, and the abduction of the sisters in *The Searchers*. Our greatest terror in 3 *Bad Men* is our fear for the forgotten baby who sits down-screen, having been left by its mother when the father fixed their wagon and then raced ahead. Helplessly we watch the thunderous approach of horses coming straight at the baby, and at us, until O'Malley leans from his horse to catch the child in the nick of time.

At the end of a hard day of riding, Hunter's men chase the group of protagonists as they seek escape through an enormous slit in the rocks. O'Malley and Lee are sent ahead, and the three bad men stay behind to stand against Hunter: they are "together for the last reunion." What follows is an overly extended sequence depicting the bravery of fools, with each bad man trying to be more sarcastic or noble than the other: cutting cards to see who will stand first, say "Adios, amigo," and atone for a lawless life. Hunter and his men successfully terrorize Lee Carleton and her protectors for some time. Every attempted standoff by the three bad men seems arbitrary and melodramatic, yet it is Ford's attempt to give each character an honorable exit. Though Hunter is killed, the price is high. The story concludes with the intertitle "As the years went on, the gold of grain grows," implying that greed will be supplanted by the discovery of good earth. Thus the sacrifice was not in vain in promoting the settlement of the West, and the good will not be forgotten. In the last sequence, O'Malley and Lee are happily farming but then go into their cabin to see their child. The parents show their baby the hats of the "best 3 bad men who ever named a baby," and the trio is then seen, in spirit, riding on horseback against the sky. The idea of using each of the three outlaws' names for the name of the baby will be repeated in Ford's later *3 Godfathers*.

After *3 Bad Men*, Ford suspended his exploration of the genre for more than a decade, not directing another Western until *Stagecoach*, in the autumn of 1938. Instead of filming in Jackson Hole, he went to Monument Valley and the Mojave Desert, locations that would give greater meaning, scope, and scale to his finest Westerns. And Ford found in John Wayne a physically imposing, psychologically compelling screen presence, the kind of actor who could reignite the slow-burning fire of both Carey and Santschi, Ford's earlier good bad men.

CHAPTER 2

Not at Home on the Range

Women against the Frontier in "The Wind"

Nature appears in most Western films as a setting, obstacle, metaphor, or source of inspiration, or as a combination of the above. In *The Wind* (1928), nature is manifested chiefly as a threatening, sinister, destructive power that transforms as well as tests the psychology and character of its human protagonist. At the symbolic level, the desert winds of the early frontier become a supernatural, erotic force that drives Letty Mason (Lillian Gish) to the brink of madness. Tautly directed by Victor Sjöström (known in Hollywood as Victor Seastrom), the film is marked by persuasive terror and sexuality, which were shaped by three extraordinary, and at that time highly successful, female talents: Gish, novelist Dorothy Scarborough, and screenwriter Frances Marion. Together they created a film that is one of the most intriguing of Westerns, especially in terms of the relationship between humans and their natural environment.[1]

The Wind remains unique among landscape Westerns in creating a female protagonist who battles hostile forces of wicked men and evil nature alone, without a hero to come to her rescue.[2] Letty does not manipulate men to destroy one another, nor does she entice them to sacrifice their lives for her. Letty has no greed to make her evil; she is not a "good bad woman." Even the virtuous heroine Jane Withersteen in *Riders of the Purple Sage*, one of the most popular early Western novels to portray a woman as an equally central character, relies upon her rescuer and principal lover, Lassiter, to stop their pursuers. And what also distinguishes both novels among Westerns—*Riders of the Purple Sage,* which was written in 1912, and *The Wind* of 1925—is the latter's metaphorical presentation of the landscape as the heroine's other lover, a demonic "stalker" of limitless psychological and physical power, a sexual tormentor eager to destroy. *Riders of the Purple Sage,* which must have been well known to Scarborough, concludes with the anticipated climactic fall of Balancing Rock, destroying the villains and bringing together Lassiter and Jane forever as the rock seals them in the hidden valley beyond Deception Pass.[3] In *Riders,* nature assists human love rather than conquering or replacing it by means of its own sensual power.

Character and community in the frontier landscape can be understood, and intriguingly so, through this focus on sexual passion. James Folsom analyzed the symbolic parallel between civilization and eros that emerges in *The Wind:*

> The novel's real strength lies in its carefully thought-out and generally skillfully developed symbolic structure, for *The Wind* is a study in symbolic opposites. . . . The wind becomes a symbol for the frontier life before the advent of civilization, and its symbolic values of wildness and freedom are emphasized by the wild black stallion to which it is often specifically compared. . . . The metaphorical opposites of Letty and the wind become symbols for the process of colonization . . . [and] the bringing of land under the plow becomes an emblem for the replacement of "Texas" by "Virginia."[4]

Folsom goes on to say that this dialectic is expressed through "the omnipresent sexual symbolism which fills the book[:] . . . the more elemental purely sexual metaphor of the wind, seen first as a great black stallion, an obvious symbol of sexual power; later, more explicitly, Letty hears the wind 'wailing' about her house 'like a lost soul, like a banshee, like a demon lover,' images which constantly reappear."[5] Letty's ultimate seducer is not a man but the North Wind, which takes the form of a ghost horse that lives in the clouds; in the novel it is a black stallion, in the film a white steed, the better to prance before dark clouds in Letty's nightmare vision. Black or white, its symbolism is clear: the wind is a powerful threat, beautiful and dangerous because forever chaotic and untamable. The wind, like the horse, is active and destructive, resisting the very civilization that women were to bring to the frontier. Scarborough's novel makes this clear:

> But long ago it was different. The winds were wild and free, and they were more powerful than human beings. . . . In the old days, the winds were the enemies of women. Did they hate them because they saw in them the symbols of that civilization which might gradually lessen their own power?

Because it was for women that men would build houses as once they made dugouts?—would increase their herds, would turn the unfenced pastures into farms, furrowing the land that had never known touch of plow since time began?—stealing the sand from the winds?[6]

Such was Scarborough's premise underlying the tragedy of a woman who fails to civilize the frontier. The Western is typically preoccupied with notions of masculinity, marked by chivalrous deeds and noble daring, and the classic westerner is traditionally male. But of course there is an occasional focus on the women of the West, and the role of Letty Mason, played by Lillian Gish, in *The Wind* is a prime example of such a focus, anticipating such characters (among countless others) as Barbara Stanwyck's Vance Jeffords in Anthony Mann's *The Furies* (1950), Joan Crawford's Vienna in Nicholas Ray's *Johnny Guitar* (1954), Vera Miles's Hallie in John Ford's *The Man Who Shot Liberty Valance* (1962), and Claudia Cardinale's Jill McBain in Sergio Leone's *Once Upon a Time in the West* (1968). *The Wind* is an effective counterexample to scholars like Brett Westbrook, who, even with certain qualifications, view the American Western as defined almost solely by the authoritative presence of the male/masculine. Westbrook has stated in an article on the predominance of the masculine in the films of Clint Eastwood:

> Despite their presence on the historical frontier, women seem to have no place on Hollywood's frontier. Given the generic requirements of unencumbered "freedom" to ride away into the sunset and the absolute necessity of participation in violence, women are not, as many feminist critics have argued, "erased" from the classic Western; there is literally no room for them in the first place. They cannot be erased because they were never there to begin with. Westerns require a landscape in which women cannot move with any liberty; Westerns require a constantly confrontational stance vis-à-vis nature and Indians that women, by virtue of their exclusion from instigating violence (as opposed to being the objects of violence), cannot take. . . . Ironically, Westerns actually need women.[7]

Scarborough's story of Letty's transformative encounter with the Western wilderness was tailor-made for the silver screen, particularly in the hands of Sjöström and Marion, and more especially as a vehicle for the talents of Gish. The theme of the struggle to establish community—to bring women from a supposedly civilized (or, alternatively, a decadent) eastern America to the raw but pure frontier—offered the actress abundant material for rich character portrayals in Westerns ranging from Griffith's *The Battle of Elderbush Gulch* (1913) to John Huston's *The Unforgiven* (1960). At the time of *The Wind,* Gish was still one of

MGM's most beloved stars, although she would leave the studio in 1927, prior to the film's release in November 1928. Years later, she said that when she signed a contract with MGM in 1925, the studio had no stories for her. Having portrayed heroines of various historical periods—first for Griffith in *The Birth of a Nation* (1915), *Broken Blossoms* (1919), *Way Down East* (1920), and *Orphans of the Storm* (1922)—Gish brought to MGM the stories of *Romola* (1924, directed by Henry King), *La Bohème* (1925, directed by King Vidor); and *The Scarlet Letter* (1926) and *The Wind* (both directed by Sjöström).

The Wind reunited Gish and costar Lars Hanson, director Sjöström, and screenwriter Marion, following their previous work together on *The Scarlet Letter*. Nathaniel Hawthorne's 1850 novel interpreted an earlier American frontier bordering on the New England wilderness of the seventeenth century. In the Puritan community, order was severely imposed through strict adherence to law and through suppression of the freedom of expression. The story's publicly humiliated victim, Hester Prynne (Gish), is seduced by the Reverend Arthur Dimmesdale (Hanson), has his child, and is punished by the community. In *The Wind,* nature is expressed almost solely in a negative and destructive manner. But in *The Scarlet Letter,* Hester regards the wilderness as a refuge or escape, its thick woods offering a glimpse of alluring freedom, since the community does not nurture or protect Hester but rather makes her an outcast from it.

Hawthorne was writing at mid-nineteenth century, long after the frontier had shifted from New England to the trans-Mississippi West, beyond the Rocky Mountains to California and Oregon, and from Virginia to Texas and the vast Southwest. The frontier was formed by rugged landscapes that became defined by the white man's continued imposition of law and settlement. In novels and stories derived from this new frontier community, women were meant to bring virtue and civilization to the wilderness and were punished if they failed. By the early twentieth century, Molly Stark in Owen Wister's *The Virginian* and Jane Withersteen in Zane Grey's *Riders of the Purple Sage* had to accept their heroes and frontier lives as they were. The rough terrain enticed brutal men to be as evil as the natural forces surrounding them, to indulge their greed for cattle, land, and women. This recurring theme of the conflict or tension between civilization and wilderness would be most powerfully imagined by Scarborough in *The Wind*. The novel depicts the landscape metaphorically as the heroine's true love, but it is a powerful and demonic seducer, determined to destroy her and, in so doing, drive away forever the feminine forces that have come to civilize the newly occupied territory.[8]

Gish thought *The Wind* would make a perfect motion picture: it was "pure motion," she said.[9] Her MGM contract stipulated that Gish would be consulted on script, director, and cast. Rights were secured, as was approval from the studio's production chief, Irving Thalberg. Gish wrote a four-page outline that she gave to Frances Marion, who developed it into a screenplay, and it was agreed that Sjöström would direct. The seamless melding of naturalism and tragic grandeur apparent in *The Wind* had also been evident in the previous collaboration of Gish and Sjöström as they worked from Marion's sensitive scripting of the Hawthorne novel. The theme of sexual entrapment, played out within the American frontier landscape, dominated *The Scarlet Letter* and *The Wind*. In both films Gish's character is an outcast: first as Hester, an adultress who raises her child in a Puritan community, and then as Letty Mason, a "useless" wife who is raped and who commits murder on the desert plains.

In Sjöström's major films, he revealed a moral ambiguity in his characters' struggles to survive their hostile surroundings. And he approached the layered renderings of sexual passion in the narratives chosen by Gish as intensely and movingly as he had when directing his earlier silent films in Sweden and Norway. The struggle of man in his natural environment, a popular theme in Swedish drama and literature, was an essential theme in this period for Sjöström as well as for his partner, Mauritz Stiller.[10] On the screen, the emotional and visual complexity of Sjöström's landscape narratives, shot on Scandinavian locations in richly rendered lights and shadows, reveals the psychological tensions and passions of the protagonists *in* nature. Personality and landscape influence each other in fundamental ways, as we also see throughout the history of Westerns: "Fate is character and landscape is fate."[11] The external natural world both conditions and metaphorically expresses an individual's interior reality and worldview. This is the core of Sjöström's brand of poetic tragedy, as these outdoor cinematic narratives blend human performance with the naturalism of the physical elements. Key to this structure is the broken or unsuccessful journey, so often endured by the westerner. Peter Cowie notes that "the idea of the journey is the catalyst of *The Wind*, as it is of most of Sjöström's films. His heroes and heroines can only learn the truth about themselves and their secret flaws by traveling; the way is difficult and strenuous."[12]

Self-transforming odysseys are measured in psychological and moral terms but also by passage through space and time. A character's physical, geographical, and temporal passage is in turn defined by the individual's changing relationship to the earth itself. The external journey through time and across terrain conditions the individual's inner journey while also expressing that transformation symbolically. For example, Sjöström's 1917 masterwork *Berg-Ejvind och hans hustru* (known in the English-speaking world as *The Outlaw and His Wife* or *You and I*) is set in the sparse, mountainous landscape of eighteenth-century Iceland. Sjöström stars as Berg-Ejvind, a thief escaped from prison, to which he had been confined for stealing a sheep. He becomes the trusted foreman of the farm of a handsome widow, Halla, played by Edith Erastoff, Sjöström's soon-to-be wife. Halla's brother-in-law insists that they should be married, to unite their fortunes, and after she spurns him he plots his revenge and pursues the thief. Halla realizes her love for Berg-Ejvind and they flee to the mountains, where for sixteen years they live as husband and wife amid nature, joyfully fishing, swimming, and washing in the high waters and falls nearby. But the rock cliffs and flowing water are both paradise and hell. In the terrible battle with her brother-in-law and his men, Halla intentionally destroys her child. Years afterward she hallucinates about her daughter as the end arrives during a fierce snowstorm. She, like Letty, flees into the wind and storm; her lover finds her and dies embracing her.

These protagonists can conquer neither the past nor the brutal forces of an unforgiving nature, but still they love each other. Sjöström and his cameraman, J. Julius (Julius Jaenzon), heighten the expressiveness of the characters' eyes through the effective play of light, while shadows sharpen the dangers of the cold, night, and storm. The filmmakers bring out the texture and feel of the elements, of the thickness and flow of the water and the wind. We see in *The Outlaw and His Wife* what Sjöström would achieve most effectively and expressionistically in the mise-en-scène of *The Wind*: both a raging world of nature and the interior of the pathetic shack where Letty will go mad as her home sways and falls apart in the storm. With *The Wind*, Sjöström put onto the screen in visual terms what Frances Marion was able to put onto the pages of her screenplay in literary form: Scarborough's brilliant fusion of an animated symbolic wilderness, the power of erotic passion, and the specter of insanity for those who could not deal adequately with a brutal frontier existence.

FIGURE 6. Letty (Lillian Gish), Roddy (Montagu Love, *center*), and Lige (Lars Hanson) during the dance sequence in Victor Sjöström's *The Wind* (1928). Courtesy of the Museum of Modern Art.

In her book *Off with Their Heads!* Marion summarized the bleak fate of Letty, explaining that she had wanted to keep it bleak in the film.[13] In Scarborough's novel the protagonist is the cyclonic wind that blows relentlessly across the vast cattle ranges in Texas. To that wind-tormented prairie comes a penniless and delicately reared southern girl seeking refuge with her cousin on his ranch. From that point on, the story slowly and inevitably reveals the trap that closes over this frightened girl: her cousin is dying of tuberculosis, she is led into marriage with Lige, a cowboy rancher, and she is forced to live the kind of life pioneer women accepted as their fate.

"It's pretty gloomy," MGM studio boss Irving Thalberg remarked to Marion after reading the script, "but I think the public welcomes a strong melodrama now and then."

"But no happy ending, Irving," Frances Marion pleaded. "Please, not that!"

"I agree with you. No happy ending."[14]

Marion's script and revision, filmed in the spring and summer of 1927, are spare and intelligent in the depiction of loneliness, as well as in the renderings of the sexual threat of the unrelenting Roddy (Montagu Love) and of the equally malevolent wind. The intertitles read as simple and direct frontier talk, revealing the characters to be, in turn, brutal and gentle. Marion alters various characters' personalities, backgrounds, and physical makeup so as to simplify motives made obvious by repetitive description in the novel and to concentrate the actions of wind, storm, restless cattle, and wild horses. The first half of the novel takes place largely at the ranch of Letty's male cousin, Beverly; she does not marry Lige and move into his shack until well after the midpoint of the novel. Scarborough evokes Letty's home back in Virginia through the lonely girl's remembrance of the sweetness of the changing seasons, in bitter contrast to the continual harshness and violence of the Texas plains. As Freedonia Paschall and Robert G. Weiner inform us in their essay "Nature Conquering or Nature Conquered in *The Wind* (1928)":

> The novel describes Letty as being "oppressed by the solitude of nature which was so different from the friendly countryside she had known at home— these vast, distressing stretches of treeless plains, with nothing to see but a few stunted mesquite bushes, and samples of cactus that would repel the touch. No friendly intimate wild animals such as she had always been used to seeing—gossipy squirrels grey or brown, chipmunks." "In Virginia there were rivers, calm and life-giving . . . and lakes with water lilies, and alder-fringed banks; and little, talkative brooks . . . (and) birds that sang and nested." Letty knew a world with servants and a carefree life where nature was something to be looked at and admired for its tranquility. The natural world of Virginia was not the world of West Texas that she saw as raw and uncivilized. Virginia was already refined and was not really the natural world, in Letty's mind. Throughout the novel she thinks of her former home.[15]

The novel sets the character of Letty, the delicate flower of the civilized South, against the magnificent beauty and strength of Cora, Beverly's wife, the ideal woman for the settlement of the Western frontier. The novel's parallel structure that is built around the contrast between these archetypal females is eliminated in the screen version, no doubt for reasons of story economy: Letty's struggles against frontier men and the frontier itself were obviously enough to fill a feature film. And so the "rivalry" between Letty and Cora is downplayed to some degree in the movie adaptation, and the plot's streamlined focus on Letty's journey into an almost otherworldly realm gives the film its special dramatic power and psychological intensity.

FIGURE 7. The delicate Letty (*left*) is confronted by the strong frontier wife Cora (Dorothy Cumming, *right*). Courtesy of the Museum of Modern Art.

The Wind gives us no wagon trains, gunslingers, or showdowns on the main street of town. There is also no role here for the Native American, neither in the novel nor in the film, since the chief antagonists are an overbearing white man and an overwhelming natural world. As Paschall and Weiner also tell us in their essay: "The film softens the novel's portrayal of Native Americans, referring to them as Injuns and describing their view that the wind was like a horse. . . . There is no reference in either version [novel or film] of *The Wind* to Native Americans as 'noble savages.' Indians are seen as a part of nature, which needed to be subdued."[16]

The film's power derives instead from the focus and pace established early in the narrative and never relaxed: the tragic events succeed one another in a swift sequence to the beat of the wind. There is but a single story, with no sustained subplots and few comic asides. Characters are introduced and then gotten out of the way so as not to distract from the central theme, a woman seduced and threatened with madness. Unlike John Ford's Westerns, such as *The Searchers,* there is little pause for relief or reflection and few leisurely scenes of sentiment or broad comedy to ease the harshness and cruelty. And unlike Howard Hawks's Westerns, such as *Red River,* there is no camaraderie or mutual love between the principals of the same sex, who in *The Wind* are female. The other woman, Cora, is depicted briefly and more narrowly in the film as jealous, hateful, and full of spite. In both novel and film, Letty's husband, Lige, has a sidekick, Sourdough, but neither man has a role in the key scenes, for this is Letty's story. Lige, an honest and decent rancher, is physically strong and steady, but rough, and he lacks the capability, psychologically as well as financially, to make frontier life bearable for Letty, to educate her and rescue her from her enemies. She is attracted not to the good people, Lige and Sourdough, but only to her enemies, the sexually potent Roddy and the wind.

Sjöström and Marion instilled in *The Wind* the edginess of a psychological drama, its claustrophobic atmosphere frightening Letty and pushing her toward insanity and murder as the focus tightens on scenes of the ranch enveloped in the never ceasing wind and blowing sand. *The Wind* is not a classic Western of chase and rescue, for Letty must rescue *herself.* In Gish's major performances for Griffith in the epics *The Birth of a Nation, Way Down East,* and *Orphans of the Storm,* the tension is built from shots of Gish in terrible danger intercut with shots of her savior's dash to her rescue. *Broken Blossoms,* arguably their finest work together, is atypical of the Gish-Griffith films, for there is no last-minute rescue. Instead, it is her father (Donald Crisp) who drives Gish's character to madness. In a drunken rage, he has locked her in a closet; as she listens to him, she realizes that he will murder her. We feel her claustrophobia and her dread in *Broken Blossoms,* just as we feel the sound and might of the norther when Gish listens, at first nervously and then fearfully, in *The Wind.* The suspense in both films is terrific, and we do not quite know what is going to happen.

Sjöström builds suspense from *The Wind*'s opening scenes, establishing the opposition between Letty and the landscape. John Arnold's black-and-white cinematography masks the light as the wind stirs the sand to block the sun. We never see the horizon, for *The Wind* is a Western that *hides* its landscape visually while highlighting it thematically. It is the intensity of this filtered light that makes the terrain of prairie and hills so threatening and terrifying throughout the narrative. The initial intertitles deride mankind's settlement of the wilderness: "Man—puny, but irresistible—encroaching forever on Nature's vastness, gradually, very gradually, wresting away her strange secrets, subduing her fierce elements—conquers the earth! This is the story of a woman who came into the domain of the winds."

And so we meet this woman who ventures into the wilderness far from her home back East—a wilderness that, while eventually conquered and subdued by human hands, fights back at times with ferocious power. Letty Mason is traveling by train through the Western prairies to live with her cousin Beverly, his wife, Cora, and their children at their ranch in Sweet Water. Wirt Roddy befriends her on the train, and she is grateful for his company. Alarmed by the wind blowing against the train windows, Letty is warned by Roddy that she will not take to life out West as the wind will get to her: "Injuns call this the 'land o' the winds'—it never stops blowing here—day in, day out, whistlin' and howlin'—makes folks go crazy—especially women!" The train arrives at night, in a fierce wind, and Letty endures a long buggy ride through the wind and sand, driven by Lige (Lars Hanson) and his buddy Sourdough (William Orlamond), friends of her cousin. Lige tells her: "Mighty queer—Injuns think the North Wind is a ghost horse that lives in the clouds." And as the buggy passes a herd of wild horses, there appears the stunning symbol of a white stallion leaping through the sky amid dark billowing clouds.

There is no mention in the intertitles that Sweet Water is in Texas. *The Wind*'s production was headquartered in Bakersfield, California, in the Mojave Desert, and airplane propellers were used to stir the wind and sand to create the terrible storm. Not only were the demands of the role hard on Gish but so were the ever present sand and sawdust blown by the propellers, and the 120-degree temperature of the location in the Mojave Desert, not to mention the smoking sulfur pots that were used in the studio for visual effects during the filming of the storm.[17] *The Wind*'s landscape is whirling sand, a mise-en-scène as claustrophobic as those of *Red River* and *The Searchers* are broad and deep. Rarely do we see a vista of ranch lands and mountains, for the constant swirl of sand and then storm blot out the sun and sky. Ultimately we do not much notice or care whether this vague, nearly abstract setting is Texas or California. The claustrophobia is relentless as the constant wash of dust turns day into night, keeping the focus on the desolate horror of the earth.

Parallel to this earthly hell are the heavens of roiling clouds, through which the symbolic white stallion gallops furiously, presenting an Olympian atmosphere of an angry and capricious god that controls nature. In this way the landscape of *The Wind* serves to break the passage or jour-

FIGURE 8. Letty envisions a white stallion galloping in the sky over a desert landscape. Courtesy of the Museum of Modern Art.

ney of its heroine; it will entrap, surround, and torment her as much as any villain would do, its goal to seduce and destroy. *The Wind* may be the ultimate landscape Western, in which the forces of nature—an evil, resisting nature—are so great that the battle to obliterate light, air, and water makes it impossible for the "invaders," the new settlers and ranchers, to survive in it. Most will surrender and leave.

Both Roddy and Lige have proposed marriage to Letty. She goes to see Roddy, who confesses that he already has a wife but wants to take Letty where the wind can never follow her. Not having another choice, and although she thinks Lige's proposal a joke, she accepts Lige, only to find out on their wedding night that as a lover he is oafish and coarse. Letty does not want to live with him; Lige pledges not to touch her again and promises to find the money to send her back East. Letty hates being left alone in their rough shack of a home, where she is always sweeping away the sand. Lige agrees to take her to a meeting with other ranchers to discuss how best to save the cattle from the terrible drought, but her horse runs away with her in the wind, and after Lige rescues her

FIGURE 9. A distraught Letty cannot close her cabin door because of the windblown sand that has entered her abode. Courtesy of the Museum of Modern Art.

she falls from his horse. Letty cannot stay out in the wind; she has to return to their ranch with Sourdough, who makes a few jokes before the men bring in Roddy, supposedly hurt. While Letty washes dishes with sand, Roddy asks why she is afraid of Lige leaving them alone together, and as the wind worsens he tries to seduce her. But Lige soon returns.

The wild horses are coming down the mountain by the thousands, and every man is needed to round them up. Lige says he is helping in order to get money for Letty, and Roddy leaves with him. But Roddy eventually drops behind and returns to the homestead as Letty shuts the door against the howling wind. The norther is coming: cattle break out of the corral, while inside the house objects are blown about and the lantern sways, casting shafts of moving light. Letty cowers in her bed, her eyes following the swaying of the light; she paces, the dog barks, objects bang, a window bursts, and the lamp is knocked over and causes a fire. Letty puts out the flames, stuffs the window with a blanket, and exhaustedly stares at the swaying lantern as everything seems to go back and forth. She sways too and is about to lose her senses when she hears a knock. Thinking it is Lige, she runs to open the door, and a smack of the wind blows Letty to the floor. Roddy enters, picks her up, and tries to make love to her. Letty runs out into the wind but is blown back again: she cannot escape, and when she sees the white stallion racing toward her, she falls into Roddy's arms and faints. He puts her on the bed and then bars the door as the white stallion, symbol of passion, gallops about in the clouds. His rape of Letty occurs offscreen.

The next morning Letty sits at the table as if in a trance, wrapped in her shawl, staring at a gun in its holster. Roddy cannot shut the door against the sand so he props it closed with a shovel, puts on his gun belt and tells her to pack, to go away with him before Lige comes back. When she refuses, he replies that Lige will kill them both, and she declares her hope that he will. As they scuffle and the dog barks, her shawl falls off; she is thrown against the table, picks up the gun, and aims it at him with both hands. Roddy smiles in condescension, moves toward her, then puts his hand on the gun to turn it away. She shoots, and looks at the gun in astonishment as Roddy falls dead. She then panics, grabs the shovel, and runs out to dig a hole in the sand so as to bury his corpse, pushing her shovel against the driving wind.

The films then cuts to Letty in the shack as she paces once more and looks out the window to see the sand blown away from the grave, revealing Roddy's head and his hands. As someone tries to enter, she picks up the gun and throws herself onto the bed in total fear. When Lige turns her over, he sees a madwoman. She confesses that she killed Roddy and points outside, but Lige sees nothing out there, nothing but sand. While Letty stands with her hair falling about her shoulders, Lige assures her that "if you kill a man in justice—it allers covers him up!" He holds her tenderly and promises that she will soon be far away from

FIGURE 10. Letty, fearful but determined, points a pistol to defend herself. Courtesy of the Museum of Modern Art.

all this. Letty begs him not to hate her, not to send her away, crying out, "Can't you see I love you?" They kiss; the door blows open and lets in the blowing sand. Lige asks her if she will always be afraid. She exclaims, "I'm not afraid of the wind—I'm not afraid of anything now!—because I'm your wife—to work with you—to love you!" As in earlier silent Westerns such as Ford's *Straight Shooting* and *3 Bad Men,* as well as Hart's *Hell's Hinges,* a moment of sudden (perhaps too sudden) self-transformation has occurred (see chapter 1).

Gish's characters had endured seductions by unworthy lovers in *Way Down East* and *The Scarlet Letter,* not to mention her roles in which she was murdered by her father (in *Broken Blossoms*), imprisoned in the Bastille (in *Orphans of the Storm*), and subjected to a fatal disease (in *La Bohème*). Few actresses had perished or been rescued more dramatically. With *The Wind,* the movie business decided that Gish's character must save herself, and so it would be a few years before the desert enticed a character played by a major actress to plunge fatally into its vastness: Marlene Dietrich, starring in *Morocco* (1930). The studio's choice of a happy ending made Western movie sense at the time, at least

FIGURE 11. Letty cowers in fear at the verge of madness as she succumbs to the psychological effects of the ever-present desert winds. Courtesy of the Museum of Modern Art.

to the bosses of MGM, even as it deprived the public of a thrilling if pessimistic climax that would have brought the melding of naturalism and melodrama to a brilliant completion. The insistence on a superficially happy ending kept the genre on hold during the transition to sound motion pictures. However unfortunate this may have been for the filmmakers, as for audiences then and now, the decision indicated it was not yet the moment for a more complex denouement that might take the Western tradition in new directions.

Letty, no less than the gunfighters later played by John Wayne in various roles or by Gary Cooper in *The Virginian* (1929), is a classic westerner: a survivor, exiled from her beloved South, moved to kill but exhausted by her ordeal, which she endures alone. She is preoccupied with all that she has lost and, by the end, faces the "reality" of a partnership with her husband in their desolate frontier home. Her giddy relief when Lige hears her confession of murder, and his unquestioning acceptance of her love—no matter that Letty is now damaged goods—are no more overly optimistic than are responses that Gish's characters are forced to make in numerous other films where an about-face in the final scenes is demanded. Letty is reconciled, by Hollywood standards. There being no production code of ethics at the time to dictate her punishment for murdering Roddy, rape appears to be sufficient justification, and Letty is easily forgiven. We cannot but wonder, nonetheless, at Letty's fate. She may have been through the worst, yet the wind will not fade and we cannot imagine that frontier life will improve anytime soon.

Following the release of the film and for years afterward, Gish and Marion complained about the forced "happy ending." Gish said, "We all felt that it was morally unjust." She blamed the exhibitors who insisted that the ending be changed after preview screenings of the film.[18] Marion said that the eastern office had insisted on the picture having a happy ending, and she later recalled: "Lillian was sent for, the interior set was rebuilt, and the 'happy, happy ending' was photographed. Discouraged, Victor Seastrom and Lars Hanson returned to Sweden, and I made some genteel remark like, 'oh, hell, what's the use?' "[19]

An analysis of Marion's numerous scripts for *The Wind,* however, refutes this claim. According to the existing scenarios of *The Wind* in the University of Southern California Warner Brothers Archives, there were six versions and a "New Ending Sequence." The fifth and sixth versions, dated, by Marion, February 11 and February 14–27, 1927, include a prologue of scenes of Letty in Virginia with her grandfather, which depicts a countryside whose setting is "so beautiful that the memory of it will remain with us long after the scene is gone." These scenes are not in the editing continuity list of October 22, 1927, in which the film begins with Letty's train ride west, when she meets Wirt Roddy and first encounters the eternal blowing of the wind. The drafts do have a happy ending, however, with Letty and Lige united by their love, and the "New Ending Sequence" of July 20 expands and alters earlier versions. Production ran from April 29 through June 24.

Thus we may conclude that the happy ending written in February was shot in the spring and revised in July. The ending was not simply created and "tacked on" at the last minute by studio directive. The editing continuity list includes the ending based on the July 20 sequence, and the final title list (of August 7, 1928) is identical to the continuity list of the previous October. The film was released in November of 1928, after further editing, and with an added sound track of music and effects, such as the wind and the barking of the dog, since MGM had begun to add music and effect tracks to films in 1928, in response to the success of the Vitaphone sound system introduced by Warner Brothers in 1926 and 1927.[20]

The film offers Letty no escape, only the choice of staying after conquering her fears. As we witness her sanity being diminished by the harshness of the Texas environment, we recall similar threats to the mental stability of such westerners as Tom Dunson in *Red River* and Ethan Edwards in *The Searchers,* both portrayed by John Wayne. In the former movie, Dunson's determination to cross Texas and reach a northern railroad town pushes him, a rancher leading a cattle drive, to become autocratic and excessive in carrying out his personal vision of frontier justice (see chapter 6). Edwards, wandering in the landscape for years, is obsessed with avenging the murder of his sister-in-law and destroying her daughter, his niece, who was taken by the Comanche warrior Scar as his woman (see chapter 8). Each of these westerners overcomes his lapse into madness but kills men along the way; each has his memories of the woman whom he once loved and who was murdered by Indians; each makes peace with a niece or adopted son; yet each is alone at the end.[21]

Letty, Dunson, and Edwards endure broken journeys and find, in their respective versions of a Hollywood resolution, that madness ends not with love but with reconciliation. Wayne's characters are allowed to struggle through long periods and endless terrain, driven by hatred and a determination to avenge.[22] Dunson and Edwards can shoot and fight it out, their endurance is phenomenal, and their wounds only slow them down temporarily: their pursuit of revenge makes them strong. Letty, though she faints and is attacked by Roddy and the wind, finds similar strength to survive: she can shoot a gun, dig a grave, and bury a man single-handedly. But all has happened so fast. How is her psyche to cope, after months of isolation in a shack on the plains, with what has taken place in less than a day, with the terror of the storm, with rape and her vengeful response, with seeing the body revealed in the sand, all during the ceaseless howling of the wind? A natural reaction to such horror is a retreat into ruthless obsession and even madness. Like Dunson and Edwards, Gish's character survives her temporary insanity. After all, this is Lillian Gish and this is Hollywood. So the Letty of the film awaits her husband and a new chance for happiness, while we are cheated of perhaps Gish's greatest exit, her dash into the stormy desert, like the Letty of Scarborough's novel.

The Wind is classically Western in suggesting contradictions in Letty's character—her innocence and her sexual passion—that point to the fate she should have had. Throughout the narrative Letty is preoccupied by memory, fear, and desire. She has no impulse to take action, no urge to ride across the landscape to complete a cattle drive or a search while in pursuit of vengeance, as do Dunson or Edwards. Nor can she decide how to flee from evil pursuers, as do Jane and Bess in *Riders* or Lee Carleton in Ford's land-rush tale, *3 Bad Men*. Instead, Letty is trapped in the wilderness, and all she can concentrate on is her desperate desire to be rescued from its evil hold over her and on her need of someone else to make possible her escape. Letty is passive, innocent, sensitive, and untrained for her duties as a frontier wife.

Jane Withersteen too suffers from her sincere goodness and from her naive trust in her fellow ranchers in *Riders of the Purple Sage*. Accordingly, the landscape might be viewed as punishing Jane by trapping Lassiter and Jane forever in an isolated valley. In the novel of *The Wind,* Cora is more complex and interesting as an archetype of the strong frontier wife, a beautiful and passionate woman as necessarily selfish as any man and just as devoted, like Jane, to her man's sexuality. The landscape cannot defeat her, for she is too domineering, too crude, and simply too forceful to be attractive to the elements. The wind and sand seem to prey instead on women who appear more vulnerable, and Cora likewise has no patience with those who are too weak, be they men or women—or so she proclaims in the novel.

The lesson to be gleaned from Cora's scorn is that women such as Letty should not leave their homes in "civilized" post–Civil War Virginia to endure frontier life in Texas until the land is settled. This is also Dunson's belief in *Red River*. He will not take his sweetheart, Fen, away from the wagon train to help him start his ranch, for he will not accept her statement that she is strong enough. She cannot persuade him, and his refusal is his biggest mistake: the wagon train is attacked soon after they part, and Fen is murdered (see chapter 6).

However, there are other eastern women who do go out West and overcome their obstacles and challenges. In *The Virginian*, the prototype of Western tradition for numerous later novels and films, Molly Stark, like Letty, crosses the country by train. She is heading to Medicine Bow to become the town's schoolmarm, and she then marries the hero. In Ford's *Stagecoach*, Mrs. Lucy Mallory (Louise Platt) travels from Virginia to Lordsburg to join her husband, a Union Army officer, because she is having a child and "won't be separated from him any longer." Clementine Carter (Cathy Downs) heads out West in search of Doc Holliday (Victor Mature) and stays to civilize Tombstone as a schoolteacher in Ford's *My Darling Clementine*. And Olivia Dandridge (Joanne Dru), visiting from the East, decides to stay and marry a young cavalry officer in Ford's *She Wore a Yellow Ribbon* (1949).

It seems that the goal of Western expansion was to make Texas another Virginia, that symbolic heart of southern gentility where women were revered, cherished, and sheltered by their men. Sentimentally, if hardly historically, Virginia stood for a prewar, civilized America back East, while Texas was the raw frontier West. Texas had southern sympathies and, like Virginia, was a Confederate state during the Civil War. As the agrarian South used up its land in plantations of cotton and tobacco, Texas grass (before the discovery of oil) was grabbed for grazing by new generations of landowners, the cattle ranchers. But the attempt to transform Texas into another Virginia was, of course, a failed one, and *The Wind* has something to say at the metaphorical level about this failure. The drought and the norther in *The Wind* ruin the soil and decimate herds. And in the post–Civil War Texas of *Red River*, Dunson must drive cattle a thousand miles to the north because the war used up all the money in the South; the landscape alone can no longer sustain the economic way of life established by the ranchers, those who forcibly took the land from the Spaniards a couple of decades before the war. In *The Searchers*, Edwards's apology to Lars Jorgensen (John Qualen), the father of Brad (Harry Carey Jr.), who was killed by Indians, is cut short with the comment: "It wasn't your fault, it's this terrible country." And near the end of the novel *The Wind*, Letty tells Roddy, "Oh, it wasn't Lige's fault! He's good. It's this country, this terrible country where it never rains, and no green things grow, and no birds sing!"[23]

Red River and *The Searchers*, both of which play out the notion that fate is character and landscape is fate, were made in the mid-1940s and mid-1950s, respectively, by which time audiences had become familiar with the Western narrative as a form of psychological epic. None of the Westerns produced before 1928 prepare us for *The Wind*'s fierceness, its passion, and its unrelenting, swirling maelstrom of wind and sand. Gish lets us hear the wind through her gestures and expressions. We do not need orchestral cues to trigger our responses, to let us know that the wind is gathering force. In the thrilling scenes of Letty's panic during the storm, the film cuts rapidly to show us the dog barking, objects banging, and a window breaking. We sense the ferocity of the howling elements.

Tom Mix's 1925 film version of *Riders of the Purple Sage* does not approach the intensity of *The Wind*, but closer to the latter is Hart's *Hell's Hinges*, which provides a roaring climax of a town in flames (see chapter 1). Ford's *Bad Men*, like *Riders*' storyline, has two heroines pursued by an evil man, just as Letty is pursued by the malevolent Roddy. The narrative of Ford's film, however, is overloaded with a meandering melodramatic plot and underdeveloped romantic leads, emotionally engaging us primarily in the redemption of the three good bad men (see chapter 1). Perhaps only *The Gold Rush*, Charlie Chaplin's 1925 masterpiece and arguably a Western landscape film in some sense, pits its hero as excitingly against the elements and storms of the frontier, the Yukon snow country of 1898, as does *The Wind*. To be sure, *The Gold Rush* is a comedy, while *The Wind* veers toward the tragic throughout much of its running time. Sjöström's film is also the impressive precursor of such later "psychological Westerns" as *Duel in the Sun, Pursued, The Furies, Jubal, The Naked Spur,* and *The Searchers*—in addition to being the last great Western of the silent era.

CHAPTER 3

"He Went That-Away"

The Comic Western and "Ruggles of Red Gap"

I'd like the West better if it was in the East.
—Chico Marx in *Go West* (1940)

Throughout the rich history of the Western film, the most enduring and successful, or at least most beloved, productions have been notable for their romanticism, comedy, or both. They have often presented comrades who joyfully and delightedly indulge those who yearn to become heroes. The Western genre has been consistently supple enough to encourage satire and parody of its formulaic plots, its expansionist themes, and particularly its notion of the westerner as an occasional antihero, put forth as early as 1911 in the delightful short *Was He a Coward?* In this D.W. Griffith production for the Biograph Company, which had a screenplay by Emmett Campbell Hall, and which was shot on location in California by cameraman Billy Bitzer, a new brand of hero appeared, the bumbling easterner who emerges as a self-possessed and capable man, played here by Wilfred Lucas. Lucas stars as the tenderfoot who arrives at Jack Rabbit Ranch to recover from a nervous breakdown and redeems his cowardly refusal to fight by bravely caring for victims of smallpox. That same year, in *Bertie's Bandit* (1911), Bertie the Botanist goes West to develop his manliness in Arizona, where part of the film was shot, only to grow peevish when a bandit ruins his specimen case. Bertie defeats the robber in the rocks overlooking the desert, as seen in a long shot of the valley from the vantage point of the cliff. A few years later, Douglas Fairbanks would perfect the role of the effete easterner come West to reveal an all-American, can-do optimism certain to vanquish every foe, in such films as *Wild and Woolly* (1917) and *The Mollycoddle* (1920).

If contradictory themes and characterizations, as well as moral ambiguities, are at the heart of the Western, they are no less important in the genre's comic modes. The comedies of violence, satire, parody, ridicule, and prejudice were all used in a variety of ways as the Western evolved—mixing and blending them in dramas, melodramas, and tragedies, as well as in comic shorts and features, though not always to the films' advantage. As Westerns relied on stereotypical characters to quickly convey messages of stupidity, danger, and evil, as well as to set up characters for easy laughs, generalized racial and gender types flourished. Along with caricatures of Apache and Comanche warriors and Mexican banditos were stereotypes such as the immigrant or foreigner who does not speak English too good, the bossy mother-in-law, the law 'n' order league of ladies, the hero's sidekick, the rustler who works in the dark, the barman, the gambler, the crooked sheriff, the tootsies who sometimes even dance and sing, the ranch or outlaw boss and his "boys," and the hired gun.

Matthew Turner nicely summarizes the nature of the Western comedy in terms of its subverting *and* sustaining of genre expectations in his essay "From Cowboys and Comedy: The Simultaneous Deconstruction and Reinforcement of Generic Conventions in the Western Parody":

> The [Western] genre is composed of a complex set of codes and images, including the lonesome hero, moral justice enforced by violence, the coming of the railroad, the shoot-out, the open prairie, hats, horses, cowboys, and guns. Even though the Western parody does not reflect the prevailing dramatic mood of the Western, it does adhere to the genre's setting and incorporates its codes and images for comedic and parodic purposes. . . . Despite the tendency of Western parodies to undermine or spoof the codes of the more traditional Western, they are still situated within the genre. . . . The Western parody mocks the codes and conventions of a distinctively American cinematic genre while commenting—directly and indirectly—on the cultural and social issues of its time. Nevertheless, in the act of subverting those conventions and calling attention to their constructedness, the Western parody creates its own set of conventions that are closely allied to, and often rely heavily on, the conventions of the Western itself.[1]

THE DEVELOPMENT OF THE WESTERN COMEDY

Among the earliest and most successful Westerns was Edwin S. Porter's *The Great Train Robbery,* a narrative dealing with a violent crime involving the murder of innocent people. Two years later Porter smartly parodied his popular Western with *The Little Train Robbery,* in which junior cowboys stage a holdup, steal candy and dolls from girls in white dresses, and are chased and captured by adult cops. Filmed at an amusement park in the convenient wilds of New Jersey, using a miniature train, the action is highlighted by pans of the train ride.

The Biograph Company's one- and two-reel Westerns—whether comedies, dramas, or melodramas—were always adventurous, packing the moral punch of the literary form of the short story and marked by a clever twist so that our heroes foil the crime or suffer a devastating loss. Filmed at the studio in New York or in the California landscape and Hollywood cityscape, the various plots relied on stereotypes in pairing the good guy (or quite often the gal) and the villains. Shot in the New York studio, Griffith's *The Road to the Heart* (1909) shows us that the road to the heart is right through the stomach, as a wealthy Mexican rancher discovers when his wife and daughter leave him. In quick succession, he hires and fires three cooks—a Chinese man, an Irish lass, and a temperamental cowboy—before humbly rejoining his family at their table. Ethnic and comic stereotyping would play a major role in many of John Ford's Westerns, most especially in his "cavalry trilogy" of the 1940s (*Fort Apache, She Wore a Yellow Ribbon,* and *Rio Grande*), in which one Irish American officer (played in all three films by Victor McLaglen) exhibits all of the overly generalized traits of his "race": he is alcoholic, bumbling, and loquacious when liquored. Mel Brooks's later landmark parody of the Western, *Blazing Saddles* (1974), would bring the blatant use of racial and ethnic stereotypes for comic effect to an entirely new level.

In the Kalem production *Driver of the Deadwood Coach* (1912, director unknown), Bad Bill's heist of a gold shipment is foiled by a clever lad who photographs the arrival of the stagecoach so as to identify the robber, developing the negative in the nick of time. And by 1916 it was time to parody the great William S. Hart, the laconic hero of action-adventure Westerns, and Mack Sennett took on this task in his Keystone Studios comedy *His Bitter Pill* (1916). The marvelous Mack Swain, Chaplin's oversized costar in *The Gold Rush* as delirious Big Jim McKay, mocks Hart in his role as a "big-hearted sheriff." Swain is joined by Edgar Kennedy, who had performed with Chaplin in Keystone's short *Tillie's Punctured Romance* (1914), and who would later master the "slow burn" in reaction to the antics of Laurel and Hardy and the Marx Brothers.

Douglas Fairbanks raised the question "Was he a coward?" to an art form. The gay blade, who is not generally recalled as a star of Westerns, made a series of comedy-adventures during the second decade of the twentieth century, contributions to the genre that are as accomplished as the features of Hart. In them, Fairbanks's incompetent urbanite is every bit as bold and brave as Wilfred Lucas's character was in the 1911 Biograph short whose title poses the "coward" question. And this is true despite the fact that his character is in disguise for a good part of each film in this series—*The Lamb* (1915), *The Good Bad Man* (1916), *The Half Breed* (1916), *Wild and Woolly, The Man from Painted Post* (1917), *The Knickerbocker Buckaroo* (1919), and *The Mollycoddle*.

Hart and Fairbanks saw themselves (and were marketed) as earnest, clean-living, virile all-American heroes even as they played the good bad man or the naive spoiled brat. William Hart's straitlaced and straight-faced gunfighter pursued authenticity and realism without speaking a word more than necessary (see chapter 1). He was the predecessor to the loner played by Gary Cooper or Randolph Scott in later Westerns, the man who chivalrously saved the female from the bad guys and eliminated his enemies at the same time, often single-handedly. In real life Fairbanks dreamily worshipped the West as a land of natural virtue. Fairbanks thought of the circumscribed domain of the "civilized" urbanite with abhorrence and sought to encourage freedom and inspiration for the pathetic, trapped clerical worker in the comic romances of his Western adventures. Fairbanks's acknowledged idol was Theodore Roosevelt, the embodiment of virtues that were honed in the late nineteenth-century West, and that enabled Americans to walk tall into the twentieth century. In his popular 1917 book *Laugh and Live,* Fairbanks's instructional manual on how to be physically and mentally fit on a diet of humor, he cites Roosevelt as a direct influence on his gung ho appreciation of good health and an expansionist America.[2]

Fairbanks produced and starred in adventure comedies in the years 1915–20, an extraordinary period in a different kind of expansionist America, during which the United States entered World War I. These films are fantasies in which a young, clever, energetic, and ever optimistic patriot conquers all, fearlessly if seemingly foolishly. Yet Fairbanks smartly satirizes his veneration of the life of the manly westerner, whose athleticism, honesty, and self-confidence enable him to put a stop to evil deeds as well as to the mockery of the villains. Few matched the talents of Fairbanks on screen. He seems to have it all, yet he looks like an ordinary man, not especially tall or imposing or handsome when dressed in city or cowboy garb (he would reveal his famous physique in later swashbucklers). His infectious gaiety, lighthearted approach to dire situations, and enthusiastic leaping-about gave him special appeal. Rather than relying on facial close-ups, he offers his whole body, which is ever in motion, suggesting the physical elegance and amusing style of the later Cary Grant or Fred Astaire and the dashing athleticism and energy of Gene Kelly, with hints of the goofy stiff-legged walks and scissors kicks of Jacques Tati. Fairbanks understood the magical fusion of timing, visual composition, and camera angle, whether he occupied center screen or was manic at its fringes and in long shots.

Spanning much of the filmmaking period prior to sound motion pictures—from the opening years of the century through the 1920s—the comedic Western was a staple of theatrical shorts and features. Comic timing reached perfect pitch before the talkies took over. Charlie Chaplin in *The Gold Rush* (1925), Raymond Griffith in *Hands Up!* (1926), Tom Mix in *The Great K & A Train Robbery* (1926), and Buster Keaton in *Go West* (1925) and *The General* (1927) offered hilarious, exquisitely fluid sequences of physical gags spiced by witty intertitles. Except for Tom Mix, basically a cowboy hero, these comic adventurers traveled west or south, or into the past, and took advantage of the codes of the Western film that were well ingrained in the funny bones of their audiences. Keaton's comic Westerns are feats of manic stunt work and elaborate sight gags, particularly his stone-faced portrayal of an inexperienced cowboy in *Go West* and his earlier short *The Paleface* (1922), in which Buster is adopted by an Indian tribe seeking vengeance against land-grabbing oil barons.

In 1924 Mack Sennett produced *Riders of the Purple Cows*, continuing his slapstick approach to the Western with gags that hardly relate to Zane Grey's *Riders of the Purple Sage*. Grey's novel (1912) had been filmed in 1918, and it relied on the clichés of a ranch owner who is threatened by outlaws, defended by his daughter, and saved by a gold prospector. In the following year, Tom Mix would star in a version of *Riders of the Purple Sage* (1925); yet more to the point is his rollicking 1926 Western *The Great K & A Train Robbery*, directed by Lewis Seiler. Mix plays a dashing detective, but his horse, Tony, is as much the hero; their daring feats and stunts take advantage of the heights and depths of the Royal Gorge of the Arkansas River in Colorado, including a preposterous underwater hangout. The most popular cowboy star of the silent period, Mix is the opposite of Hart: frenetic where Hart is slow, self-mocking where Hart is deadpan serious, and a daredevil of stunts in escapist stories in which he seeks authenticity and realism.

John Ford exploited yet struggled with comical stereotypes throughout his career. He did not favor exclusively comedic sound Westerns, but as early as *Straight Shooting* (1917) and *Just Pals* (1920) he relied on the wisdom of truths revealed comically, whether uttered by the hero, by a drunken journalist or doctor, or by certain female characters played by such actresses as Olive Carey and Mildred Natwick. Ford used the comic approach in most of his Westerns to strengthen or balance his themes, at times with genuine warmth, as in *My Darling Clementine* (1946) and *She Wore a Yellow Ribbon* (1949), or with savage hilarity or bitterness, as in *The Searchers* (1956) and *The Man Who Shot Liberty Valance* (1962). He also indulged in broadly farcical, if at times overly sentimental, exchanges between inebriated Irishmen, such as the banter between Victor McLaglen's Sergeant Quincannon and Francis Ford's bartender in *She Wore a Yellow Ribbon*. Indeed, the consumption of spirits and attempts at abstinence are characteristic of many of the principal and secondary characters in Ford's (as well as Hawks's) Westerns. Certainly Thomas Mitchell as Doc Boone in *Stagecoach* and Edmund O'Brien as newspaper editor Dutton Peabody in *The Man Who Shot Liberty Valance* are, together with heroes played by John Wayne, the most perceptive observers and speakers of truth in Westerns. Other characters—including villains, self-righteous ladies, and bartenders—may be funny, but it is the inebriated who are the most highly educated professionals, who manage to do their jobs however sloshed they may be, and who are the only truly witty characters, the only ones to play consciously with language and meaning.

Easily recognizable characters are deemed as necessary for the success of comic Westerns as for any other blend of film genres, just as the traits of the gunfighter or cowboy—in behavior, costume, and setting—adhere to established if overly well worn codes. Ford's *Stagecoach* is a comedy-drama whose narrative economy is built on the deliberate tensions between the expected and the unexpected, as well as on the audience's familiarity with clichéd personalities (see chapter 4). Such characters are quickly understood because they are cleverly cast, overtly costumed to type, and directed in a kind of cinematic shorthand to emphasize strong gestures and familiar expressions. We have no difficulty in grasping the frustrations and self-obsessions of these traditional characters. The tense interactions between these peculiar and not always civilized Americans, in constant conflict with one another and helped by the fast-paced editing of the verbal exchanges, make the comic segments of *Stagecoach* as sharp and satisfying as the narrative of Hawks's contemporaneous screwball comedy *His Girl Friday* (1940). The rhythm of comic editing, too, is crucial, as essential to our ability to grasp the layers of meaning and humor as are the clichéd personalities. The infinitesimal pauses around and between words and gestures give us the time we need to get and savor the point.

The comic Western became perfected in the period of the mid- to late 1930s with movies such as Leo McCarey's *Ruggles of Red Gap* (1935), *Stagecoach,* and George Marshall's *Destry Rides Again* (1939). The satirical thrusts of these films and their strong comic elements may have been factors in the revival of interest in the Western genre, which had languished following the end of the 1920s and during the first half-decade of the Great Depression, when audiences preferred crime stories and glamorous comedies.

Along the pathway of the developing humor-laced sound Western, famous comedy actors took their turns in reviving the types of Western spoofs that had been pioneered by Fairbanks and Keaton. That popular pair of bumblers Stan Laurel and Oliver Hardy appeared in the hilarious *Way Out West* (1937), one of their best films. In it, they travel into uncivilized territory to deliver a mining deed to the daughter of a recently deceased prospector, only to face villains and other obstacles. The Marx Brothers went west in *Go West* (1940), filled with their typically zany humor as well as a plot involving land deeds and a diabolical saloon owner. Bud Abbott and Lou Costello wound up at a dude ranch and rode the range in *Ride 'Em Cowboy* (1942); they once again appeared way out west in *The Wistful Widow of Wagon Gap* (1947), this time teamed with Marjorie Main.

Droll wiseguy Bob Hope, playing cowardly dentist "Painless" Peter Potter, found himself unwittingly married to sharpshooting Calamity Jane (Jane Russell) and in the middle of her battle with Indians in *The Paleface* (1948). A few years later, Hope and Lucille Ball enjoyed their best teaming in George Marshall's *Fancy Pants* (1950), a loose remake of Leo McCarey's infinitely superior *Ruggles of Red Gap* (discussed later in this chapter). In this version of the Harry Leon Wilson novel, Hope is an actor playing a butler, eventually mistaken for an earl, and caught up in various trials and tribulations while his town awaits the visit of none other than President Theodore Roosevelt. While Bob Hope's Western comedies do not reach the heights of Fairbanks's or Keaton's, these films present viewers with further variations on the stereotype of the effete westerner who stumbles naively through a land of savages (both red and white). Hope's audience-friendly style and popularity also helped to pave the way for many of the humor-filled Western television series of the 1950s and 1960s, including the successful series *Maverick* (beginning in 1957) with Jack Kelly and James Garner.

The role of the hero's sidekick would become a ubiquitous feature of comedic Westerns in films and television shows. Whether comic or straight man, he might be Spanish, as in numerous versions of *The Cisco Kid* in film (1940s) and on TV (1950–1956), or Indian, like Jay Silverheels as Tonto in *The Lone Ranger* TV series (1949–1957).[3] A useful fellow as loyalist, front man, or spy, he usually lacked his pal's daring or enforcement skills. The sidekick might be physically slowed by his weight, as with Andy Devine in the 1950s television series *The Adventures of Wild Bill Hickok*. Edgar Buchanan (who appeared in countless Westerns in film and television) played good guys and bad guys as equally sympathetic, funny, and nasty where need be, as did the popular Slim Pickens and Chill Wills. Walter Brennan's most enduring interpretations on screen were in the role of reliable sidekick in Howard Hawks's Westerns, where he played the wiser, long-suffering older friend and sometime deputy sheriff whom the hero could not do without. Such a sidekick was portrayed by Brennan in Hawks's *Red River* (1948) and *Rio Bravo* (1959) and by Arthur Hunnicutt in Hawks's *The Big Sky* (1952) and *El Dorado* (1967) (see chapter 6).

By the 1960s the comedic Western had become a beloved and familiar component of the overall genre. At the very start of the decade, John Wayne tried his hand at rugged outdoor comedy in Henry Hathaway's *North to Alaska* (1960), alongside an eclectic cast that included Stewart Granger, Ernie Kovacs, Capucine, and Fabian. Wayne had already delved into comedy in Ford's classic parody of Irish culture, *The Quiet Man* (1952), and also played lighthearted straight man to Walter Brennan's hilariously cantankerous "Stumpy" in Hawks's *Rio Bravo*. A few years later, Wayne continued in comic mode with Andrew McLaglen's *McLintock!* (1963), where he reteamed with Maureen O'Hara, his previous costar in Ford's *Rio Grande*, *The Quiet Man*, and *The Wings of Eagles*.

Some films began to revel in their parodies of the Western genre's conventions. Elliot Silverstein's *Cat Ballou* (1965) stars an engaging Jane Fonda as the title character, a female westerner who seeks vengeance against land-grabbing railroad-builders for her father's murder. In the process she hires a drunken ex-gunslinger, Kid Shelleen, played hilariously and charismatically by Lee Marvin, who won an Oscar for Best Actor in his dual role here as Shelleen and his "evil twin," Tim Strawn.

Some may have been surprised by Marvin's masterful display of comic talent, but his performance is the clear extension of his bold and outrageous villain in Ford's *The Man Who Shot Liberty Valance* and, more especially, of his drunken, brawling "Boats" Gilhooley (alongside Wayne) in Ford's tropical comedy *Donovan's Reef* (1963). The humor of *Cat Ballou* is also enhanced by the presence of Nat King Cole and Stubby Kaye, smiling balladeers who wander throughout the proceedings with their banjos and narrate the ongoing story in infectious bursts of song.

For Western comedy of the 1960s, *Cat Ballou* was most closely rivaled by Burt Kennedy's successful *Support Your Local Sheriff* (1969), in which James Garner plays an enterprising sheriff amid an impressive roster of familiar Western character actors, including Harry Morgan, Jack Elam, and none other than perennial sidekick Walter Brennan. As with James Stewart's lead character in *Destry Rides Again,* Garner's lawman is a combination of naïveté and cleverness, an expert marksman who nonetheless prefers to use his wit instead of a weapon when he can do so. A few years later, director Kennedy, star Garner, and a near-identical cast (minus Brennan) joined forces for another enjoyable, though somewhat less successful, Western comedy entitled *Support Your Local Gunfighter* (1971). And in 1970, old friends and accomplished Western stars Jimmy Stewart and Henry Fonda teamed up with Shirley Jones for an enjoyable, modest little Western comedy entitled *The Cheyenne Social Club,* directed by Gene Kelly.

The stage was set, of course, for a turn to comedy in the works of the revisionist Western filmmakers of the later 1960s and the 1970s (see chapter 9 for an exploration of this period). The revisionist, or "post-classical," Western is adept, almost by definition, at the same type of genre subversion that is the hallmark of the traditional Western comedy, and so their combination is an aptly fitting one. One of the most successful of these fusions is George Roy Hill's *Butch Cassidy and the Sundance Kid* (1969), starring Paul Newman and Robert Redford as rambunctious outlaws who rob one train too many and then head to Bolivia to escape, or attempt to escape, a posse in pursuit. The film features some hilarious lines of dialogue and occasions frequent smiles because of the antics of its charismatic leads. By 1983, the movie had become the second-most popular Western ever made in terms of American box office returns, second only to *Blazing Saddles,* which arrived in 1974.[4]

Also notable is Sam Peckinpah's surprisingly relaxed and pleasant *The Ballad of Cable Hogue* (1970), in which the violence-oriented director shifts moods radically after his brilliant but bloody *The Wild Bunch*

FIGURE 12. Cleavon Little (*right*) as Sheriff Bart and Gene Wilder (*left*) as his sidekick, Jim, in Mel Brooks's *Blazing Saddles* (1974). Courtesy of the Museum of Modern Art.

of a year before. The title character (Jason Robards) is left to die in the desert by his two former partners and, nearly dead of thirst while trekking across scorching sands, discovers a patch of land with a source of freshwater. Cable eventually purchases the property and turns it into a successful way station for stagecoach passengers, a vestige of pioneering enterprise in a West that is quickly changing. While waiting patiently to enact revenge against the pair of double-crossers who had left him for dead, hoping that they will happen by in order to quench their thirst, Cable befriends a preacher, Joshua (David Warner), and takes up with local prostitute Hildy (Stella Stevens). The movie features a memorable performance by Strother Martin and is ornamented with impressive cinematography by Lucien Ballard, along with superb original songs by Jerry Goldsmith. Most of all, it is graced with a clever script by John Crawford and Edmund Penney, one that radiates the kind of brash wit and eccentric charm that mark the best Western comedies of the sound era.

Finally, we have Mel Brooks pushing the genre to the extreme limit in *Blazing Saddles*, which may be the funniest parody in the history of

Western movies. Some of the filmgoing public deemed it a tad too crude because of its indulgence in raunchy revelry, but its considerable number of viewers made *Blazing Saddles* one of the top-grossing Westerns of all time. In this clever and audacious satire, the black sheriff of Rock Ridge (Cleavon Little) encounters bigotry at every step in his brief career as a law enforcer, though he triumphs because he is clever and cool. His sidekick is the eccentric, alcoholic Jim (Gene Wilder, who also scored as the mad genius in Brooks's other classic spoof of 1974, *Young Frankenstein*). Together they must confront the villainous land-grabbing politician Hedley Lamarr (Harvey Korman) and a band of idiotic gunfighters hired by Lamarr and led by trail boss Taggart (the reliable Western character actor Slim Pickens). Madeline Kahn nearly steals the show as seductive dance-hall performer Lili von Shtupp in a parody of Marlene Dietrich's performance in *Destry Rides Again*. Director Brooks enjoys two small roles: as Governor William J. Lepetomane, who only has eyes for female cleavage, and as the idiotic Indian chief.

No Western comedy has since topped *Blazing Saddles* for its sheer zaniness and willingness to push the envelope in terms of convention-mocking. There were not as many instances of comedic Westerns during the 1980s and 1990s, with the most notable example being Ron Underwood's *City Slickers* (1991), in which actor-comedian Billy Crystal portrays a man who goes on a two-week cattle drive, along with his two buddies (Daniel Stern and Bruno Kirby), in the attempt to overcome, or at least temporarily escape, his midlife crisis. Along the way they learn inspirational and hard life lessons from the weathered cowpoke Curly Washburn (Jack Palance). The film was successful enough to merit a sequel and also earned Palance, who was the archetype of Western villainy in 1953's *Shane*, an Oscar for Best Supporting Actor in his role as an experienced cowboy guru.

CASE STUDY: *RUGGLES OF RED GAP*

Comic Westerns continued yet broadened the Western tradition in the sound era, quite apart from the dramas of racial, political, and expansionist themes that characterized visually ambitious and intellectually critical Westerns in the decades following World War II, when the Cold War and Vietnam spurred meaningful commentary in Western narratives. Western comedies could be delightfully subversive, satirizing modern society through stories set in earlier times and taking on issues such as racial and social tolerance. In the middle and late 1930s, several Westerns, such as *Stagecoach* and *Destry Rides Again,* parodied or satirized the traditions and mores of the late-nineteenth-century West and were hugely successful at the box office and with critics. These films blended genres in their attempts to rely on sex or romance in the way that made screwball comedies so popular.

A notable and oft-neglected comic Western is *Ruggles of Red Gap.* Directed by Leo McCarey for Paramount and produced by Arthur Hornblow Jr. from a screenplay by Walter De Leon and Harlan Thompson, *Ruggles* stars Charles Laughton and features notable performances by Mary Boland, Charlie Ruggles, ZaSu Pitts, Roland Young, and Leila Hyams. The film relates the story of the emancipation of Ruggles (Laughton), a perfect gentleman's gentleman, from his slavishly loyal status in English servitude. He eventually becomes a successful entrepreneur in America, the proprietor of the Anglo-American Grill in the town of Red Gap in the state of Washington. The original story, set in 1908 and published in 1915, winks at snobbery and social pretension. A comedy that is a Western in at least a broad sense of the term, *Ruggles* blends satire, sentiment, and social commentary and has consequently been considered an odd little masterpiece, off to the side of the classic screwball comedies of the 1930s.

Leo McCarey's oeuvre is equally impossible to classify and categorize. His sharp-edged spoofs and the brilliant comic performances he elicited from actors in this period are the opposite of the melodramatic tearjerkers and sometimes treacly sentimentality of his later films, such as *An Affair to Remember* (1957). McCarey had been a gag writer for Hal Roach, and many of the shorts in which he teamed Laurel and Hardy were ones that he wrote and directed. Laughton's paralyzed grin at the denouement of *Ruggles of Red Gap* seems the heir to Laurel's famous facial expression. In the 1930s McCarey directed such other masterful comedies as *Duck Soup* (1933) with the Marx Brothers; *Six of a Kind* (1934) with W. C. Fields; *Belle of the Nineties* (1934) with Mae West; *The Milky Way* (1936) with Harold Lloyd; *The Awful Truth* (1937) with Irene Dunne and Cary Grant; and the sophisticated yet wonderfully corny drama *Love Affair* (1939) with Irene Dunne and Charles Boyer (remade by McCarey in 1957 as *An Affair to Remember* with Deborah Kerr and Cary Grant).

McCarey was friends with and learned from Charlie Chaplin and Ernst Lubitsch, before and while Lubitsch was head of production at Paramount. He was compared to Frank Capra and was even brought over to Columbia in 1937 to make *The Awful Truth* as a Capraesque film for the studio that wanted to show that Harry Cohn could get along without Capra. James Harvey noted in his book *Romantic Comedy in Hollywood*: "The McCarey stamp on a picture has been described as being 'somewhere between the Capra and the Lubitsch touch.' "[5] At first glance, *Ruggles* seems indebted to both Lubitsch and Capra. Like the former's *Trouble in Paradise* (1932), *Ruggles* is a social comedy at its silliest, where the rich are frivolous and useless while their male and female servants are much wiser and more capable of maintaining successful careers, whether as crooks in Lubitsch's contemporary Venice and Paris or as the denizens of McCarey's Wild West. Although the stories are set two decades apart, both films tweak Gallic glamour, the importance attached to fashionable and expensive dress, and the appearance of the appreciation of art and culture. In addition, each film offers a performance by Charlie Ruggles. And like Capra's sagas of the very American male, *Ruggles* contains messages about fundamental American concepts of democracy and equality and about the supposedly little man who can make a difference in people's lives.

Ruggles of Red Gap is not really a parody, although in its own delightful way it mocks the classic Western story of the good bad man come to town to rid it of evil, as does *Destry Rides Again* and *Blazing Saddles*. In *Ruggles* the barriers are set by the socially ambitious nouveaux riches. While Laughton would never be convincing in country gear, he comes to master the raw frontier like any Virginian from the civilized world, becoming a man of property and settlement through a quintessential Anglo conquest of new territories. The theme of freeing oneself from servitude and refusing to keep to one's place in a rigid, prescribed society, a society marked by snobbery and prejudice, is as central to *Ruggles* as it is to *Blazing Saddles*.

A highly accomplished work of social observation, this movie is a critique of class distinctions in which the characters are given sparkling individuality through their eccentric responses to every challenging situation. They are more fully developed than are the sometimes clichéd and sentimentalized characters of Capra's comedies or those of Ford's *Stagecoach*. But this is not to denigrate such stereotypes. Watching a Ford or a Capra film, we readily respond with passion, tears, jitters, or sighs to the troubles of the easily recognizable characters as we note the populist sympathies of the directors and their scorn for hypocrisy.

Rather different is our affectionate response of grins and belly laughs, free of anger or bitterness, when we watch the antics of Ruggles and his

FIGURE 13. English butler Ruggles (Charles Laughton) is led along a Paris boulevard by his new "owner," Egbert Floud (Charlie Ruggles), in Leo McCarey's Western comedy *Ruggles of Red Gap* (1935). Courtesy of the Museum of Modern Art.

masters and friends. The laughter we find in daily life in the movie's Paris and Red Gap is not that of Lubitsch's Paris and Venice. *Trouble in Paradise* was, fortunately, directed by Lubitsch in precode Hollywood in 1932 and thus uncensored: gloriously amoral, its plot turns Herbert Marshall's Gaston Monescu, world-famous thief, into a good bad man at the last minute, to ease the cynicism of his double game and allow him to save Madame Mariette Colet (Kay Francis), the wealthy beauty he has robbed, from an even bigger crook (C. Aubrey Smith) so that he can keep the stolen goods for his first love Lily (Miriam Hopkins). *Trouble in Paradise* is a sexual romp disguised as a romantic comedy, or vice versa, and that is its beginning and end. Its three main characters are stunningly attractive and witty, and its supporting characters (as played by Charlie Ruggles, Edward Everett Horton, C. Aubrey Smith, and Robert Greig) are all-male, foolish, pompous, or long suffering. Preston Sturges—who wrote the screenplay for *Easy Living,* the satire of rich and deliciously foolish New Yorkers directed by Mitchell Leisen in 1937—would carry on the Lubitsch tradition in *The Lady Eve* (1941) and *The Palm Beach Story* (1942).

Ruggles of Red Gap has an affectionate and generous heart, but one less obviously devoted to sexual romance than these other films. Its numerous male and female characters, excepting the party-giver Nell, are all people as silly and stubborn as we could ever hope to meet. McCarey has a magic touch of his own in illuminating personalities with a quip or an unexpected kick in the pants, shifting fluidly from raucous to gentle, from slapstick to subtle. His timing can be exquisite.

Ruggles has been praised for Laughton's fine performance and for the ease with which the director and actor collaborated. Laughton offers gestures and expressive reactions with a physicality that embodies the character in awkward, jerky, but slyly rhythmic movements, ever on tiptoe. His soft yet crisp voice conveys his deep intelligence and powers of observation as well as his simultaneous assertiveness and humility. Laughton's Ruggles, loyal to English rule or at least to the tradition of servitude, is the errant knight, the effete European who comes to the West and learns the American way. In Red Gap he acquires the courage to be his own man, to stand up to hypocrisy and falsehood, even to criticize the cooking of the woman he loves. As such, Ruggles is a successor to Douglas Fairbanks's European-raised American mollycoddle who learns to be a man and a hero, the son who triumphs in *Wild and Woolly*. Trapped in his urban surroundings, Fairbanks's character would dream of adventure and excitement not to be found in New York City's parks, and he could not wait to rush out West. In *The Mollycoddle* Fairbanks is initially a reluctant traveler, kidnapped and stowed on board a boat for a transatlantic journey to Arizona via Galveston. His odyssey is broken as abruptly and violently as that of any Western hero, yet his triumph seems easily achieved because of his optimism and acrobatics.

Ruggles, too, through no will of his own, undertakes a journey after he is "won" by Egbert Floud (Charlie Ruggles) in a poker game in Paris and thus must accompany Mr. and Mrs. Floud (Mary Boland) to Red Gap. His journey is far more frightening than that of Fairbanks in *Wild and Woolly,* for he lacks courage and assertiveness in all but the social and sartorial skills of a gentleman's gentleman. His terror at the concept of living in the untamed wilderness that is Washington State gives us an early clue to the movie's structure, in which his timidity initially yields to humiliation and domination by the self-obsessed. Ruggles will subsequently encounter a frontier of snobbery and social climbing by the nouveau riche "boorgeoisy" of Mrs. Floud, her brother-in-law, Mr. Belknap-Jackson (Lucien Littlefield), and the town's prominent hostesses. But he will also hear about democracy and equality from the simpler, loud-mouthed, hard-drinking but genial circle of Egbert Floud, his mother-in-law, Ma Pettingill (Maude Eburne), and a prominent hostess of quite another kind, Nell Kenner (Leila Hyams).

Also giving memorable performances here are Roland Young as the butler's previous and presumably lifetime employer (the nonsensical Earl of Burnstead) and James Burke as fellow Red Gap native Jeff Tuttle, who thirstily arrives in Paris after having traveled, he says, "all over Europe, *and* Italy. Cathedrals, just one church after another." No less than to these gentlemen, *Ruggles of Red Gap* belongs to the ladies. Mary Boland as Effie Floud (she is also superb as the Countess De Lave in George Cukor's classic all-female comedy *The Women* of 1939) is tightly corseted and overdressed to kill in striped, puff-sleeved outfits that must have been borrowed from Mae West's wardrobe. When she swishes the train of one of her alarming gowns as she turns in frustration to confront her husband or any other member of "the opposition," she commands center stage like no one else. Her mispronunciation of French may be her greatest talent as she fractures every word and phrase with clarity and ease; we do not miss any of her comments on the Parisian "*oh-tee mon-dee.*"

Effie's origins are clear from the moment we meet her mother, Ma Pettingill, a loud-laughing, cigarette-puffing oil millionairess who has paid for the family's palatial, heavily columned, vulgar Victorian mansion and who enjoys the follies of her daughter and son-in-law as they obsess about social esteem. Mrs. Judson, as interpreted by ZaSu Pitts with gentle charm and perfect timing of expression and voice, represents reason and sanity; in her quiet way she is keenly observant when not fearful that she has pushed too far. Where Charlie Ruggles's Egbert laughs at himself and his friends, Pitts delivers Mrs. Judson's asides directly to us, sharing her deadpan commentary so that we do not miss a beat.

Mrs. Judson and Egbert Floud are the wisest citizens of Red Gap, unafraid to question the fears of Ruggles and to tell him to stand up for himself. From the time Egbert takes possession of Ruggles in Paris on the morning after the poker game, the reluctant master lectures his new valet on the principle of American egalitarianism: that all men are created equal. (At the same time, Egbert demonstrates a libertarian approach to his wardrobe, a collection of boldly checked suits that assert his individuality and constitute one of his few rebellious ways of dealing with his beloved wife.) "Oh, no," replies the British Ruggles to Egbert's pronouncement of his democratic views. "That may be all very well for America, sir, but it would never do with us." Thus we are told that this social comedy will be more than a witty exposé of the manners of the Old World rich.

Carl Van Doren notes of the original novel: "If the new [twentieth] century had no humorist of the stature of Mark Twain, it still had Harry Leon Wilson, whose *Bunker Bean* (1912), *Ruggles of Red Gap* (1915), and *Merton of the Movies* (1922) pleased a hearty public with an excellent fun which has been overlooked by short-sighted, low-spirited criticism."[6] Wilson's story of the triumph of Ruggles in the Wild West was not overlooked by the movie industry, which produced versions in 1918, 1923, and, as mentioned earlier, in 1950 as a vehicle for Bob Hope, titled *Fancy Pants*. In 1915, the year *Ruggles* was published, America recognized the fiftieth anniversary of its Civil War while Europe was engaged in its Great War. The survival of democratic ideas and the reasons why the nation nearly split permanently in two have much to do with universal principles of equality and freedom, as Floud keeps reminding Ruggles. And the acknowledgment of this connection becomes the film's centerpiece: Ruggles's recitation of the Gettysburg Address at the Silver Dollar Saloon. This surprising oration takes place only after various triumphs and failures for Ruggles, as well as after a few lessons in servitude. It reminds us of a key lesson at the heart of the social and political development of the Old West: the lesson that human freedom cannot forever remain the unrestrained freedom of the warrior or conquering frontiersman but must become ordered within a democratic system of officially respected rights and liberties.

As if to remind us of the ever present emphasis on the principle of equality and the idea that no one is fundamentally "better" than another in terms of our basic humanity, *Ruggles of Red Gap* contains frequent moments of humiliation experienced by one or another of the characters. Classed with the screwball romantic comedies of the 1930s and early 1940s, its narrative may seem to be structured according to the classic formula for entertaining Depression audiences, where one engagingly loopy character takes a character of the opposite sex down a few pegs. In these other films most everybody gets to enjoy sexual play or else suffers frustration. Beautiful people who wear gorgeous clothes in luxurious surroundings experience glam romance. But *Ruggles* is more complex, less formulaic, and its humiliations are less obvious, less vengeful, and less concentrated on rivalry between the sexes or on submission to seduction. Its narrative is structured around serial humiliations spread thickly on all sides so that we laugh at everyone at one moment or another.[7]

FIGURE 14. Ruggles the butler (*far left*), Egbert Floud (*center*), Ma Pettingill (Maude Eburne, *second to right*), and Prunella Judson (ZaSu Pitts, *far right*) ponder the principle of equality and recall Lincoln's Gettysburg Address. Courtesy of the Museum of Modern Art.

Early films of Laurel and Hardy, the Marx Brothers, and even W. C. Fields taught us how any one of their characters could win in one scene, only to lose in the next. In *Ruggles,* McCarey is more deceptive, disguising a key goal, which is to bring us to a state of thoughtfulness after passing through layers of comic silliness. There is deep humanity behind his comedy, perhaps because of the great humanness of his characters, for McCarey conveys a profound affection for humankind, an uncynical acceptance that allows him to get away with warmly sappy endings that flow with sincere feeling. He accomplishes this not only in *Ruggles* but also in *Love Affair* and *An Affair to Remember,* leaving us a little teary as we watch the misty-eyed characters accept their fate. This is a comedy of *feeling;* and the endings, after all the humiliations, are joyful. McCarey does not define the principal couples in *Ruggles* and *Love Affair* solely in terms of the battle of the sexes, so fundamental to the screwball films of the 1930s and early 1940s. Nor does he conclude with sly asides on the unlikelihood of a successful marriage, as does

FIGURE 15. Ruminating at the Silver Dollar Saloon: Prunella Judson, Ruggles, Egbert Floud, and Ma Pettingill try to come up with a fitting name for Ruggles's future restaurant. Courtesy of the Museum of Modern Art.

Alfred Hitchcock in films such as *Rear Window* (1954) and *To Catch a Thief* (1955).

The romantic leads in *Ruggles,* played by Laughton and Pitts, and in *Love Affair,* played by Dunne and Boyer, are unique in two ways: the characters actually *like* each other and they respect each other's intention to have an independent career. Although *Love Affair* seems at first to be an entirely sexual romp, its narrative shifts away from the tricks by which one character tries to seduce the other or to use him or her to get rich. Instead, as in *Ruggles,* each character attempts to succeed at a profession and accordingly to win self-esteem as well as the respect of a partner in this endeavor. Here are people trying to figure out how to work for a living, to do honest work rather than toil in slavery as household servants (as in *Ruggles*) or as gigolos or kept women (as in *Love Affair*). These characters indeed do love each other, quite passionately in their ways, but the films seem chaste because the romance, however tender, is not central like the issues of freedom and independence, professional worth and self-respect. This is part of the reason why *Ruggles* should not be viewed as a romantic comedy, but this is also attributable to the fact that Laughton and Pitts are scrappy yet tender, not glamorous in the manner of Boyer and Dunne, Grant and Kerr. Nonetheless one can argue that McCarey ranks among the most romantic of film artists, putting his yearnings on the screen in deep and subtle ways, behind obvious comedic or melodramatic gestures and actions. His comedies carry the sharpest truths inside them, and silliness is not to be dismissed as idle laughter.

In sum, *Ruggles* waltzes pleasingly between satire and parody. The screenplay comments on social mores and political values while scoffing at essential conventions of the Western genre. As Turner tells us: "A parody is a comical imitation of a genre that uses its existing codes to examine the subject in a humorous way. Parody often exists simultaneously with satire, but it can be distinguished from satire, which is designed more specifically to point out vices, follies, or problems with conventional beliefs, whereas parody is generally more lighthearted."[8] Both satire and parody depend on a certain incongruity or tension between one's conceived expectations of a given situation and one's actual experience of that situation.[9] The Western comedy is typically effective because its viewers' expectations and preconceptions are so firmly determined by their familiarity with this genre's well-established conventions. The great success of *Ruggles* revolves around its willingness to play off such conventions with warmth and wit while also expressing sincerely our deepest convictions about the occasional pretensions of aristocracy and the eternal truths of a democratic America.

CHAPTER 4

Landscape and Standard-Setting in the 1930s Western

"The Big Trail" and "Stagecoach"

Western mythology had emerged and been given shape by author James Fenimore Cooper, and then by storytellers in the years following the Civil War, as much as a half century before Griffith and Ford staged their first filmed shoot-outs. By concentrating on this not-too-distant past, the last half of the nineteenth century, the Western has led people to believe that it is a vital record, or at least a meaningful interpretation, of America's expansionist history. That history began well before the Civil War and was intimately connected with the geography of the country. All told, no breed of film developed as rich and universally popular an appreciation for a regional or national geography as did the Western.

The American nation has long been preoccupied by the manipulation of its spaces. Historically, if the frontier wilderness has been a major preoccupation of the colonies, territories, and nation, it is because Americans value themselves as adept organizers of their spaces, with the goal of structuring space so as to accommodate a broad range of needs and desires. Politicians, military strategists, fur traders, gold-seekers, explorers, naturalists, geologists, and engineers grappled with organizing the wilderness, paving the way for ranchers, farmers, and townspeople. Since the time Columbus and other explorers reached North and Central America in the fifteenth century, America has been a frontier culture, or perhaps better said, a culture of many frontiers.

By its explorers, geologists, photographers, and painters, the American West was perceived as a wilderness, rich in natural monuments and awesome in scale. To its settlers, it offered a landscape, a "vast unit of human habitation, indeed a jurisdiction," the kind of landscape to which the historian Simon Schama's tracing of the term *landskip* can be applied. This term appeared in colloquial English not long after Columbus reached the New World and revealed, to the acquisitive and highly competitive European empires of the sixteenth century, new lands to be taken.[1] Deborah A. Carmichael summarizes the settlement process in the introduction to her collection *The Landscape of Hollywood Westerns: Ecocriticism in an American Film Genre*:

> In the stories of settlement on a new continent, which appeared first in literature and then in the movies, the natural world posed the possibility of both danger and profit. . . . The need for land began the move from spiritual to secular goals of nation-building in a new world, and this adjustment also changed the American relationship with the environment. Westward expansion grew as the population grew (early in the tentative settlement of the continent). Thomas Jefferson took delight in the increase of Virginia inhabitants, noting, "In Europe the object is to make the most of their land, labour being abundant: here it is to make the most of our labour, land being abundant." Thus began the independent, landowning tradition that underpins American identity—a yeoman agriculturalist (albeit, today, a gardener in a suburban backyard) ready to advance and conquer a limitless continent of natural resources.[2]

The expansionist movement that opened the American continent to settlement by colonists and pioneers concluded around the time of the birth of the motion picture in America. The Western spaces created or found by the filmmakers, inside the studio or on location in particular landscapes, repeatedly combined artificial, contrived, and natural forms in ways that were deliberate. These filmmakers paralleled those painters who created portraits of frontier landscapes and the activities of cowboys and Indians: Albert Bierstadt, Thomas Moran, Frederic Remington, Charles Russell, and Charles Schreyvogel, to name but several.[3] There were also those influential landscape photographers—including Carleton Watkins, Eadweard Muybridge, Jack Hillers, and Timothy O'Sullivan—who "recorded" mountains and plains, valleys and canyons and rivers, often in the manner of the European Romantic painters.[4] It is not surprising, then, that certain filmmakers assembled shots of actual locations and of studio settings to convey a sense of a real Western terrain that followed in the artistic tradition suggested here. And so the American public's aesthetic appreciation of the Western landscape had its own pattern of cultural evolution, as Edward Buscombe makes clear in his book on Ford's *Stagecoach:* "Many of the cultural meanings we now invest in landscapes are of comparatively recent origin. Prior to the late eighteenth century, the aesthetic sensibility was not pleasurably stimulated by vast panoramas, towering cliffs, limitless vistas. The absence of human habitation was regarded with distaste."[5]

Preoccupied by frontier myths and histories, writers depended on descriptions of terrain to distinguish character and to color personality. Sometimes the landscape is but incidental background, but in other works it is an active force, as with Dorothy Scarborough's *The Wind* (see chapter 2). The landscape seems like nothing without its inhabitants; the people and the wildlife are inseparable from their physical environment. It may be sparsely populated, but an entirely empty West can have no meaning for us—though the temporary sense of emptiness as evoked by a barren landscape can have a powerful and alienating emotional effect. The land exists to be occupied, or so humankind determined long ago, with its spaces to be organized for use.

LANDSCAPE AS A PHYSICAL AND MORAL UNIVERSE

A landscape-oriented movie may be called a "filmscape" in the sense of the "wedding" of a filmmaker and region. In the Western genre, examples are Ford and Monument Valley, Hawks and the Missouri River, John Sturges and wooded terrain, Anthony Mann and the mountains, and Eastwood and the Northwest. Other landscape-oriented movies, beyond the parameters of the Western genre, include the breathtaking German mountain films of Leni Riefenstahl and her mentor Arnold Fanck; the masterfully crafted documentaries of Robert Flaherty; Satyajit Ray's lovingly made films depicting everyday life in his native country of India; Akira Kurosawa's samurai masterworks; and Jean Renoir's exquisitely photographed portraits of the French countryside in *Day in the Country* (1936) and *Rules of the Game* (1939), not to mention his gorgeously framed shots of India in *The River* (1951).

The contemporary German director Werner Herzog, a dedicated filmscape-creator who has crafted such awe-inspiring adventure movies as *Aguirre: Wrath of God* (1972) and *Fitzcarraldo* (1982) and such fascinating documentaries as *Grizzly Man* (2005) and *Encounters at the End of the World* (2007), got to the heart of the Western genre's intimate affinity for landscape when he was asked about his own particular usage of a jungle setting in *Aguirre:*

In my films landscapes are never just picturesque or scenic backdrops as they often are in Hollywood films. . . . It [the jungle] is not just a location, it is a state of our mind. It has almost human qualities. It is a vital part of the characters' inner landscapes. . . . I like to direct landscapes just as I like to direct actors and animals. People think I am joking, but it is true. Often I try to introduce into a landscape a certain atmosphere, using sound and vision to give it a definite character. Most directors merely exploit landscapes to embellish what is going on in the foreground, and this is one reason why I like some of John Ford's work. He never used Monument Valley as merely a backdrop, but rather to signify the spirit of his characters. Westerns are really all about our very basic notions of justice, and when I see Monument Valley in his films I somehow start to believe—amazingly enough—in American justice.[6]

Authentic Western landscapes had certainly been used as far back as D. W. Griffith's Biograph Westerns after 1910, when Griffith's company of actors and crew members began to make regular treks to California in order to take advantage of the climate, particularly during the winter months. Ford and Raoul Walsh, two landscape-oriented directors, had made scores of films in the silent era, and Ford's early *Straight Shooting* is a clear example of a pre-1920 Western that takes advantage of outdoor shooting so as to convey some sense of the Western terrain (see chapter 1). Ford's *The Outcasts of Poker Flat* (1919) was praised by the film periodical *Photoplay* for its main actor's performance, but especially for its director's special gift for outdoor imagery: "Two remarkable things [about the film] are Harry Carey's rise to real acting power, and director Ford's marvelous river locations and absolutely incomparable photography. This photoplay is an optic symphony."[7] And as noted in chapter 1, Ford made brilliant use of authentic Western terrain in his two great silent epics of the 1920s, *The Iron Horse* and *3 Bad Men*.

The filmscape as a fusion of human nature and natural setting came to special prominence with the rise of the big-budget A-Western, most especially in the late 1930s and early 1940s. Film scholars have established a familiar distinction between large-scale, typically superior-quality A-Westerns and their usually less costly, mediocre-quality counterparts, the B-Westerns. B-Westerns, especially those churned out by the Hollywood studios at an astonishing rate during the 1930s, were primarily low-cost, quickly produced profit-makers geared toward weekend matinee audiences who were satisfied with rapid action, hokey dialogue, and familiar stars such as Roy Rogers and Gene Autry. And it was the 1930s B-Western that gave John Wayne a frequent home between his starring roles in two major A-Westerns that bookended the decade:

Walsh's *The Big Trail* (1930) and Ford's *Stagecoach* (1939), two films that serve as focal points of this chapter.

A good many of the A-Westerns, because they were chiefly funded by the major studios, tended to be filmed, at least partly, in the great outdoors of the West and Southwest. Because of travel and transportation costs, on-location shooting in distant places was typically far more expensive than filming in a studio, therefore requiring major investment. Authentic Western landscapes became more and more prominent in many of the A-Westerns of the 1930s and 1940s, particularly when contrasted with the cheaply made B-Westerns.[8] It is true that *some* of the B-Westerns of the Depression era took advantage of outdoor location shooting in the immediate sunny Southern California terrain, primarily because it was ready to hand and required little effort or expense in making these landscapes anything other than secondary backdrops for action sequences. In the B-Westerns, however, there was usually no reach for jaw-dropping beauty or a sense of the sublime. And there were also few attempts to make the landscape a thematic component of a B-Western narrative, whether as obstacle, inspiration, or metaphor.

But with the A-Western "renaissance" of the late 1930s and early 1940s came a renewed emphasis on the photographic use of real-world environments that could play as significant a role in a motion picture as the performances of the lead actors. Despite the occasional insertion of fairly artificial shots and scenes that were filmed on the studio lot, many of the World War II–era A-Westerns contain scenes of such authentic natural beauty that they sometimes seem like quick-moving slideshows of masterful landscape paintings by the likes of Thomas Cole or Albert Bierstadt. Several of the influential A-Western directors of this period— Ford, Walsh, Henry King, William Wyler, King Vidor, Fritz Lang—had long exhibited a painterly sensibility, beginning with their work in the era of silent film.

The connection between Romantic landscape artistry and cinematic Westerns is more than a loose analogy. In his epic biography *Searching for John Ford*, Joseph McBride offers evidence of the Ford-Remington connection when he describes one of Ford's early silents, *Hell Bent* (1918, with Harry Carey Sr.), as beginning with a writer who admires Remington's 1897 painting *A Misdeal,* an artwork that the movie then attempts to "imitate" to some degree.[9] The biographer discusses Ford's familiarity with Remington and Russell when he describes the making of Ford's silent epic *The Iron Horse,* the story of the building of the transcontinental railroad. He also reveals the strong influence of the Western paintings of

Remington, Russell, and Schreyvogel on Ford when the director came to make the first two films of his cavalry trilogy, *Fort Apache* and *She Wore a Yellow Ribbon*.[10] McBride informs us:

> Ford acknowledged that his principal visual influence for *Fort Apache* was Frederic Remington, whom he had first imitated in the 1918 *Hell Bent*. Remington's starkly beautiful paintings of cavalrymen, often tragic in tone, provided inspiration for the entire Cavalry Trilogy, along with the more romantic Western paintings of Charles M. Russell. Russell's colorful landscapes and Indian scenes were imitated by Ford in his magnificent imagery of Indians on the march in *She Wore a Yellow Ribbon*. The Western painter Charles Schreyvogel, a rival of Remington's, also left his imprint on the director. "My father kept a copy of a collection by Schreyvogel close by his bedside," Pat Ford recalled. "He pored over it to dream up action sequences for his films."[11]

It is true that natural settings in many of the paintings by artists like Remington, Russell, and Schreyvogel are subordinated to the human action occurring within them, and so these artworks are less Romantic than the non-human-centered artworks of, say, those of the Hudson River school painters. Sometimes Remington's depictions of Western landscapes even appear abstract in contrast with the detailed attention afforded to the human figures placed against those backdrops. But this does not diminish the fact that such paintings taught filmmakers like Ford and Walsh to appreciate the visual ways in which westerners and their natural environments are typically conceived or imagined simultaneously. And such artworks also inspired certain filmmakers to capture the sense of gritty authenticity that these painters evoked when capturing the physical action and motion of westerners and their animals.

In a retrospective interview that he gave late in his life at the American Film Institute, Walsh was asked about the visual similarities between his depictions of some of the action scenes featuring General Custer (Errol Flynn) in *They Died with Their Boots On* (1941) and the depictions of similar Custer-related scenes in paintings by Remington and Russell. Walsh declared, "I'd seen all the Remingtons and I knew Russell. When I was a young boy, my father introduced me to Remington, and I knew the groupings [of people] and the different things."[12] And while Walsh-directed Westerns such as *Dark Command* (1940), *Pursued* (1947), *Cheyenne* (1947), *Silver River* (1948), and *Colorado Territory* (1949) gave visual evidence of the influence of such painters, it was Walsh's earliest A-Western, *The Big Trail* (1930), that truly demonstrated the director's affinity with these artists and, at least indirectly, with the Romantic landscape painters who had inspired them.

THE BIG TRAIL

Almost a decade before Ford's landmark *Stagecoach,* two movies helped to blaze a path into the history of the Old West's wagon train pioneers. Wesley Ruggles's adaptation of Edna Ferber's *Cimarron* (1931), starring Richard Dix and Irene Dunne, was successful at the box office and won the Oscar for Best Picture, the first Western film to win this award (the second was Kevin Costner's *Dances with Wolves,* almost sixty years later). But the other tale of settlers on "prairie schooners"—Raoul Walsh's *The Big Trail* of a year earlier—was the more accomplished film in terms of its on-site utilization of the natural landscape and its subsequent emphasis on the intimate connection between frontier folk and the land.

If *The Wind* masterfully brought to a close the silent Western of the 1920s, *The Big Trail* daringly initiated the epic sound Western. An ambitious undertaking, it failed financially, causing the genre to endure a decadelong eclipse until the release of Ford's *Stagecoach* and other classic A-Westerns of 1939, such as Henry King's *Jesse James,* Michael Curtiz's *Dodge City,* and Cecil B. DeMille's *Union Pacific.* Walsh—like Ford, Vidor, King, Wyler, and other great directors of Hollywood's studio era—got his start in the formative years of silent cinema, where he worked as both actor and director. D.W. Griffith, his mentor, cast him in an uncredited minor role as John Wilkes Booth in his landmark *Birth of a Nation* (1915). During that same year Walsh directed well over a dozen short features, which included three Westerns: *The Lone Cowboy, A Bad Man and Others,* and *The Greaser.*

For *The Big Trail,* Walsh utilized Twentieth Century Fox's new seventy-millimeter Grandeur widescreen process to hold steadily and boldly a series of broad panoramic views of such natural wonders as monstrous cliffs near the Sierra Nevada that challenged the pioneers in the film's most thrilling sequence.[13] The narrative follows a wagon train from the Missouri River to Oregon Territory in the 1840s. Walsh took cast and crew on locations for months: Yuma, Arizona; Sacramento, Sequoia National Park, and the Sierra Nevada in California; Jackson Hole and Yellowstone National Park in Wyoming; Montana; and Utah. As the wagon train crosses the country, we experience the mess and mud of the camps along with the harsher tasks of avoiding stampeding buffalo and defending against Indian attacks.

Walsh cast John Wayne in his first starring role, that of a scout who leads the wagon train as he seeks frontier justice. He hunts down the men who killed his best friend, establishing a revenge-motivated character

FIGURE 16. John Wayne is the revenge-seeking and nature-loving frontiersman Breck Coleman in Raoul Walsh's epic *The Big Trail* (1930). Courtesy of the Museum of Modern Art.

FIGURE 17. Frontier settlers gather and enjoy a communal dance, enclosed by their covered wagons and the surrounding forest, in *The Big Trail*. Courtesy of the Museum of Modern Art.

whom he would portray most meaningfully in later Westerns directed by Ford (*Stagecoach, The Searchers*) and Howard Hawks (*Red River*). Before *The Big Trail*, Wayne worked primarily as an extra and a bit player, especially in Ford's films of the late 1920s. Wayne served as an uncredited extra (as well as prop assistant at times) on Ford's *Mother Machree* (1928), *Four Sons* (1928), *Hangman's House* (1928), *The Black Watch* (1929), *Salute* (1929), *Men without Women* (1930), and *Born Reckless* (1930). Wayne got to know Ford and thought of him as something of a role model.[14] It was most likely the combination of Ford, Walsh, and silent Western star Harry Carey Sr.—three similarly self-assured and life-loving men—who gave Wayne his blend of folksy charm, quiet bravado, and wry humor.

Walsh was a master storyteller with an unpretentious visual style and unmannered pacing that gave his Westerns a sense of seamlessness and a deceptively easy beauty. He knew as well as any artist where to place river, mountain, and sky. What distinguished his vision of a country waiting to be made into a landscape was his grasp of scale, depth, and light. The camera looked at and across wagons and terrain; the resulting compositions revealed a calm majestic spread of natural features. Another Western epic derived from an actual event, and as sweeping and visually engaging, would not be made until *Red River*. In that one, which depicts the first cattle drive from Texas to Abilene, Wayne and the character of the mythical westerner, following his youthful adventures in *The Big Trail* and *Stagecoach,* become forever joined (see chapter 6).

The Big Trail's production was as burdened as its fictional pioneers. Each scene of the film was shot several times for different versions: first shot in Grandeur widescreen, and then in standard thirty-five millimeter in multiple-language versions with different casts. If this were not complicated enough, there were also the great challenges, physical as well as financial, of hauling cumbersome equipment, of filming with sound using microphones hidden among barrels and wagons, and of moving hundreds of cast, crew, and animals. Studio boss William Fox had initiated the use of this widescreen process and owned the equipment that could project the film stock required by the new method. It was a major investment on his part that in many ways was far ahead of its time, anticipating the widescreen technology of the 1950s like Cinemascope, VistaVision, and Cinerama. Unfortunately, because of the high costs involved and the advent of the Great Depression, the Grandeur method led to financial failure. At the time of its release only a handful of theaters in America, mainly those owned by Fox, could purchase the equipment necessary for the exhibition of Walsh's film in its most spectacular dimensions and quality.[15]

But even in its thirty-five-millimeter versions—those made with different casts in four different languages—*The Big Trail* contains scenes of natural majesty and splendor that surpass anything that had come before.[16] And some of the stills or shots from the film rival the kind of breathtaking vastness of nature that had been depicted in the artworks of the Hudson River school, the first official branch of American Romantic painting. More than a few of the on-site backdrops for various shots in the movie—and especially those toward the end of the film where Breck Coleman points to the "Great White Mountain" and the lake-filled valley before him—could be mistaken for black-and-white copies of masterpieces by Cole and Bierstadt.

Above all, as epics of trail-blazing and nation-building, many of the A-Westerns had something to say about America's mission of expansionism under the banner of Manifest Destiny. In his book *The Invention of the Western Film*, Scott Simmon discusses *The Big Trail* as a clear example

FIGURE 18. Romance in the wilderness: Breck Coleman (John Wayne) and Ruth Cameron (Marguerite Churchill) in *The Big Trail*. Courtesy of the Museum of Modern Art.

of this type of wilderness-conquering, frontier-settling story. He reminds us that, in the "social world" of "old Europe," there is little or no empty farmland, and so everything is private property to *someone*. By contrast, Westerns deal with the idea of empty fertile land waiting to be claimed by homesteaders who must get there and work the land. It is "God's garden," waiting to be settled and harvested. As Simmon states, "*The Big Trail*'s purest argument for the existence of empty land on the American continent is made silently through camera angles and bodies. Pushing further the high-angle shots of *The Covered Wagon* (1923) and a century of landscape painting, *The Big Trail* is punctuated with God's-eye widescreens of wagons snaking across valleys and deserts, with shimmering mountain vistas extending to the edge of the horizon."[17]

According to Simmon, there are several reasons why the "wagon-train emigrants can expect to come to own the land themselves," and these reasons have "common-law traditions behind them."[18] As the English philosopher John Locke pointed out in his *Second Treatise on Government*, a strong influence on the political thinking of America's founding fathers, private property results from the attachment of human labor to previously unclaimed land. *The Big Trail* is essentially the story of the labor that was required, not merely to cultivate a desired plot of land, but to reach it in the first place. The movie does ignore, however, the important ethical and political issue raised when one acknowledges that native peoples had once possessed many of these lands-to-be-claimed.

The trek westward is always a deadly struggle, Wayne's Breck Coleman warns his fellow travelers in *The Big Trail*. But it is worth it once you get there, as he describes it to them: "the bounteous natural wonders" of a land "north of Oregon."[19] Coleman is the only member of the wagon train who has been there before and who can convey the wonders and dangers lying ahead of them. Here the landscape becomes both an occasion for risk, adventure, and struggle and a source of inspiration and faith. Like the human being, the natural world should be viewed as multifaceted if it is to be properly appreciated.

Aside from giving us a genuine epic that takes full advantage of its natural landscape, and that also focuses its story of wagon train pioneers by centering on a revenge plot, *The Big Trail* reveals two aspects of a certain philosophy of nature. As Simmon elaborates, while most of the film shows us the oppressive ("hard") aspects of nature that produce pain and suffering and struggle for the wagon-trainers, it also gives us a brief speech by John Wayne's character that stresses the magic and mystery of the landscape and the reasons why it entices him to spend nights alone on the moonlit desert. When asked whether he fears the risks and dangers that loom before him as he rides through the wilderness, Coleman replies (in what is, for a Wayne character, a surprisingly articulate and even poetic meditation), "Lord, no. I love it. Especially now that it's Spring, and everything's so happy. Why, there's trees out there, big tall pines, just a'reachin' and a'reachin', as if they wanted to climb right through the gates of heaven. And there's brooks too, with water smiling all day long. . . . Birds singing, brooks lapping, and the wind sort of crooning through the forest like some great organ."[20] This "soft," or appreciative, view of nature, as Simmon labels it, recalls the Romantic perspective expressed in Griffith's early East Coast–made Westerns before he moved his company out West and made films in which nature is oppressive and deadly ("hard") rather than lush, nurturing, or inspirational (see chapter 1). According to Coleman's speech, nature can be serene and sublime, even while serving as a deadly obstacle and challenge to human settlers.

The scope and drama of *The Big Trail* echo Cruze's earlier epic *The Covered Wagon* (1923) and Ford's silent epic *The Iron Horse* (1924). But Walsh's own presentation of the wagon train theme is a vast photographic-technical improvement on those films. *The Big Trail* is, especially in its second half, as visually elegant and cinematically adventurous as any film made up until that time. And this is even more clearly the case when one views the seventy-millimeter widescreen version, now made accessible by Twentieth Century Fox's two-DVD special edition of the film that was released in 2008.

It is fitting that a film that puts such emphasis on the use of authentic natural landscapes and that tells the story of the rigors of pioneer life was produced in a novel widescreen process. Widescreen films are in many ways more true to the human eye's field of perception, most especially when one is pondering a landscape where the breadth and depth of one's field of vision is much greater. And in most Westerns—in which the stories are often closely tied to the land, and in which exterior scenes are crucial in providing an authentic sense of the natural terrain—the wider the screen, the more visually realistic the film appears. Western landscapes are stunning in their beauty and vastness, and the best one can do is to try to capture them realistically rather than distort them, as might happen with a more expressionistic technique of filmmaking. In Westerns there is a need for wide-eyed vision when glimpsing action across vast spaces and against distant horizons. And so the widescreen process, beginning with early innovations like *The Big Trail*'s Grandeur method, is especially apt for Western films that attempt to convey some sense of authenticity in depicting life on the American frontier and in making the landscape itself a primary character.[21]

The commercial failure of *The Big Trail* gave rise to a decade likewise defined chiefly by economic failure, in which B-Westerns dominated the American movie market and appealed to a strong desire for entertainment and escapism on the part of Depression-era audiences. Between the two great John Wayne Westerns that bookended the decade—*The Big Trail* and *Stagecoach*—the iconic star found a home in the "factory" of the Hollywood B-Western and began to develop his heroic but folksy persona. Most of these popular movies mixed action and comedy in a broad manner, but more than a few also depicted the kinds of conflict that would have resonated with audience members who were struggling amid a long-running national depression. A good number of the low-budget, quickly made B-Westerns of the 1930s did not shy away from populist stories of economic survival and of clashes between decent, hardworking folk and greedy corporate land-grabbers, those who were hell-bent on taking away individuals' property or acquiring water rights.[22]

John Wayne starred in many of these low-budget but socially aware Westerns. For example, in his film *Two-Fisted Law* (1932), in which Walter Brennan plays a deputy sheriff, "Duke" (Wayne) works for a rancher who loses his property to a crooked, cattle-rustling banker. In some of these stories, cowboy heroes sometimes unveil themselves as government-appointed lawmen or agents who help those in need for the sake of the common good, echoing the general sentiments behind Roosevelt's "New Deal" programs that attempted to rescue the American people from economic catastrophe. In *The Big Stampede* (1932), for example, Wayne plays a marshal appointed by the governor to bring law and order to a town in New Mexico where killers and cattle rustlers reign. In *Riders of Destiny* (1933), Singin' Sandy Saunders (Wayne) is an undercover government agent who helps ranchers outwit a man who both controls the local water supply and seeks to drive them out of the area unless he is paid handsomely for use of the water.

Wayne's character in *Riders of Destiny,* apparent from his very nickname, is one of the traditional "singing cowboys," clean-cut heroes who put their feelings into song while riding the range and battling evil (luckily Wayne was dubbed by a genuine singer). A significant branch of the B-Western overlapped with the genre of the movie musical and featured such famous crooning stars as Gene Autry, Tex Ritter, and Roy Rogers—the latter was a cofounder of the Sons of the Pioneers, a popular cowboy singing group featuring actor-singers like Shrug Fisher and Ford regular Ken Curtis.[23] Film scholar Peter Stanfield has done some highly welcome research that helps us to reevaluate the oft-overlooked 1930s B-Western, in his books *Hollywood, Westerns, and the 1930s: The Lost Trail* and *Horse Opera: The Strange History of the 1930s Singing Cowboy.* Edward Buscombe summarizes the surge of B-Westerns in the 1930s:

> During the 30s the collapse at the box office caused by the Depression had led exhibitors to seek out any gimmick to lure patrons back. Bingo, popcorn, free gifts, all were tried. An enduring legacy was the double bill, in which audiences got two pictures for the price of one. A host of minor studios rushed to cash in on the opportunity this provided, supplying product for the lower, or "B," half of the programme. Thus was born the B-Western, the dusty vineyard in which John Wayne laboured throughout his early manhood. Wayne's career showed that it was possible to make the leap up from the lower depths into the sunlit pastures of stardom, but for the most part

the two worlds kept themselves apart, two parallel industries supplying product for two polarized markets.[24]

Despite the typical major differences between these two categories of Western, especially in terms of cinematic quality, there are occasional instances of overlap or transition between the B-Westerns of the 1930s and those A-Westerns that began to emerge at the tail end of the decade. Films like James Cruze's *Sutter's Gold* (1936), Cecil B. DeMille's *The Plainsman* (1936), King Vidor's *The Texas Rangers* (1936), and Frank Lloyd's *Wells Fargo* (1937) helped to establish a serious effort by the big studios to rise above the generally lower artistic levels of their B-Western productions. But these movies also failed to reach the levels of cinematic artistry attained by the classic A-Westerns that were soon to come. The latter helped to constitute a "partial A-Western renaissance," a category coined by George N. Fenin and William K. Everson in their landmark survey of the cinematic genre, *The Western: From Silents to the Seventies.*[25]

It was with Ford's *Stagecoach*, however, that the realism captured by Walsh in *The Big Trail* became fused with visual poetry as well as with archetypal character portraits, playing upon the genre's underlying dialectic between gritty authenticity and mythic grandeur. The landscapes in *Stagecoach* are as majestic as those in *The Big Trail,* but Ford gives us characters who are far worthier objects of our attention and intrigue than are the stilted caricatures in Walsh's earlier film. *Stagecoach* presents Western folk whose gestures and intonations are as nuanced and symbolic as the natural world around them. With Ford's greatest Western yet, we begin to see signs that the Hollywood Westerns of the Depression era were mere stepping-stones to the standard-setting classics to come.

STAGECOACH

Lillian Gish had correctly guessed that Dorothy Scarborough's *The Wind* would make a wonderful movie because it was "pure motion," suggested by the very title of the novel and by the subsequent script based on it (see chapter 2).[26] John Ford must have had a similar intuition when he planned for the production of *Stagecoach*. The Western film tends to be, in a manner of speaking, more "cinematic" than the more theatrical and dialogue-laden genres. This is because film is chiefly defined as an art of the *moving* image, and the Western typically involves such essential action-and-motion-oriented elements as rapid horse riding, last-minute escapes from enemy threats, suspenseful chases, and determined desert crossings. While it is true that all film images "move," technically speaking, Western movies frequently highlight imagery that affords the viewer a dramatic sense of being transported across great spaces and distances, a feeling of immediacy not provided by other art forms such as painting, theater, and literature. By its very title and basic plot, *Stagecoach* lets the audience know that it will be "on the move" for much of its duration.

Stagecoach was Ford's first Western of the sound era and marked his return to the Western genre for the first time since *3 Bad Men* of 1926. A twelve-year gap ensued before he went to Monument Valley in the autumn of 1938, and few Ford films of the intervening years used landscape to meaningful effect.[27] More important, *Stagecoach* was the first of many Westerns Ford shot in Monument Valley and the first Ford film with John Wayne as its star.[28] With *Stagecoach*, Ford helped to transform the genre and to shift the Western from its 1930s status as "B" picture to the "A" category, paving the way for his own and other Hollywood directors' masterful Westerns of the next three decades. While Walsh's *The Big Trail* was really the first sound Western to give its audiences a genuine sense of the breathtaking vistas that were regularly witnessed by the settlers of the Old West, it was Ford's *Stagecoach* that incorporated the landscape into a character-driven Western of truly classic proportions and quality. Not since *The Big Trail* had a director selected sites for on-location shooting with as self-conscious an intention, though Ford had always been attuned to the importance of place and terrain.

Ford had shot most of his early Westerns for Universal in California's river-and-ranch country and the Mojave Desert. These films included the Cheyenne Harry films *Straight Shooting* (1917), *Marked Men* (1919), and *The Outcasts of Poker Flat* (1919). Ford's first film for William Fox, *Just Pals* (1920), was set on the Wyoming-Nebraska border. His two feature Westerns of the 1920s, *The Iron Horse* and *3 Bad Men*, were set in the central West but not actually filmed in that region. For *The Iron Horse*, the territory of the transcontinental railroad; the settlements of the North Platte and Cheyenne, Wyoming; and the hidden pass not far from Smoky River were shot in the Sierra Nevada. For *3 Bad Men* Ford consciously chose the mountainous panorama of the Grand Tetons to provide a strong horizontal backdrop to the more static drama of the fortune hunters at camp and in the territorial town of Custer. And he needed the vast flatness of the California desert to set off the huge sweep of wagons and horsemen in the land rush depicted in the latter film (see chapter 1).

Ford's evocation of an authentic landscape, so beautifully realized in the mountains and desert of *3 Bad Men,* became poetic in *Stagecoach.* Ford chose to film neither in the familiar California country of his early Westerns nor in Wyoming, but in the landscape of the Southwest. He selected Monument Valley to represent a country of settlements and Indian tribes of the 1880s, an enclosed but seemingly vast desert landscape that is part of the Monument Valley Navajo Tribal Park, crossing from Arizona into Utah.[29]

Monument Valley provides a seemingly eternal canvas against which the variables and vagaries of human existence can be etched. Many a classic Western film depends on its capacity to create the illusion of spatial and temporal passage, a passage that is emblematic of the wider notion of the transience of human life.

Monument Valley so impressed Ford that he would shoot *Stagecoach* and part or all of six later films in the valley's locations: *My Darling Clementine, Fort Apache, She Wore a Yellow Ribbon, The Searchers, Sergeant Rutledge,* and *Cheyenne Autumn.*[30] Whether shooting in black and white or in color, Ford captured panoramic vistas of earth and sky that stretch more than thirty miles, a singular universe that suited his notion of a deep but contained space, at once trapping and freeing the characters of his stories. As Ford related in an interview done in 1964: "I think you can say that the real star of my Westerns has always been the land. . . . My favorite location is Monument Valley. . . . It has rivers, mountains, plains, desert, everything the land can offer. I feel at peace there. I have been all over the world, but I consider this the most complete, beautiful, and peaceful place on earth."[31]

Stagecoach relates a desperate two-day journey in an area along the Arizona and New Mexico border with Mexico—from Tonto to Lordsburg through Dry Forks and Apache Wells—as the coach races to elude Geronimo and his Chiricahua Apaches. Ford read Ernest Haycox's story "The Stage to Lordsburg" in *Collier's* magazine in 1937 and bought the movie rights. Dudley Nichols wrote the screenplay, changing names and adapting characters, and Ford added his own touches to the story and dialogue. Ford had almost always collaborated actively with his screenwriters, and Nichols was particularly open to Ford's suggestions. There were exceptions, of course, where this type of collaboration did not occur: Ford's filming of screenplays by Nunnally Johnson (*The Prisoner of Shark Island, The Grapes of Wrath, Tobacco Road*) and by Philip Dunne (*How Green Was My Valley*).[32] Nichols, who veered toward the theatrical and literary and therefore provided a good balance with the visually oriented Ford, had already worked with the director on pre-*Stagecoach* productions such as *The Lost Patrol* (1934), *Judge Priest* (1934), *The Informer* (1935), *Steamboat around the Bend* (1935), *Mary of Scotland* (1936), *The Plough and the Stars* (1936), and *The Hurricane* (1937). After *Stagecoach*, he wrote the screenplay for Ford's *The Long Voyage Home* (1940), based on several one-act plays by Eugene O'Neill, and concluded his career with Ford by writing the script for the highly symbolic and commercially unsuccessful *The Fugitive* (1947).

Stagecoach's musical score and the passage of coach and riders through the landscape are inseparable; their complementary rhythms form the beat of the movie. Adapted from American folk tunes of the early 1880s such as "I Dream of Jeanie," the musical themes are simple and familiar, striking up each time the coach starts to pull its weighty load as if encouraging the teams of horses in the race to safety. Musical motifs also alert us to the terrors of Geronimo and his war party. Music, and especially music derived from the traditional American folk songbook, has always played an important role in Ford's films (his Western *Rio Grande* even borders on being a musical in certain scenes), and the director allegedly immersed himself in period music when undertaking the research for many of his movies.[33] In *Stagecoach*, music provides an almost subconscious connection with America's past while also affording an upbeat accompaniment to the journey of the stagecoach passengers. As Kathryn Kalinak tells us in her enlightening book *How the West Was Sung: Music in the Westerns of John Ford*:

> Film music's power to return us to a general idealized past is transformed through folk and period song into a specific idealized past, the nineteenth-century American West, a mythic past that never actually existed. Bruno David Ussher, in his 1939 review of the film, recognized this power, noting that the American music makes *Stagecoach* "more of a correspondingly true portrayal of life as it was on the middle-border half a century ago." Folk and period songs not only make the imagined past real, however, they create nostalgia for it, harnessing the pleasures and plentitudes of film music, its ability to offer a utopic alternative to experiential reality (more integrated, harmonic, and aesthetically pleasing), to Ford's particular vision of a moment in America's past.[34]

The pleasurable excitement and the rollicking mood of *Stagecoach* are established with the opening credits sequence. Credits appear over shots of the army troop riding through Monument Valley, followed by Indians on horseback, all moving from left to right and accompanied by gay music, then by a shot of the stagecoach traveling through the valley, a shot which carries the final credit "Directed by John Ford." We cut to riders coming into camp to tell of hills filled with Apaches, stirred up by Geronimo, who has jumped the reservation and gone on the warpath. Placed at a low vantage point, the camera shoots up at the valley's famous features, its high and deeply carved buttes—its monuments—rising from the valley floor. Above two of these, the Mittens, move high, puffy white clouds, creating strong shadows. The impact of the rock buttes seen against a low horizon and big sky is startling and staggering, richly expressive of mood and effect, a mise-en-scène in black and white of such contrast and beauty that we are thrilled.

With *Stagecoach*, Ford revealed his visionary talent for rendering landscape in ways quite different from the expansionist themes of *The Iron Horse* and *3 Bad Men*. Each of these latter films depicts large groups of people engaged in activities that take them over plains and the mountainous terrain of the vast West. These people have a specific purpose, and they are building the new nation. The horizontality of the background with the looming Tetons in the first half of *3 Bad Men* emphasizes the tense waiting among newly arrived wagons before the land rush. These people are going somewhere, in a hurry, but not for some time, and Ford establishes character and motive on a broad and static set.

The theme of *Stagecoach*, however, is tied to quite another theme in conjunction with quite another expansionist goal: class conflicts within white society, as well as the removal of the Indians by the United States Army. The story is not about building communities, for they already exist in Tonto and in Lordsburg. It is about keeping control of these communities and defending them against external threats while also overcoming social conflicts, such as those resulting from class-based prejudice, that are internal to these societies.[35] As the drunken physician Doc Boone (Thomas Mitchell) declares to the prostitute Dallas (Claire Trevor) as they are being exiled from Tonto for their "degenerate" lifestyles, they are "the victims of a foul disease called 'social prejudice.' "

The protagonists do not aim to settle the Southwest; they go forth in uneasy relation to the land and they try desperately to survive in areas where they clearly are not wanted. Several of the passengers—Ringo, Dallas, and Doc—also go forth in uneasy relation to society itself, given their outcast status and their treatment by others. The landscape does not welcome the transients; it threatens them. Its rocks and hills hide hostile Apaches bent on killing them. The travelers are trapped, and much of the story is a sequence of chase and escape before they reach the dubious safety of the raucous and not particularly law-abiding

Lordsburg. Kalinak, in fact, shows us how the different parts of the film's musical score clue us in (subconsciously, at least) to the conflict between the whites and their Indian enemies: "The Anglo passengers are represented by what is perceived by most listeners as folk song. Because of the immense cultural investment in folk music as a distinctly American art form, especially in the 1930s, its use confers Americanness on whom it accompanies: the Anglo passengers inside the coach, the towns they emerge from and move to, and even the wilderness itself."[36]

Ford is interested in the passage of individuals through space and time, and he wastes little energy on the towns of Tonto and Lordsburg, concentrating instead on the cinematography of the supposedly treacherous landscape. Within the sharp-edged frame, Ford creates an impression of limitless depth and height. This merging of subject and setting, rather than a view of the landscape as merely a backdrop, characterizes the Western genre at its best and is integral to Ford's vision and narrative. In *Stagecoach* Ford joins character, action, and setting in a seamless, cliché-filled narrative, cutting between scenes that are melodramatic yet broadly comic and shots of the stagecoach being frantically pulled along below the valley's buttes.

If *Stagecoach* joins *Destry Rides Again* (released the same year) as one of the two wittiest Westerns to date, this is in part because of the contradictions it sets before us with such delight. The towns, supposedly civilized communities, are full of the white people's chicanery, thievery, hypocrisy, and murderous intent, while the landscape—vast, beautiful, and unspoiled—is nonetheless home to the terrors of the fiercest of Indians: Geronimo. At the end of Ford's *Stagecoach*, Ringo and Dallas ride off to Ringo's ranch just across the border, "free from the blessings of civilization"—as Doc Boone (Thomas Mitchell) laughingly tells Sheriff Curley (George Bancroft) in the movie's final line. Their flight into Mexico will, we can hope, bring newfound freedom and opportunity (the reverse of today's current border situation, in which the arrow of hope tends to point north rather than south). Ringo and Dallas, while apparently fleeing "civilization," are the kind of good-hearted romantic pair who might nonetheless help to initiate a more benevolent form of society in the Old West, one that has overcome the kind of pettiness and prejudice that they had experienced in Tonto and along their journey to Lordsburg.[37]

Ford's depiction of the birth of Lucy Mallory's baby, the emotional center point and central transformative event of the film, includes shots of Ringo and Dallas staring at each other lovingly over the newly delivered child which has been nicknamed "Little Coyote"—a child born in the wilderness but to a woman who represents an aristocratic southern culture. The scene of a baby's birth amid a savage wilderness (one might also think here of a similar plot element in Ford's later *3 Godfathers* of 1948, as well as in his final feature film of 1965, *7 Women*) gives us the clear sense that the escape across the border to Ringo's ranch at the end of the film will result in new life and the creation of a family, the basic building block of any stable civilization. Ringo's ranch, never seen, is the offscreen symbol of a pastoral, settled existence, one in which the need for gunslinging and revenge has been overcome.[38] Like Gary Cooper's Cole Harden in Wyler's *The Westerner,* released a year after *Stagecoach,* Ringo has been a lone drifter and gunslinger who tires of his solitude and desires to build a home, most especially after having found the woman of his dreams (see chapter 5). Ringo and Cole are therefore atypical westerners, since such figures usually remain solitary and independent.

With all of the essential and traditional elements of the genre in place, *Stagecoach* garnered upon its release a general critical response that was as enthusiastic as its box office reception, an appraisal that has only grown over the years. Frank S. Nugent, a film critic-turned-screenwriter who later collaborated with Ford on many a script (from *Fort Apache* and *The Searchers* to *Donovan's Reef*), wrote about the film in the March 3, 1939, issue of the *New York Times*:

> John Ford has swept aside ten years of artifice and talkie compromise and has made a motion picture that sings a song of camera. It moves, and how beautifully it moves, across the plains of Arizona, skirting the sky-reaching mesas of Monument Valley, beneath the piled-up cloud banks which every photographer dreams about. . . . Mr. Ford is not one of your subtle directors, suspending sequences on the wink of an eye or the precisely calculated gleam of a candle in a mirror. He prefers the broadest canvas, the brightest colors, the widest brush and the boldest possible strokes. He hews to the straight narrative line with the well-reasoned confidence of a man who has seen that narrative succeed before. He takes no shadings from his characters; either they play it straight or they don't play at all. He likes his language simple and he doesn't want too much of it. When his Redskins bite the dust, he expects to hear the thud and see the dirt spurt up. Above all, he likes to have things happen in the open, where his camera can keep them in view. . . . This is one stagecoach that's powered by a Ford.[39]

Film scholar and theoretician André Bazin describes the film's artistry in similarly effusive terms: "In seeing again today such films as *Jezebel* by William Wyler, *Stagecoach* by John Ford, or *Le Jour se lève* by Marcel Carné, one has the feeling that in them an art has found its perfect balance, its ideal form of expression. . . . In short, here are all the characteristics of the ripeness of a classical art."[40] As Bazin further says about this masterwork's merit as a model that sets the standard against which other movies should be judged, "*Stagecoach* (1939) is the ideal example of the maturity of a style brought to classical perfection. . . . *Stagecoach* is like a wheel, so perfectly made that it remains in equilibrium on its axis in any position."[41] No wonder, then, that Orson Welles studied Ford's movie rigorously in preparing to make the movie that has been rated by many film scholars as one of the greatest ever made: *Citizen Kane* (1941). Welles admitted once in an interview: "John Ford was my teacher. My own style has nothing to do with his, but *Stagecoach* was my movie textbook. I ran it over forty times. . . . I wanted to learn how to make movies, and that's such a classically perfect one."[42]

The "classical" qualities of *Stagecoach* would be echoed and amplified by many other A-Westerns of the World War II period, especially those made between 1939 and 1942—just before the war film began to replace the Western as the dominant genre during the height of America's involvement in the global conflict. Two highly different masterworks of this period—*Northwest Passage* and *The Westerner* (both 1940)—are discussed in the next chapter. After 1945, as we shall see, the Western film began a gradual transition from classical to postclassical, a transformation brought about by filmmakers who sought to transcend the traditional parameters of the genre, particularly given the psychological and existential climate of the postwar world.

CHAPTER 5

Indian-Fighting, Nation-Building, and Homesteading in the A-Western

"Northwest Passage" and "The Westerner"

Some students of Western cinema have argued that the sudden rise in the number of high-quality big-budget Westerns between the years 1939 and 1942—what has been labeled as "the A-Western Renaissance" and described in chapter 4—had much to do with a growing recognition on the part of studios and filmmakers that the Western was able to reflect a contemporary culture caught in a process of intense transition and self-definition. The Western could represent in a dual fashion both the new seeds of optimism in the late 1930s, given that the Great Depression was coming to a close, and the collective memory of hardship and struggle that had been experienced by the average moviegoer throughout that decade. The surge in A-Western production might be related to the complex spirit of its times by encompassing both prospective and retrospective feelings about the recent social, political, and economic situation.

Rather than dealing directly with the problems of the Depression and the collective project of national renewal in the Roosevelt years, many of the A-Westerns of this period offered a vicarious way of reflecting on hard times, mainly because a good number of Westerns were set in the post–Civil War Reconstruction era. In such an era, those who had been most negatively affected by the destructive effects of the war—mainly southerners, who were coping with a great sense of loss— had fled to the frontier in order to rebuild their lives and even to seek fortune. At the same time, an entire nation was attempting to mend its wounds after such a devastating conflict. And the Western film was especially apt for expressing such conflicts and reconciliations. Film scholar and theoretician André Bazin has commented on the rise of the A-Western from 1937 to 1940 and the return, to the Western form, of established directors who had started their careers in this genre. "This phenomenon," he says, "can be explained by the widespread publicity given westerns between 1937 and 1940. Perhaps the sense of national awareness which preceded the war in the Roosevelt era contributed to this. We are disposed to think so, insofar as the western is rooted in the history of the American nation which it exalts directly or indirectly."[1]

At the surface level, Western films provided simple escape from the everyday worries of those coping with the effects of a national economic disaster: better to let the mind occasionally escape to golden sands and the mythical realm of cowboy heroes rather than to face reality on a strictly full-time basis. At the same time, while providing escapist fare on one level and reflections of a difficult existence on another level, the Western was also capable of providing a feeling of hope for optimistic resolution and closure. In most cases it was the "good guy" who prevailed, and certainly not the crooked banker or corporate land-grabber or the gunslinger hired by him. Since many A-Westerns took the form of trail-blazing and community-building frontier epics, reminding their audiences that a great nation had arisen eventually and successfully from a savage wilderness and a constant struggle against adversity, these films also provided a sense of idealistic faith for viewers who had wearied of economic devastation.

It is not surprising, when one considers the evidence, that A-Westerns of the immediate pre–World War II period offered their audiences as much cultural self-reflection as escapist entertainment. One needs only to consider here that Ford's *Stagecoach* of 1939—the film that in many ways helped the most to revive the genre, despite its occasional reliance on certain B-Western conventions—had as much to do with themes of social prejudice and class distinction as it did with Geronimo and revenge (see chapter 4). Henry King's popular *Jesse James* of that same year—starring Tyrone Power as the title character and Henry Fonda as his brother Frank—explained the legendary outlaw's initial motives in terms of an act of revenge against banks and railroad companies who had hired thugs to harass the James brothers' poor mother (played by the ever maternal Jane Darwell) in order to acquire her property. And in Wyler's *The Westerner* of 1940, a portrait of the ruthless Judge Roy

Bean is set within the wider context of a feud, with ranchers and cattle-men set against farmers and homesteaders. This context would resonate with movie viewers who had recently witnessed a nation's struggle for economic survival and who had found themselves on the threshold of another battle between good and evil, that of World War II.

The B-Western was indeed alive throughout the 1930s, and hundreds of these lower-budget movies had been churned out. Often these B-Westerns reflected Depression-era realities by dealing with the land ownership problems of struggling individuals, especially those who faced the threat of greedy capitalists out to acquire their land.[2] The large number of A-Westerns produced during the first few years of World War II can be explained, at least partially, by the long-running success of the B-Westerns, as well as by the A-Westerns' occasional suggestion of the wider political and economic realities that America had been facing. A-Westerns such as *Jesse James* and *Destry Rides Again* deal explicitly with cheating land-grabbers who attempt to swindle innocent families out of their property (Brian Donlevy plays the greedy heavy in both of those movies). And certain non-Western classics of this era—Fleming's *Gone with the Wind* (1939) and Ford's *The Grapes of Wrath* (1940), in particular—also express a similar theme of survival amid great economic despair. Many of the A-Westerns and B-Westerns of the mid- to late 1930s also helped to restore, for those Depression-era folk who had recently migrated to the cities, a nostalgic sense of authentic origins. The rural Old West became a symbolic substitute for rural America in general.[3]

From an even broader perspective, and as history has taught us, hard times and crisis situations can bring about serious reflection on the virtues, vices, and variables of human nature itself. Most Western films appear, on the surface, as simplistic stories about fights between cowboys and "Injuns" or between heroic and villainous gunslingers. But the majority of A-Westerns produced by the major Hollywood studios have had something deeper to say about the human condition, usually because of thoughtful screenplays, and they have done so despite their primary commitment to action-packed narratives meant to thrill as well as to enlighten their audiences. In reflecting upon recent trials and tribulations—as well as upon our acts of overcoming such obstacles—we are often led to broader ruminations about what it means to be a human individual caught within time and history. The Great Depression and its aftermath cried out for such reflection.

Two underappreciated A-production Westerns that were released in 1940 and that exemplify the national optimism *and* cultural retrospection of the time are Vidor's *Northwest Passage* and Wyler's *The Westerner*. They are two very different types of Western featuring two very distinct kinds of Western hero, thus revealing the richness and diversity of the genre at this crucial stage in Hollywood's classical Golden Age. Vidor's film is an epic frontier saga centered on themes of Indian-fighting and wilderness survival; its protagonist is a military hero who provides a model of strength and perseverance amid the greatest adversity. Wyler's movie portrays a humble westerner who knows how to use a pistol but does so only when absolutely necessary, and who enters into a range war between homesteaders and the villainous Judge Roy Bean, the defender of cattlemen's interests. Both Westerns are as impressive for their dialogue as for their action, and both represent the highest qualities of the A-Western Renaissance.

NORTHWEST PASSAGE

An especially intriguing example of a high-quality, landscape-oriented A-Western of the World War II era is King Vidor's *Northwest Passage* (1940), a colorful and visually rich portrait of frontier survival. The film was based on Kenneth Roberts's epic novel (published in 1937, but first serialized in the *Saturday Evening Post* in 1936) that deals with the real-life trail-blazing adventures of a band of men known as Rogers' Rangers. While the exploits depicted in the novel and film were undertaken in northern New England and the Saint Lawrence River region, the filming was done chiefly around Payette Lake in Idaho and in the forested mountains of Oregon.[4] The movie exhibits the kind of appreciation for the natural world that reminds us once again of the influences of nineteenth-century landscape photography and landscape painting. But it also revolves around the kind of optimism and faith that was required in the early part of the struggle to build a nation and that might have resonated with viewers who had recently experienced a decade of countrywide economic depression and who were now pondering the possibility of America's involvement in an ever spreading battle between good and evil in Europe.

Above all, *Northwest Passage* depicts in a graphic way the suffering and struggle of colonial soldiers undertaking frontier battles during the French and Indian War (1754–1763), the North American extension of the war between Britain and France (eventually known as the "Seven

Years' War"). The story's hero, Major Robert Rogers (Spencer Tracy), commands a band of rugged colonists who fight for the British against the French and their native allies. Rogers is the epitome of the stoic military leader who must mask his own sympathies and weaknesses in order to inspire his men to greatness, always with the goal of victory in mind. The titles of the novel and film reflect the later life of the historical Rogers (1731–1795), after his active military career, when he was appointed by King George III as a royal governor in a fur-trading area of Michigan. One of his primary missions was the organization of expeditions to discover and chart the legendary "Northwest Passage" that would provide a trading route across the continent.[5]

Susan Paterson Glover observes in her essay "East Goes West: The Technicolor Environment of *Northwest Passage* (1940)," in reference to the vision of Rogers that was expressed in his own writings: "Rogers's account of the colonies in his *Concise Account of North America* had prophesied for the northwestern frontier the possibility of 'a rich and great kingdom, exceeding in extent of territory most of the kingdoms in Europe, and exceeded by few, if any, in the fertility of its soil, or the salubrity of its air, and in its present uncultivated state, abounding with many of the necessaries and conveniences of life.' "[6] The combination of Rogers's earlier military accomplishments and his later involvement in frontier exploration, plus his writings about such events and deeds, makes him an apt symbol of America's early efforts in realizing its idealist project of nation-building—even if Rogers sometimes sympathized more with the British than with the colonists, especially during the course of the American Revolution. While he had been convicted by the British of being a traitor (though he was later pardoned), been suspected by American leaders of being a spy for the British, and died as a broken alcoholic in debt, Rogers lives on in Roberts's novel and in Vidor's film as a man filled with strong faith in the idea of an expansionist America.

The movie is both historical Western saga and heroic odyssey. A sequel had been planned but was never realized; it was to continue the story of Rogers by detailing his attempt to discover the fabled passage to the Pacific, a route that had been sought by explorers for centuries. With the continuation of the story in mind, MGM had subtitled Vidor's film "Book I—Rogers' Rangers." One of the apparent reasons why the studio canceled plans to undertake a sequel had to do with lower box office returns than expected and high cost overruns, especially as a result of the many physical and logistical obstacles encountered in the production of the first film.

The movie's use of Technicolor impresses the viewer (and must have certainly impressed its audiences in 1940) with its rich palette and deep hues. Certain scenes of men paddling canoes down sapphire-blue rivers and against forest-green backdrops remind one of landscape paintings by Bierstadt and color-soaked illustrations by N.C. Wyeth (as in the latter's contributions to an edition of Cooper's *The Last of the Mohicans*).[7] The choice of Technicolor adds to the movie's magic but gave Vidor and the studio more than a few headaches when the enchanting colors of his on-site settings did not always translate into film as intended, especially when the first rushes were seen. As Glover tells us, "All color processes to that point that been unable to accurately reproduce hues of green, and considerable work went into finding a dye for the green Ranger uniforms that, on film, would blend in to the green of the natural surroundings. In his autobiography Vidor recalls the early production tests, when the dull green of the Rangers' uniforms appeared on the film as a 'brilliant Kelly green.'"[8]

Vidor honed his talents as a director during the silent film era; his two masterworks of this period are *The Big Parade* (1925) and *The Crowd* (1928). The latter was an authentic portrait of the American common man, a film that depicted the shining dreams and gritty hardships of the Roaring Twenties with the same tension between realism and romanticism that Vidor brought to the story of frontier struggles in *Northwest Passage*. Later sound films by Vidor include *The Champ* (1931), *Stella Dallas* (1937), *The Fountainhead* (1949), *Ruby Gentry* (1952), and *War and Peace* (1956). His other Westerns include *Billy the Kid* (1930), *The Texas Rangers* (1936), *Duel in the Sun* (1946), and *Man without a Star* (1955). Vidor concluded his long career as director in 1980 with a brief documentary titled *The Metaphor,* which features painter Andrew Wyeth. It was perhaps only natural that Vidor, another "painterly" director in the vein of Ford and Walsh, returned to filmmaking in his final years to discuss painting.[9]

Northwest Passage is not a typical Western, by any means, in that it is set much farther east than most Westerns, starting off in Portsmouth, New Hampshire, and then bringing its viewer to an early version of the "Western" frontier—that of the northern New England region surrounding Lake Champlain and extending upward into the terrain around the Saint Lawrence River in Quebec. And rather than being set in the familiar post–Civil War era that historically frames many Westerns, the story here takes place during the French and Indian War of the 1700s. Like John Ford's *Drums along the Mohawk* (which was released a year before *Northwest Passage,* in 1939, the same year as *Stagecoach*), Vidor's film was shot in strikingly brilliant Technicolor, constitutes an "eastern" Western of sorts, and is one of the few successful and well-crafted movies to be set in the colonial period of American history. Also much like Ford's film, *Northwest Passage* is the story of those individuals, whether militia-forming settlers (*Drums*) or frontier warriors (*Northwest*), who must confront savage enemies and overcome natural obstacles while protecting their families and fellow fighters at all costs. *Northwest Passage* and *Drums along the Mohawk* fall within the broad parameters of the Western genre because they revolve around themes of wilderness conquering, Indian-fighting, and frontier settling. If the Western is primarily the story of American expansionism and the struggle against primal adversity, then movies like *Northwest Passage* and *Drums* belong fittingly to the genre, despite the qualms of any genre guardians concerning geography and historical setting.

Above all, these are films in which, like many of the great A-Westerns, the landscape plays a dual role as both inspiration and obstacle. This is especially true of Vidor's movie, where the brave crew of Indian-fighters must travel vast distances through dangerous territory, haul their boats over hilltops, trudge through swamps, ford raging rivers, and above all, seek to survive in a rugged terrain where food is scarce. There are other Westerns, of course, whose primary theme is survival in the face of extreme hunger, thirst, and the threat of a hostile enemy. But *Northwest Passage* depicts the rigors and dangers of the wilderness more explicitly than most other Hollywood Westerns of this era. Here, Vidor reveals the great beauty of the terrain, but also the ways in which the suffering involved in the attempt to trek through that land leads at times to possible madness and death.

In the end, a sense of spiritual faith is the only thing left to give the Rangers (or at least most of them) a vestige of hope. Many are on the verge of complete mental and physical collapse and a few have already crossed that threshold. Up to this point, it is their sense of duty, dreams of an expanded civilization, and hatred of a common enemy that keep Rogers's men going. The story of American territorial expansionism has its dark underbelly, and Vidor's film (as well as Roberts's novel on which it is based) does not shy away from describing that side of the tale, showing both the romantic power of the mythic ideal and the deadly costs and sacrifices in pursuing that ideal.

As with the rigors and challenges of shooting *The Big Trail* (see chapter 4), the production of *Northwest Passage* involved countless hurdles that sometimes echoed the ordeals faced by Rogers's frontiersmen. Shooting began in Idaho in June 1938, but filming ceased soon after and was postponed until the following spring, mainly because of "logistical and management problems." Technicolor technology had been enhanced during the months in between the two shoots, and so the footage from the previous summer (under the direction of W. S. Van Dyke) was not used and Vidor took over as director when filming recommenced in the spring.[10] Other production obstacles ranged from the need to inoculate the entire cast and crew against tick fever to the necessity of reshooting scenes because of changes in the physical environment, such as fluctuating foliage colors and water levels.[11] As yet another example of the obstacles that occurred, part of the on-site filming in the summer of 1938 involved the initial shooting of the thrilling scene in which the Rangers create a human chain across perilous river rapids. The filming had been started at the Yellowstone River, but the task proved too dangerous for cast and crew and the rest of the scene was shot on the MGM studio lot using a massive water tank.[12]

Northwest Passage begins with an emphasis on geography, giving a "lay of the land" in the most literal sense: a series of maps of colonial North America during the time of conflicts among the British, the French, and their Indian allies. Maps and mapmaking, in fact, figure prominently in the plotline of the film and remind us of an essential expansionist theme: the American drive to conquer and organize natural spaces. The narrative officially begins in colonial Portsmouth in 1759, and one may recall the opening of Ford's *Drums along the Mohawk,* which starts with the wedding of Gil (Henry Fonda) and Lana (Claudette Colbert) at Lana's elegant European-style family home in Albany. Here a clear contrast is drawn between the cultured, commercial, colonial East, on the one hand, and the raw frontier wilderness, on the other.

We see men on the Portsmouth waterfront, preparing the rigging of a ship and laboring at other tasks. One worker who sits on a crossbeam spots the Boston stagecoach arriving. We now see that it carries young Langdon Towne (Robert Young), who has returned home from Harvard after going there at his family's behest to study for the clergy. We learn right away that Langdon is an aspiring artist who wishes to practice his vocation at all costs. Above all, he desires to develop his craft as an "American" painter by portraying, not the civilized colonist, but the Indian as he exists in his natural setting.

After arriving back in Portsmouth, Langdon runs into Hunk Marriner (Walter Brennan), who has been put into stocks for, as the accompa-

FIGURE 19. Spencer Tracy as Major Rogers (*second from right*) converses with new recruits Langdon Towne (Robert Young, *center*) and Hunk Marriner (Walter Brennan, *left*) in King Vidor's *Northwest Passage* (1940). Courtesy of the Museum of Modern Art.

nying sign states, "Disloyal Conversation." Given Langdon's report about his expulsion from Harvard for having published a politically controversial caricature, there is a parallel to be drawn here: both men are not afraid to flout authority in their desire to speak their minds. They are especially apt exemplars of the archetypal easterner who becomes a westerner, particularly since they are men who feel constrained and frustrated by the conventions and restrictions of a rigid Puritan lifestyle in old New England. Langdon and Hunk yearn for freedom, yet they unfortunately wind up in a regimented existence amid a savage wilderness and a brutal war.

It does not take long before our protagonist lands in serious trouble yet again after he insults a representative of the Crown while highly inebriated at a local tavern. Langdon and Hunk (who has come to his friend's rescue) escape, even though Langdon must leave his beloved Elizabeth (Ruth Hussey) behind. They make their way by canoe to a small outpost on the frontier, Fort Flintlock, where they meet up with Major Rogers and help him sober up a besotted Indian guide. Langdon soon tells Roberts that he has drawn maps of western territories because he wants to go there to paint Indians "as they really are"—saying this even as the viewer is treated to a wholly negative and stereotypical portrait of an Indian. Langdon appears initially to be someone who is sympathetic with "the red man." He and his sidekick, Hunk, are, at this point in the film, heading to Albany—supposedly where "the West" begins—so that he can travel with traders and thereby fulfill his dream of seeing and painting the "real" West.

Rogers wants Langdon to join his company because he desperately needs a man who is good at drawing to be the mapmaker for his next expedition. He tells Langdon that he may be a bit too educated for the rough woodsmen who make up the Rangers, but Hunk retorts, "He's not *that* educated." Langdon scoffs at Rogers's invitation: "I want to paint live Indians, not dead ones." Rogers then explains why Langdon may someday need to kill the native he may be painting, because of the real threat involved, telling him that his aspiration is merely some romanticized dream. As we will soon see, Langdon proves Rogers right and the artist winds up killing Indians rather than painting them.

As Armando Prats points out in his book *Invisible Natives: Myth and Identity in the American Western,* Langdon's initial artistic goal and his subsequent forsaking of that goal during his Indian-fighting adventure are especially symbolic of the ways in which the Native American is referenced in Hollywood Western narratives. They are referenced, but only to be vanquished, forgotten, and erased via these movies' various forms of "cultural appropriation."[13] Prats, in fact, uses *Northwest Passage* as his chief cinematic example in introducing and outlining his book's overall argument about the treatment of the Indian in American Western films.[14] As revealed by his sketchbook when shown to Major Rogers, Langdon has been content to render drawings of his beloved Elizabeth and of Rogers and selected other Rangers. But the Indians against whom he is fighting are never depicted, dead or alive.[15] Langdon gradually comes to view the natives through Rogers's eyes: as savage enemies, as possibly deceitful scouts, or as hopeless drunks who, like Rogers's inebriated and inarticulate guide, Konapot, have been partially assimilated to white society.[16]

This pattern, according to Prats, follows the general trajectory of the overall myth of conquest, the master narrative that underlies much of the genre from the silent era (see chapter 1) up until today. This myth is part of a wider one that Richard Slotkin has called "the myth of America" and "the Myth of the Frontier."[17] The shaping of the very idea of America as a cultural entity, argues Prats, depends on such an appropriating, distorting myth, along with its implicit principle that the Indian must be made "present" in a given Western narrative—but presented always as the Other, an Other who must inevitably be made "absent." The making-absent of the Indian echoes, of course, the historical genocide against the native. But Prats is chiefly concerned with the specific ways in which the evolution of American cultural identity depends on those dialectical tensions (same/Other, presence/absence) that help to constitute the Western mythos and the story of its expansionist consequences—most especially in terms of how that story is articulated through the cinema's treatment of is victims. According to this interpretation, it is in its very act of representing the Indian that the traditional Western movie relegates the native to a realm of absence and alterity. As Prats tells us, "If the *opposition* [to the Indian Other] is essential to the national self, so too is the *elimination* of it. Perhaps the ambiguity explains why the Indian is the Western's everlasting revenant: the Western had to save the Indian so that it could destroy him."[18]

Langdon's ignoring of his original artistic goal and his adoption of Rogers's vision of the Indian is one of many ways in which this kind of narrative pattern is manifested, according to Prats. The native can never be rendered "as he is" as long as his depiction is subsumed under the broader myth of expansionism and conquest, a myth that has been central to the story of America. Another example of this pattern occurs when the Western narrative defines the Indian through the words of the white frontiersman, the man who knows the native well enough to interpret the latter's motives, actions, and very existence.[19] The apparent expert, a "provisional savage" of sorts, is usually put into the position of needing to explain the ways of the Indian to a naive counterpart. Here again, the Other is referenced or made present, as is necessary in the dialectic of conquest, but he is simultaneously made *absent* by a distorting form of mediation, by the very act of being represented by his knowing enemy.[20] In *Northwest Passage*, it is Major Roberts who acts as this type of substitute, instructing Langdon about the kind of people these natives really are and the types of bloody deeds that they have enacted. We might also think here of Ethan Edwards in Ford's *The Searchers*, who knows enough about his Comanche enemies to speak their language, guess their strategies, understand their spiritual beliefs, and mirror to some degree the dreaded Chief Scar (see chapter 8).

Lured into the company of the Rangers after the oblivion of a drunken night, Langdon and Hunk soon become accepted to some degree by the rough-hewn Rangers. They soon venture as new soldiers

FIGURE 20. "All for one and one for all" in the exciting river-fording scene from the frontier epic *Northwest Passage*. Courtesy of the Museum of Modern Art.

through a wild but majestic terrain that poses danger as much as it affords beauty. The idea of the landscape as an obstacle to be conquered emerges specifically when we witness the Rangers toiling to transport their boats over a hillside so as to avoid being spotted by the French and their Indian allies. These enemies are camped just down the shoreline, obstructing their voyage, and the men groan and sweat as they lift their boats with a massive rope. Vidor shows us each step of this burdensome task, including the eventual lowering of the wooden vessels down the hillside and the boats finally sliding into the river, now beyond the place where the French ships are waiting. Rogers has outwitted the enemy with his trademark determination and his expert coordination of collective labor.

Soon after, Rogers tells his men what their mission really is, using a map painted on the stone face of a hillside. They have been assigned by their British superiors to destroy the Abenaki village of Saint Francis in Quebec, given the destruction wrought by the Abenakis' past raids on the whites. Rogers clearly explains why they need to go after the Indians, calling upon one of the Rangers who describes in brutal detail how the

Abenakis had torn his brother's skin upwards from his belly and then hanged him from it while he was still alive. This description of torture cements in the men's minds the fact that the Indians are animal-like savages who must be destroyed. Ruthless revenge becomes a duty and a matter of justice.

It would appear on the surface that the attack on the Abenakis is justified from what Rogers and his Ranger have to say about the bloodthirsty deeds of their Indian enemies. It is this surface-level view that undoubtedly led Western experts George Fenin and William Everson to point out that this film holds a special place in the genre because of its unrelentingly negative depiction of the Indian enemy: "*Northwest Passage* has a place in the general history of the Western for being one of the most viciously anti-Indian films ever made. . . . The Indian's side of the question is never presented."[21] Or, as Prats has argued, the Indian perspective is presented here, but through the words of Rogers and his men—and so presented only through a distorting, appropriative, and deeply biased interpretation that renders the native's "genuine" viewpoint completely absent.

However, as Susan Glover argues, things are not quite so simple as they would at first appear. That is because, while we *hear* about the Abenakis' brutality, the movie actually *shows* us the brutality of the Rangers. The scene of the massacre of the Abenaki village is graphic enough to make the viewer wince at the fierce violence waged by Rogers's men. While the film concentrates on the military goal of the Rangers in the face of an Indian enemy, it also chooses to communicate the savagery of the enemy in words—a clear distancing device—while demonstrating the vengeance of the hero and his men in direct, violent images. While Prats may emphasize the ways in which the film's "white" mediation of the native's perspective inevitably displaces and even "erases" the native himself, what the viewer ultimately experiences is a narrative in which Indian violence is presented in a deliberately detached manner and the Rangers' acts of violence are conveyed in immediate, horrifying imagery. Such an observation certainly qualifies, at least to some degree, the criticism that *Northwest Passage* is purely "anti-Indian." At the very least, there is an implicit dialectic in place here between the different modes of presenting these opposing perspectives, one that complicates the film's presentation of its basic subject matter.[22]

Vidor proceeds to provide regular glimpses of the landscape as the Rangers then journey to Saint Francis and avoid detection by the French and Indians. After the massacre of the Abenakis at Saint Francis, Rogers's men journey homeward and suffer from extreme hunger. There were no substantial provisions to be found at the village they just destroyed, and they have only a few kernels of corn to sustain each man. We then experience a highly morbid element of the film's narrative that points to the harshness of the Rangers' lives and the extreme personal costs of conquering a land for the sake of building a nation.

At one point during the battle at Saint Francis, a Ranger named Crofton (Addison Richards) had begun to show signs of having suffered severe psychological effects from such a brutal existence. He was about to kill a native child, but another Ranger prevented him, saying the child is "too young" and must simply be taken prisoner. As if to channel his rage, Crofton savagely attacks an already dead adult Indian with a hatchet. After the battle, the increasingly deranged Ranger soon shows himself to be more than disturbed, mocking the hunger of his comrades and carrying a mysterious bundle around with him as if it were a sack of treasure. Not long thereafter, the demented Ranger steals away to feed off the contents of his treasured sack: the head of the Indian whom he had viciously massacred. We are not shown this gruesome event, of course, but the horror of this scene is increased by the fact that Vidor leaves the act of cannibalism to the power of the viewer's imagination. Eventually Crofton leaps off a cliff in a suicidal frenzy, leaving a stunned Rogers to offer a eulogizing salute to a formerly loyal member of his band.

Despite the splendor of the natural scenery around them, the Rangers have suffered greatly, even been driven to madness, by their lack of food and their expenditure of energy in conquering a hostile foe. They would gladly trade the beauty of their surroundings for a bit of sustenance. Fort Wentworth, their long-desired destination, winds up being a deserted outpost. Rogers rushes ahead to investigate the fort, finds it empty just before the men arrive, and for once expresses signs of weakness, breaking into a momentary crying jag before he hears his men approaching. An exemplar of stoic dignity, Rogers quickly regains his composure and then demands that the men march into camp. They are starved and exhausted, at the threshold of death's door, with the dream of food having kept them going until this point. Rogers then refers to the Biblical example of Moses, who allegedly went hungry for forty days without food and water, and he cites a few verses from scripture (a paraphrased amalgam of Isaiah 40:3 and Isaiah 43:19–20): "The voice of Him that cryeth in the wilderness. Prepare ye the way of the Lord. Make straight in the desert a highway for our God. Behold, I will do a

FIGURE 21. Langdon Towne (*left*) has transformed himself into a determined Indian fighter in *Northwest Passage*. Courtesy of the Museum of Modern Art.

new thing. Shall ye not know it? I will make a way in the wilderness and rivers in the desert. And the highway shall be there, and a way. And wayfaring men, though fools, shall not go astray therein."

In the end, of course, hope is answered and British soldiers appear in boats, arriving to help the ragged Rangers after Rogers had earlier sent a few of his men back to their starting point to seek help. Rogers tells his men in their dilapidated attire to stand proud and straight with eyes front. We suddenly transition to the near future: the surviving Rangers march into town to great fanfare, with the citizens out in the streets to greet them upon their homecoming. The British commander wastes no time in giving Rogers his new orders—to find the fabled Northwest Passage. Langdon and Hunk, however, have decided that they will not join the men on their next adventure. Langdon tells his sweetheart, Elizabeth, who had been patiently waiting for him, that Rogers and his men are now marching off to make history. When she asks Rogers if there really is a Northwest Passage, he tells her: "There's bound to be." And Rogers promises Langdon, before departing: "I'll see you at sundown,

Harvard." Langdon looks on as Rogers and his men march off, and he proclaims to Elizabeth, "That man will never die."

The film concludes with a shot of Rogers silhouetted against the sky at the end of a dark road—not unlike the concluding iconic shot in Ford's *Young Mr. Lincoln* (1939). The chiaroscuro image reminds us that the road ahead will be a mixture of darkness and light. But as long as the light exists, there will be a mission to fulfill and a nation to build. Once again, the memory of suffering and sacrifice is combined with a sense of optimistic faith and historical destiny in order to do justice to the story of American expansionism. And yet the film clearly shows us—even if it does not *say* so—that the story of America and its ideal of Manifest Destiny are inevitably intertwined with death and loss, with racism and conflict. We may want to cheer Rogers on at the end of the film as he embarks on his new mission, but we also witness the refusal of Langdon and Hunk to join in, as they opt instead for a settled and civilized existence.

THE WESTERNER

There are epic A-Westerns in the World War II era—those like *Union Pacific* (1939) and *Northwest Passage* (1940)—that deal with the expansion and unification of an entire country. There are other A-Westerns of this period that emphasize the more intimate and local building blocks of nationhood: the theme of building a permanent home and starting a family, even against great odds. This theme is suggested by the struggles of Gil Martin (Henry Fonda) and his wife, Lana (Claudette Colbert), in building a frontier home in Ford's *Drums along the Mohawk* (1939). Home and family are the seeds of civilization-building. However, as Patrick McGee points out in his *From* Shane *to* Kill Bill: *Re-thinking the Western,* while the family is often viewed as the most basic social and economic unit that nurtures individualism, it also engenders "the contradiction between individual desire and social conformity, to which the Western frequently offers an imaginary resolution."[23]

In many stories of the settling of the Old West, homesteading and home-building lead to the establishment of a stable form of agrarian existence. A tranquil farming life is the reward for the toil and tribulation of journeying from the civilized East to the wilderness of the West. This is especially evident in Wyler's *The Westerner,* in which saddle tramp Cole Harden (Gary Cooper) comes to ally himself with a community of farmers and finally triumphs over the ruthless Judge Roy Bean

(Walter Brennan). Harden seeks to bring peace to the homesteaders after they have been terrorized by the cattle ranchers and their hired guns, those who want to keep the land as free range for grazing. The conflict between settlers and ranchers is a recurring theme in Western cinema and emerges as early as Ford's silent Western *Straight Shooting* of 1917 (see chapter 1). It is the central conflict in George Stevens's *Shane* (1953), and the battle with wealthy ranchers also frames the plots of later Westerns such as Arthur Penn's *The Missouri Breaks* (1976), Michael Cimino's *Heaven's Gate* (1980), and Kevin Costner's *Open Range* (2003).

In Wyler's film there is an explicit discussion of the virtues of having a permanent home, something that Harden does not readily concede, as he is a man of the open range. He is accustomed to making his "home" beneath sun and stars, as he proudly states. But by the end of the film, Harden has settled down with his beloved Jane Ellen Matthews (Doris Davenport), a young woman who had always dreamed of a stable house to call her home. Harden has finally been domesticated willingly, much like Ringo at the end of *Stagecoach* (see chapter 4). As Cole and Jane Ellen stare out the window of their new home in the concluding scene, they see a procession of familiar homesteaders returning to the area, those who had departed after Bean's men destroyed their corn crops. Harden proclaims quietly but firmly, "Yep, the promised land." There are biblical connotations here, of course, but also the idea of Manifest Destiny, a near-religious ideal in the name of which empty land became eligible for claiming and for building a community, all for the purpose of expanding a nation to the very limits of its continent. Ultimately, it is the dream of a future home and the labor of creating it that is the real engine of progress, helping to ensure that this collective ideal becomes a reality.

Harden is no Ethan Edwards, who at the end of Ford's *The Searchers* must remain excluded from family and home, banishing himself once again to solitude amid the wilderness (see chapter 8). Since Harden is a man who actually surrenders his role as a lone westerner, he may be compared with William Munny (Clint Eastwood) at the start of Eastwood's *Unforgiven*, a man who has hung up his rifle (for a stretch of time, anyway) to start a family and care for his children (see chapter 10). Harden is also similar to Tom Doniphon (Wayne again) in *The Man Who Shot Liberty Valance*, a gunslinging rancher who desires above all else to marry his beloved Hallie (Vera Miles) and settle into a happy, comfortable existence (see chapter 8). Edwards, on the other hand, never hangs up his gun or his role as westerner, even if at times he may desire strongly to do so. He saunters away, reluctantly but inevitably, in the famous closing shot of the movie, back to the desert from whence he came.

As Fenin and Everson point out in their survey *The Western: From Silents to the Seventies,* Wyler was one of the more intriguing and talented directors of Westerns to emerge from the silent movie period. While Wyler made only two sound-era Westerns aside from *The Westerner—Hell's Heroes* (1930, at the advent of talkies) and *The Big Country* (1958)—he directed a good number of silent Westerns and knew the fundamentals of the genre quite well. In 1925, Wyler's first two-reeler for Universal, *Crook Buster,* was released, and he directed twenty of these Universal Western shorts (which were called "Mustangs") in all. He also contributed to the script for another Western, *Ridin' for Love* (1926), which was the only time he ever accepted script credit. Film reviewers at the time rated Wyler's *The Ore Raiders* (1927) as one of his "best and most action-packed films."[24] In addition, Wyler directed five of Universal's "Blue Streak" Westerns (typically five-reelers), including *Lazy Lightning* (1926), and he later made several other feature Westerns for Universal as part of the studio's new "Adventure Series."[25]

Wyler directed *The Westerner* for producer Sam Goldwyn amid an impressive run of filmmaking that included such other masterworks as *Jezebel* (1938), *Wuthering Heights* (1939), *The Letter* (1940), *The Little Foxes* (1941), and *Mrs. Miniver* (1942). The many merits of the film include Wyler's superb direction, Gregg Toland's memorable cinematography, the accomplished performances of Brennan and Cooper, and expert dialogue by Niven Busch.[26] This Western (like others, ranging from *Stagecoach* to *Unforgiven*) deglamorizes the West and shows the hard struggle involved in forging a civilized community amid barren desert and villainous gunslingers. *The Westerner* blends gritty action, visual poetry, and occasional comedy in the way that the best A-Westerns have always managed to achieve.

There are no Indians to be battled here, since the unjust ranchers led by Judge Bean give the homesteaders enough to worry about. The plot of *The Westerner* also includes heartfelt scenes of romance and mourning, along with the decisions of a hero who (shades of *Destry Rides Again*) seeks rational negotiation before resorting to his gun. Busch—who authored the novels *Duel in the Sun* and *The Furies,* the bases of two later "psychological" Western films (see chapter 7)—rooted his script in a story by Stuart N. Lake. Lake had authored the novel *Wyatt Earp: Frontier Marshal,* which was the foundation of two different movie adaptations titled *Frontier Marshal* (1934, 1939) as well as the basis of Ford's *My Darling Clementine* (1946), which also starred Brennan as a villain. In addition, Lake penned the story for the later Western classic *Winchester '73* (1950), directed by Anthony Mann.

In *The Westerner* Cooper wears his familiar persona of the quiet but charismatic hero. Brennan won an Oscar for Best Supporting Actor for his mesmerizing performance as the tyrannical Bean (it was his record-breaking third Oscar win). The characters are broadly drawn, almost caricatured at times, but the director and his actors add unexpected nuances at just the right moments, particularly in shaping the peculiar relationship formed between Harden and Bean. There are several spell-binding face-to-face confrontations between the two men, with each representing, respectively, the good and evil sides of the archetypal Western gunslinger.

Bean is a continual and unpredictable threat. But at the same time, the hard-drinking judge seeks to form a friendship with Harden, and his heart turns to mush every time he glances at a picture of his beloved, the music hall actress Lily Langtry (Lilian Bond), after whom he decides to name his town. One might mistake Bean's occasional friendliness toward Harden and his love for "Miss Lily"—not to mention his gruff charm—as evidence of this character's moral ambiguity. But though Bean is not a simple man, he is always a ruthless and self-centered one, even to the bitter end, and his signs of sociability or dependency point more to his need for selfish marriages of convenience than to any inherent humanity. It is yet another lesson that wolfish tyrants can be beguiling at times, especially when they are the makers of their own rules and laws.

In fact, of the many memorable actors who played villains in the history of Western cinema—Tyrone Power Sr. in *The Big Trail* (1930), Brian Donlevy in *Destry Rides Again, Union Pacific,* and *Jesse James* (all 1939), Jack Palance in *Shane* (1953), Robert Ryan in *The Naked Spur* (1953), Henry Brandon in *The Searchers* (1956), Lee Marvin in *The Man Who Shot Liberty Valance* (1962), and Henry Fonda in *Once upon a Time in the West* (1968), to name but several—Brennan gave two of the very best performances in this category, including his role as the coldhearted Pa Clanton in *Clementine*. As Roy Bean, Brennan portrays one of the most snakelike of all Western villains—one who is later echoed by Karl Malden, with his venom-soaked charm as Dad Long-worth in Marlon Brando's *One-Eyed Jacks* (1961), and Gene Hackman

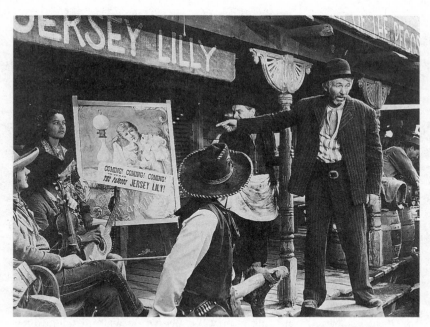

FIGURE 22. Walter Brennan as the ruthless Judge Roy Bean (*standing*) points to a poster advertising the arrival of his beloved Lily Langtry ("The Jersey Lily") in William Wyler's *The Westerner* (1940). Courtesy of the Museum of Modern Art.

as Little Bill Daggett in Eastwood's *Unforgiven*. Despite his moments of displaying humor, affection, and folksy charisma, making it difficult for the viewer to despise him outright, Bean is rotten to the core, and anyone who forgets that basic fact is liable to suffer his wrath at some point.

But *The Westerner* is not solely a portrait of Judge Roy Bean. It is, in many ways, a depiction of the primitive politics of the Old West. In his essay "Country Music and the 1939 Western: From Hillbillies to Cowboys," Peter Stanfield points out that *The Westerner* is one example of the way in which "the Western was able to negotiate the contradictions and conflicts of what it meant to be an American," most especially as a reflection of the post-Depression, pre–World War II period in which the movie was made. This is clear, for example, in the overall theme of the conflict between homesteaders, who are dedicated to their agrarian livelihood, and the cattlemen (defended by Bean), who view these migrants and their pursuit of property as a threat to the free ranges on which the cattle can roam and feed. As Stanfield tells us of *The Westerner* and its place within this wider context:

The Westerner . . . is not so much concerned with the frontier, as with the establishment and defence of a Jeffersonian pastoral idyll. Gregg Toland's photography manages powerfully to evoke the destruction of homes, families, crops and the ever-present threat to the land, as Judge Roy Bean . . . does all he can to drive out the homesteaders. . . . The sense of loss in *The Westerner* is palpable and the heroine's determination not to give up is every bit as convincing as Scarlett O'Hara's. After the crops and homes have been devastated, we witness a long procession of wagons leaving the territory.[27]

The economic theme of struggle amid hardship is central in *The Westerner,* as is the battle between good and evil, themes that would resonate with audience members, who, at the time of the film's release, might have been thinking of the growing war in Europe and the possible external threats to America. The movie is clearly history-minded, with some loose allusions to Wyoming's Johnson County range war of 1892; and Toland's documentary-like shots of homesteaders and cornfields remind one of Depression-era photographs of rural devastation in the Midwest.[28] Yet the film is also laced with mythical moments, both visually and narratively.

The movie begins with majestic shots of a cloud-covered desert appearing beneath the title credits, and in one of these initial shots a silhouetted horseman suddenly appears under Gary Cooper's name. We know right away that this will be the story of an archetypal personality, the type of individual who bravely helped to make the Old West what it was. The solitary figure is "the westerner," the hero of our tale, and the very title of the film summons us to ponder this type of character. After the credits we turn to the image of a covered-wagon train making its way past the camera. We know from this symbolic shot that the story about to unfold will be set within a larger social situation, in this case that of traveling homesteaders who have braved the threats of the wilderness and of the free-range-protecting cattlemen, all in order to reach their goal of establishing permanent homes at the edge of a constantly shifting frontier.

Words begin to roll down the screen, establishing the historical and biographical contexts that are fused within the wider narrative of the film. After the end of this literary prologue, there emerges a black-and-white map of Texas. The camera zooms in, with the name *Pecos* clearly visible, and we switch to a shot of cattle being herded. Obstructing the cows are barbed-wire fences that have been erected by the farmers to protect their claimed property. We then see cattlemen cutting the fence wires, and a gun battle erupts between the homesteaders and cattlemen.

One farmer runs through the fields, trying to escape a cattleman who has ridden after him. He is captured and taken to meet his punishment; the stage for conflict is set.

We soon find ourselves at the scene of an unfair lynching of the fleeing homesteader. The homesteader who is to be hanged is convicted of "the most serious crime west of the Pecos, to wit, shooting a steer," and he protests that he had been trying to shoot a man in self-defense and had simply missed. Roy Bean, the presiding judge, responds by blaming the man for being a typical "sodbuster" in that he does not know how to "shoot straight." The judge then kicks the horse out from under the poor man, who has a noose around his neck. Immediately thereafter Cole Harden is brought into the saloon with his hands tied, accused of stealing one of Bean's men's horses, just before Jane Ellen Matthews arrives to ask after her friend Shad Wilkins (Trevor Bardette), the man who was lynched unjustly. The judge tells Miss Matthews that Wilkins had broken the law: "It's agin' the law to build fences hereabouts." But she challenges him fearlessly: "*What* law? *Whose* law? . . . You're no more judge than I am. [You] just *call* yourself a judge."

Bean is now irritated and orders Miss Matthews to sit down. He then returns to trying Harden and asks that the allegedly stolen horse be brought into the saloon to stand witness to prove if Harden really stole him or not. We now have a real sense of Bean's psychotic parody of a justice system. And yet while one of his men goes outside to retrieve the horse, Bean does express some attempt at "reasonable" discourse when he turns back to Jane Ellen and explains some basic practical logic: homesteaders will not be allowed to build fences and thus hold private property because cattle die when they cannot make it to water. Jane Ellen retorts that there are miles of river on each side of the homesteaders' property and Bean snarls that the land had always been quality free range for cattle grazing: "This country's unfenced range land. Always was and always will be." Later in the film, after explaining to Harden why he had his men burn the farmers' crops, Bean repeats the argument that the homesteaders must go because the grass needed for the cattle has been ruined. While the movie does not shy away from depicting Bean as a vicious tyrant and his men as obsequious simpletons, the story also makes clear that there are arguments on both sides of the conflict.

After hearing Bean's case for the ranchers, a spirited Jane Ellen then gives a fiery response, proclaiming that no matter what Bean does to the homesteaders, they will keep fighting for what is theirs and what is right. It is the kind of speech in defense of justice that one might expect of Tom Joad in *The Grapes of Wrath*. She tells him, "You thought you'd starve the homesteaders out but you didn't. You can pester us and rob us and kill us, but you can't stop us. 'Cause there'll always be more coming, more and more. And we'll stay on our farms in spite of you and your courtrooms and your killers."

Soon thereafter Harden takes note of Bean's deference to Lily Langtry and the many images of her hanging on the wall behind the bar. Harden deceives Bean by telling him that he has met Lily many times and immediately wins Bean's attention, respect, and curiosity. Harden refers to her as an "angel" and then says that he will never forget the night they met, knowing that he may well satisfy Bean's thirst for more intimate knowledge while not saying so much that he will raise his jealous ire. Bean is enraptured by the story, and Harden adds that he possesses a locket of Lily's hair, knowing how much this will entice Bean. The dazzled judge suggests that Harden could ride to El Paso, where Harden claims to have left the locket, even if it might take weeks for the locket to arrive back to Bean by mail coach. Bean seems to have forgotten that he has already convicted this alleged horse thief, even though his "jury" is still "deliberating" (i.e., drinking and playing cards in the back room). When Bean's men return and deliver the expected verdict of guilty, Bean concurs but states that the sentence shall be suspended for a few weeks until he has time to weigh the evidence further. This puzzles and angers his men, but Bean holds sway and Harden is obviously let off the hook for the time being, his ruse having proved successful.

Toland's genius for cinematography and Daniel Mandell's effective editing are on display when we witness Bean, still suffering a debilitating hangover after drinking heavily all night with Harden, eventually chasing after Harden on horseback. There is rapid crosscutting between shots of the galloping horsemen in order to build a brief burst of suspense. The landscape is prominent throughout the scene, with luminous white and gray clouds towering above a tree-dotted prairie. Elegant bands of darkness and light play off each other as Bean gallops wildly after Harden. In each shot the camera is positioned and pans effectively, sometimes slightly above the rider and sometimes slightly below, creating a quick-moving and almost musical rhythm of visual information. The scene culminates with a crescendo-like convergence of the two men out in the wilderness, beyond the borders of town. But rather than a conventional duel in the sun, we get a conversation—a momentary lull after this heart-pounding chase, in which Harden outwits Bean once again, steals his pistol, and then gallops away.

FIGURE 23. Cole Harden (Gary Cooper, *left*) continues to outwit the villainous Judge Roy Bean after a rousing horseback chase. Courtesy of the Museum of Modern Art.

We then cut to a scene of some of the homesteaders in the kitchen of the Matthews's farmhouse. (The actors who play these homesteaders include the young Dana Andrews.) Very few of the men want to fight a war against Bean and his gang, for understandable reasons. Harden soon enters the room, in which he finds Jane Ellen with her dad, Caliphet Matthews (Fred Stone). It is nighttime, and Harden, after appearing suddenly at the kitchen window, enters the kitchen to tell them that he has come to thank Jane Ellen for her assistance in defending him. Harden informs them that he is on his way to California, and they invite him to have dinner with them. As Mr. Matthews says a blessing over the meal, we notice that Harden appears to be out of place, not accustomed to a religious invocation or even to sitting at a dining room table. He is the consummate westerner here, a benevolent outsider who wishes to help innocent community-builders, but who, initially at least, cannot feel at home in such a community and must soon move on.

Harden joins Jane Ellen again in the kitchen after dinner as she washes the dishes. The dialogue here concerns their divergent views on the idea of home, one of the central themes of the movie. She asks him

FIGURE 24. Cole Harden and Jane Ellen Matthews (Doris Davenport) ponder the landscape and a future together in a romantic scene from *The Westerner*. Courtesy of the Museum of Modern Art.

whether he would not prefer to spend more time in some places rather than wandering all the time, and he answers: "It's much like the turtle: carry their houses with 'em. If I had to build a house, I'd have it on wheels." She responds firmly, "Not me. I'd want my house so that nothing could ever move it, so down deep that an earthquake couldn't shake it and . . . a cyclone would be just another wind goin' by."

Our protagonist decides against leaving and becomes committed to the cause of helping the homesteaders in their fight against Bean. A bit later on, Cole and Jane Ellen continue their discussion about the importance of a permanent home, just after the homesteaders are shown kneeling in front of the vast field of cornstalks and giving their benediction and thanksgiving. Jane Ellen follows in the footsteps of such strong-willed Western women as Letty Mason in *The Wind* (see chapter 2) and Dallas in *Stagecoach* (see chapter 4); for all three characters, a stable home and family life amid the frontier wilderness is their light at the end of the tunnel. In his book *From Shane to Kill Bill: Re-thinking the Western,* Patrick McGee compares Jane Ellen with Dallas, as well as with the spirited Frenchy (Marlene Dietrich) of *Destry Rides Again.*

According to McGee, while Jane Ellen may be more traditional and less charismatic than the other two female westerners, she is the perfect heroine for post–Depression era audience members who had also recently been forced to realize, more than ever, the value of a secure home and income, not to mention the value of a strong female presence.[29]

A celebration with music and dancing follows the blessing of the crops, reminding us of similar communal celebrations in Ford's *The Grapes of Wrath*, *My Darling Clementine*, and *Wagon Master*. Close-ups and long shots of people and cornstalks are alternated with images of a cloud-filled sky stretched above them as a visual manifestation of the deity to whom they pray. It is a scene that stresses the centrality of land and community in the overall narrative of the settling of the Old West. As the music of the thanksgiving celebration begins, Cole and Jane Ellen stroll beyond the outskirts of the cornfields. She points out a stretch of land below their hilltop perch and declares: "Look, Cole—the best piece of homestead land in all the country. It used to belong to one of the hired men that left us and now it's anybody's. You just claim it." She glances at him in a way that suggests she is drawing an intentional parallel between herself and the land, indicating that he can "claim" her if he would like to do so.

She asks whether he knows how to "build a home," and he does not disappoint her, moving to sit on a nearby log and then describing the design of his imaginary house. Predictably, they kiss passionately. But then, in the film's sudden turn from optimistic romance to destructive tragedy, Cole notices that the crops in the distance behind them are on fire. We see Bean's men dragging piles of burning brush along the perimeter of the cornfields as the homesteaders quickly notice the flames in the distance and scramble to respond. Harden now feels that he must eventually confront Bean in a showdown: any chance for rational negotiation has proven futile.

The crop-burning scene is a suspenseful fusion of rapid-fire crosscutting, masterful camera framing, and memorable visual effects—the latter involving the work of Archie Stout, who would demonstrate his own highly nuanced cinematography in Ford's *Fort Apache* (1948). In the background we see flames reach for the heavens as homesteaders in the foreground are interrupted from their celebration and turn to face the sudden horror. We witness Bean's men on horseback, trampling over Jane Ellen's father, who had just stepped before them with his arms raised in utter rage at the evil that is being enacted. We see Harden riding frantically and calling out after his beloved, but he pauses momentarily to watch as homesteaders run desperately for safety while buildings burn to the ground. There are echoes here of the fiery ending of William Hart's *Hell's Hinges* (see chapter 1). Peter Stanfield remarks on this scene when contrasting the movie's way of presenting the conflict between settlers and ranchers with that of George Stevens's later classic *Shane*: "*Shane,* in its highly affected self-reflexivity, doesn't give the same weight to the issue of farming and land that *The Westerner* does, instead displacing the audience's attention more firmly onto the hero. And the scenes of destruction wrought by the cattlemen on the land are nothing compared to the apocalyptic vision that Gregg Toland's camera creates."[30]

Harden knows that he must eventually kill Bean in order to obtain the settled life that he now desires. He is a man who realizes what it takes to live in a better world, one in which reliance on another person is necessary, and he is willing to use bullets rather than bluster only when words will no longer persuade. Anticipating Ford's *The Man Who Shot Liberty Valance,* released twenty-two years after *The Westerner,* Wyler's film gives us in Harden a unique precursor to Ransom Stoddard, the idealistic lawyer who seeks to overcome violence diplomatically but who eventually learns that justice must be backed with the threat of bullets (see chapter 8). Harden embodies the necessary transition, one spelled out so clearly in Ford's later film, between wilderness and garden.

CHAPTER 6

Howard Hawks and John Wayne

"Red River" and "El Dorado"

RED RIVER

Howard Hawks's greatest contribution to the art of the Western is *Red River,* which he produced and directed in a protracted period from 1946 through 1948. His three other major contributions to the genre are *The Big Sky* (1952), *Rio Bravo* (1959), and *El Dorado* (1967). Hawks had told stories about real heroes before, as in *Viva Villa!* (1934), *Sergeant York* (1941), *The Dawn Patrol* (1930), *Air Force* (1943), and *Only Angels Have Wings* (1939). But *Red River* was a major departure for Hawks as a storyteller of American culture. This time he focused on the expansion of the frontier, if not of the Western genre itself. In many ways it is his most ambitious film, certainly since *His Girl Friday* (1940). *Red River* was hugely successful at the box office, ranking number one when it was finally released in 1948 after many difficulties.

Hawks's first completed Western accompanied a number of visually and psychologically expressive Westerns released during the second half of the 1940s and in 1950: *My Darling Clementine* (Ford), *Canyon Passage* (Jacques Tourneur), and *Duel in the Sun* (King Vidor), all in 1946; *Ramrod* (André de Toth) and *Pursued* (Raoul Walsh) in 1947; *Fort Apache* and *3 Godfathers* (both Ford) and *Yellow Sky* (Wellman) in 1948; *She Wore a Yellow Ribbon* (Ford) and *I Shot Jesse James* (Sam Fuller) in 1949; and in 1950, *Broken Arrow* (Delmer Daves), *Rio Grande* and *Wagon Master* (both Ford), *The Gunfighter* (Henry King), and *The*

Furies and *Winchester '73* (both Anthony Mann). These were the kinds of Westerns that tend to yield more thoughtful reflection by the viewer because they posit a more complex morality in which the good bad men (or bad good men) do not achieve easy resolutions, and in which the narratives avoid the clichés of stock villains and fierce Indians. (See chapter 7 for further exploration of the post–World War II Western.)

Red River is Hawks's first complete sound Western after *Viva Villa!* (1934) and *The Outlaw* (1943), neither of which he finished. *Red River* begins and ends outdoors; there are but half a dozen interior scenes in the entire movie.[1] Most of *Red River* is set in and shaped by the vast open landscape of the trail. It is the story of Tom Dunson (John Wayne), Matthew Garth (Montgomery Clift), and their cattle drive from Texas to Kansas through tough terrain and inclement weather. As is usual in a Hawks film, where the director is as interested in the overall subject matter as in the interrelationships of the characters, much of the film is given over to depicting the process of the cattle drive. The script was adapted from the Borden Chase novel *The Chisholm Trail,* an epic story of a cattle empire's role in the expansion of the west. Chase's novel was serialized in the *Saturday Evening Post* in December 1946 and January 1947. Dunson's drive eventually takes the trail established in 1867 by Jesse Chisholm, which provided a shorter, more direct route north from Texas to the railroad that reaches as far west as Abilene, Kansas. The cowmen do not know this when the drive begins; they think they are going on a long trek to Missouri. But the choice of routes becomes the heart of the story and triggers the dramatic twist that takes the film along its darker, deeper narrative.

What makes *Red River* one of the most enduring of Westerns is the director's and his collaborators' achievement in balancing a story full of historical sweep. The narrative, replete with tensions between individualism and expansionism, concentrates all elements of the film within a broad, unending landscape. *Red River* does not actually follow the Chisholm Trail, nor was it even filmed in Texas and Kansas. Location shooting took place entirely in southern Arizona, not far from the Mexican border, on ranch land owned by C. H. Symington. The terrain, including the Whetstone Mountains and Apache Peak, offered a variety of landscapes, enabling the cast, crew, and fifteen hundred cows to work close to camp. The only set built was that of the streets of Abilene, while all the night and interior scenes were shot on Goldwyn Studio stages when the cast and crew returned to Hollywood.[2] Even the dialogue between Dunson and his first love, Fen (Coleen Gray), was shot at the studio against a rear-projection screen. Todd McCarthy, in his biography *Howard Hawks: The Grey Fox of Hollywood,* notes that the "entire film is marked by this technique [of combining studio-created and on-location shots], something numerous other pictures, such as *The Treasure of the Sierra Madre,* were guilty of during this transitional period from traditional studio work to vastly increased location shooting."[3] Chris Nyby was brought in as editor, fresh from cutting *Pursued* for Walsh, to give shape to the episodes and to shorten the total footage. Dimitri Tiomkin, who had scored Hawks's *Only Angels Have Wings,* again composed a lush score, this time incorporating themes of Western and cowboy songs.

Among the choices made by directors of Western films at this time was the decision to shoot in color or black and white. *Red River* was shot in black and white, and McCarthy reports that "Hawks debated at length whether or not to shoot in color, as Selznick had done with his giant Western *Duel in the Sun,* but he felt that color film at that time still looked 'garish' and was not as conducive to evoking a period look as black and white."[4] Hawks hired Russell Harlan as cinematographer; Harlan had shot black-and-white B-Westerns in the 1930s and 1940s, as well as *Ramrod* for André de Toth. He would later film *Rio Bravo* and *El Dorado,* both in color, for Hawks. Hawks may have preferred black and white to give consistency to the nighttime scenes—which start with a Comanche raid and include meals at camp around the chuck wagon—as well as to provide consistency with the indoor scenes, shot on a studio stage in contrast with the expansive scenes on the trail.

Once again the key chapters of a Western epic take place immediately after the Civil War. The Confederacy's defeat is acutely felt by Texans, and Dunson tells Garth, newly returned from the war, that the market for beef in the territory has collapsed. "The war took all the money out of the South," says Dunson's longtime companion Groot (Walter Brennan). So after building the biggest cattle ranch in Texas, Dunson is now broke, and that is why he must take his (and any neighbor's) cattle a thousand miles to Missouri. Garth, the boy Dunson found fourteen years earlier and raised as his son, has spent the past four years fighting on the Southern side, where he polished his skill with a gun.

In *Red River* we have not one but two classic westerners: a good man gone wrong in Dunson, and a young good-hearted southerner in Garth. Dunson and Garth are natural leaders, respected and, in Dunson's case, increasingly feared. Garth is perceived as "soft," with affectionate regard for Dunson and then Tess Millay (Joanne Dru); he must prove he has

FIGURE 25. A procession of covered wagons is dwarfed by the vast landscape in Howard Hawks's *Red River* (1948). Courtesy of the Museum of Modern Art.

guts when it becomes clear he cannot run from the fight. Dunson is the most complex character in *Red River* and is splendidly realized by Wayne. Here Wayne plays Dunson at two ages, a man of his own years (at the start of production Wayne was thirty-nine) and a gray-haired man of middle age, fourteen years later, full of aches and pains after long days in the saddle. Equally successfully in 1949, Wayne starred as an army officer old enough to retire in Ford's *She Wore a Yellow Ribbon*. Like other Hawksian heroes, including Cary Grant's Jeff Carter in *Only Angels Have Wings* (1939) and Humphrey Bogart's Steve Morgan in *To Have and Have Not* (1944), Dunson has a hard time expressing love, in this case for Garth. But we are never in doubt about this love, and this makes the film's climax somewhat puzzling, as we will see.

Stubborn and willful, Dunson loses his first great love, Fen, in the film's opening scene on the trail. Because he doubts that she is strong enough to ride with him and then to help build his ranch, he rejects her desperate plea to go with him, and she stays with the wagon train that is massacred by Comanche just hours later. She seems capable enough to us, as well as beautiful and passionate, which makes her loss the more deeply felt. "That's too bad," Groot says when he and Dunson see the far-off smoke of the burning wagons. That night they prepare for an attack by the same Comanche, whom they dispatch easily with knife and gun. Dunson finds on a brave's wrist his mother's bracelet, which he had given Fen in parting and which confirms her death; he in turn will give it to young Garth, who fourteen years later will put it on the arm of Tess Millay. Tess is strikingly similar to Fen in beauty and outspokenness.

The dialogue between Fen and Dunson at the outset establishes their characters in the straightforward but suggestive manner we expect from Hawks. Fen is tender and more sexually alive than Tess is in the latter's later exchanges with Garth. Dunson has just told the leader of the wagon train that he is going his own way, and he turns to embrace Fen, making his departure from her certain, despite her protests. *Red River* thus opens with the protagonist's mistake, the biggest of his life. Like Fen, Garth and Groot love Tom but must tell him when he is wrong.

Dunson is not a typical good bad man like Hart's Blaze Tracy (*Hell's Hinges*), Santschi's Bull Stanley (*3 Bad Men*), or Wayne's Ringo Kid (*Stagecoach*)—men on the other side of the law who are redeemed by their love for, and subsequent devotion to, women of strength and character (see chapters 1 and 4). By contrast, Dunson, in his determination to be a successful rancher at any cost whatsoever, becomes a tyrannical "bad" man. As Hawks once noted, Dunson's rejection of the woman who could have softened and civilized him "would make him all the more anxious to go through with his plans. Because a man who has made a great mistake to get somewhere is not going to stop at small things."[5] Dunson hates weakness, complaining to Garth later in the film: "You're soft, Matt." Yet Dunson raised Garth as his son. This is the contradiction of character essential to the Western, as the film narrative retains the men's love for one another despite Dunson's later fury. In the novel as well as the film, Dunson's affection for Garth dissolves into hatred and then into an attempt to kill the son who took away his cattle and his pride.

In his essay "Beyond the River: Women and the Role of the Feminine in Howard Hawks's *Red River*," John Parris Springer analyzes the characters of Dunson and Garth in terms of gender—specifically the masculine and feminine qualities that play a role in their respective personalities—and the underlying "homoerotic subtext" occasioned by the deep love that the two men share. Springer argues that, despite the strength and determination shown by the characters of Fen and Tess, Hawks focuses almost entirely on the men's "love story," especially in terms of each man's need to develop the psychological characteristics that are dominant in the other man. According to this interpretation, Dunson and Garth come to recognize through each other the traits that each lacks. As Springer tells us:

> The homoerotic subtext is quite strong in many of Hawks's films, which often deal openly with what Hawks himself called "a love story between two men." Here the devotion to profession and loyalty to an elite group of male comrades who practice a way of life defined by constant danger and the threat of death create a strong, often physical bond between the characters that can be seen either as a heroic, existential link between men or as macho posturing of the rankest sort. But in *Red River* Matt Garth functions as an alternative to Tom Dunson's stern masculine ethos, and he becomes the embodiment of "feminine" characteristics and values that are most apparent in his more compassionate and humane treatment of the men on the cattle drive.[6]

Garth comes into the story the morning after the Comanche attack. Dunson and Groot hear the mutterings of a young boy who is out of his senses from witnessing the horrors of the massacre. He stumbles along leading a cow until Dunson slaps the youngster to bring him about and takes his cow and gun. "But don't ever try to take it [the pistol] away from me again," the boys warns. Dunson turns to Groot: "He'll do." Later, after crossing the Red River into Texas, Dunson decides that he has found the land he has been seeking. With everything a man could want—plenty of good water and grass—he will establish the greatest ranching empire in all of Texas. He draws a brand in the soil: two lines like the banks of a river along with the letter D.

As they start to brand his bull *and* Garth's cow—"I'll put an M on it when you earn it," Dunson tells him—two Spanish riders come along, attracted by the smoke of the fire. The land is Don Diego's, they say, and reaches far south some four hundred miles, beyond the Rio Grande. Dunson declares that the land is his and orders them to tell Don Diego that all the land north of the Rio Grande belongs to Dunson, especially since Don Diego probably took it away from someone else. One of the riders is unwise enough to go for his gun and is shot dead by Dunson. "He went for his gun first," says Garth, as if to reassure himself as well as the viewer, but it is a questionable moment that never leaves us feeling quite comfortable about Dunson's later worries over being broke and stuck with too many cattle. Dunson tells the surviving rider to bury the dead Spaniard and he will "read over him" from the Bible. This happens each time Dunson kills somebody, until his employee Simms (Hank Worden) later points out to us the irony of this ritual, in case we might not get it: "Plantin' and readin', plantin' and readin'. Fill a man full o' lead, stick him in the ground, and then read words over him. Why, when you killed a man, why try to read the Lord in as a partner on the job?"

Red River's dialogue usually clues us in just before or just after a twist or turn so that we will not be left behind. Surprisingly for such a visually engaging, expressive landscape film, *Red River* relies on verbal explanation almost as a silent movie typically depends on intertitles. Two versions of the film were released: one with text, the other with voice-over narration. In the "book," or diary, version, the film cuts all too often to pages of a handwritten text that tell us what is going on every ten days or so on the drive, particularly noting the changes in Dunson's demeanor as he becomes a tyrant. We know he can kill easily, and he does, punishing without compunction anyone who stands in his way. And, guided by the text, we know he will go too far one day, the day of his undoing. No doubt the explanatory passages of the text were thought to be necessary to bind together the episodic wanderings of the story. Curiously, the early editing and postproduction of the two versions of *Red River* were completed with little input or supervision from the director. The earlier "book" version is longer than the other version, which has, instead of the text, a voice-over narration by Groot along with a briefer conclusion.[7]

In terms of dialogue, Hawks's characters frequently antagonize each other with humorous jabs to disguise their mutual attraction. The relief of these exchanges in *Red River* and Hawks's other adventure films differs importantly from the humor of his screwball and later comedies. From *Twentieth Century* (1934) through *Bringing Up Baby* (1938), *His Girl Friday*, and *I Was a Male War Bride* (1949), Hawks pits one sex against the other. The plots consist of attempts to humiliate and frustrate the objects of desire, to hilarious effect; the rapport and sexual gratification come with the clinch, at the end. *Only Angels Have Wings, To Have and Have Not,* and *Red River* are as much about affectionate relationships between male comrades as they are about romances between male and female protagonists. This is especially true of the three finest films of his later career, in the 1950s and 1960s, and all are Westerns: *The Big Sky, Rio Bravo,* and *El Dorado.* The camaraderie is there from the start or develops quickly, for it is a necessary point of departure for Hawks. The broad comedy in these films deepens and strengthens the depiction of courage and the stoic endurance of hardships. In the earlier struggles of *Red River,* such comedy serves to offset, in a compensatory way, the growing anger and fear, the enmity forming between the boss and his crew.

Red River has been called a Western version of *Mutiny on the Bounty,* in which the men of the former are bound to the desert and plains as much as sailors are confined on a ship, and their leader is as single-minded and ruthless as Captain Bligh. Mutiny is inevitable. But the comparison is not entirely apt: *Red River*'s concerns are not cruelty and punishment and isolation, but rather hard work and maturity and accomplishment. Dunson does not start the drive as a man removed, aloof, rigid—qualities that earned Bligh high marks by the Royal Navy—but rather as a man facing his last chance, desperate to survive. Dunson is ruthless, and we witness the manner in which he claims his land. But this is smoothed over as he brands his bull and Garth's cow to start the herd, telling the young Garth about his dream—an idealistic, quintessentially American dream, one that any corporate leader would admire: "Ten years and I'll have the 'Red River D' on more cattle than you've looked at anywhere. I'll have that brand on enough beef to feed the whole country—good beef, for hungry people, beef to make 'em strong, to make 'em grow. But it takes work, it takes sweat, it takes time, lots of time, it takes years."

As Dunson conveys his dream of establishing a cattle empire, we see a vision of the ranch and the vast herds. Then we cut to fourteen years later and a gray-haired Dunson explains to a grown-up Garth what happened while Garth was off fighting in the war. As Dunson organizes the drive, it is clear that he is a boss who is admired and respected by his men and his fellow ranchers. And although Dunson subsequently loses the respect of his men and becomes feared for punishing them excessively during the long drive, Garth never ceases to love him, and it is his love that enables them both to survive.

While the relationship between the two men is certainly the emotional axis of the movie, Dunson's obsessive desire to establish an empire gives the narrative its metapersonal backdrop and ties it to the expansionist ideal that is central to the story of America. As Springer observes, "From the very beginning of *Red River,* with its framing device of the expository titles and the manuscript called 'Early Tales of Texas,' Hawks announces a much larger historical and cultural frame for this film than is typical of his work. . . . Clearly, this is a theme with social and political implications."[8] And in his book *Cowboys as Cold Warriors: The Western and U.S. History,* Stanley Corkin argues that *Red River,* like Ford's *My Darling Clementine,* should be understood not merely in terms of the wider context of empire-building in the nineteenth-century Old West but also in terms of the parallel context of America's Cold War ideology—especially given that these Westerns were released right after the start of this period in U.S. foreign policy. Beginning right after the Allied victory in World War II, the anti-Communist agenda was anchored by a deep conviction in "American exceptionalism" and by a firm opposition to any possible threats to our democratic and capitalist system. One can indeed make the case that certain Cold-War-era Westerns express the prodemocratic ideals and procapitalist values that are central to the evolving view of America as a "shining city" or "city on a hill."[9] Corkin summarizes his interpretation:

> In *Red River* and *My Darling Clementine,* we view the economic outcomes that *should* emerge from the effective assertion and visceral acceptance of the core terms of national identity. In *Red River,* heroes emerge and perform their morally desirable actions, and, as a result, the cattle industry is born; in *My Darling Clementine,* Tombstone becomes a place where an entrepreneur need not fear the forces of chaos. . . . These economic goals are mystified by their association with character traits that resonate within the national mythos. At their most explicit level, both films are character driven and focus on the power of the (male) individual to bend conditions to his will by exercising the prerogatives of freedom; thus, we can boil down much of the ideological thrust of these presentations to the powerful terms 'freedom' and 'individualism,' which, not coincidentally, are the focal terms of [Frederick Jackson] Turner's essay ["The Significance of the Frontier in American History"].[10]

It is natural, at first glance, to think of *Red River* as a movie that expresses core principles of American ideology and idealism—not merely because of its themes of empire, frontier, and individual ambition, but also given the fact that this is a John Wayne film. As William Beard reminds us, Wayne's iconic screen persona has been associated with the ideas of American exceptionalism and individualism in the minds of many viewers over the course of his career, and most especially in his war and Western movies: "Wayne's power sustains the dominant ideology but is also derived from it."[11] And as Corkin further tells us, "In ways that are fairly typical of the genre, *My Darling Clementine* and *Red River* present the annexation of western lands as a matter of inevitability. Specifically, the question they present is *how* parts of Arizona and Texas will be integrated into the national fabric, not whether they will be or whether they should be."[12]

Yet despite Corkin's illuminating comparisons between nineteenth- and twentieth-century forms of American idealism and expansionism, there are certain limits that must be drawn here. This is especially the case with Hawks's film, in which Dunson's obsessive determination and excessive ruthlessness in his pursuit of empire-building brings about the near-collapse of his cattle drive team, a severed relationship with his own "son" (Garth), and his own subsequent exile from and revenge against those who had once served him so faithfully. One chief problem is that, while Dunson clearly embodies the ideals and values around which Corkin's analysis revolves, he is also a seriously flawed and narrow-minded figure, as the movie demonstrates. If anything, Dunson's unquestioning dedication to his mission makes him *less* democratic, in that he rarely listens to his men (even Garth and Groot are typically ignored). It is Garth who elicits the opinions of his fellow drovers and who relies on consensus in pushing the team ahead. Once Dunson, however, has garnered sworn oaths from his men, oaths to complete the cattle drive no matter what obstacles may lie ahead, he becomes purely autocratic.

If there is a lesson to be drawn from the film, it is that blind adherence to such a mission is personally destructive, and that humane values should never be forsaken—values that are expressed by Garth, not Dunson. At the end of the day, Dunson's individuality and the freedom that he needs to forge his empire are not shown to be intrinsically preferable to the collective interests of his men. *Red River* is not so much the expression of a prodemocratic, procapitalist ideology as it is a warning signal about the dangers involved for those who do not recognize the limits of such an ideology. The movie emphasizes the consequences of an idealistic ambition that forsakes its roots in a common humanity.

Patrick McGee, in his book *From* Shane *to* Kill Bill: *Re-thinking the Western*, critiques Corkin's interpretation for precisely these reasons. According to McGee, *Red River* demonstrates the contradictions that can emerge when democracy and capitalism do not easily blend—and this is shown especially in terms of the conflict between Dunson and Garth. The film is not simply a cinematic embodiment of American ideals, as Corkin might have us believe, but is rather a dramatized lesson about the possible consequences when our adherence to these ideals are pushed to the extreme. In fact, when relating the film to the anti-Communist efforts taking place in Hollywood around the time of its release—efforts involving the Motion Picture Alliance for the Preservation of American Ideals, of which John Wayne served as president, succeeding Ward Bond—McGee suggests that *Red River*, the movie that "almost single-handedly invented the myth of John Wayne," also put into question the kind of oppressive ideology and patriarchal authoritarianism that Wayne willingly represented in his political life around that time.[13] The film does so, not merely by pointing to Dunson's increasing tyranny over his men, but by showing that Dunson has very little regard for private property (as when he takes Don Diego's land and seizes others' cattle by force) and that he has grown his cattle herd beyond the demands of his local market, thus producing an "economic crisis" for himself.[14]

As McGee states in regard to the problems and limits of Corkin's interpretation, particularly when one looks beyond Dunson's determined empire-building: "Corkin argues that the conflict between Dunson and Garth is ultimately nothing more than a clash over 'management theory.' . . . Though this thesis has a good deal of merit . . . there is a tendency toward reduction in Corkin's reading of these Westerns [like *Red River*] that ignores or downplays those elements that point toward contradiction rather than the pure expression of nationalist ideology."[15]

To take but one example of the tension that grows along the drive, there is the stunning scene of the cattle stampede. On a night when the cattle are especially restless, a cowhand (Buck Kenneally) tries to steal sugar from the chuck wagon and knocks over pots and pans, triggering a stampede. There follows an exciting sequence, terrifying in the sweep and swiftness of the panicked herd. We see the faces of the cowboys, just as we did at the start of the drive, as they grab their saddles and race to do their jobs. This sequence was the work of the assistant director, Arthur Rosson, who supervised most of the film's action sequences with the herds.[16] The stampede takes place at night, with a stream of cattle flowing through the camp, across the grassland, up and over a rise, and down into a draw, all below a cloud-streaked sky. At times the camera is set low, at the level of the stampeding cattle or even in a hole in the ground to catch the steers running overhead. Medium shots bring us close to the riders and the herd. The stampede follows its course, in tracking shots that keep pace with the movement of the herd. Then the camera is placed on a rise, front and center, to film the steers racing below and up toward us, passing by to the right. We are never far from the stampede: we see it up close, almost as close as the cowboy stunt men, and we feel intimately involved with it. The sequence is marred only by the artificial-looking process shots showing the stampede in rear projection behind Garth and Dunson.

The young and sympathetic Dan Latimer (Harry Carey Jr.) is killed during the stampede. "We'll bury him, and I'll read over him in the morning," Dunson declares, instructing Garth to pay Latimer's widow his wages for the entire drive. Again we hear the familiar words from the Bible, delivered always beside a grave set back on a rise or slope, at a respectful distance from us. Dunson then grabs a whip to punish the sugar-stealing cowboy, and Garth quickly intervenes. By now we know that whenever Garth tries to treat the men decently, he must confront Dunson. Dunson soon goes for his pistol but Garth outdraws him, wounding the cowhand so as to keep him from being killed outright, and says to Dunson: "You would have shot him right between the eyes." "Just as sure as you're standing there," Dunson confirms, and then barks to Groot: "Go ahead, say it." Groot replies firmly and predictably: "You was wrong, Mr. Dunson."

As Groot, Walter Brennan joined Hawks's cast for the fourth time, following *Barbary Coast* (1935), *Sergeant York* (1941), and *To Have and Have Not* (1944). A veteran of Westerns, he had acted in dozens of oaters before receiving an Academy Award as Best Supporting Actor for his interpretation of Judge Roy Bean in Wyler's *The Westerner* (see chapter 5), and he was notable as Pa Clanton in Ford's *My Darling Clementine* (see chapter 7). Brennan's first Western for Hawks was *Red River;* his second and last would be *Rio Bravo* in 1959. His performance as the physically impaired and loyal but critical older friend of Dunson is key to the Hawksian comic tone. In *Red River* he sets this tone in the opening scene when he explains why he is quitting the wagon train to accompany his friend: "Me and Dunson—well, it's me and Dunson." No other explanation is necessary. Groot loses his "store-bought teeth" to Quo (Chief Yowlatchie) in a poker game the night before the start of the drive; his Cherokee friend, having won a half-interest in them, decides to give Groot his teeth only at mealtimes. The joke is carried throughout the film; Groot's mumbling caused by his lack of teeth irritates Dunson, who makes him repeat, slowly and defiantly, his opinions and criticisms. Groot talks to himself about the problem of keeping dust out of his toothless mouth: "Bet I et ten pounds in the last sixteen days. 'Fore this shenanigan's over I'll probably et enough land to incorporate me into the union, the state of Groot."

The Texas landscape is unforgiving: it goes on and on, and the drive lasts month after month, before the men and cattle reach the Red River, the northern border of Texas that Dunson and Garth crossed fourteen years earlier. The trail is dry and full of dust, or the rain is hard, and the men are exhausted. A cowboy rides into camp, having barely survived a Missouri border raid. He reports that his outfit should have turned north at the Big Red because an Indian trader, Jess Chisholm, told him that he blazed a trail clear to Kansas. He even reports that there was a railroad there, at Abilene. He has not seen it himself, though, and Dunson will not risk diverting to a possibly shorter trail on hearsay alone.

FIGURE 26. Cattle drive meets "iron horse" in *Red River*. Courtesy of the Museum of Modern Art.

Three cowhands then tell Dunson that they have had enough, and they are soon dead. They were quitters: "not good enough," says Dunson, who will tolerate no more disobedience or opposition. He reminds the other men that, since they signed on, they have to finish the drive. But he is jumpy, and the men see it.

Dunson is now alone, and as the men turn from him, there is a subtle shift: we become slightly and problematically sympathetic for the hardships he has endured. Although we are supposed to feel the men's fear of Dunson, it is not easy to dismiss their nervous and vulnerable leader without empathy. That night, three more cowboys rebel and leave the drive. Dunson sends Cherry Valance (John Ireland) to bring them back and the mood shifts again, with the herd moving slowly along toward us and away from low hills. Under a magnificent Western sky and to the rhythm of the Tiomkin score, the Red River is reached at last. As the cows sweep down to the river, the theme of the cowboy song "My Rifle, My Pony, and Me" mixes with the principal music theme (and will be sung to great effect by Dean Martin and Ricky Nelson in Hawks's later *Rio Bravo*). During a pause at the riverbank, Garth and Dunson share their last peaceful moment together; he says that the crossing will keep the men worn out (and therefore less likely to rebel against him) until Cherry gets back. The movement of the herd through the river is depicted with Hawksian calmness, the narrative drama pausing to let us watch and enjoy at a leisurely pace, providing the feeling of a lengthy and mighty task. Like the stampede, the men ably handle the crossing under Dunson's increasingly oppressive leadership; they still obey their trail boss.

It becomes clear, however, that Dunson intends to kill the men who ran away, and when Cherry brings back two of the three men, the most horrifying of Dunson's brutal moves is declared: he will not shoot but rather hang the deserters. For Garth, this is the limit; he cannot accept Dunson's judgment or carry out the punishment. He is the true rebel: he takes over the drive from Dunson, and he does it without firing a shot. Instead, Cherry shoots Dunson in the hand. This is the point of passage in the film: the emergence of Garth into manhood. The "son" has humiliated the "father" in front of the others, and so quickly is it done that Hawks must provide a moment to reflect on the loss of camaraderie and the severing of every bond. There is no turning back. Dunson stands by his horse, about to be left behind, and his fury is coldly put: "Every time you turn around, expect to see me, 'cause one time you'll turn around I'll be there. I'll kill you, Matt."

This declaration by the trail boss who has become too brutal, too exhausted by his efforts, is calmly delivered by Wayne, surprisingly subtle in his ferocity. And it scares the hell out of Garth, quietly registered in Clift's expressive eyes and slight grimace. Dunson watches as his cattle and men leave, the sequence ending with a shot of the landscape. To the right is Dunson, his back to us, unable to stand erect, a wounded man left alone. It is an exceptionally beautiful moment and we hold on to it, for it is in this pause that we sense everything that this westerner has lost. Dunson is a man defeated, and his stance, his sagging physicality, conveys his tragedy, his second great loss after Fen. This time it is his friend (Groot), "son" (Garth), and cattle: all he possesses.

A big sunny sky sits over the cowboys and cattle for much of the rest of the drive. Flat-bottomed clouds familiar to the Western mountains and southwestern desert fill the screen above a low horizon. The cinematography of the landscape of the Red River and the country to the north, while actually the same Arizona terrain throughout the film, seems deeper and more tranquil as they approach Kansas. Garth can now make his own decisions, capably taking charge as his "father" has failed. He commits the drive to the shorter route to Abilene although he has no proof that the railroad has reached that far west; it is still only hearsay. But for the sake of his men, Garth is willing to take the risk, unlike Dunson. Along the way, the men dash into an Indian raid to save a wagon train (and there are a few dreadful moments, cinematically speaking, when we see the cowboys up close, riding their mechanical studio horses). Garth meets Tess Millay, who is hit by an arrow, and by the time Garth has pulled out the shaft and has sucked the poison from her shoulder, she seems to be in love with him. That foggy night she learns the story of Garth and Dunson from Cherry and Groot. When she finds Garth and snuggles with him for a spell, she tells him that she knows he loves Dunson.

A week later, Garth having now departed, Millay meets Dunson, gives him dinner and a couple of drinks, and asks about the woman *he* left behind. Dru is not a bad match for Wayne. She is given the mannerisms Hawks likes his women to use: a kind of loose sexiness in the movement of their arms, their hands clasping the tiny waists of their period costumes, their posture daring the men to try something. Lauren Bacall in *To Have and Have Not,* Angie Dickinson in *Rio Bravo,* and Charlene Holt in *El Dorado* are similarly provocative. Tess gets right to the point, startling Dunson in his remembrance of Fen as she talks of wanting Garth so much. Dunson has seen the bracelet on her wrist, the one he gave Fen fourteen years earlier. He lost the only woman he ever wanted, and all he desires now is a son. "I thought I had a son," he complains. Then he offers her half of all he has if she will bear him a son, especially in looking ahead to the future of his planned empire, and also undoubtedly out of spite. She tells him she will do so, most likely as a ruse, if he promises to stop now, turn around, and go back. She begs him to take her along to Abilene. "Nothing you can say or do . . . ," he begins—but then he consents, no doubt remembering Fen, the woman he once left behind in a similar situation.

Gradually, during this last phase of the drive, we become less convinced of Dunson's threat, even as Garth and his men jump at every noise and calculate how many days it will be before Dunson catches up with them. The threat seems contrived if we listen carefully to the intimacy of the conversation between Millay and Dunson, and we cannot believe that either Clift, in his first starring role, or Wayne, forceful as ever, will die at the end of this tale. In fact, according to McCarthy's biography of Hawks, the climax had not been decided when production began. In Chase's novel, Dunson is wounded by Cherry Valance, whom he then kills, and Dunson is too weak to hold his aim on Garth. Chase concludes his novel with an epilogue in which Garth and Millay take Dunson home in a wagon, and when they cross the Red River he dies on Texan soil. Charles Schnee was brought in to revise Chase's narrative, and he made important changes and improvements, such as the introduction of Fen. It was Hawks, however, who no longer wanted to kill off sympathetic characters, as he did to Thomas Mitchell's Kid Dabb in *Only Angels Have Wings*.[17]

It would also seem odd, by Hollywood standards of the time, to allow a hero such as Garth to fall in love at this stage in the film and kill him off a few scenes later. The introduction of the romantic interest serves another purpose: it clues us into a change in mood and temper, a shifting away from violence and tragedy and an emergence of the Western's traditional view of the woman as an agent of civilization. Whether for a bad man trying to reform, like a Hart character, or a good man gone bad, like Dunson, it is never too late for a westerner to listen to a wise woman. Tess is not a new type of Hawksian heroine, but she sets the character mold (for *Rio Bravo* and *El Dorado*) of the card sharp who is very much a caring woman: strong-willed, talkative, and ready to fall in love at first sight. Like Bonnie Lee (Jean Arthur) in *Only Angels Have Wings* and Slim (Lauren Bacall) in *To Have and Have Not,* Tess does not hesitate to speak her mind and she is a forceful participant. The Hawksian woman is intelligent enough to figure out the man she loves pretty quickly and to tell him so in her own determined, sexy way. A critic of the stubbornness and wrongheadedness of the principal male character, she centers the film morally and acts as a civilizing influence. In early Westerns the female character tended to be a schoolmarm (even as recently as Ford's *My Darling Clementine*), and, in becoming a gambler, as Tess is, she has come a long way. In Chase's original story and in the script, Tess and her wagon train companions were prostitutes. The change from prostitute to gambler imposed by Joseph Breen's Production Code Office (along with numerous other script changes) seems absurd in the mid-1940s, since Claire Trevor was clearly a woman of the night in *Stagecoach* and Marlene Dietrich was a brash saloon singer in *Destry Rides Again* (both 1939).[18]

The drive, the first to take the Chisholm Trail, arrives in Abilene on August 14, 1865, and Garth quickly sells the herd to Melville (Harry Carey Sr. in one of his final performances), who represents the Greenwood Trading Company of Illinois. And so we come to the end of the four principal sequences depicting the movement of the cattle, scenes that mark the film's rhythm like the opening and closing of acts in a play. First, the launch of the cattle drive is joyous, sweeping us along in the excitement and anticipation of the cowboys. The stampede is the second sequence that calls on the cowboys' professional expertise; their skill, daring, and swift action, no matter how weary they are, prove the effectiveness of Dunson's leadership. The drive of the herd across the Red River is the next meaningful passage, not only marking the physical departure from Texas and Dunson's lands, but also psychologically reinforcing his relentlessness. Though men and cattle have passed into new territory, the trip is far from over. The final extended phase of the cattle drive, as the steers move slowly into Abilene, is relaxed and leisurely, the music track revving up the now familiar theme of this huge effort, accompanying the men on their last ride of the long trail and bringing the drive itself to its successful conclusion. The sequence would be a coda to the main theme, were it not for the cowboys' worry about Dunson showing up.

Typical of many Westerns, *Red River*'s final scene takes place in the sunshine, on the main street of Abilene. But the crowding of the cattle onto the stage gives it a comic edge. The steers are carefully left in the streets the night before, since there are no pens large enough to hold even half as many. So there is an unusual moment of densely occupied landscape to enhance the effect of the ending. They are a tired bunch of steers after their long trek, and they are not about to be agitated by Dunson or a gunfight. The happy conclusion of the drive is undercut by the anticipated fight with Dunson, who is on his way with men and ammunition. Although Dunson reaches Abilene on the same night that Garth signs the contract, just a few hours after the cattle are brought into the town, the denouement is instead set in the early morning of the following day. Dunson bursts forth in an extraordinary, purely Hawksian lead-in to the final scene: he rides into the herd, dismounts fast, and shoves the cattle aside as he strides purposely toward Matt. Nothing can stop him now. It may be the most thrilling sequence of strutting in the cinema: Wayne at his most physically imposing and the music enhancing the tension.

Wearing his black hat, Dunson makes his pigeon-toed strut through the herd and across the railroad track and starts shooting around and past Garth, who will not fire back. The crosscutting between increasing close-ups of their faces builds to a crescendo as Dunson strikes Garth with his fist. "You're soft," he tells Garth. "Won't anything make a man out of you?" As the long-awaited fight begins, we look patiently for Garth to respond, which he soon does satisfactorily, despite being much smaller than Dunson. Dunson is knocked down by Garth's punch, to his surprise, and Groot gleefully tells Millay, "It's all right. For fourteen years I've been skeered, but it's gonna be all right." And we know it, too. Then, after shooting a couple of bullets past Dunson and Garth, Tess keeps their attention with an angry speech about how killing each other is the last thing they would do; anyone would know the two love each other, she proclaims. Once again Hawks has a character explain more than is necessary. Millay nonetheless makes emphatic a happy ending: by surprising them, she provokes Dunson to say, "You'd better marry that girl, Matt." Dunson soon draws the design of a cattle brand that will symbolize their new partnership. "You've earned it," he adds affectionately.

Sudden moral transformations are typical of the genre, dating back to Griffith's Biograph oaters (see chapter 1), and we may accept Dunson as a psychotic tyrant temporarily gone mad, eager to kill his men. Yet there are a few clues to his essential humanity. He is a man who has forged his way through the frontier and forced the landscape to bend to his will. When the land fought back, through drought and obstacles all along the drive, it cost him his strength and his sanity, not unlike what happened to Letty Mason in *The Wind*. But Dunson never quits, for Hawks created this Western as an illustration of movement forward, as the broken journey that must be completed.

Dunson's concluding shift in mood—his lightning-quick switch from ferocious avenger to affectionate father figure—is indeed jarring and does not seem to fit well with the foregoing. Tess's sudden act of mediating between the two "enemies" is supposed to help transition the viewer, even if overly quickly, from tragic to comic mode. As Springer observes about the peculiar emotional dynamic involved in the odd conclusion of the film: "It should be observed at this point that Millay's intervention in the conflict between Dunson and Matt and the comedic resolution that makes it possible (the film's ending in the promise of marriage) are clearly inappropriate in terms of the conventions of the Western genre, according to which one of the two men should be killed. Nor is this ending in any way commensurate with the depth of the conflict established between the two characters over the course of the film."[19]

In looking back at the film, Hawks admitted that the ending was "rather corny": "If we overdid it a little bit or went too far, well . . . I didn't know any other way to end it."[20] But Hawks, who with *Red River* had become thoroughly engaged in the Western genre, was not so much interested in a happy ending as he was in broadening and deepening his own humanistic approach, merging comedy and drama in new and more profound ways. The problems of the lengthy production, Hawks's first and last independent production, make it difficult to discern this shift, for many collaborators were involved here in script development, deletions and changes were imposed by the censorship office, the initial running time (which was considered too long, and the film required extensive editing) needed to be reduced, and the issue of two versions (the book and the voice-over narrative) had to be resolved. Hawks's efforts to mold the genre to his style and intent are nonetheless consistent within the body of his work.

Prior to *Red River, Air Force* and *To Have and Have Not* show the beginnings of a new direction for Hawks's films of action and adventure after the taut brilliance of *Only Angels Have Wings*. Until the end of his career he continued as a master of comedies, directing *I Was a Male War Bride* two years after *Red River.* But his great Westerns of the next two decades—*The Big Sky, Rio Bravo,* and *El Dorado*—are very much of a piece with various notions surfacing in *Red River.* (*Rio Lobo* of 1970, his last Western, is something of a disappointment when compared with these other films.) In these Westerns, as in *Red River,* the portraits of stubborn, strong men and women who are hard on each other because they love each other are enriched by acerbic, sympathetic commentary from friends and sidekicks. The secondary leads are, like Garth, pushed to *their* limits so that they will become the men the westerner wants them to be. Rich humor infuses the three later films, more so than in *Red River,* and the comedy is expressed directly and unsubtly. These later Westerns become not satires but comedies of the human spirit in which men have to make choices and often fail.

Hawks eases up on the killings and moves away from the slaughters that will mark a number of other Western films from the 1950s forward. No comic-book adventure stories for this director: his Westerns are character studies and we never tire of them. A good part of their appeal comes from observation and commentary by both sexes, whose rapport and affectionate jibes are more engaging than the plots. And in both *Rio Bravo* and *El Dorado,* Wayne plays a unique double role: sometimes the activist or gunfighter-turned-lawman who leads the group and makes most of the decisions, and at other times, the passive observer who looks over his friends with affection, amusement, and concern. In the latter role, Wayne enjoys some of his most laid back and contented moments on the screen.

EL DORADO

Inseparable from *Rio Bravo* and directed by Hawks a decade later, *El Dorado* is generally regarded as the weaker of the two films, derivative, and possessing less of the warmth and camaraderie that is found among *Rio Bravo*'s brilliantly eccentric cast: Dean Martin, Ricky Nelson, Angie Dickinson, John Wayne, and Walter Brennan. *El Dorado* seems cooler, more detached, more amusing. The characters suffer and endure their hardship in calm, rueful awareness. Wayne as Cole Thorton and Robert Mitchum as J. P. Harrah fill their roles as middle-aged, drunken westerners, one a gunfighter and the other a lawman. They are smoothly comic, building our sympathy and our laughter by twisting their big frames into knots of hangovers and stomach pains, their thick bodies and rugged faces expressing their irritation at the fixes into which they get themselves.

James Caan is a self-assured sidekick, like Mitchum. He is conscious of the ways he can move and shift his large lean body in relation to the physical presence and force of Wayne's gunfighter, on or off his horse. Cheeky, as was Ricky Nelson, Caan plays Alan Bourdillion "Mississippi" Traherne to provide counterpoint and give rhythm to the careful maneuvers he carries out with Thornton. Together, they are the outsiders who come to El Dorado to back up the other male couple, Harrah and Bull (Arthur Hunnicutt), the town's lawmen who are urgently in need of help in defeating landowner Bart Jason (Ed Asner) and his hired gun, Nelse McCleod (Christopher George), in their fight against the MacDonald clan. In the Martin-Wayne pairing in *Rio Bravo*, Wayne's character chastises and prods Martin's "Dude," the lesser man, toward regeneration. But Dude remains weak and humble when not self-loathing. In *El Dorado*, Harrah and Thornton are equals, both first-rate with a gun, and old friends from the Civil War years. They do not hesitate to exchange insults as only those men do who have affection and respect for each other.

In an atmosphere remarkably relaxed, given the seriousness of the hostilities (for this is a typical Western struggle for control of water rights), the narrative makes two points clear. The first is that Thornton is the observer, the much larger-than-life hero who can stand to the side and take real pleasure in watching and listening to others. While Thornton gives good advice and strong criticism at times, and goes into action if necessary, Wayne plays the lead character as if it were a supporting role. It is a unique kind of performance for so strong a screen actor; it is his gift to the motion picture. Wayne has brought to perfection here his long-running characterization of the relaxed and friendly (but ruthless when necessary) gunfighter. Harry Carey Sr., as Cheyenne Harry in some twenty-five early Ford silent Westerns, had sharpened a screen persona that helped to shape that of the young Wayne, and it is Carey's on-screen naturalism and openness to others that are also Wayne's hallmarks as an actor.[21] And while he is forceful and dominant in many of his best remembered leading roles, Wayne played substantial supporting roles in films such as Ford's *They Were Expendable* (1945) and *Fort Apache* (1948). He could easily play characters who listened closely to others and gave them his support, even if reluctantly.

A second major point conveyed in *El Dorado* is that friendship and mutual support in the Old West are governed by certain unspoken rules. Harrah is the sheriff of El Dorado, and his position must be respected, even when he becomes a drunk. It is Harrah who makes the decisions, who controls or tries to control the actions of villains and victims. Thornton consistently turns to Harrah and asks him what he plans to do, though there is a low point when Harrah is too hungover to get his gun in his holster and Thornton leaves him behind. Harrah, however, catches up and behaves like a sheriff, even though a sick one. These two aging gunfighters, one a sheriff and one for hire, were once equally fast on the draw. They become equal again, as Thornton is weakened by a bullet lodged near his spine, the result of being shot by Joey MacDonald (Michele Carey) as an act of revenge against Thornton for having fatally wounded her brother. Increasingly, the bullet pressing on his spine causes sharp pain in Thornton's back, followed by moments of paralysis that make him vulnerable at key moments of the plot. He and Harrah are well matched: middle-aged, hurt, no longer invincible, needing their sidekicks and each other. By the end of the film, their friendship has survived and ripened. The final scene follows Thornton and Harrah on their evening patrol of El Dorado, each leaning on his crutch, with Harrah telling Thornton sarcastically: "We just don't need your kind around here."

Despite the gunfire, *El Dorado* is partly a comedy about the difficulties of staying at the top of one's profession. Hawks rejected Leigh Brackett's initial script, a drama of guilt, justice, and sacrifice adapted from the novel *The Stars in Their Courses* by Harry Brown. Hawks had asked Brackett, to her dismay, to revise the original screenplay so as to create a character study of another kind: the aging gunfighter who can no longer go it alone.[22] The movie's plot and its personalities are freely borrowed from Hawks's earlier *Rio Bravo* and *The Big Sleep* (1946).[23] As we are never in doubt about the fate of the leading characters, Hawks indulges his comedic predilection to humiliate the heroes throughout the narrative, to challenge their wit and intelligence and humanity so that we can then watch them survive, if not triumph. We are reminded loosely of the series of comic humiliations that are experienced by different characters in McCarey's *Ruggles of Red Gap* (see chapter 3).

Wayne is not really funny except when he is the commentator and can punch out his one-liners. In *El Dorado* he addresses a hired gun as "Hey, fancy vest!" or complains, "They're no gud," just as he repeatedly and amusingly exclaims, "That'll be the day," in Ford's *The Searchers*. In *Rio Bravo* and *El Dorado,* Wayne is humbled not by his costars' characters but by the families fighting for control. Not even Angie Dickinson's love interest can really bring him down to size in *Rio Bravo,* and it frustrates her to tears. *Red River* is an exception, in which Garth humiliates Dunson almost beyond recovery. But *Red River* is hardly comedic, at least not until its last scene and except for a few moments of levity resulting from Walter Brennan's usual way of turning on his folksy wit, noted earlier in this chapter. Like Ford's later *The Searchers* and *The Man Who Shot Liberty Valance, Red River* brings out, indeed introduces, the ornery side of Wayne's screen persona: his stubborn wrongheadedness, his bitterness over the loss of love and youth, his thirst for revenge. Nearly twenty years later Hawks wanted, for *El Dorado,* more readily likable characters to enact his human comedy of repeated failures and occasional successes amid attempts at survival, self-recognition, and friendship.

If *Red River* and Hawks's later *The Big Sky* are landscape Westerns, frontier epics set in wide-open spaces, *Rio Bravo* and *El Dorado* are most meaningful at night. They are films shot predominantly on a studio set, emphasizing an intimacy, an easy humor, and a playful give and take, all within Hawks's straightforward mise-en-scène. *El Dorado* takes place in and around the town of the same name, deep in the Southwest and not far from the Sonora border: ranch country where water is gold. The film opens in the washroom of the Saloon and Lodging, where Thornton and Harrah meet again after their last adventures during the Civil War. Their friendship and mutual goodwill immediately transcend a misunderstanding, and Thornton agrees to turn down the job offered by Bart Jason, who seeks the MacDonalds' water rights. Standing with rifle in hand, pointed at Thornton, and with one foot on

FIGURE 27. Cole Thornton (John Wayne) and Maudie (Charlene Holt) observe with amusement the bathing Sheriff J.P. Harrah (Robert Mitchum) in Hawks's *El Dorado* (1966). Courtesy of the Museum of Modern Art.

the bathtub, Harrah explains the way it is. Mitchum's posture and sleepily deep-voiced delivery set the comic tone that will dominate the film. Maudie (Charlene Holt) barges in and bursts out laughing at seeing her two former lovers at once; she and Harrah affectionately share their views of their loyal and supportive friend Cole.

The plot is given shape by Thornton's visits to two ranches: first to that of Jason, where he tells the rancher he will not be working for him after all, and then to the MacDonalds' spread, where he brings the body of the boy Luke (Johnny Crawford) whose death he accidentally caused along the way. Thornton is in control as he returns the pouch of his wages to Jason, yet wary when he leaves, making his horse step backward along the low buildings so he can keep an eye on Jason's men. At the MacDonalds' family compound, Thornton relates in simple spare sentences the shooting and subsequent suicide of Luke. In a few wrenching moments, Thornton speaks almost breathlessly. However difficult it may be for him, he handles the father's questions with grace and the sister's anger with terse dignity. It is a quiet, serious, beautifully realized scene, with Wayne once again revealing his heroic and stoic stature.

The latter scene had been in both the novel and initial screenplay, but the film narrative subsequently goes in another direction. Thornton's first visit to El Dorado ends with the death of Luke MacDonald and a send-off by friends, with a bit of bugling by his old army buddy Bull, for he decides to drift down Sonora way in search of another job. Wisely, his former gal knows he cannot stay in El Dorado until he can forget what happened to Luke. Some months later, his wanderings are cut short when he arrives at night in a town filled with cantinas. Here he learns that Harrah has become a drunk and Nelse McLeod has been hired as Jason's gunfighter.

Sitting quietly by is the young "Mississippi": he has come to kill one of McLeod's men who is responsible for the death of Johnny Diamond, the man who had raised him. Mississippi encounters Thornton and the narrative segues into a leisurely ride, during which the experienced man and the maturing youth become partners. They ride through a desert of cholla and saguaro cactus, indicative of Arizona-Mexico territory. The setting may be Texas, but Old Tucson provided most of the filming locations.[24] The ride reveals to Mississippi Thornton's disability, and the younger man is in turn shown to be inept with a gun. A friendship has begun, and the narrative reverts to the comic mode. As their horses trot through the desert in bright sun, Thornton attempts to educate Mississippi about the etiquette of gunplay, then listens to the younger man's recital of the first and last verses of Edgar Allan Poe's poem *Eldorado*, written in 1849 at the height of gold fever:

> Gaily bedight,
> A gallant knight,
> In sunshine and in shadow,
> Had journeyed long,
> Singing a song,
> In search of Eldorado . . .
> Over the Mountains
> Of the Moon,
> Down the Valley of the Shadow,
> "Ride, boldly ride,"
> The shade replied,
> "If you seek for Eldorado!"

The young knight is warned by his more experienced pilgrim shadow that the dreams of the soul are not to be found easily. Thornton's immediate response—"Ride, boldly ride? Well, it don't work out that way"— expresses not only his wise acceptance and understanding of the knight's, or gunfighter's, spurious quest, but it also startles us into grasping the theme of the film. It does not work out that way, at least not in one's lifetime in the Old West. Nothing goes quite as planned, certainly not for J.P. Harrah, Jason, or the MacDonalds, nor for Nelse McLeod, perhaps the most gallant knight of all because of his noble adherence to a code of honor, even among killers.

Beginning with the scene of the midnight arrival of Thornton and Mississippi in El Dorado, the film mixes location shooting and studio production to create the narrow streetscape running from jail to saloon. This setting dominates the rest of the story, serving to enhance the immediate dangers and absurdities of the plot. Like other Western communities, El Dorado is a tightly enclosed town: a locus of hostility, action, and romance, with its own hybrid culture of ranchers, Mexicans, gamblers, and troublemakers. Its small world is a cosmos unto itself, though you will not find it on a map. One reaches the town by riding over and around various sizable rocks, crossing a stream (the MacDonalds' water source) and riding by flat ranch land. El Dorado is both somewhere and nowhere. It is a town out of a dream, slyly constructed in the last fully realized film by the master storyteller Hawks, who himself was growing older (he was seventy at the time).

Except for the death of the youngest MacDonald, the subsequent shootings and killings have a darkly comic edge. Hawks injects surprise and eccentricity into the mix of his law-enforcing quartet's efforts to exterminate Jason and his hired killers. Bull's bugle, a holdover from his Civil War days, marks his individuality, as does his bow and arrow. So too do Mississippi's prowess with a knife and incompetence with a gun. Bull is an old pro whose talents are never in doubt, unlike those of Mississippi, who will never make it as lawman or gunfighter. Their talents must be seen and enjoyed close up, on the set and at night. The dangerous activity in town takes place after dark, when the streets are full of traps and the saloon is lit up with bad guys and tinny music. To enhance the after-dark ambiance, cinematographer Harold Rosson studied, at Hawks's request, Frederic Remington's paintings of nighttime saloons, where light escapes through doors and windows and spills onto the otherwise darkened street.[25] A yellow light infuses the town, with the ac-

FIGURE 28. Cole Thornton (*right*) prepares to deliver a sobering blow to his old friend Sheriff J.P. Harrah in a comic scene. Courtesy of the Museum of Modern Art.

tors highlighted by a bright white light so as to stand out against the buildings.

The threat of McLeod and his quick gun hand moves the story along, and the film reverts to the theme of the gallant knight. At the first encounter between McLeod and Thornton in the cantina, McLeod shows his respect for a colleague: "Call it professional courtesy." When McLeod kidnaps Thornton to exchange him for Jason, he emphasizes his regret

EL-58-4

FIGURE 29. Pardners again: old buddies Cole Thornton and Sheriff J.P. Harrah.
Courtesy of the Museum of Modern Art.

for Thornton's disability and offers his apology, saying that it is not his fault, for he would never do anything to hurt a fellow gunfighter except kill him in a draw. In contrast, during the final shoot-out, Thornton resorts to a trick, hiding his shotgun and then shooting McLeod, who is not prepared for it. Thornton thus reveals his occasional willingness to violate the gunfighter's code of honor, demonstrating his strength of will to survive to a potentially peaceful old age. McLeod was the professional knight who wanted to live and die by the code, and Thornton cheated him. Thornton had neither the wish nor the need to prove who was fastest.

Such is the stuff of drama, and *El Dorado* is above all a rueful, amused depiction of self-knowledge. "I'm paid to risk my neck, and I'll decide where and when I'll do it," Thornton tells Jason earlier in the film. And he does just that, turning down Jason at the start of the story because, he says, he does not want to go up against his old friend Harrah. Later, accepting the greater risk of going against McLeod out of friendship with

Harrah, Thornton makes no unnecessary plays, instead figuring out a way to kill McLeod most unfairly.

McLeod certainly falls into the camp of "good bad men" who challenge us to distinguish the good from the bad in their personalities and conduct. The more complex Westerns mix traditional notions of good and bad, as we have already seen in discussing Wayne's Dunson in *Red River,* a man whom we come to love as well as hate in the very same film. Sam Peckinpah's superb *Ride the High Country* (1962), like *El Dorado,* is a tale of former partners who reunite but in quite different ways, and we root for both Joel McCrea's and Randolph Scott's respective characters, even when we find them morally opposed. In *El Dorado,* we know that Thornton has pulled a fast one on McLeod at the end, killing a man who adhered to the principle of a fair and honest fight. It does not seem like the type of thing that John Wayne is supposed to do, but as Hawks teaches us here, it is survival and friendship that really count in the end.

CHAPTER 7

The Postwar Psychological Western (1946–1956)

"My Darling Clementine" to "Jubal"

Let us call the ensemble of forms adopted by the postwar western the "superwestern." For the purposes of our exposé this word will bring together phenomena that are not always comparable. It can certainly be justified on negative grounds, in contrast to the classicism of the forties and to the tradition of which it is the outcome. The superwestern is a western that would be ashamed to be just itself, and looks for some additional interest to justify its existence—an aesthetic, sociological, moral, psychological, political, or erotic interest, in short some quality extrinsic to the genre and which is supposed to enrich it.

—André Bazin, "The Evolution of the Western" (1955)

Hawks's *Red River,* as mentioned at the outset of the previous chapter, hit theaters on a wave of visually and psychologically expressive Westerns released between the end of World War II and 1950. These ranged from John Ford's *My Darling Clementine* and King Vidor's *Duel in the Sun* (both 1946) to Delmer Daves's *Broken Arrow* and Anthony Mann's *The Furies, Devil's Doorway,* and *Winchester '73* (all 1950). These films typically summon the viewer to consider complex situations in which characters struggle with their own demons and desires in attempting to realize their goals or in trying to justify the righteousness of those aims. Focusing on the inner contradictions and dilemmas of protagonists and antagonists alike, the narratives of many of the postwar Westerns tend to avoid overly simplified portraits of heroes and villains. For example, and as we have seen, *Red River* explores the problematic morality and psychology of its "antihero," the increasingly tyrannical Tom Dunson, even while taking full advantage of such classical elements of the genre as the journey narrative and on-location shooting in breathtaking Western landscapes (see chapter 6). It is one of a number of major Western films made just after World War II that utilize the conventions of the genre while also deepening and complicating the characters and dramatic situations framed by those familiar patterns.

The second half of the 1940s marked an important transition point in the evolution of the Western film. This gradual transformation of the genre was undoubtedly an effect of new audience expectations, the result of the "maturing" of America's public self-consciousness both during and after the nation's multifaceted wartime experience. Despite the Allied victory and a revived sense of "American exceptionalism" in some quarters, many Americans were nonetheless conscious of the costs in human life and the bleak lessons about human nature that World War II had occasioned. A skeptical and even pessimistic sensibility often lay beneath the public roar of military triumph, and this tension was clearly reflected in the postwar use of the Western genre in a more critical, demythologizing manner. Hollywood producers were certainly aware of their audiences' increasing need for more complex "adult" movies that reflected the public's gradual disillusionment with traditional myths of unfailing heroes and inevitable communal progress. At the same time, filmmakers like John Ford had participated in the war—in Ford's case, as head of the Office of Strategic Service's Field Photographic Branch—and had witnessed its brutal reality firsthand.[1] Such artists were conscious of their roles in conveying the collective awakening that had taken place.

As we have seen, the genre had always blended history and fiction in re-creating the kind of struggles amid adversity that took place (most often) in colonial as well as Reconstruction-era America. The Western's usual depiction of courage and hardship, along with its recurring emphasis on the conflict between good and evil, had resonated with audiences at the beginning of America's involvement in the war. But starting in 1946, many Western movies offered more expressive ways of presenting stories of struggle and conflict, stories that frequently centered on morally ambiguous characters and psychologically complex situations. This deepening of the genre in response to the war and its aftermath also paralleled audiences' heightened interest in film noir and in narratives that recognized the irrational aspects of human existence. Eventually, the postwar transformation of the genre paved the way for the more psychologically and existentially charged Westerns of the 1950s.

TRANSITIONS: FORD'S POSTWAR WESTERNS

My Darling Clementine presents us with a traditionally heroic lawman (Wyatt Earp, played in cool, stoic fashion by Henry Fonda) who chooses to take revenge at just the right moment against those villains (the Clanton clan) who have murdered his younger brother, thereby bringing a sense of enforced law and order to the formerly chaotic town of Tombstone. The process of revenge-taking is slow and deliberate, and the narrative structure tends to make the viewer think that Earp has chosen to delay action against the Clantons for a long spell of time because of some Hamlet-like reason of conscience or melancholy—though one might conclude that there are also convenient *dramatic* reasons for the postponement of the climactic shoot-out. As Jim Kitses points out, in actuality the course of events in *Clementine* unfolds over the course of only a few days, but given the leisurely pace of the movie, the audience would be surprised to figure that out.[2] It is Ford's unrushed pacing and structuring of the events that occur over a long weekend in Tombstone that make the movie's narrative appear on the surface to extend for weeks rather than days and hours.

Intriguing parallels can be drawn between Ford's Westerns of the later 1940s (*My Darling Clementine,* his "cavalry trilogy," plus his 1948 Western *3 Godfathers*) and his 1945 war film *They Were Expendable.* What is so distinctive and comparable about these films—especially in contrast with Ford's pre–World War II pictures—is their slow, careful, and even meditative tempo. Ford's *Stagecoach,* by contrast, is designed and crafted in a manner that delivers action moments, punch lines, and dramatic peaks in an almost steady stream. Ford's more deliberate method of pacing in his postwar Westerns is partly the result of the movies' respective screenplays and final editing, but Ford chose to emphasize extended moments of reflective quietude that provide time for the viewer to absorb moments of action and dramatic decision making. Such moments have been referred to as "grace notes," seemingly ornamental shots or scenes that are not designed to advance the narrative but rather are included so as to create a refined dialectic between action and stasis. In *Clementine* Ford expresses a heightened appreciation for a more contemplative form of pacing, with shots or scenes that are not always narrative driven, and a sense of timing that makes the viewer experience a

FIGURE 30. A celebration of community and town-building against a wilderness landscape (Monument Valley) in John Ford's *My Darling Clementine* (1946). Dancing together at center are Wyatt Earp (Henry Fonda) and Clementine Carter (Cathy Downs). Courtesy of the Museum of Modern Art.

feeling of waiting. This type of studied rhythm may well have been the result of the fact that Ford's direct wartime experiences had occasioned, at least subconsciously, a more reflective stylization of his storylines.

Clementine certainly contains many classical elements of the genre in terms of its visuals and narrative. And at least one Ford expert has interpreted the film, perhaps too metaphorically, as an allegory for the recent conflict of World War II or even as an anticipation of Cold War politics. As Tag Gallagher puts it in his book on John Ford, "Wyatt Earp (the U.S.) gives up marshalling in Dodge City (World War I), but takes up arms again to combat the Clantons (World War II) to make the world safe. Victory is horrible, and Wyatt must return to the wilderness, to his father (confession; reconstruction), leaving innocence, hope, and civilization (Clementine) behind, 'lost and gone forever,' a distant memory (the long road) in Tombstone (the world of 1946)."[3] It is an intriguing reading of the film, dependent on a view of the traditional Western in terms of the inevitable showdown between good and evil. Flights of allegorical interpretation are always possible, but most relevant to *Clementine*'s subtle way of providing a transition between classical and postclassical forms of the Western is the movie's emphasis on the troubled and morally ambiguous personality of the physician-turned-outlaw Doc Holliday (Victor Mature). Holliday is in some ways a clear transition point in the path that takes us from heroic gunslingers like Cheyenne Harry and the Ringo Kid to Eastwood's antiheroic William Munny in *Unforgiven*.

Kitses has interpreted the film's attention to the problematic character of Holliday as a symbolic precursor to the more revisionist, pluralistic, and hence "postmodern" Westerns of later decades. Kitses qualifies this reference by pointing out that *Clementine* remains mostly within the confines of the traditional or classical Western, particularly with its chief focus on the heroic Earp, his iconic community-celebrating dance with his darling Clementine, and his final horizon-gazing departure.[4] Nonetheless, it is the integration of Holliday's psychological and moral tensions within the main narrative that provides an exemplary bridge of sorts between classical and revisionist modes of the Western film. The lingering shadows of World War II's global carnage undoubtedly had a role to play in the "darkening" of the Western genre around this time, and *Clementine*'s inclusion of Holliday's inner complexity, as well as its presentation of a shadowy, wild Tombstone in its opening segments, have even led some film scholars to categorize the film as a "noir Western" that heralded later movies fitting this label.

Some postwar Westerns that include genre-revising components in terms of both narrative and visuals—leading to the more existentialist, psychological, and expressionist Westerns of the 1950s—tend to downsize or even eliminate the explicit historicizing of the more traditional Westerns of the Depression era and World War II period. This is not always so clear-cut, of course, as is evident in *Red River*'s complicating of its protagonist, Dunson, and his relationship with his "son," Matt, against the backdrop of a massive cattle drive that is framed by the theme of empire building. We can again draw on the postwar work of Ford in pointing out some hybrid examples of history-minded Westerns that nonetheless modify and expand the genre in influential ways.

Fort Apache (1948) is the only Ford Western to feature both of the director's favorite actors, John Wayne and Henry Fonda. The film expresses an implicit criticism of the Indian-fighting missions conducted by the United States Cavalry, particularly given the troubling and dangerous leadership practiced by the fanatical Lt. Col. Owen Thursday (Fonda). *Fort Apache*'s partially sympathetic portrayal of the Native

FIGURE 31. U.S. Cavalry officers converse with their enemy against a desert landscape in John Ford's *Fort Apache* (1948). Included in this shot are Ford regulars Victor McLaglen (*second from left*), John Wayne (*third from left*), Henry Fonda *(to the right of Wayne)*, and George O'Brien *(to the right of Fonda)*. Courtesy of the Museum of Modern Art.

American as a noble warrior defending himself against America's ruthless expansionism anticipates, at least in part, the later revisionist Westerns that attempt in their ways to reverse Hollywood's previous demonization of "the red man" (e.g., Delmer Daves's *Broken Arrow,* Samuel Fuller's *Run of the Arrow,* Ford's own *Cheyenne Autumn,* Eastwood's *The Outlaw Josey Wales,* and Costner's *Dances with Wolves*). In addition, *Fort Apache* anticipates Ford's later masterwork about the fading away of the Old West, *The Man Who Shot Liberty Valance* (see chapter 8), in that it reveals the intentional deceptions and falsehoods that lie behind the myth of the Western hero—in the case of *Fort Apache,* the military frontier hero. At the end of the day, the film presents a noble portrait of the "average" cavalry soldier suffering the trials and tribulations of daily existence on a perilous frontier while adhering to duty and a higher cause. And yet the movie criticizes those decision-making commanders (and by indirect inference, the politicians who give them their orders) whose obsession with national and military ideals causes unnecessary bloodshed and who endanger their loyal men.

At the conclusion of *Fort Apache,* Captain Kirby York (Wayne) chooses to defend the honor and reputation of Lt. Col. Thursday (a character who echoes George Armstrong Custer) before a group of reporters who stand admiring a heroic portrait of this dogmatic, arrogant, and racist military leader. York is all too well aware (as is the audience) that Thursday had knowingly led his men to their deaths in a suicidal battle against Cochise and the Apaches. Thursday's charge ends in tragic destruction, similar to the devastation of Custer's loss at the Battle of Little Big Horn in 1876, for the vastly outnumbered cavalry soldiers who fulfill their duty while expecting their impending doom. York stares out a window into his own (and the American public's) imagination: ethereal images of proud soldiers ride by. He tells the reporters gathered behind him: "The faces may change, and the names, but they're there, they're the regiment, the regular army—now and fifty years from now. They're better men than they used to be. Thursday did that. He made it a command to be proud of." York decides to uphold the legend at the expense of the facts, but the clear presentation of the deception involved is a revisionist lesson for any viewer who otherwise accepts her Western "history" while wearing blinders. The film gives us Ford's "dual vision," as Kitses puts it, involving a critique as well as mythologization of American militarism. Kitses observes in his book *Horizons West: Directing the Western from John Ford to Clint Eastwood:*

> *Fort Apache* is a film of antithetical energies, a liberal critique of militarism that culminates in a conservative defence of tradition, at once revisionist and reactionary, a film that employs Ford's dual vision to have it both ways. The cloud of dust that frequently hovers over the film's military actions hints at the ambiguity with which they are seen. . . . Ford simultaneously exposes the Custer/Thursday myth as bankrupt and attaches Thursday to the noble traditions of the military. . . . By demonizing the Apache as savage and inferior, Thursday had given himself permission to surpass them in violence and unscrupulous action, while wrapping himself in the banners of duty and glory. Ford ruthlessly analyses this process, but by an ideological sleight-of-hand suggests that his behaviour was aberrant rather than dominant national policy.[5]

Unfortunately, Kitses views this tension between the movie's critical and constructive tendencies as undercutting the overall coherence of the film. To the contrary, this double-edged treatment should be appreciated for its complicating of the story of the cavalry—not to mention the story of American idealism. Kitses holds that *Fort Apache* does not go far enough in critiquing the imperialist and expansionist policies of American government—policies that frame the film's overall narrative—particularly in light of the fact that York continues fighting against Geronimo at the movie's end, despite all that we have witnessed. Kitses concludes: "Suppressing the historical economic determinant for the action leaves the film with a void, which it fills with the suicidal vainglory of Colonel Thursday, whom it finally recuperates. Ford's selective history, allowing him to affirm his idealized America, strains and finally tears apart *Fort Apache*."[6] To read the film's conclusion in such a way, however, is to diminish not merely the fascinating complexities and moral ambivalences that run throughout the movie, aspects of this Western's greatness, but also the great irony of its final scene. It is York who decides to paint a rosy picture of Thursday and the recent battle, not Ford. The movie as a whole gives us both sides of a messy, tragic historical situation and also provides a profound lesson about the general dangers of idealism and nationalism gone wrong.

Fort Apache's theme of "glory in defeat," suggesting practical limitations to the ideals of American exceptionalism and Manifest Destiny, is also evident in Ford's *They Were Expendable,* released a year earlier. The PT squadron members in that unique war film are courageous and duty-driven, even as they face imminent defeat by the enemy. The theme of the individual's heroism amid collective loss governs the entire narrative of *Expendable,* as well as the conclusion of *Fort Apache*. It also emerges conspicuously in Ford's sequel to the latter film, *She Wore a Yellow Ribbon* (1949), the second in his postwar "cavalry trilogy"—the third being *Rio Grande* (1950).

Yellow Ribbon's breathtaking Technicolor cinematography by Winston Hoch rivals and at times surpasses Archie Stout's impressive black-and-white visual artistry in *Fort Apache*. For many Ford fans, it is the consummate expression of the classical, myth-governed Western, especially in terms of its style of photographic grandeur. And yet, when one pays close attention to its storyline, *Yellow Ribbon* proves to be an example of the partial transitioning of the Western toward revisionism, not unlike *Fort Apache*. *Yellow Ribbon* is the story of the retiring Captain Nathan Brittles (Wayne again, playing an aging character with echoes of *Red River*'s Tom Dunson). During the final days of his command, Brittles experiences one failure after another as time passes quickly. He nonetheless maintains the deep respect of his men, who present him with a special retirement gift: a pocket watch inscribed with the sentiment "Lest we forget." By continuing with the idea of glory in defeat, a recurring Fordian theme noted by Peter Bogdanovich in his interviews with Ford, *Yellow Ribbon* celebrates the heroism of its frontier soldiers in a

FIGURE 32. John Wayne as retiring cavalry officer Captain Nathan Brittles in John Ford's *She Wore a Yellow Ribbon* (1949). Ben Johnson, as Sergeant Tyree, is to Wayne's left. Courtesy of the Museum of Modern Art.

mythical fashion; but beneath the mythical surface lies a gritty reality.[7] In spite of the dedication and courage of Brittles's soldiers, the military's attempts continually fail, as if thwarted by negative fate rather than positive destiny.

There is also some attempt to show sympathetic communication between the "white man" and the "red man," as in the dialogue between Brittles and Chief Pony That Walks (Chief John Big Tree), in spite of otherwise stereotypical portraits of the Indian enemies. Though Brittles attempts to avoid battle through dialogue with the old chief, the Indian's response is a fatalistic one: it is "too late" for "old men" such as the captain and the chief to stop wars. As crystallized in this one bit of dialogue, the mood of the entire film becomes one of quiet resignation to a life of imposed duties and threats, despite the great valor and perseverance of Brittles's soldiers. These men must learn to accept death and loss just as they have learned to accept the monotony of

FIGURE 33. Captain Nathan Brittles "converses" with his deceased wife at her desert grave. Courtesy of the Museum of Modern Art.

their daily existence at the military outpost—and just as Brittles and Chief Pony That Walks must acknowledge the impossibility of life without war.

Fort Apache and *Yellow Ribbon* teach us that myths point to their own implicit sets of ideals, that these ideals should never be accepted uncritically, and that reality and history are not always guaranteed to accommodate the realization of such ideals in a manner that is easy or inevitable. Ford's cavalry trilogy is part of a postwar phase of Western moviemaking in which the costs of American expansionism and the limitations of American idealism were beginning to be recognized more explicitly, even beneath a façade of mythmaking, and in which the plight of the frontier hero was being presented in a more complex and less optimistic manner. Above all, this was the start of a period in which the conventional parameters of the genre were being transcended by integrating themes, lessons, and dramatic situations that had been the focus of other types of cinema—not only to enrich and revitalize the genre, but so as to assist in turning a more critical eye on the genre's underlying mythos.

DUEL IN THE SUN AND THE FURIES

The "psychological Western," a mode of enriching and challenging the genre by complicating the figure of the westerner, was initiated with Sjöström's silent masterpiece *The Wind,* as discussed in chapter 2. But it was in the sound era, and more especially the immediate post–World War II period, that the Western became a popular narrative vehicle for the exploration of human instincts, emotions, and desires. The protagonist had to contend with the inner battle between his ego and id while also confronting external adversaries. The struggle to repress his libido or curb his will-to-power sometimes became as challenging as his struggle for survival or justice. The westerner slowly came to recognize that his own psyche might be as chaotic and labyrinthine as the wilderness surrounding him.

The first big-budget post–World War II Western to explore the devastating power of human passion and lust was *Duel in the Sun,* King Vidor's grandiose, visually sumptuous, and often corny soap-opera-on-the-range. Other directors such as William Dieterle and Josef von Sternberg were allegedly involved in the production but went uncredited, and producer David O. Selznick took an expected active hand in shaping the film, though Vidor (*The Big Parade, The Crowd, Stella Dallas, Northwest Passage, The Fountainhead, Ruby Gentry*) was the chief artistic creator of this lavish epic. The psychological complexity exhibited in this type of Western was echoed by noir Westerns of the period such as Raoul Walsh's *Pursued* (1947), with Robert Mitchum and Teresa Wright, and Anthony Mann's *The Furies* (1950), with Barbara Stanwyck and Walter Huston. These "Freudian oaters" led to later emotion-charged Westerns such as Nicholas Ray's fascinatingly eccentric *Johnny Guitar* (1954), starring Joan Crawford and Mercedes McCambridge as ruthless rivals; Robert Aldrich's *The Last Sunset* (1961), with Rock Hudson and Kirk Douglas as competing adversaries; and Marlon Brando's oft-underrated *One-Eyed Jacks* (1961).

Duel in the Sun deals with the rivalry between two brothers, Lewt (Gregory Peck) and Jesse (Joseph Cotten) McCanles, and their love for the seductive "half-breed" Pearl Chavez (Jennifer Jones), recently arrived at the ranching empire of the brothers' father, "Senator" Jackson McCanles (Lionel Barrymore). Pearl's father, Scott Chavez (Herbert Marshall), has just been sent to prison and to his eventual execution for having killed his cheating wife and her lover, and so his daughter goes to live with the senator and his wife, Laura Belle (Lillian Gish), the long-ago lover of Pearl's father. Set against a Technicolor-soaked landscape constructed of both on-location shots and studio settings, Vidor's film deals, first and foremost, with the Freudian tension between instinctual self-expression and its counterforce, the repression of subconscious impulses, along with the racial and class differences between Pearl and the McCanles family.[8]

Given that the movie begins with the sultry dancing of Pearl and with the subsequent shooting of her adulterous mother by her jealous father, we realize immediately that we can expect a narrative built around themes of unbridled desire and explosions of previously bottled-up passion. We also come to witness the festering anger of the patriarch Senator McCanles in dealing with the betrayal of his son Jesse, as well as Jesse's half-concealed disappointment when he catches his beloved Pearl in an intimate moment with his wild brother, Lewt, after an apparent session of lovemaking. These examples of barely self-contained psychological energy are contrasted with the reckless lustfulness of Lewt and Pearl. The sensual Pearl, even when Lewt has wronged her, always manages to seek him again because of her intense physical longing, until the time when she feels that she must kill him for what he has done to her. And even then, she manages to fire shots at Lewt while climbing across jagged rocks to reach his dying body, wavering between bloodthirsty vengeance and sexual passion. One might say that Pearl is torn between Eros (desire) and Thanatos (death or destruction), the two basic principles, or "drives," of human nature, according to Freud's *Civilization and Its Discontents*.[9]

Duel in the Sun also highlights the enduring self-denial of Laura Belle McCanles, whose love for her husband reaches its limits after she has dealt for a near-lifetime with his hard-hearted ruthlessness and icy ambition. There is a stagy yet touching scene in which the dying Laura Belle crawls across the expanse of her bed to offer her affection to a husband who is absorbed in his own sudden release of guilt and emotion. The senator has confessed at long last that he had ruined their marriage (and his own legs) years earlier when he had suffered a horse riding accident while pursuing his wife in a jealous rage after she had run away from him. Following his confession and her attempt to embrace him, Laura Belle falls from the bed to the floor, dead, while trying to express her love for her emotionally stunted husband. The senator takes a stilted moment to notice almost casually that she has fallen by the side of his wheelchair. It is an almost ludicrously dramatic moment, charged with sentiment and yet elevated by the copresence of these two screen legends.

FIGURE 34. "Lust in the dust": The aggressive Lewt McCanles (Gregory Peck) embraces a momentarily resistant Pearl Chavez (Jennifer Jones) in King Vidor's *Duel in the Sun* (1946). Courtesy of the Museum of Modern Art.

This tension between smirk-inducing dramatic exaggeration and charismatic theatrical acting is the virtue *and* vice of the movie: we waver constantly between incredulity and fascination, and the result is magnetizing, to say the least, especially when combined with the highly expressive and deeply colorful visuals. What makes this particular scene intriguing for any viewer with a sense of cinematic history is the fact that Barrymore and Gish enjoyed an opportunity to ham it up after having worked together for Griffith in the early Biograph years—most notably in *The Battle of Elderbush Gulch* of 1913 (see chapter 1).

While dramatically "overbaked" in more than a few scenes, *Duel in the Sun* should be praised for its boldness in reviving a psychologically motivated and artfully symbolic utilization of the genre that had not been seen since *The Wind* and that would soon be equaled by Mann's *The Furies*. The latter Western, centered on a power struggle between cattle baron T.C. Jeffords (Walter Huston) and his overly doting daughter Vance (Barbara Stanwyck), is a clear example of the fruitful cross-pollination of the Western genre with the category of dark-toned movie known as film noir. Director Mann, astonishingly productive at this point in his career, was no stranger to either brand of motion picture. The year 1950 saw, in addition to *The Furies,* the release of Mann's *Winchester '73,* with James Stewart—the start of a successful series of Westerns on which the filmmaker and his favorite star collaborated—and his underrated *Devil's Doorway* with Robert Taylor, not to mention his non-Western film noir *Side Street* with Farley Granger. Mann had also directed such previous (and mainly overlooked) noir movies as *Desperate* (1947), *Railroaded!* (1947), *T-Men* (1947), and *Raw Deal* (1948).

Film noir is typically characterized in a stylistic sense by its expressionistic use of stark lighting (lots of chiaroscuro effects with dramatic contrasts between shadowy darkness and sobering light) and symbolic camera angles that often create a feeling of heightened tension or even disorientation. Film noir's basic stylistic devices recall those of German expressionistic cinema. It is no coincidence perhaps that one of the true masters of German expressionism, Fritz Lang—who created such classics of that tradition as *Metropolis* and *M*—came to America in the mid-1930s and eventually directed a string of influential film noir classics in the 1940s and 1950s (e.g., *Ministry of Fear, Woman in the Window, Scarlet Street, Clash by Night, The Blue Gardenia, The Big Heat, Human Desire*). But before immersing his talents in the world of American film noir, Lang crafted a few notable and fairly traditional Westerns: *The Return of Frank James* (1940) with Henry Fonda, and *Western Union* (1941) with Robert Young and Randolph Scott. Lang later made *Rancho Notorious* (1952) with Marlene Dietrich and Arthur Kennedy, a Western that reveals more obvious traces of the director's blossoming engagement with film noir.

In terms of narrative, a noir film tends to emphasize the ambivalence and alienation of its main characters amid an environment or world that is uncertain and often threatening. As screenwriter, film theorist, and director Paul Schrader (*Hardcore, Mishima, Affliction*) observes in his seminal article titled "Notes on Film Noir," the "overriding noir theme" is "a passion for the past and present, but also a fear of the future. Noir heroes dread to look ahead, but instead try to survive by the day, and if unsuccessful at that, they retreat to the past. Thus film noir's techniques emphasize loss, nostalgia, lack of clear priorities, and insecurity, then submerge these self-doubts in mannerism and style."[10]

It is not surprising to find an intermingling of film noir and the Western, as in *The Furies*, in more than a few films of the post–World War II period, particularly because earlier Westerns had often practiced an implicit form of expressionism when evoking the implicit bond between characters' rugged, hard-edged, often dangerous personalities and their rugged, hard-edged, often dangerous physical settings. And many previous Westerns, while shying away from overt psychologizing, had nonetheless centered on lone, alienated westerners who were not afraid to stand apart from the nearest community, at least for a time, and who migrated between acts of heroic chivalry and cold-blooded killing in a brutal land where a sense of jaded pessimism was easily bred. While film noir had originally taken shape within the crime and private eye genre, it was *The Furies* that demonstrated—perhaps more than any other Western of this era—that the noir style of filmmaking could be fruitfully channeled in exploring the dark "underbelly" of tales about cowboys, ranchers, and wilderness warriors. Mann specialized in Westerns in which the protagonist feels estranged from and threatened by his environment, doomed by a troubled past and by oppressive external forces to a life of simply "keeping on." These feelings usually evoke a similar sense of nervousness, tension, and alienation in the viewer, and it is precisely this kind of pessimistic and fatalistic sensibility that helps to define film noir.[11]

Certain genres or styles of filmmaking typically attract, on a recurring basis, talented individuals who are intrigued by and experienced in these types of cinema. More often than not, major studios recognize success in a certain domain of filmmaking and hire those who have excelled in this area to repeat the application of their talents. *The Furies* is a clear case of this in its fusion of Western and film noir. Charles Schnee wrote the screenplay for *The Furies* after having collaborated a few years earlier with Borden Chase on the script for *Red River*; he had also penned the screenplay for Nicholas Ray's noir classic *They Live by Night* (1949).[12] Furthermore, Schnee's screenplay for *The Furies* was based on the novel of the same title by Niven Busch, who had also written the novel that was the basis of *Duel in the Sun,* not to mention screenplays for the Western noir *Pursued,* the 1940 Western classic *The Westerner* (see chapter 5), and Tay Garnett's 1946 noir classic *The Postman Always Rings Twice* (cowritten with Harry Ruskin).

As if these connections were not enough to guarantee that *The Furies* would be sure to capture the type of visual style, sense of ambiguity, and feeling of tension that were primary characteristics of 1940s film noir, the producer of the film, Hal Wallis, had been responsible for producing or executive producing several previous noir and quasi-noir classics. These included John Huston's *The Maltese Falcon* (1941), Raoul Walsh's *They Drive by Night* (1940) and *High Sierra* (1941), and Michael Curtiz's *Casablanca* (1942). Wallis had also produced two previous film noirs starring Barbara Stanwyck: Lewis Milestone's *The Strange Love of Martha Ivers* (1946) and Robert Siodmak's *The File on Thelma Jordon.* The latter film was also released in 1950, but earlier than *The Furies,* and starred Wendell Corey, who plays vengeful Rip Darrow opposite Stanwyck's Vance Jeffords in Mann's tragic Western.

Stanwyck might be regarded as the "queen" or "doyenne" of lead actresses who made their mark in American film noir, given her several roles in such films (e.g., *The Strange Love of Martha Ivers, The File on Thelma Jordon, No Man of Her Own, Clash by Night*), and most especially her memorable performance as the paradigmatic femme fatale Phyllis Dietrichson in Billy Wilder's *Double Indemnity* (1944). Walter Huston, who gave his final screen performance as the spirited and free-spending T.C. Jeffords in *The Furies,* also played a fire-and-brimstone preacher with a touch of lust in his heart for Pearl Chavez in *Duel in the Sun.* Judith Anderson portrays Flo Burnett, Jeffords's gold-digging love interest who sparks the wrath of his daughter. Anderson had also played Mrs. Callum in *Pursued* and, more notably, Stanwyck's cruel aunt in *The Strange Love of Martha Ivers.* Anderson, like Stanwyck, had been an effective staple in several film noir classics.

There are three crucial scenes in *The Furies* that highlight the noir-like emphases on moral complexity and psychological tension, elements that later became integral to such Westerns by Mann as *The Tin Star* (1957), *Man of the West* (1958), and most especially his series of Westerns with James Stewart (including *Winchester '73, Bend of the River, The Naked Spur,* and *The Man from Laramie*). The first of our selected scenes takes place early on in *The Furies* and suggests the Freudian Electra complex that serves as the core of the film's narrative. This scene

FIGURE 35. Anthony Mann's "neurotic" Western *The Furies* (1950): Vance Jeffords (Barbara Stanwyck) prepares to hurl a pair of scissors at the intrusive Flo Burnett (Judith Anderson), who stands reflected in the mirror alongside Vance's father, T.C. Jeffords (Walter Huston). Courtesy of the Museum of Modern Art.

involves a tight close-up shot of Vance and her father, T.C., as they discourse about the possibility of Vance's future husband and T.C.'s doubts that she will ever find a man who will live up to the standards of manhood set by T.C. himself. As they converse, Stanwyck and Huston portray the characters as if they were lovers rather than father and daughter. If one were to watch the scene with the sound turned off and no knowledge of the rest of the plotline, one might assume that this is a movie about a May-December romance, with the characters about to kiss.

Here Mann demonstrates that he is not afraid to foreground such controversial themes, even within the parameters of the otherwise traditional Western narrative. And it is Vance's convoluted love for her father, veering from emotional codependence and hyperinflated idol worship to jealousy and rage, that gives the film the kind of discomforting and fascinating tension that can be found in many a film noir, ranging from a gangster son's obsessive love for his mother in Walsh's *White Heat* (1949) to the disturbing revelation of an incestuous father-daughter relationship in Roman Polanski's *Chinatown* (1974)—with none other than Walter Huston's son John starring as the tyrannical, pathological father in that latter masterpiece.

Another crucial scene, occurring later in the film, centers on Vance's sudden explosion of repressed resentment against her father's new lover, Flo Burnett, a woman who is as greedy and power hungry as Vance herself. Burnett has gone so far as to intervene in the management of T.C.'s vast ranching business, a role previously assumed quite willingly by his ambitious daughter. The newcomer has also taken the liberty of visiting the former bedroom chamber of Vance's dead mother, a "sacred space" within the Jeffords mansion that had previously been reserved for visits only by T.C. and his daughter. Vance stands before her mother's bedroom mirror and listens, eyes glowing with hatred, as we see reflected in the mirror T.C. and Flo, the latter attempting to console in an irritatingly artificial manner. Vance erupts into an act of destructive wrath, violently hurling a pair of formerly concealed scissors into the face and neck of her father's lover. A horrified T.C. assists the bleeding victim while expelling Vance from the bedroom, threatening to kill his own daughter should Flo die from her wounds.

The third of our selected scenes centers on T.C.'s decision to order Vance's longtime friend and romantic interest Juan Herrera (Gilbert Roland) to be hanged once a standoff with the squatting Mexicans, including Juan's family, has ended to the cattle baron's advantage. Vance, who has accompanied Juan and his family during their brief battle with her father and his men, tells Juan that T.C. is only doing this to force her to beg, and that she is nonetheless willing do so in order to spare his life. Vance knows that T.C. is punishing her for her alliance with Juan, but also quite probably because of her disfiguring attack against Flo. Juan willingly (*too* willingly, it may seem to some viewers) accepts his fate, knowing that T.C. will hang him anyway and that Vance's pleas will only partially satisfy T.C.'s desire to punish his daughter for her insubordination. The hanging commences and Vance tearfully swears vengeance against her father for what he has done, setting in motion a chain of events that will lead to an expected tragic conclusion. Vance is transformed here from an Electra-like father-worshipper to an "Oedipal" father-destroyer. Her retribution will be methodical and patient, a strategic harnessing of her repressed rage.

The figure of the Mexican and the setting of the U.S.-Mexican border recur throughout many Western films. *The Furies* affords a thought-provoking conception of "the Mexican," given that the plot presents the Mexicans as seemingly undeserving squatters on private property and

FIGURE 36. Vance Jeffords stands with pistol ready as she joins in the Mexicans' stand-off against her own father and his men. Courtesy of the Museum of Modern Art.

yet also as stoic, long-suffering laborers who are the victims of T.C.'s overly primitive, egocentric sense of justice. The role of the Mexican in the Western movie has not received the same type of detailed treatment that has been accorded the role of the Native American. It is safe to say, given Mann's ambivalent portrait of the Mexican in this film, that he offers an appreciation (even if a limited one) of the injustices faced by those who slave for a man who would rather drive them from his "land of plenty" than accommodate them—and for purely self-centered reasons. Vance's long-standing friendship with Juan, and her willingness to stand by his side during the battle, provides a stark contrast to her father's worldview. Much like Ford's treatment of the Indian in *Fort Apache* and *She Wore a Yellow Ribbon,* an intentional stereotyping of the "Other" emerges alongside an attempt to provoke reflection on the dangers of such stereotyping.

The title of the film (the same as that of Busch's novel) refers to the vast spread of T.C.'s ranching empire, but it also summons the name of the vengeful sisters of Aeschylus's Greek trilogy *The Oresteia.* Mann, a former stage director whose experience in the theater had undoubtedly helped to shape his recurring interest in crafting modern versions of classical epics and tragedies, brings to this film the same feeling of exaggerated emotional turbulence that can be found in many ancient dramas. Aeschylus's Furies symbolize the innate instinct for primal retribution that gives rise to an irrational and primitive form of justice, one that is articulated by such basic principles and laws as Hammurabi's code ("an eye for an eye"). Two of the main characters in Mann's film, Vance and Rip Darrow, are as driven by the need for revenge as are Clytemnestra and Orestes in *The Oresteia.* Aeschylus's tragic drama winds its way to the eventual founding of the Athenian system of rational civic justice (with the assistance of the gods, of course), but we are always reminded that human nature is defined as much by our subconscious instincts and ego-driven passions as it is by our aspirations to reasonable coexistence. Mann's *The Furies* teaches a similar lesson.

CASE STUDY: *JUBAL,* OR "OTHELLO ON THE RANGE"

Delmer Daves's underrated *Jubal* (1956) follows in the wake of earlier Westerns, like *Duel in the Sun* and *The Furies,* that explore the darker side of human nature through their tales of wild desire and repressed passion. It is worth exploring this oft-forgotten film, particularly in terms of its narrative details, because this movie serves as a clear model of the midcentury psychological Western and provides a basis of specific comparison with several other Westerns of the period.

The movie's screenplay was written by Delmer Daves and Russell S. Hughes and was based on a novel by Paul Wellman, whose novels *Apache* and *The Comancheros* had also been made into films, by the same titles. While *Jubal* is far from being a noir Western in terms of its visual style (it is far more classical in that sense), it does revolve around characters, themes, and situations that echo the dark vision of film noir narratives. And the title character is played by Glenn Ford, who had recently starred in several noir films, including Fritz Lang's *The Big Heat* and *Human Desire*—not to mention such other Westerns as George Marshall's *Texas* (1941), Charles Vidor's *The Desperadoes* (1941), Henry Levin's *The Man from Colorado* (1948), and Budd Boetticher's *The Man from the Alamo* (1953).

The film—shot mostly in the gorgeous and rugged terrain of Jackson Hole, Wyoming—starts off with breathtaking forest and mountain scenery. Jubal Troop (Ford) emerges from the wilderness, alone and exhausted, and stumbles down a steep hillside, falling onto the dirt roadway below.[13] Rancher Shep Horgan (Ernest Borgnine) happens upon him while driving by in a horse-drawn carriage, as thickly forested hillsides and distant mountaintops serve as an eye-catching backdrop. Shep brings the unconscious man home, and the troublemaking ranch hand Pinky (Rod Steiger) immediately denigrates the stranger by saying he smells of "sheep dip," thus suspecting him of being a "lousy sheep herder." They revive Jubal, and Shep asks him if he is a cowhand and where his horse is. Jubal tells them that his horse fell from under him while he traveled through a pass in a blizzard on the way from Montana. After Jubal mentions quietly and solemnly that his horse cried like a human when it fell, Sam (Noah Beery Jr.), another worker for Shep, declares in a friendly manner that "most horses are better than humans." Jubal, still groggy, gives Sam an appreciative smile and concurs, seemingly sharing his view. Although Jubal is still a mysterious stranger to the ranchers and to the viewer, we can guess that he has suffered some dramatic and perhaps even traumatic experience that has forced him into the role of a loner in the wilderness, one who is also a skeptic about human nature.

When Jubal awakens the next morning and asks where his clothes are, Pinky tells him that he burned them because they stank: a clear antagonism between these two men, initiated by Pinky, has been established from the very start. Shep gives Jubal clean clothes and offers him a job, but while Jubal offers thanks for the opportunity, he is clearly ready to leave. Shep, who has taken a shine to the stranger, asks him point-blank if he is running from something. Jubal at first denies this but then replies reflectively, "Maybe I am running from something . . . bad luck . . . I carry it with me." Jubal is initially the archetypal lone westerner troubled by a mysterious past, at least until we get to know him better. Shep tells him that there comes a time when a man should stop running from bad fortune and instead "fight it out." He advises Jubal,

"You know, there comes a day, Jubal, when a man needs to decide where he's going." This is sage advice for a man who until now appeared to be an aimless drifter and whose chief goal in life is to escape his past.

Shep is persuasive, and Jubal soon proves himself to be a loyal worker who has found a place where he can escape temporarily from his troubled history. Much like Cole Harden in Wyler's *The Westerner,* who eventually desires to settle down and give up his wandering ways (see chapter 5), and contrary to Ethan Edwards in Ford's *The Searchers,* who remains an eternal outsider (see chapter 8), Jubal is ready for a place to hang his hat for a spell. Despite the fact that we (along with Shep) recognize Jubal as an apparently decent man who has been down on his luck for a time and who wants to stay out of trouble—with Ford's "average Joe" portrayal supporting our initial intuitions—the hints about his problematic past remind us that his personality is still too opaque to allow us to render a complete judgment.

Jubal meets Shep's wife, Mae (Valerie French), and we easily recognize that Mae has romantic leanings toward Jubal, even at first sight. Mae, the embodiment of barely repressed erotic passion, soon attempts to seduce Jubal when he comes to heat his branding iron in the ranch house, but Jubal wisely departs. Pinky, having seen him leave Mae's presence, enters the ranch house and reminds her of their former affair in an aggressive, pent-up, and violent way. He warns Mae not to invite Jubal up to the house again and to always call on *him* to satisfy her desires when Shep is away from the ranch. Mae appears rightly terrified of the hostile and domineering Pinky. Steiger's performance is an intriguing precursor of sorts to his brilliant later portrayal of the ruthless, self-centered, repressed, and lustfully jealous Komarovsky in David Lean's epic *Doctor Zhivago* (1965). Much like Borgnine, Steiger is a very physical performer and uses his stocky body to dramatic and highly expressive effect here, easily evoking a sense of threatening menace.[14] We know that there will be a showdown between Pinky and Jubal because of the former's jealousy over Mae's new affections for the latter. But we also anticipate that there may be a possible confrontation between Shep and Pinky because of the complicated romantic and power relationships developing at the ranch.

Later, as Jubal dines with Shep and Mae, Shep asks Jubal to be his new foreman since he will be away at many meetings of the Cattlemen's Association. He needs someone trustworthy to run the ranch, admitting that he has faith in Jubal and that he recognizes various weaknesses in his other men, despite their experience. Shep turns on his player piano and

FIGURE 37. Mae Horgan (Valerie French) lustfully clutches ranch hand Jubal Troop (Glenn Ford) in Delmer Daves's *Jubal* (1956). Courtesy of the Museum of Modern Art.

encourages Mae and Jubal to dance while he remains absorbed by his musical toy. The ranch owner, a wholly decent and trusting man but also naive when it comes to his wife, seems oblivious to the possibility that Mae could be interested romantically in their new foreman. When Shep eventually goes upstairs and out of their view, Mae plants a kiss on Jubal.

Shep makes it known the next day that Jube will be the new foreman, and Pinky predictably objects, asking for the reason. Shep replies, "I trust him." There is immediate resistance from Pinky, and after Jubal rides over the ridge on his horse, Pinky shoots over the hill close to Jubal, releasing his anger about the recent turn of events. Jubal rides quickly back to confront Pinky and fires his pistol at a tree directly next to Pinky to put him in his place. We now have an emotional dynamic in place that has conspicuous parallels with that of *Othello*. Pinky is a scheming Iago-like villain who envies his colleague's recent promotion and who possesses the jealous lust of a Roderigo to boot. Jubal is the loyal Cassio-like victim of others' machinations, and Mae is a Desdemona-like figure, but one who in this case has truly adulterous intentions. Shep, of course, takes the place of the duped and doomed title character of Shakespeare's classic tragedy.[15]

Love triangles, especially those that breed conflict between rival westerners, tend to be a recurring dramatic situation in the genre. This adds extra emotional tension to narratives that are already highlighted by action-packed physical confrontations and heart-pounding showdowns between gun-wielding opponents. And these situations also remind us of the important role of the female in the Western. Typically the woman either represents the domestic virtues of civilization—and so the man who fights for her struggles symbolically for the sake of a future society where violence has been tamed—or she is the wanton woman who has succumbed to the primitive ways of the Old West.

Going back to the very early days, we may recall the competition between Standing Rock and Little Bear for the hand of their beloved Rising Moon in D.W. Griffith's 1909 tale of Indian romance, *The Mended Lute*, along with the story of how reckless Joe's desire for a married girl leads him to seek revenge against her husband in Griffith's 1912 one-reeler *Under Burning Skies* (see chapter 1). As discussed in chapter 2, both Lige and Roddy pursue Letty Mason in *The Wind*, and as mentioned earlier in this chapter, there is the rivalry between brothers Lewt and Jesse in their shared desire for Pearl in Vidor's *Duel in the Sun*. In Ford's *My Darling Clementine*, the title character grows closer to Wyatt Earp as her former love, Doc Holliday, pushes her farther away, angered that she has come all the way out West to seek him. Vance Jeffords is torn between her affections for Juan Herrera and her tangled feelings for Rip Darrow in Mann's *The Furies*, while Howie Kemp begins to fall in love with Lina Patch, even as he must bring her current companion, Ben Vandergroat, to justice, in Mann's *The Naked Spur* (1953). And perhaps the greatest of all Western love triangles is offered in Ford's *The Man Who Shot Liberty Valance*, in which Hallie is torn between idealistic Ransom Stoddard and pragmatic rancher-gunslinger Tom Doniphon (see chapter 8). Also like *Jubal, Valance* is a Western that demonstrates the powerful psychological effects of the past on a man's current conception of himself.

Pinky later tries to stir up serious trouble by telling Shep that Jubal had interfered with his attempt to expel a group of Mormons from his land, and that Jubal did so because he took a liking to a girl in the group. Shep, sharing his new foreman's sense of compassion and decency, expectedly takes Jubal's side, saying that he had already heard that there were sick people in the group. Meanwhile, Mae runs out to the barn to meet Jubal, but he rebuffs her advances. She explains to Jube that she is in an unhappy marriage and confesses that Shep regards her as little more than a "heifer." After Jube asks why she has not left her husband, Mae tells him that she once had many men after her but that Shep told her he was a "cattle king." Mae is presented as an unsatisfied wife who married for comfort and money rather than for authentic love and true passion. She tells Jube that her life at Shep's ranch is a "thousand acres of loneliness," and these words recall the dismal life and marriage of Lillian Gish's Letty Mason in *The Wind* (see chapter 2), not to mention Gish's Laura Belle McCanles in *Duel in the Sun,* as discussed earlier in this chapter. Mae attempts to continue her seduction of Jube, but he tells her that Shep is his friend and that this encounter is the "last time." Mae then expresses envious resentment over the recent gossip that Jube has found himself a new girl with the Mormon clan.

We soon witness a character-revealing scene between Jube and the Mormon girl, Naomi (Felicia Farr)—a scene to which the story has been slowly building, at least in terms of its references to Jubal's troubled past. He finally discloses a crucial event from his childhood that has had a lasting influence on his adult life. Jube's "therapy session" with Naomi is brief but highly illuminating. In the pursuit of attaining greater self-knowledge and personal wholeness through sustained introspection, an individual may come to discover that certain past experiences, perhaps long repressed and forgotten, have played a crucial role in shaping his present personality. One of the essential components of Freud's psychological theory is the strong influence of childhood experiences, especially traumas, on the adult psyche.[16] *Jubal,* while hardly the story of a "cowboy on the couch," is nonetheless the story of a man who has looked deeply within his heart and who comes to share the fruits of his reflection with another human being, particularly with someone he can trust.

Jube tells Naomi that he has never had a real home, and that in childhood, while he and his father shared a close bond, he had nevertheless been hated by his mother, no doubt because of his unintended birth. He and his parents had once lived on a riverboat, and when he came close to drowning in the river on one occasion, his mother had merely stared down at him, hoping he would drown and doing nothing to save him. The background music becomes tense and dramatic as Jubal describes how his father, having heard his cries, jumped into the water to save him but in doing so was struck by the propeller blade of an approaching riverboat while holding his young son away from danger. His mother then looked down at his father's retrieved body and asked her son why he could not have been the one who died rather than her husband. After conveying this former secret of his past, Jubal ponders self-reflectively why he has said all of this in front of someone he barely knows, something he has never done before. Naomi, now in tears and trying to comprehend such unnatural behavior on the part of a mother, declares that his story has made her "beholden" to him. A Brando or a Clift would have undoubtedly brought a more dramatic intensity to such a scene and would have also contributed a greater aura of initial mystery and danger to the character of Jubal Troop. However, Ford does a solid job of conveying the type of stoic dignity and ordinary decency that explains why Shep and Naomi trusted Jubal and expressed affection for him in the first place.

The idea of the past shaping the future in psychological terms plays a key role in many a Western, but most especially in the "neurotic" and "Freudian" Westerns of the 1950s.[17] In these character-oriented Westerns, the protagonist (like Jubal) becomes more identifiable for the viewer once this figure becomes better known to others (and even to himself), typically through the revelation of an incident from the past that has played a major role in making him the kind of person he is at present. *Jubal* is a clear example of this in that the title character, an enigmatic stranger whose motivations and worldview are only minimally exhibited during the first half of the film, eventually conveys a revealing autobiographical fact that reaches far back into his past—in Jubal's case, back to a childhood trauma. The viewer feels from the outset that Jubal is a generally decent man who has compassion for others and who deeply desires to settle down, but we now know the reasons for his world-weariness, self-protective sensitivity, and occasional doubts about human nature.

A similar narrative unfolds in Mann's *The Naked Spur* (1953), for example, where the audience is held in a temporary state of unknowing about the reasons why the bounty hunter Howie Kemp (James Stewart) is so fiercely determined to find his prey, Ben Vandergroat (Robert Ryan), and bring him back to civilization. Is the protagonist driven by greed for the bounty offered, by a desire for personal revenge, by a sense of justice, or all three combined? We do not find out for sure until later in the movie, when it is revealed that Howie's wife had left him for another man and sold his treasured ranch while he was away fighting in the Civil War. Kemp knows that Ben is a no-good outlaw, but he is primarily out for the bounty because he needs the money to repurchase his ranch, not necessarily for the sake of adhering to some code of justice. It is the past trauma of having lost his wife, home, and chosen livelihood that has turned Howie into a stubborn, desperate loner with only one goal on his mind as a means to, he hopes, a redemptive end. He is a man who becomes eventually torn by his competing values.

The character Howie Kemp in *The Naked Spur* and the title character in *Jubal* have, in their respective ways, been shaped by a significant, life-altering experience in their past—though Jubal is haunted by an incident that extends all the way back to his youth and, most problematically, includes his experience of a mother's hatred. In each film we encounter a main character, solitary and weary of his life in the wilderness, whose intentions and choices remain enigmatic to a degree until a moment of revelation occurs. In addition, both movies make highly effective use of the landscape, perhaps to draw a contrast between the perpetual beauty of nature and the occasional ugliness of human nature—and also to show that humans are as molded and limited by their physical environment as they are by their own personal histories.

Opposed to the character-revealing narratives in many of the films by Daves and Mann, there are the more traditional Westerns where we basically know a westerner's character or personality from the outset. In these films we watch as a protagonist, whose past we either know right away or never really know, has a moment of inner transformation. For instance, we know nothing about the past of William S. Hart's Blaze Tracy in *Hell's Hinges,* or that of Cheyenne Harry in *Straight Shooting,* and yet we become acquainted with them as fearless gunslingers who undergo their respective moral awakenings after feeling sudden compassion for an innocent woman in trouble (see chapter 1). In such films, the westerner's character or personality, or the dramatic experience that helped to shape it, is not *unveiled* after first posing a mystery for the audience; the westerner simply changes from "bad man" to "good man" at a certain point in the narrative, and that is that.

In Ford's *Stagecoach,* Ringo (John Wayne) also presents us with no great personal enigma; Hatfield (John Carradine) is the only character in the group of passengers who seems to possess some secret from the past. Most of what we need to know about Ringo is delivered from the start: he is a young, good-hearted gunslinger who has recently busted out of jail in order to avenge the murder of his brother. We do witness the demonstration of Ringo's inherent dignity and compassion as the movie progresses, particularly through his love of Dallas, but it takes no more than a few moments after meeting him to know his basic character.

At the other extreme of the genre, and contrary to the process of character disclosure that forms the core of many 1950s Westerns such as *Jubal* and *The Naked Spur,* there are those postmodern films in which westerners remain enigmatic (or even abstractly superficial) throughout the entire narrative. These are in many ways "antipsychological" films, in that they attempt no substantial exploration of the protagonist's psyche, present no major transformation of self, and tend to be style-driven rather than character-driven. The clearest example is the "Man with No Name" character that Clint Eastwood portrays in Sergio Leone's "Dollars" trilogy (*A Fistful of Dollars, For a Few Dollars More,* and *The Good, the Bad, and the Ugly*), along with those mysterious and archetypal strangers whom Eastwood plays in a few of his own Westerns—primarily *High Plains Drifter* and *Pale Rider.* These are characters who are there simply because they are there, having emerged almost supernaturally from a misty horizon or blur of desert haze, and who typically return there, having done what they needed to do in the situation at hand (see chapter 10 for a fuller discussion of these and other Eastwood Westerns.)

It is true that such Westerns may be compared in at least one important way with many of the more psychological Westerns of the postwar and Cold War period, in that they too tend to reduce or eliminate references to social-historical contexts and primarily focus on individuals and their immediate situations of drama or action. However, the abstract and static characterizations of the westerners in these more contemporary Westerns must ultimately set them apart from the deep concern with character and personality that were the hallmarks of midcentury films by such directors as Mann and Daves.

French film scholar and theoretician André Bazin suggests precisely this kind of distinguishing quality of the postwar Western in his 1955 essay "The Evolution of the Western." Bazin chooses the terms *sincerity* and *novelistic* in order to capture some of what distinguishes the 1950s "super-Western" (as he categorizes this kind of film in the quote at the beginning of this chapter) from other movies in the genre, particularly in terms of the extra "something" (usually a serious consideration of moral, existential, or psychological themes) that is intentionally integrated into these films so that they may transcend the traditional parameters and constraints of the genre. Bazin tells us:

> I have hesitated a great deal over what adjective best applies to these westerns of the fifties. At first I thought to turn to words like "feeling," "sensibility," "lyricism." . . . It is with an eye on the style of the narrative, rather than on the subjective attitude of the director to the genre, that I will finally choose my epithet. I say freely of the westerns I have yet to name—the best in my view—that they are "novelistic." By this I mean that without departing from the traditional themes they enrich them from within by the originality of their characters, their psychological flavor, an engaging individuality, which is what we expect from the hero of a novel.[18]

The character-revealing nature of many of the midcentury Westerns, especially those like *Jubal*, is one of the primary qualities distinguishing these more novelistic films from earlier classical and later postmodern Westerns. The eventual disclosure of the westerner's inner self through crucial decision making, demonstrative action, and confession puts emphasis on the principle of individuality. This disclosure reminds us that, even amid America's collective projects of frontier taming and civilization building, there could be no community or nation without the unique individuals whose interior lives were shaped by their pasts as well as by their physical environments. At a time in history when the idea of America was still being realized, these individuals were forced at special moments to confront the personal task of their own *self*-realization.

CHAPTER 8

John Ford's Later Masterpieces

"The Searchers" and "The Man Who Shot Liberty Valance"

THE SEARCHERS

The great master of the American Western film, John Ford, played a key role in the transformation of the genre that took place between the end of World War II and the mid-1960s. Ford's postwar cavalry films, as discussed in chapter 7, introduced narrative-related elements of revisionism that included critical views of expansionist idealism, Western heroism, and the confrontation with Native Americans. His classic *My Darling Clementine* is noirlike in certain aspects of its visual scheme and most especially in its focus on the morally and psychologically complex character of Doc Holliday. It should not be surprising, therefore, that Ford deepened this kind of exploration in two later masterpieces, *The Searchers* (1956) and *The Man Who Shot Liberty Valance* (1962).

The Searchers features Monument Valley and John Wayne in equal and glorious measure. Frank Nugent, in his collaboration with director Ford, crafted a brilliant screenplay that was based on a novel by Alan Le May. The landscape and the reluctant hero are inseparable; in the relentless sun of the desert valley, the toughness and intractability of the one infuse the other. Ethan Edwards (Wayne) had left this land to fight in the Civil War. His current and constant roaming among the majestic rocks, in a tireless search for his captured niece, is in furious response to all that he has lost. His quest becomes a search for his lost soul. The movie is more complex in moral structure than Ford's earlier Westerns, specifically in regard to its pair of male protagonists: one is white and racist, the other mostly white but "one-eighth part Cherokee." The taint of Indian blood lends tension to their desperate efforts to protect and defend two white girls from death or, worse, defilement by "savages." And while some, like director and film scholar Lindsay Anderson, have criticized the way in which Ford heavy-handedly juxtaposes intense drama and broad humor in certain sequences of *The Searchers,* the film in fact draws even more attention to its sense of tragic loss by contrast with the scenes of comic relief.[1]

The movie gained mixed reviews upon its release but has grown exponentially in stature over the years; it is now rated widely as one of the great American films. As Edward Buscombe has stated in his book on *The Searchers,* summarizing general reasons for the greatness of the film: "At the dawn of the second century of cinema *The Searchers* stands, by general assent, as a monument no less conspicuous than the towers of stone which dominate its landscapes. The strength yet delicacy of its *mise en scène,* the splendour of its vistas, the true timbre of its emotions, make it a touchstone of American cinema. *The Searchers* is one of those films by which Hollywood may be measured."[2]

Prior to *The Searchers,* Ford had filmed five Westerns (entirely or in large part) in Monument Valley, which belongs to the Navajo Tribal Park. So attached were Ford and the Navajo people to each other that Ford was given an honorary nickname by the tribe: "Natani Nez" or "Tall Soldier." Wayne was nearly as familiar with the valley, having starred in four of these films. Aside from two other superb Ford Westerns of the mid-twentieth century that were mostly shot in other locations (*3 Godfathers* and *Wagon Master*), these five films—*Stagecoach, My Darling Clementine, Fort Apache, She Wore a Yellow Ribbon,* and *Rio Grande*—constitute as fine and as accomplished a body of work as any Hollywood director's career Westerns (those of Hawks, Mann, Boetticher, and Peckinpah included). Yet these movies precede Ford's two most meaningful Westerns and cannot fully prepare us for the awesome scale, scope, beauty, harshness, terror, and cruelty of *The Searchers.*[3]

In the later phase of his career, Ford brought a more critical approach, not only to his depiction of the westerner, but also to the overall story of the evolution of the Old West. Ford had already hinted at this deromanticizing turn, in *Fort Apache,* in which the conflict between heroic ideal and flawed reality is emphasized, and in *Yellow Ribbon,* where the military hero meets with repeated failure before retirement (see chapter 7). *The Searchers, Sergeant Rutledge* (1960), *The Man Who Shot Liberty*

FIGURE 38. The funeral rites for the Edwards family are about to be interrupted by a westerner's angry impatience in John Ford's classic Western *The Searchers* (1956). *From left to right:* Ethan Edwards (John Wayne), the Reverend Captain Samuel Clayton (Ward Bond), Martin Pawley (Jeffrey Hunter), and an unidentified woman. Courtesy of the Museum of Modern Art.

Valance, and *Cheyenne Autumn* (1964) were the results of Ford's later desire to complicate and demythologize such a story. *Sergeant Rutledge* explores issues of racism and injustice in the western cavalry, and *Cheyenne Autumn* empathizes with the perspective of the suffering Indians who attempt to journey homeward after being confined and dehumanized.[4] But *The Searchers* and *Liberty Valance* are the true masterpieces within Ford's later project of disclosing the dark underbelly of the American West's progress from wilderness to civilization.

Despite the losses, sacrifices, and obstacles that the Western hero must overcome, and along with an acute awareness of the morally questionable side of the westerner's personality, Ford almost always offers us an overall sense of optimism about the social and political advances that the Western communities depicted in his films are undertaking in their quest for a more rational order of existence. For example, even though *The Searchers* presents us with a clear portrait of the horrors and struggles that the settlers and ranchers in the West often had to face, there is a notable expression of forward-looking determination given by Mrs. Jorgensen (Olive Carey, the real-life wife of early Western star Harry Carey Sr.) to her husband (John Qualen) and guest Ethan Edwards. Despite the deaths of her son and of the Edwards family at the hands of the Comanche, and in spite of the fact that they must now endure the ongoing brutality of such a hard land, Mrs. Jorgensen predicts better things to come if they stay the course: "It just happens we be Texicans. 'Texican' is nothing but a human way out on a limb, this year and next . . . maybe for a hundred more. I don't think it'll be forever. Someday this country is going to be a fine good place to be. Maybe it needs our bones in the ground before that time can come."

The Searchers is hardly a nihilistic movie, especially if we take as our guidelines Mrs. Jorgensen's prediction and Ethan's act of self-redemption at the end of the film. It is a film about heroic sacrifice and retribution, with an underlying lesson about the need to hope for better days to come. But as much as this film teaches us about the beauties and triumphs of the human spirit, it does not shy away from the specter of death and destruction. Beyond the borders of family and community reside the emptiness and danger of the desert and mountains. The film continually reminds us of the abyss of nothingness that always lies on the other side of our desire to persevere. With such a realistic and pragmatic lesson in mind, we learn a newfound respect for those larger-than-life figures, like Ethan Edwards of *The Searchers* and Tom Doniphon of *Liberty Valance,* who have helped to clear a path in the wilderness so as to make way for a more ordered and civilized world.

It is 1868 when Ethan, an ex-Confederate soldier, returns to the Texas home of his brother Aaron (Walter Coy), his sister-in-law Martha (Dorothy Jordan), and their three children. He appears out of the desert suddenly and inexplicably, first glimpsed by Martha as she exits her front door in the opening shot to get a better view of the approaching "stranger." We view her as she moves from pitch-black interior to gloriously sunlit exterior, a rectangular-framed ode to the beauty of Monument Valley and presented in a manner (a frame-within-a-frame) that implicitly emphasizes the way in which theater audiences will experience the landscape of this film through a similar rectangular "window" onto the world (i.e., via the movie screen in a darkened cinema). The film's recurring use of doorways and cave or tepee entrances as framing devices invites multiple interpretive possibilities, ranging from a straightforward contrast between home and wilderness to the more intriguing suggestion

FIGURE 39. The iconic closing shot of *The Searchers*: Ethan Edwards departs once again into the desert, framed by the doorway of the Jorgensen home. Courtesy of the Museum of Modern Art.

of the interior as a kind of "womb" from which Edwards (and other solitary, celibate westerners like him) are typically excluded.

Some avid students of *The Searchers,* and Peter Lehman most notably, have proposed various ways in which the opening shot of the film, with its obvious contrast between interior and exterior, should be understood symbolically—especially given the recurrence of this kind of contrast in other framing choices throughout the movie, including the famous closing shot that parallels the opening of the film.[5] However, in his persuasive article "Ways of Knowing: Peter Lehman and *The Searchers,*" Tom Paulus argues that Ford's use of the aperture shot in such scenes might be more convincingly understood as a pragmatic way of dealing with the widescreen VistaVision process used for this movie, a process that welcomes strategies for dividing up the screen and focusing the audience's attention—and possibly also as a tribute to Ford's own similar use of such framed shots (for practical filmmaking purposes) in his earlier silent Westerns.[6] Either way, Ford's recurring use of such a framing method makes for magical images that allow the viewer to sometimes feel as if she were viewing, or even being drawn into, a Romantic landscape painting.

FIGURE 40. "The searchers" confer over a recently discovered Comanche spear, framed against the Monument Valley landscape. *From left to right:* Brad Jorgensen (Harry Carey Jr.), Ethan Edwards, and Mose Harper (Hank Worden). Courtesy of the Museum of Modern Art.

Ethan's arrival is a moving homecoming as the family wonders where he has been for the three years that have passed since the Civil War ended. He is uneasily welcomed back into the family structure, and he awkwardly recognizes Martin Pawley (Jeffrey Hunter), the part-Cherokee youth who was adopted by the Edwards family when his parents were massacred. In the few brief opening scenes, Ethan is revealed as the classic westerner: a southerner who fought in the Civil War on the losing side and who has no choice but to become a westerner. He is the epitome of the gunslinging hero who is a "good bad man"—a person who has been on the wrong side of the law for a while (presumably as a gunfighter)—as well as an outsider, a loner with no lover, partner, or best friend to need or guide him.

In a conversation with Peter Bogdanovich, the irascible Ford made it clear that Ethan's true love had been Martha, now his brother's wife: "Well, I thought it was pretty obvious—that his brother's wife was in love with Wayne; you couldn't hit it on the nose, but I think it's very plain to anyone with any intelligence. You could tell from the way she picked up his cape." This explains the degree of awkwardness in the homecoming and suggests one of the possible reasons for Ethan's reluctance to return to his brother's home for so long after the end of the war. Ford also indicated in his interview how we might imagine Ethan's background in the years following the war: "He's the man who came back from the Civil War, probably went over into Mexico, became a bandit, probably fought for Juarez or Maximilian. . . . He was just a plain loner—could never really be a part of the family."[7]

The viewer is nevertheless left with an intentional mystery concerning Ethan's past, and most especially what he has experienced during and just after the war. And unlike other 1950s Westerns such as *Jubal* and *The Naked Spur,* discussed in the previous chapter, *The Searchers* does not provide us with any character-revealing secrets about the main character's recent past, other than the fact that he fought in the war and returned home with a suspicious stash of newly minted gold coins. Ethan's psychological complexity is demonstrated through his present words and actions; and the movie's "strategic opacity" about Ethan's biography (other than his past love for Martha and his ingrained familiarity with the landscape and with his Indian enemies) makes that complexity even more pronounced.[8]

Ethan is the knowing westerner who grew up in the wilderness of the southwestern Texas desert and profoundly understands the terrain, its dangers, and its inhabitants. He is an expert on the Comanche, especially their tricks and their murderous methods; equally well does he recognize and mistrust the white man who will kill for gold. He is a descendant of Lassiter, Zane Grey's rider of the purple sage who was also a gunfighter preoccupied with finding *his* niece. Like Lassiter, Ethan is at one with the landscape; he is ever impatient to be in it, on the move to somewhere. He, too, is a man of violence, who lives by the use of his gun.

Ethan cannot stay indoors, whether during his initial homecoming, when he goes out on the porch as the family retires to bed, throughout his years of wanderings, or at his final homecoming, when he stands outside the sheltering doorway and turns away, stepping off the porch into the desert, alone. Ethan is *in* the landscape, and he is *of* it as much as the Comanche he despises; but he is the more skilled survivor, facing death at the Indians' hands again and again, seemingly without fear. He was an experienced rebel soldier, after all, and perhaps also was a gunfighter in Mexico, as Ford had suggested to Bogdanovich. We are fearful for him, though this extrasized hero replies calmly and comically to such threats—"That'll be the day"—just as he does to Martin Pawley's anguished attempts to be a grown-up. So fearless is Ethan that he never hesitates in his pursuit. He is cunning and cruel, and the pursuer becomes as frightening as the pursued, and just as vengeful.

Lassiter and Ethan belong to different eras of American culture and are products of different perceptions of the West. Lassiter is taught forgiveness by Jane Withersteen. A wealthy rancher, Jane is a kindhearted, generous, and gentle heroine who naively opposes vengeance and retribution until her love for Lassiter conquers her better self. Redemption for Lassiter and Jane is achieved by Lassiter's rolling of a very large stone, Balancing Rock, which murders the villains and locks the lovers forever in the hidden valley beyond Deception Pass. Ethan has no such redeemer. His story is the tragedy of a loner, told at mid-twentieth century—and consequently more pessimistic, perhaps, because its absolutes are shaded in modernist colors. For Edwards is an angry man, angry in every muscle of his towering body and grim face. His gestures are big: his arms swoop to quickly fire his rifle or six-gun or to indicate another meaning of Comanche strategy. He seems immensely powerful, yet he is also swift and graceful as both gunfighter and rider. He speaks in clipped sarcastic phrases, punching out words to emphasize his bleak perception of people and their frailties.

Ethan is, in a name, John Wayne. We cannot imagine another Ethan Edwards; like landscape and character in *The Searchers,* Wayne and Edwards are one. Not since *Red River* has Wayne played a character so driven by anger, pain, and the sheer will to survive the challenges of a harsh Old West. In *Red River,* Wayne's Tom Dunson loses his true love early in the narrative; he is saved, in part, by a young girl, Tess, who carries on the spirit and beauty of his lost Fen, and he ultimately forgives the young Garth, his adopted son, because of Tess (see chapter 6). In *The Searchers,* Ethan's love, Martha, was lost to him, first through her marriage to his brother, then by the brutality of the Comanche. Ethan has little to sustain him throughout his wanderings to find Martha's two daughters—no gal of his own to write to as Martin Pawley has in Laurie Jorgensen (Vera Miles), though Martin sends her but one letter in five years.

Not unlike the Ringo Kid in *Stagecoach,* Ethan is driven by a deep desire for revenge. He is hardly a kid, however, and he often exhibits questionable traits, such as intolerance and an absence of sympathy. Ethan gives in to his rage-filled impulses at certain moments and also reveals his inability to settle down, as is conspicuous in the famous final shot of the movie. Ethan is highly unpredictable, as when he shoots bullets into the eyes of a dead Indian so as to make his spirit wander forever. He is also quite willing to put others' lives at risk when the situation demands it, as when he uses Martin as a sitting (in this case, sleeping) duck, knowing that they will most likely be ambushed by the greedy Mr. Futterman (Peter Mamokos). Ethan does not seem to care whether using an unsuspecting Marty as a decoy might endanger the younger man, and Futterman does indeed get off a shot before Ethan kills him. Luckily, Futterman misses, and Marty quickly realizes that Ethan has callously imperiled his life.

The violence in the film—ranging from the Comanche massacre of the Edwards family and Ethan's discovery of Martha's ravaged corpse to Ethan's finding of Lucy's body and his later scalping of an already dead Scar—always takes place offscreen, leaving such horrific acts and scenes to the power of the viewer's imagination. This is a movie about violence that does not reveal its violence directly to the audience. As Buscombe correctly observes in his book on the movie: "The most heart-wrenching scenes in Ford are when the emotion is only half expressed. 'Heard melodies are sweet, but those unheard/Are sweeter,' Keats wrote. Ford knew the same applied to moments of anguish. It's extraordinary how many moments of violence are suppressed."[9]

Ethan is undoubtedly Ford's most complex and problematic hero. This has much to do with Ethan's commitment to avenging his loved ones' murders, and this desire for retribution is fueled most intensely by his hatred of "the red man" and, later on, by his fear that his niece Debbie (Natalie Wood) has been sexually defiled by Chief Scar (Henry Brandon). We would not regard Ethan as morally ambiguous, most likely, if he were simply a killer bent on revenge solely for justified purposes, but his thirst for vengeance is mixed with blatant racism. Ford (along with screenwriter Nugent) makes this clear throughout the film. Marty, for example, tells Laurie that he fears what Ethan might do to Debbie when he finds her, based on the way that Ethan looks when he even hears the word *Comanche*. And Ethan later confirms our worst fears when, pistol drawn, he orders Marty to "stand aside" so that he can get a clear shot at Debbie after she has run to rejoin them. While revenge against Scar for the murders of Ethan's loved ones may earn our sympathy, his urge to destroy his niece if she has been assimilated by the "Other" tends to raise major questions about his morality. Such questions lend psychological depth and complexity to the character of

Ethan. The viewer already feels troubled, in fact, by the very possibility that a character played by *John Wayne* even contemplates such an action—just as some viewers may be disturbed, say, by the idea that Cary Grant plays a potential wife-killer in Hitchcock's *Suspicion* (1941).

Ford's camera zooms in on Ethan's face as he visits a fort where white females who have been rescued from captivity are being sheltered. Ethan voices his view that these women are now "Comanche": he equates physical defilement with total assimilation. Ethan turns at one point and offers a sober glance back at one white woman who has visibly lost her mind after such horror and suffering. The woman plays with a doll, blank-eyed and insane, evoking a nightmarish analogy with Debbie, who had also clutched a doll when she was taken by Scar. The rapid zoom-in that allows us to focus on Ethan's disturbed reaction makes for a powerful shot, and Wayne's facial expression connotes what Ethan is really thinking, without the need for words—true to Ford's great talent for substituting images for dialogue.[10] Ethan confirms for himself here that by killing Debbie—if she indeed still exists, and if he *does* finally find her—he would be doing her a favor after she has been, in his eyes, so dehumanized, so "scarred." He now sees Debbie as little more than an inanimate object, symbolized perhaps by the doll clutched by the mad woman in the fort as well as the doll held by Debbie when she was a little girl.

Ford and *The Searchers* have often been charged with racism, given that the director along with his screenwriter mythologizes a violence-prone westerner who harbors such a deep hatred of his Indian enemy. The film appears, on the surface anyway, to justify Ethan's obsessive desire to destroy Scar and the Comanche, given the horror of what has happened to the Edwards family. That seeming justification is complicated, however, by the fact that Scar later claims to have massacred the white people in the area because his own sons were killed by the whites. And what truly amplifies the movie's emphasis on the portrait of Ethan as an avid racist is his eventual desire to destroy Debbie rather than to save her. The idea of her sexual defilement at the hands of Ethan's enemy, an enemy who has killed (and may also have raped) his beloved Martha, is too much for him to bear. He would rather see Debbie's "infected" body dead and her soul liberated than continue imagining her at the side of Scar. Ethan's concern with the possibility of Debbie's physical impurity and his implicit goal of saving her soul harkens back, in fact, to the start of the movie, when the Reverend Captain Samuel Johnston

Clayton (Ward Bond) asks little Debbie (Lana Wood) whether she had been baptized. If Ethan is willing to kill his own niece, someone for whom he has searched for seven long years, chiefly because of her sexual union with a Comanche, then it is clear that he has come to view one's assimilation to another race as a defining property of that person.

Further, Ethan's attitude is doubly complicated because he and Scar seem to mirror one another as creatures of the wilderness. As Edward Buscombe states, "Scar, the Comanche chief whom Ethan pursues, is in some sense Ethan's unconscious, his id if you like. In raping Martha, Scar has acted out in brutal fashion the illicit sexual desire which Ethan harboured in his heart."[11] Jim Kitses similarly observes, "When the family is massacred and Debbie abducted by the Comanche, their leader, Scar, comes into focus as a distorted reflection of Ethan himself."[12] And as Tag Gallagher tells us, "For the white Ethan Edwards (John Wayne), the Comanche Scar is the 'Other' that he can stare at but cannot see. Worse, he is Ethan's doppelgänger, everything in himself that he despises. . . . Thus Ethan must kill Scar in order to destroy the complex of violence within himself."[13]

Gallagher views Ford's film as filled with clearly intentional examples of racist distortions and demonizations of the "Other"—including Ford's very use of a white actor as Chief Scar—and yet maintains that the film is not *itself* racist. This is because *The Searchers* makes this theme prominent and invites the audience to reflect on such a theme, an invitation that is especially pronounced in terms of Ethan's own "mirroring" of Scar. This is a convincing reading of the movie, one that does justice to the complexities of the narrative. Such an interpretation is also supported by obvious tensions and contradictions in the movie—such as the fact that Ethan and Marty treat Marty's newly acquired "wife" ("Look"), the Indian woman whom he had unwittingly purchased, in a highly derogatory fashion, and yet they both show clear signs of mourning her death later in the film.

Ford and Nugent make us pause elsewhere at times when we are called on to judge the Comanche as pure savages who deserve their fate. Ethan is not the only racist in his community, since Laurie later tells Marty that if Debbie were indeed living with Scar, then she (along with Martha, were she still alive) would have also wanted her dead. Debbie, when Ethan finally finds her, appears as a serene and well-assimilated member of Scar's tribe, not having suffered the kind of mistreatment and cruelty that drove the rescued females at the fort to lose their minds. And perhaps the most puzzling examples of contradiction or peculiar juxtaposition in the movie are the radically sudden transformations in thinking that are undertaken by both Ethan and Debbie at the very end of the film. Debbie, who steadfastly told Marty that she did not want to leave her "people," quickly changes her mind almost overnight; and of course Ethan decides in a split second to save Debbie rather than destroy her once he has elevated her in his arms.

There is therefore good evidence from the intricacies and complexities of the film that Ford, who had played upon and against stereotypical characters throughout his long career, created a movie that is not itself a racist "object" but rather is one in which racism is made a thematic subject of consciousness-raising, evoking questions rather than delivering absolute value judgments. Kitses also follows this approach in his analysis of the movie, though he wisely qualifies this interpretation by emphasizing that the movie provides a highly "unequal treatment of white and Indian worlds," given the focus throughout the film on the perspectives of those assaulted by or pursuing the Comanche.[14] As Kitses puts it, "Ford's design is to force the audience to confront its own racist inclinations as Ethan's extreme state becomes clearer. . . . Any claim that the film embraces racism and demonises the Comanche must account for Debbie's assimilation and the film's dark portrait of its hero."[15]

The character of Ethan reminds the viewer that the path to civilization begins in the heart of the wilderness, and that the establishment of what is "reasonable" and "good" sometimes demands acts and methods that might be deemed "irrational" or "evil" according to society's conventions. The instincts that lead to necessary or praiseworthy actions may also result in the eruption of chaotic, dangerous impulses at times: they emerge from the same subconscious wellspring of emotion. For instance, in one notable scene where winter snows have fallen and the searchers' hunger has become intense, Ethan shoots at a herd of buffalo with the need of sustenance clearly in mind. Yet Ethan continues firing wildly at the herd even after the animals have scattered. Marty, shocked by Ethan's sudden release of irrational energy, recognizes that this act of useless shooting makes no sense. He attempts to knock Ethan's rifle to the ground and the older man, half-crazed and eyes blazing, strikes Marty to the earth and grabs another rifle so as to continue the frenzied firing. Ethan expresses his desire to keep the Comanche from feeding on these same buffalo by destroying the herd, a visibly futile task, and his demeanor is no longer that of a rational man.

FIGURE 41. Ethan Edwards returns to the Jorgensen home with the rescued Debbie (Natalie Wood). Courtesy of the Museum of Modern Art.

We witness Ethan's fury unleashed, but it is this type of anger that drives him continuously toward his goal of finding Debbie and killing Scar. It is also the kind of passion and determination, no matter how excessive it may become, that was sometimes required in eliminating a threat from a savage land and in clearing a way for the arrival of civilization. In conquering a wilderness and building a nation, the power of ideals is inherently limited, even fragile, given the resistance of reality. And brutal violence is often required in removing obstacles to progress, or so the Western myth often tells us. Ford's later *The Man Who Shot Liberty Valance* makes this point even more emphatically.

After his Comanche enemies have been eliminated, Ethan brings Debbie home; he does not, as Martin fears, kill her. It is as if the physical act of picking up Debbie in his arms once again, as he did during his homecoming when she was a little girl, is enough to convince Ethan that he has been wrong in wanting "Debbie" (i.e., her defiled body) dead.[16] According to such an interpretation, this is a moral awakening triggered by a nostalgic remembrance that is in turn occasioned by the physical embrace of a specific individual. Ideologies and stereotypes do not matter here as much as direct human contact and the value of a unique person, especially if she is the daughter of a loved one. And Ethan and Marty are, at the end of their long journey together, reconciled.

The final return of Ethan, Martin, and Debbie to a safe homestead must be in memory of Martha. Though hearth and happiness are unattainable by Ethan, he has overcome his hatred, and he acts, finally, out of love. In this sense, Wayne completes the portrait of the classic westerner that was conceived by Harry Carey Sr. and William S. Hart: the "good bad man" who responds to a woman in a way that reforms his character and makes him do what is right, even if it means riding off alone at the end. In the final shot, Ethan turns away from the house, grasping his arm as he steps off the porch—most probably in tribute to silent Western star Harry Carey, who made such a gesture his trademark.[17] Ethan turns away from the present into his memories of the past, and most especially his memory of Martha. It is a moment he must hold alone; it cannot be shared. Such reflection covers the deepest emotion, and it almost overpowers Ethan as it does us, for here we have reached the deepest layer of the Western, the sense of what has been lost in the struggle. The search may have helped Ethan find some part of his soul, but he will never recover from all that he has lost as soldier, brother, and lover.

THE MAN WHO SHOT LIBERTY VALANCE

No longer mourn for me when I am dead . . .
Do not so much as my poor name rehearse,
But let your love even with my life decay,
Lest the wise world should look into your moan
And mock you with me after I am gone.
—William Shakespeare, Sonnet 71

Ford's *The Man Who Shot Liberty Valance* is perhaps the most meaningful, the most tragic, and the most emotionally powerful of all Western films. It takes on the notions of myth and legend and the theme of nation-building, with all the complexities and contradictions that come with imposing new law on an older and more primitive order. The movie is full of ambivalence and sorrow but leavened with comic villainy and journalistic wit. With *Liberty Valance,* Ford brought Shakespeare to the screen, as he had begun to do with *My Darling Clementine.* But unlike many other Ford Westerns, this one is not as visually striking and hardly makes use of any on-location shooting in authentic

Western terrain. Most likely Ford meant for us to focus exclusively on the tragedy and its characters and ideas. The action is shot in black and white and set on a small stage, tight and compressed so its protagonists cannot escape into the depth of the landscape.

In creating a dialogue between truth and myth, *The Man Who Shot Liberty Valance* sets a tone of intense nostalgia and loss. The code of the Old West must be superseded by a system of law and order based on the ideas of state and federation; the knight with a gun gives way to the scrivener of law. Overriding all else is the notion that the new is possible only through the sacrifice of the old. The irony is unmistakable: true nobility is shown by the gunfighter who kills the outlaw but lets the credit go to the lawyer, the man who literally cannot shoot straight. *Liberty Valance*, which presents the late-nineteenth-century phase of the settlement of the West through the imposition of law and the growth of an ordered society, nonetheless mourns the loss of a heroic past and questions the results for modern times. It is a revisionist film, growing out of the transformation of the genre that began in the immediate post–World War II era and that was developed through the works of directors such as Mann, Daves, and Boetticher (see chapter 7). And while the movie is visually stylized in the manner of one of Ford's early silent Westerns, it is revisionist in terms of its narrative trajectory—particularly given its critical questioning of the Western mythos and its eventual "deflation" of the two men who otherwise would have been its heroic exemplars. As Jim Kitses remarks, "If *Liberty Valance* appears to be Ford's ultimate personal statement, it is because the film evidences a post-modern complexity, at once nostalgic and critical, a celebration of myth and its deconstruction, a radical recycling, the director's dual vision brought here into its sharpest focus."[18]

As we have seen earlier in this chapter, *The Searchers* is obsessed with loss, but there is a kind of rebirth or redemption through mutual forgiveness. Edwards has survived, though he must go on alone. Hawks's *Red River* also concludes with forgiveness, or at least understanding, among Tom Dunson, Matthew Garth, and Tess Millay, through a final scene twisted into a comic mode (see chapter 6). *Liberty Valance* offers no such comfort: its opening and closing scenes are the Western's most melancholic. At the start we see that symbol of modern civilization, a train, bringing Senator Stoddard (James Stewart) and his wife, Hallie (Vera Miles), from the East to Shinbone in their home state to attend a private funeral; the time is the early twentieth century. Later that same day, after their visit and the senator's telling of the "true" history of their lives, another train takes them away again. As the locomotive pulls its passenger cars out of town, we see the politically important man and his wife seated together, aged and tired, not at all heroic but rather deeply, sorrowfully aware of what has been lost.

The central narrative is tightly enclosed between the arrival and departure of this elderly couple. Their mourning, and ours, can only be understood once we have learned of their earlier years in Shinbone, for this is a mystery story as much as it is a Western. The true hero (John Wayne as Tom Doniphon) has died before the film begins, and his story is unfolded in flashbacks during the wake for this forgotten man. Introduced by Stoddard, the principal and extended flashback begins with the robbery of a stagecoach. The holdup is brutally carried out by the archetypal outlaw, the man with no morals known as Liberty Valance (Lee Marvin), who rampages throughout the territory, unchecked by local law. Stoddard, a young lawyer brimming with moral idealism, is whipped and his law books are torn apart. Out of this humiliating start he will become a hero, considerably helped along by Doniphon, who is another kind of gunfighter, thoroughly unlike Valance.

After the holdup and beating, Doniphon finds Stoddard and brings him to Shinbone. Later he will rescue Stoddard at the moment of crisis, the inevitable showdown. Since it is Wayne who portrays this enigmatic savior, he should be the true hero of our story, even if a reluctant one. But since Jimmy Stewart plays the lawyer, *he* must *also* be the hero, though his self-righteously angry character makes us occasionally squirm (as do Stewart's expert portrayals in Hitchcock's thrillers and Mann's Westerns, expressing what David Thomson aptly calls "his suppressed malevolence as an adventurer hero").[19] Here is a struggle of mythical dimensions. The gods' favorite heroes have strength and power but are flawed; egocentric and jealous, their ultimate duel is with each other. But the struggle takes a surprising direction when love comes up against reason, and he who loves the most makes the necessary sacrifice.

Doniphon's love is the old-fashioned kind, a seemingly selfish and possessive love for Hallie, a pretty but uneducated woman. He intends for her to work hard at his side to build a ranch and raise a family. Stoddard's love is that of the teacher, who gives his heroine a new life by instructing her to read and write. Hallie will be *his* helpmate in his future career as a major figure in the nation's government. But there is no doubt where Hallie's heart lies, both at the beginning and the end of *Liberty Valance,* and her tears are ours as we come to understand her personal loss. The new civilization, of which our lawyer-hero is a leader, has taken Hallie far from the land and the people she loves. She is the wife of the first governor of the state, who subsequently becomes its senator and is viewed as a future vice president. But life in Washington has offered Hallie no cactus roses.

We see the rose in bloom but not its color, since this is a black-and-white film. *Liberty Valance* opens on a brief shot of the landscape, intimate and contained—pretty enough to be Ford's landscape of memory, his beloved Ireland, but for the sagebrush. We watch as that great instrument of Western progress, the train, comes round the bend carrying easterners in comfort and security to a newer, safer, more modern society. Interestingly, in this Western we are not told the date or which state this is (although the short story that is the source of the film declares the date of the funeral as 1910).[20] A couple arrives quietly in Shinbone: too quietly for the press, who will demand an explanation, on our behalf as much as their own. But we already know, because of the sorrowful stillness surrounding this pair and the silent anguish of the woman clutching a large hatbox, that this is a journey into the past. This film wrenches the heart at its beginning, in its deceptive simplicity, its economy of dialogue, and its deliberate pace that is enhanced by the whistle of the train. There is no major musical theme to clue us in; the opening scenes are all the more powerful for their strong contrast to the Cyril Mockridge score played heartily through the credits. There is no preamble of jolly, bustling town folk tipping hats, no "Howdy, Ma'am" outside the general store, no kids playing with dogs, no happy ranchers driving up in their wagons.

Liberty Valance is all business—and a sorrowful, bitter one it is indeed. An old man, Link Appleyard (Andy Devine), greets Senator and Mrs. Stoddard at the station, and she is achingly glad to see him, moving along to his buckboard wagon and holding her hatbox tightly. A youthful reporter excitedly telephones his boss about the senator's arrival and then begs Stoddard for an interview. It does not take much to distract the senator from the purpose of his visit. When the editor of the *Shinbone Star* adds his request, the senator becomes the pompous glad-hander and tells Hallie that he is "back in business again—politics." He asks Link to take his wife for a drive while he mends "a few political fences."

Hallie sits in the buckboard, her steady gaze quietly registering her sorrow, not bothering to respond to her husband's change of plan. As a politician's wife she must be used to it, yet it cannot matter to her, wrapped as she is in her solitude, nearly overcome with her remembrance of the past. Hallie talks to Link of the changes in Shinbone, and with a catch in her voice she observes its "churches, high school, shops."

Without even looking at each other, the old friends exchange thoughts and decide to ride out "desert way" to have a look around. As Link and Hallie arrive at a burned-out ranch, music slowly rises with the mournful air "Ann Rutledge," the haunting theme from Ford's earlier film *Young Mr. Lincoln* (1939) and a song that therefore symbolizes (for Ford fans, anyway) the death of a loved one. Hallie points to the cactus roses and looks at Link. He knows, without any words spoken, that she would like for him to retrieve one of the roses so she can put it on Tom's coffin.

The metaphor of the garden will play an essential role throughout the film, especially when contrasted with the idea of the wilderness, that primitive chaos from which a cultivated civilization ("the garden") will, one may hope, emerge. It is true that the town of Shinbone, back in the early days when Valance still threatens the townspeople and statehood is yet a distant dream, should certainly not be confused with some Hobbesian "state of nature," a completely lawless condition in which humans are always on the verge of potential warfare with one another as a result of ego-driven competition for limited resources. There are many good-hearted people in Shinbone who, while not fully capable of defending themselves against Liberty Valance, have already entered into an unwritten agreement (what English political philosophers John Locke and Thomas Hobbes would call a "social contract") to get along and live together within an ordered community. There is also a sense of basic law, even if the enforcer of that law, Link Appleyard, is a coward. Nonetheless, with Valance on the prowl and the sheriff a lazy oaf, the town is caught in a limbo between wilderness and garden, between lawlessness and law-governed civilization.

This is precisely the type of tension-between-opposites that the entire film revolves around, particularly when it comes to the Old West's difficult transition to a modern democracy as an ordered system of rights and liberties. As Robert Pippin has demonstrated in his enlightening study *Hollywood Westerns and American Myth: The Importance of Howard Hawks and John Ford for Political Philosophy*, there is much that we can learn here from *Liberty Valance* (and others like it, such as *The Searchers* and *Red River*). These movies instruct us in the nature of legal authority, the significance of passions and desires in individuals' public lives, the idea of the state's legitimate exercise of violence in maintaining justice, the roles of heroism and mythmaking in a democratic society, and the ways in which human beings are either suited or not suited to the political structures that help to govern their lives.[21] Above all, *Liberty Valance* presents an implicit argument that public and private happiness cannot be easily divorced, and that the old order of primitive justice, despite being transcended in large part by the new order of a rights-based democratic republic, is nonetheless retained to some degree in modern society's continuing need to satisfy personal vengeance in terms of state-sanctioned violence.

Stoddard has talked to the newspapermen for some time but cuts off his visit to join Hallie and Link on their return. The Stoddards walk slowly through a back alley to the undertaker's, Link tenderly carrying the hatbox as he limps along after them. Through a carpentry shop, past a dusty stagecoach inside it, they reach a tiny room filled with a plain wooden coffin. There is barely enough space for a bench, and on it sits the stooped, white-haired Pompey (Woody Strode), friend and servant of the deceased, who sheds tears when Hallie takes his hand. We are trembling now with the desire to know who lies in the pine box, but we are not about to see him. We will find out soon enough. The senator looks into the coffin and is shocked to find that there are no boots, spurs, or gun belt on Doniphon's corpse. Link explains that Tom had not carried a handgun for years. Here movie mythology takes over, for this is not a role in a play or an opera that could be performed by any number of well-known artists: we are talking about John Wayne. For Wayne's westerner to be lying in a coffin at the start of the film is so unexpected that we are reluctant to believe it.

The gentlemen of the *Shinbone Star* are wondering the same thing: Who is Tom Doniphon? Why did the senator and his wife come all this way for the funeral of a man completely unknown to them, nowhere mentioned in their newspaper records? The editor refuses to leave them alone, claiming that the readers of his statewide circulation have a right to know and that he has a right to have the story. Here, the editor defends a right to public knowledge, and the movie is in many ways about the rights of individuals and the liberties to which those rights lay claim, the same rights that are at the core of the development of democracy and civilization in the Old West. Stoddard looks to his wife for permission and she nods. Stoddard and the newsmen retreat to the carpentry shop where they will talk in front of the stagecoach, an old relic that has been stored there. A quick cut to a tearful Hallie shows her taking the hatbox, which contains the cactus rose that Link had retrieved for her, and starting to open it. This is the last we will see of the little room with its coffin for some time. The flashback, the narrative heart of the film, is about to begin. Assuming a senatorial posture in the carpentry shop, Stoddard says that the story concerns not only him but also Pompey and

Link. He wipes the dust off the stagecoach and claims it is most likely the same one that brought him to Shinbone. He sets the tone for the flashback as he claps the dust off his hands. The flashback opens on the robbery of the stage with a terse request from Liberty Valance: "Stand and deliver!"

The distinction between truth and legend becomes the subject of this return into the past. Ford and his screenwriters, James Warner Bellah and Willis Goldbeck, concentrate our attention on the ironies that accompany such broad progress, on such a passage from frontier wilderness to justice and order through the imposition of law. We see little wandering through the Western landscape, for the flashback is a journey through time alone, within a precise, fixed space, rather than through time and space as in *The Searchers*. In that earlier film, the Southwest, central to Ford's other Westerns set in Monument Valley, was only one of the locations Ford used to create the long journey of Ethan Edwards. We see less freedom for the protagonists in *Liberty Valance;* their interweaving conflicts are confined within a small moral universe, their destinies determined amid the cramped or tightly framed spaces of the underdressed sets.

Liberty Valance is a Western *without* a regular glimpse of the landscape, unlike many of the classic Westerns, including Ford's *The Searchers* and Peckinpah's *Ride the High Country,* the other great American Western released in 1962. The only examples of natural beauty we see in the flashback are the cactus rose, a symbol of the wilderness before it becomes a garden, and the plain ranch of Tom Doniphon. There is no escape and chase through canyon and desert. Since many of the scenes occur indoors, *Liberty Valance* emerges as a Western drama acted as if on a stage—part mystery, part Shakespearean tragedy, part morality play, characterized by rich dialogue and reflective silence, without the robust physical activity we have come to expect of the genre. Neither the landscape nor extended fights with fists or guns will distract us from the encircling, mournful contemplation of perception and truth. *Liberty Valance* has been accused of being studio-bound, claustrophobic, and visually dull or downright ugly. Nothing seems more deliberate about the film, however, than Ford's choice to shoot in black and white, at the Paramount studio.

The film has the look of Ford's earliest Westerns of the second decade of the twentieth century, such as *Straight Shooting,* which was Ford's original intention.[22] And even from the late 1930s forward—

when color cinematography was first thought preferable, and the camerawork in Ford's productions would be equally stunning in color or black and white—he filmed some of his most meaningful Westerns in black and white: *Stagecoach, My Darling Clementine, Fort Apache, Rio Grande,* and *Wagon Master.*[23] Budgetary constraints, including the producers' possible refusal to spend money on Technicolor, may have influenced or dictated the decision to shoot in black and white. But Ford also explained that the scene of Liberty Valance's death, featuring the showdown between Stoddard and Valance in the shadowy confines of Shinbone's main street, would have never worked in color. In addition, Ford later claimed a personal aesthetic preference. He told Peter Bogdanovich, "Black and white is pretty tough—you've got to know your job and be very careful to lay your shadows properly and get the perspective right. . . . For a good dramatic story, though, I much prefer to work in black and white; you'll probably say I'm old-fashioned, but black and white is real photography."[24]

We are not prepared for a *Rashomon*-like structure, and we do not anticipate that we will see and hear another flashback within the principal flashback. But the closeness and crowdedness of the scenes keep us uncomfortable as the film edges us toward each protagonist's reversal of fortune. Nothing is going to turn out the way we might hope from seeing the flashback's key early scenes in the kitchen of Peter's Place, the town's leading restaurant. The personalities of the four protagonists are sharply drawn: Valance is the most-feared gunslinger of the territory; Doniphon is one of its best-liked and most-respected ranchers; Stoddard is a naive, stubborn idealist, "duly licensed by the territory" to practice law; and Hallie is lovely but unsure of herself and her admirers. Stoddard's character is pegged instantly by the two westerners: Valance calls him "Dude" when he encounters Stoddard's resistance during the robbery, and Doniphon later dubs him "Pilgrim." *Dude* refers to a person from an urban environment, an easterner who has arrived in the West and is presumed to be inexperienced. *Pilgrim* indicates a person who journeys in an alien land, a wayfarer who travels to a given destination, often a shrine or holy place; it can also denote a stray steer, as well as a newcomer to a given region.

Early on, Tom Doniphon shifts from the foreground to the side, and back to stage front again when he wants Hallie's attention. After bringing Stoddard to Peter's Place, where Hallie works as a waitress, Doniphon notices her sympathy for the badly wounded man, who would

FIGURE 42. John Ford's *The Man Who Shot Liberty Valance* (1962): Hallie (Vera Miles, *center*) assists the wounded Ransom Stoddard (James Stewart, lying), as Pompey (Woody Strode, *far left*) and Tom Doniphon (John Wayne, *second to left*) look on. Courtesy of the Museum of Modern Art.

have died had Doniphon not found him and brought him into town. Tom tells Stoddard that he can use Doniphon's credit at the restaurant until he gets back on his feet. But Stoddard wants to arrest Valance, put him in jail, and Doniphon replies that if that is what he has to do, he had better start carrying a gun. Tom follows this up with his succinct encapsulation of the code of the West: "I know those law books mean a lot to you, but not out here. Out here a man settles his own problems." Ranse is appalled and compares Doniphon to Valance, asking what kind of a community he has come to if law and order do not prevail. We might recall here Wyatt Earp's similar question, early in Ford's *My Darling Clementine,* after he arrives in a wild Tombstone: "What kind of town is this?" Ranse tries to continue but collapses, and Hallie angrily declares that a little law and order would not hurt the town. We then witness the arrival of "Mr. Law and Order himself," Link Appleyard, the clownish marshal who enters the kitchen for breakfast, only to learn from Ranse that he should put Valance in jail. Doniphon begins to mock them and to tease Hallie, drinking his coffee and smoking a cigarette, genuinely enjoying himself and his role as a passive observer. Tom calls Stoddard a "tenderfoot," declaring that Valance is the "toughest man south of the Picketwire, next to [him]."[25]

Next comes one of the great confrontation scenes in all of Western cinema. We have been waiting for the moment when Doniphon and Valance will face off, and Ford certainly delivers the goods but denies us an actual gunfight. Intriguingly, this memorable confrontation between our two gunslingers occurs in one of the most domestic of places: Pete's Place. Westerners have large appetites, and the restaurant is already mobbed on Saturday night before the town drunks come to dine. Enter the *Shinbone Star*'s founding editor, Dutton Peabody (Edmond O'Brien), the intellectual drunkard who lectures Hallie about the proprieties concerning the cutlery. Peabody is the quintessential Fordian philosopher, the educated man who, despite his weakness for the bottle, is at the moral center of the story; he may fail or he may succeed, but alcohol never dims his intelligence. Such a character was incarnated as Doc Boone (Thomas Mitchell) in *Stagecoach* and, in part, as Doc Holliday (Victor Mature) in *My Darling Clementine*.

In the kitchen, Stoddard concentrates more on his law book than on washing the dishes, a chore that he does in exchange for his meals. His wet hands cause him to ask Hallie to read the passage he discovered that will put Valance exactly where he needs him (legally speaking, that is). Reluctantly, Hallie admits that she cannot read or write and cries in frustration. He apologizes and offers to teach her, but she asks him what reading and writing has done for him, since he stands there looking foolish in an apron. But Hallie then smiles at Stoddard's reassurance that she can learn quickly: it is her first moment of real happiness in the film.

Doniphon suddenly enters the kitchen, spruced up and ready to go a-courtin'. He has brought Hallie a cutting from the cactus rose bush in bloom at his ranch, and she thanks him, a bit flustered. While Pompey plants it for her in the backyard behind the restaurant's kitchen, Doniphon spots Stoddard's shingle hanging near the door: "Ransom Stoddard, Attorney at Law." He advises Ranse that if he posts such a sign in public he will have to "defend it with a gun." We begin to wonder not merely whether Ransom should stick to his law books or pick up a gun, but also whether an ordered system of rights and liberties requires violence (or at least the *threat* of violence) to maintain and protect it from external challenges. Doniphon leaves the kitchen and enters the crowded dining room. He stops at Peabody's table, and in response to Peabody's inquiry about the seemingly impending engagement of Tom and Hallie, he tells the editor not to rush him. Tom's delay in asking Hallie is his biggest mistake, but he does not see it. As observant as Doniphon is about Stoddard, he is stubbornly obtuse about declaring himself to Hallie, preferring to court at a slow pace.

In the ensuing sequence Doniphon segues from commentator and insecure lover to heroic activist, reassuring us by taking charge during Valance's sudden appearance at the restaurant. He confronts Valance and protects Stoddard after Valance has tripped the "new waitress" (Stoddard), causing Tom's steak to fall to the floor. Tom demands that Valance pick up the steak and the long-awaited confrontation, thick with tension, ensues. Doniphon challenges Valance with his usual sardonic humor and restores order, with the help of the nearby Pompey and his rifle, so that the customers can get on with their meals. The film then takes an abrupt turn at this point, as if suddenly bringing to an end the first act of a play, for Ransom becomes enraged, berating Tom for always resorting to violence in resolving a dangerous situation.

Stoddard decides to stay in Shinbone without purchasing a pistol—at least for the time being. For the moment he opts to be a man of principle, even if it may eventually cost him his life. And thus the first act closes. We have reached a point of crisis in the impending tragedy, one that is at the core of the expansion of the West. Stoddard is convinced that he can bring the civilized East to the West if everyone will just do what he says. He believes that he will transform the West with his law books and his schooling of Shinbone's citizens, young and old. Anyone with a sense of film history realizes that James Stewart was the perfect choice to play this role of a man caught between his dedication to civic justice and his possible need to resort to violence, since we remember him not only as the gun-wary lawman of *Destry Rides Again* and as the idealistic senator in Capra's *Mr. Smith Goes to Washington* but also as the psychologically and morally complex protagonists in Mann's Westerns (e.g., *Bend of the River, The Naked Spur, The Man From Laramie*) and in Hitchcock's thrillers (e.g., *Rear Window, Vertigo*).

As the second act of the film opens, Stoddard pursues his new role as civilization builder, as a lawyer trying to drum up business. Working out of Peabody's office, he supports the editor's defense of homesteaders who want statehood. From this point on, *Liberty Valance* interweaves the larger political story of the settlement of the West with the narrative of the restless trio of Doniphon, Stoddard, and Valance. They are headed toward a showdown of their own desires and grievances. Shinbone is a growing community in a territory that seeks statehood and thereby civilization, but Doniphon wants no part of it. Ever the individual, he cares about his ranch and about finishing the new room in his house so that Hallie and he can marry and start a family. He stays to the side, but he is watching every move, and we begin to feel that he is the only one who understands the truth, the reality of the way it *is*. His methods, however, are clumsy and brutal, at least to Hallie. When he takes Pompey away from the school Stoddard has set up, his blunt talk of the dangers of Valance frightens Stoddard into shutting the school. Furious with Tom, Hallie turns away from him—forever, as we will learn. And Stoddard, as we soon realize, begins to wonder whether Tom may not be right after all.

Westerns may be ambivalent in siding with ranchers or homesteaders, for they often deal with the settling of the Great Plains by cattlemen who prepare the way for the farmers and, eventually, towns and cities. Not all ranchers are land-grabbing villains, as Tom demonstrates, and the heroic progress they make is integral to the settlement of the West. Ford, whose Westerns typically embrace the inevitability of progress, likes to take a populist perspective and to defend "the little people." Statehood will do the most good for the largest number of people, and Stoddard, the lawyer from back East, will be the most effective advocate for change. And so we soon witness a mass meeting for elections that is held at Hank's Saloon, and all is in disorder.

Doniphon bangs the meeting to order and proposes that Stoddard should run the meeting. As Stoddard explains, they are to elect two delegates who will represent them in the territorial convention for statehood. Ranse nominates Tom, but after the rousing applause dies down, Doniphon refuses the nomination—because he has other plans, personal plans.[26] Valance enters at this point, and he sees the news report of his killings. He shoves people out of the way and asks the "hash-slinger" (Stoddard) why he is standing there looking so "high and mighty." Doniphon, immediately assuming his role as protector, proclaims that Stoddard is running the meeting. Ransom is then nominated and Tom seconds it; Ranse accepts hesitatingly, a reluctant candidate.

Here again, Doniphon is required as the necessary "good bad man" who exists amid historical and political transition—as the threat of violence that is needed to secure the establishment of a democratic system of ordered freedom. Valance insists that he aims to be "the delegate from south of the Picketwire," and his sidekick, Floyd, nominates him and moves that the nominations be closed. Doniphon restores order, saying

FIGURE 43. Tom Doniphon (*center*) calls a town meeting to order while newspaper editor Dutton Peabody (Edmond O'Brien, *sitting to Doniphon's left*) and lawyer Ransom Stoddard (*standing to Doniphon's immediate right*) look on. Courtesy of the Museum of Modern Art.

they need two *honest* men, one of them being Stoddard. Valance's name is put down anyway, and then Peabody is nominated. Peabody comically protests, saying that he is a newspaperman and champion of the free press, not a politician. Stoddard and Peabody are elected, Valance is not, and Valance tells Stoddard that he has been hiding behind Doniphon for too long: "You got a choice, dishwasher: either you get out of town, or tonight you be out on that street alone. You be there, and don't make us come and get you." Tom tells Ransom that come dark, Pompey will be there with a buckboard so that he can escape.

That night, a drunken, frightened Peabody—who earlier informed the surprised Hallie that Ranse had begun practicing with a borrowed pistol out in the countryside—notices a typographical error in his newspaper and, before trying to fix it, goes to the Mexican saloon to fill his jug. Back in Peabody's office, Valance and his men are waiting. The editor drunkenly returns and is forced to eat a copy of his own newspaper; he is also beaten with Liberty's trademark silver whip, and his files and type are destroyed. Leaving him for dead, Valance puts a newspaper over his face and then smashes the windows. After hearing the bullets, Stoddard rushes across the street from the restaurant to find Peabody brutally beaten but still alive.

Stoddard has been delaying his departure but now he decides to face Valance, looking genuinely heroic for the first time in the film. After seeing Peabody in such a pathetic state, he returns to the restaurant and retrieves his recently acquired gun from a carpetbag under his bed. Hallie runs to Pompey, who is waiting nearby, and tells him to get Doniphon. Stoddard walks out into the street, holding his gun, looks into the newspaper office and moves along in the shadows, waiting. Valance then exits the saloon, yelling, "Hash-slinger, you out here?" Stoddard and Valance walk toward each other, and Valance tells him to come closer where he can see him. Valance fires at a jug hanging by a hook, splattering its liquid on Stoddard, and then shoots the lawyer in his arm. Ranse's gun falls, and we watch Stoddard grab his bloody elbow and begin to move back to pick up his gun. Valance shoots at the gun and allows Stoddard to pick it up with his left hand: "All right, Dude, this time, right between the eyes." Liberty aims his gun while the men are not far apart: each fires, but it is Valance who falls in the street, dead. Stoddard walks back into the kitchen, holding his arm, and collapses on the bed just as he did after the beating, dropping the gun before Hallie and her parents treat him tenderly.

Hallie looks at Stoddard and wraps his wound while crying; he looks back at her, knowing she is in love with him. The camera cuts to Doniphon in the doorway, who has seen and heard all, knowing now that he has lost his girl to Ranse. Tom tells Hallie indignantly that he will "be around" and slams the door on his way out. He lights a cigarette, walks past the saloon and Valance's body being taken away in a buckboard, and then begins drinking quickly at the bar. Valance's men, also in the saloon, talk of hanging Stoddard, and Doniphon easily subdues both of them. Pompey comes to take Tom home. "Home," Tom says drunkenly. "Home sweet home. You're right, Pompey, we got plenty to do at home." He drives home, yelling, and staggers from the buckboard, still drinking. He then runs into the house and lights a lamp, taking it into the new room he was building for Hallie and then smashing it. As the fire takes hold, he sits in a chair and Pompey rushes in, carrying him outside as the house and tree burn. This is the end of act 2.

There is no pause to introduce act 3, which explains the mystery and concludes the tragedy. Instead there is a quick cut to Capitol City and the convention. Major Cassius Starbuckle (John Carradine), a pompous

FIGURE 44. The final showdown as depicted in a flashback-within-a-flashback: Doniphon (*foreground left*) has shot Valance (Lee Marvin, *kneeling in background left*) as Stoddard (*background center*) stands wounded. Courtesy of the Museum of Modern Art.

blowhard, nominates a territorial representative to Congress, the right honorable Buck Langhorne, while Peabody nominates Stoddard. Peabody's oratory is sharp and funny. He is fully a match for Starbuckle, eloquently and slyly talking of progress in the territory, beginning with the days of the "savage redskin," people who were governed only by "the law of the tomahawk and the bow and arrow." He speaks of "the westward march of our nation," from the pioneers and buffalo hunters and greedy cattlemen to the railroads and the hardworking homesteaders and shopkeepers. He speaks of the need for someone to represent them in Congress, someone who can help them to build cities, dams, and roadways and to protect the rights of all. The editor nominates the "honorable" Ransom Stoddard, who has become known across the territory as "a great champion of law and order."

The farmers cheer, the cattlemen boo, and Starbuckle takes his turn. While he carries on, claiming that Stoddard's only claim to fame is that he killed a man and now bears the mark of Cain, a dusty-jacketed Doniphon bursts through the swinging doors and sits on the lobby stairs, dirt-smudged and mean-looking, smoking and getting angry. When Stoddard leaves the hall in disgust at his own reputation as a killer, Doniphon follows him and asks him where he is going. Stoddard replies that he is going home, back East where he belongs, since he hardly wants to build a life on such a reputation. "You *talk* too much, *think* too much," Doniphon proclaims as he strikes another match, and we see him in the light, with a scraggly beard and bleary eyes. "Besides, *you* didn't kill Liberty Valance . . . Think back, Pilgrim. Valance came out of the saloon. You were walking toward him when he fired his first shot. Remember?"

The entire movie thus far has indeed been a process of remembering, and here begins a flashback within a flashback. As the camera zooms in close and holds on Doniphon, he takes a deep drag from his cigarette and blows out smoke that elides the cut to the flashback within the flashback, the moment of truth. We have experienced the true climax of the film—not the shoot-out between Stoddard and Valance, but the "telling it true" by Doniphon. In a manner as blunt as his behavior throughout the film, and in pure Wayne-ese, Doniphon has let Stoddard have it. Doniphon killed Valance and Stoddard did not—he could not have done so, as he was not good enough with a gun, plus he was already wounded by Valance. Doniphon did it for Hallie, since she loved Ranse and wanted him alive. Tom sacrificed his own personal happiness for that of the woman he loved and kept his mouth shut about it. Stoddard could hardly be capable of such heroism himself.

As we watch, we feel much all at once. Doniphon's acknowledgment engages our sympathy for this twisted act of heroism. It is over for Tom, and we are devastated once again. We do not see Tom again. Unlike in the conclusion of *The Searchers,* there is no healing process, nor is there a last glimpse of Doniphon as there was of Bull Stanley in Ford's silent *3 Bad Men,* riding with his pals in the sky: *Liberty Valance* offers no such flight of fancy. We learn from Pompey that Doniphon never used his gun again and from Link Appleyard that he never rebuilt his ranch. We know that he endured long, lonely years between his sacrifice and his death. It was Appleyard who wrote to the Stoddards to inform them of Doniphon's passing. Sadly there was no more contact between the Stoddards and Doniphon after the couple married and went to Washington.

The flashback over, Stoddard tells the newspapermen that they know the rest of the story. Shinbone's current newspaper editor (Carleton Young) tears up his notes. Stoddard asks him, "Well, you're not going to use the story, Mr. Scott?" The editor proclaims, in one of Hollywood's most famous lines: "No sir. This is the West, sir. When the legend becomes fact, print the legend." This line is a crystallization of the Western's perennial tension between myth and reality, between realism and romanticism: a dialectic that underlies the genre as a whole. The train whistle blows and Stoddard looks at his watch, returning to the room with the coffin. He tells Hallie it is getting late and gives Pompey some spending money; as he leaves the little room, he turns to close the door and sees the cactus rose on top of the coffin. The camera closes in on the flowers, a recurring symbol of love and passion throughout Ford's oeuvre.[27] Once we learn that Doniphon is the man who shot Liberty Valance, we understand that he is the subject of the film after all, its hero. After confessing his true story to the gentlemen of the press, Stoddard learns that they will not use it, and so Stoddard can safely return to Washington with his reputation intact.

We cannot safely return, however. In a coda, *Liberty Valance* quits us with meaningful realizations of the tragedy endured by these two aged people, who look back over their lives with such sorrow and reflect on the nation that the wilderness has become. During the train ride out of Shinbone, Ransom suggests that they return to the land Hallie so loves. As Ford scholar Joseph McBride has pointed out, the film and Ford pose the same question to their audience at this point: Are *we* proud of our American civilization and what has become of it?[28] With such simplicity, Hallie lets Ranse know the truth, and he pauses before he asks her about the cactus rose on Tom's coffin, for he was too self-deluded to face the realization earlier. It is an awakening for him, a realization of what he has done to make the wilderness a garden—what he, and civilization, have done to the West, both positively and negatively—as well as what he has personally lost, or indeed never had.

The settlement of the West, for the American, has been the route in discovering a new destiny, replete with conflicts and contradictions. Ford was suspicious, too, of the new society of the Western frontier. From *Stagecoach* forward, Ford would deride the hypocrisy of the Law and Order League and the "blessings of civilization," and he put populist views into the dialogue of his characters. *Liberty Valance* presents the uncertainties and ambiguities dear to Ford's own maturing interpretations of the West. That the new order is not necessarily better in all respects goes against the American grain, yet Ford's Westerns are distinguished by these partial regrets, which are themselves an amalgam of his and his screenwriters' reworking of fictional sources and expansionist history. These views characterized novels and stories on which Western films were based, as James Folsom tells us in his *The American Western Novel:* "The conflict in the Western novel, in its broadest terms, is an externalized debate which reflects the common American argument about the nature of, in modern parlance, the 'good life.' . . . The American mental hesitation between the values of urban and rural life is mirrored in the Western novel; whether the coming of civilization is good or ill is the burden of Western fiction."[29]

The "pilgrim" in *Liberty Valance* is on a mission, similar to the "errand into the wilderness" described by Perry Miller in the mid-1950s.[30] If *errand* means "mission," it also signifies wandering or losing one's way. Folsom points out: "Miller shows that quite early in the American experience both of these meanings come to inhere in the term. Whether in his errand into the wilderness the American has lost his way became the burden of Puritan sermons. It is the burden of much later American writing as well, not the least of which is the fictional writing about the West. For the West is unequivocally the wilderness, and it is there that the nature of the errand may best be seen."[31] The portrayal of the pilgrim as a wanderer is key to the Western film, as it is to Western literature, particularly in various Ford Westerns, from *Straight Shooting* through *Fort Apache,* from *The Searchers* to *Liberty Valance.* By focusing on the errand of Ransom Stoddard in *Liberty Valance,* we can grapple with the tragedy of Tom Doniphon in another way. He, too, was on an errand, and Hallie (as well as Ford) knows that both of her heroes have succeeded as much as both have wandered or lost their way. Doniphon is the greater hero because his loss was much the larger: he lost his one great love and, with it, the best part of his very soul.

CHAPTER 9

The Existential and Revisionist Western

"Comanche Station" to "The Wild Bunch" and Beyond

Along with Anthony Mann, Delmer Daves, and John Ford, one of the most important directors in the postwar transformation of the genre was Budd Boetticher, who directed a cycle of films that has become known as the "Ranown cycle" because of the films' production company name. Film scholars Jim Kitses and Peter Wollen similarly describe Boetticher as a dedicated individualist whose Western hero, played by the reliable Randolph Scott in all of the Ranown movies, confronts obstacles with a stoic self-reliance and pragmatic self-centeredness. These are not movies framed by ideals of American expansionism or the building of transcontinental railroads or the range wars between ranchers and settlers. Boetticher, working on many of his Ranown pictures with screenwriter Burt Kennedy, limits his storylines to a small group of people who, while contending with threats by others (outlaws, Indians, etc.) and with the challenges of the natural landscape, also contend with themselves. Like the Westerns of Mann and Daves, Boetticher's films remind us that human beings are always individuals because of their inherent freedom and the choices they make, even when reality impinges on their dreams and desires. Though some may view Boetticher's characters (whether heroes or villains or somewhere in between) as passive victims of fate, buffeted about the deserts and prairies like tumbleweeds blowing in the wind, his movies in fact remind us that humans are by nature autonomous, and that we become more human by resisting the forces that would otherwise make us weak and passive.

There are existential moments in Boetticher's Westerns in which characters—and not only his heroes or villains but also secondary characters—are faced with choices, both between right and wrong and between authenticity and inauthenticity. These are not moments when a character, as in Ford's cavalry films, must decide merely between conformist duty and individuality, with the former usually trumping the latter in Ford's postwar Westerns. On the contrary, characters in Boetticher's films experience existential moments because, as with Jean-Paul Sartre's conception of our radical autonomy, there are ultimately no pregiven, collectively determined values that measure a certain course of action.[1] Rather, there is only the individual and reality, typically in tension or conflict, and the human as a subjective agent must always decide according to his own self-created beliefs and standards rather than according to any that have been imposed by society or some higher power. In Boetticher's Westerns, there is no force of history or nature or God that can erase the fundamental truth that all humans are capable of choosing between various life-altering options, even when those options are severely limited.

In his book *Horizons West: Directing the Western from John Ford to Clint Eastwood,* Kitses has said about this filmmaker's Westerns and their emphasis on the principle of individuality: "At an ideological level the Western is deeply attractive for Boetticher in its insistence on an archaic world where the ambiguous drama of individualism can be played out. . . . The vulnerable men and women and the isolated swing stations that characterize Boetticher's frontier have little to do with history. Boetticher's West is quite simply *the world,* a philosophical ground over which his pilgrims move to be confronted with existential choices wholly abstracted from social contexts."[2] This type of approach to Boetticher's underlying philosophical concerns echoes that of Peter Wollen, who expounds upon Boetticher's own following self-reflection: "I am not interested in making films about mass feelings. I am for the individual." As Wollen elaborates: "The central problem in Boetticher's films is the problem of the individual in an age—increasingly collectivized—in which individualism is no longer at all self-evident, in which individual action is increasingly problematic and the individual is conceived as a value per se."[3] Wollen also points to the director's emphasis on the importance of personal decisions in concrete contexts, particularly since he views the director as conceiving moral value in terms of the *quality of an action* rather than as an *end in itself.* Action as a value per se becomes the goal as an authentic response to the reality of the circumstances, and not merely as the expression of some obligation to a preestablished ethical principle or social code of justice. Wollen tells us:

> The question of good and evil is not for Boetticher a question of abstract and eternal moral principles; it is a question of individual choice in a given situation. The important thing, moreover, is the value which resides in action of a certain kind; not action to realize values of a certain kind. Evidently, this is a kind of existentialist ethic, which by its nature is impure and imperfect, but which recognizes this. Hence the irony which marks Boetticher's films and particularly his attitude to his heroes. The characters played by Randolph Scott are always fallible and vulnerable; they make their way inch by inch, not at all with the sublime confidence of crusaders. . . . Boetticher sympathizes with almost all of his characters; they are all in the same predicament in which the prime faults are inauthenticity and self-deception, rather than infringement of any collectively recognized code. The fact that some end up dead and some alive does not necessarily indicate any moral judgment, but an underlying tragedy which Boetticher prefers to treat with irony.[4]

COMANCHE STATION

Comanche Station (1960) is the last of Boetticher's Ranown Westerns and, like *Seven Men from Now* (1956) and *The Tall T* (1957), one of his best and most exemplary. It reveals an accomplished cinematic sensibility that appreciates the importance of landscape and the complexity of the human being, most particularly in terms of how individuals must learn to deal with adversity and loss—or else suffer the consequences. His heroes can be as obsessive about their need for retribution as his villains are driven by their greed and ambition. And yet these obsessions remain mostly concealed behind a facade of cool calculation and steely self-control. Often Boetticher's heroes and villains wind up mirroring one another in certain ways, not merely because of their courage or facility with a gun, but because they can be equally patient and methodical—at least up until the final showdown, where the villain finally commits a fatal error because he has replaced reason with desire. This emphasis on moral-psychological duality and the mutual mirroring of protagonist and antagonist is also echoed, for example, by pairings such as Wyatt Earp and Doc Holliday in Ford's *My Darling Clementine* (and by those two characters as portrayed in George Cosmatos's 1993 *Tombstone*), Ethan Edwards and Chief Scar in Ford's *The Searchers,* and Dan Evans (Van Heflin) and Ben Wade (Glenn Ford) in Daves's *3:10 to Yuma* (1957) (and in James Mangold's 2007 remake of that latter film with Christian Bale and Russell Crowe).

Jefferson Cody (Randolph Scott) is a solitary wanderer of deserts and canyons who, whenever the opportunity arises, trades goods (mainly sacks of calico, and occasionally guns) with the Comanche in exchange for abducted white women in order to save them from captivity. After having recently rescued a woman named Nancy Lowe (Nancy Gates), the pair reaches a stagecoach way station in the middle of nowhere. As is typical in these Ranown Westerns, the lone hero soon joins with a tiny wandering community, whether it is a gang of outlaws or a married couple or both (as in *Seven Men from Now*). No sooner have Cody and the formerly abducted Mrs. Lowe arrived at the way station than they meet up with Ben Lane (Claude Akins) and his two younger protégés, Frank (Skip Homeier) and Dobie (Richard Rust), who ride quickly toward the swing station while firing at a group of pursuing Comanche. Cody throws Nancy into a trough of water to protect her and joins the men in their shoot-out. He and Lane trade quick glances and the latter smirks: it is suggested that they know one another, and this is quickly confirmed after the Indians have been defeated. And so a formerly solitary westerner finds himself suddenly accompanied by a small ragtag band of outlaws and victims. There is no official society in most of Boetticher's Westerns, for the most part—merely individuals, otherwise out for themselves, who have been thrown together for a time by chance.

The Ranown films tend to repeat similar storylines with intriguing variants. For example, in the earlier *Seven Men from Now*, Lee Marvin's outlaw Bill Masters comes into conflict with Scott's Ben Stride and sparks the hero's anger, not merely by riding along with him in search of a possible bounty that lies at the end of the journey—thus making a final showdown with the hero inevitable—but more especially by taunting the female character in a lewd manner. Practically the same narrative pattern occurs in *Comanche Station*, and in both cases the leader of the outlaws is a former acquaintance who knows a thing or two about the protagonist's past. There is obvious tension between Cody and Lane, especially when the former observes firmly that it is high time that the latter and his men depart. Lane tells Cody, however, that they are going to stick around nonetheless and accompany them to Lordsburg. Lane then converses with Frank and Dobie at nightfall and makes it clear that a substantial reward has been offered for the finding of Nancy Lowe, a reward that has been offered by her husband back home, and that he is after the reward and is in fact planning to kill Cody along the way. To make matters worse, Lane suggests to his counterparts that Mrs. Lowe does not necessarily have to be returned alive, since he has

FIGURE 45. Jefferson Cody (Randolph Scott, *foreground center*) kneels over the dying victim of an Indian attack (Rand Brooks) in Budd Boetticher's *Comanche Station* (1960). *Behind them, from left to right:* Nancy Lowe (Nancy Gates), Frank (Skip Homeier), Ben Lane (Claude Akins), and Dobie (Richard Rust). Courtesy of the Museum of Modern Art.

heard from others that Mr. Lowe would pay the reward whether his wife is brought back "dead or alive."

Like Mann and Daves, Boetticher gives his characters rare but telling opportunities for individuation and character transformation—where the choices are not, as in many traditional Westerns, primarily conditioned by concern with social norms, political ideals, historical goals, or shared codes of honor. Their choices are occasioned primarily by personal moral awakenings and chances for self-realization. Boetticher's Westerns deal with an increasing need for self-knowledge rather than with goals of conquering the wilderness or fighting Indians or establishing a system of law and order. Many of his Westerns, like many of those by Mann and Daves, take place in nearly ahistorical contexts of individual struggle (apart from simply being set in the Old West) and emphasize the morality and psychology of the individual.[5] Only a few of Boetticher's Westerns, mainly those outside of the Ranown cycle with Randolph Scott, involve immediate historical settings and situations:

primarily *Seminole* (1953), dealing with the tensions among settlers, Indians, and the military during the Indian wars in the Everglades in 1830s Florida; and *The Man from the Alamo* (also 1953), in which a soldier (Glenn Ford) leaves his post at the Alamo for personal reasons during that famous 1836 fight for Texas's independence from Mexico.

In addition, the self-transforming choices that are dramatic highlights of the Ranown narratives are not typically undertaken by his protagonists or antagonists, but rather by secondary characters who either accompany the hero or wind up involved in the villain's greedy machinations. In *Seven Men from Now,* for example, it is the character of John Greer (Walter Reed), a married wagon-driver making his way through the wilderness, who undergoes a noticeable character transformation toward the end of the film. Greer is a passive, weak-willed man who depends on the expertise and bravery of former sheriff Ben Stride to help him and his wife (Gail Russell) make it through the challenges of rugged Indian-infested terrain. When Stride first comes across the couple, Greer and his wife are attempting to remove their wagon from a patch of deep mud into which they have unwittingly driven. Stride saves the day and agrees to accompany them, at least temporarily, on their journey southward. The husband increasingly reveals his cowardly and obsequious nature, most clearly when he refuses to take issue with Bill Masters as the outlaw speaks offensively to Mrs. Greer while Masters, Stride, and the couple share coffee in a wagon during a rainstorm. It is Stride who reacts to Masters, following him out of the wagon and knocking him to the ground for his insolent behavior. Mr. Greer sits cowardly, doing nothing.

However, by the end of the film, Greer finally takes a stand and makes the courageous choice to seek out the town sheriff so as to obtain help for the wounded Stride, even though he must pass by a brazen outlaw to get to the sheriff's office. Greer winds up shot in the back, and yet he has managed to impress even the onlooking Masters, who remarks: "I was wrong. He wasn't just half a man." While Stride has remained morally consistent throughout the film, and while Masters has never wavered from his greed-driven goal, it is Greer who expresses a dramatic change of will and character. Perhaps we can criticize him for having risked his life so recklessly at this moment, given that his nearby wife loves him and still needs him in their journey west. And yet, from an existential perspective, he has finally acted from passionate conviction in a way that he had never dared to do before. Here it is a secondary character who serves as the locus of anguished decision making. The hero and villain exist as contrasting models and thereby define the choices more clearly;

they have already committed themselves to *self-chosen* ways of life, whether for good or ill. As the director once stated, "I prefer my films to be based on heroes who want to do what they are doing, despite the danger and the risk of death. . . . In war, nobody wants to die, and I hate making films about people who are forced to do such and such a thing."[6]

As we have seen in previous chapters, going all the way back to silent oaters such as *Straight Shooting* and *Hell's Hinges,* dramatic moral choices and life-altering actions are not new to the Western film. Mid-twentieth-century directors like Boetticher and Mann did not invent the conception of the Western as a morality play, but they amplified that conception in intriguing ways. What makes *certain* 1950s Westerns intriguingly different from *certain* previous Westerns is twofold. As suggested earlier, many of the midcentury Western films tend to divorce their dramas and characters from overt social and historical contexts. In addition, the midcentury Westerns (particularly those of Mann, Daves, and Boetticher) are more likely to emphasize the inner realities and ambiguities of their characters. As opposed to traditional or classical Westerns, the narratives of certain 1950s Westerns explicitly express a situation in which a character-altering decision may be made. This is typically accomplished through overt dialogue about the intentions and motivations that help to constitute the dilemma at hand, and about the possible consequences, both positive and negative, of the choices and actions involved. Attention is drawn to these choices *as* individual choices—as opportunities for moral, existential, and psychological self-realization—and not merely as stepping-stones in advancing the narrative.

Westerners such as Cheyenne Harry (*Straight Shooting*), Blaze Tracy (*Hell's Hinges*), the title characters of *3 Bad Men,* and the Ringo Kid of *Stagecoach,* for example, do make character-defining decisions, and yet there is no serious *deliberating about* or even *agonizing over* these decisions as an essential thematic focus. It is as if these westerners are destined to make these kinds of decisions in precisely these kinds of situation. Compassion, sympathy, love, and desire for revenge tend to be the recurring motivations in play, and yet there is little attempt in these earlier films to point out the processes of the inner self, including regret and even anguish, that result in dramatic choices of action. William Hart's Blaze Tracy (like Ford's "three bad men") sees an angelic young woman, and Harry Carey Sr.'s Cheyenne Harry witnesses a grieving family, and they suddenly choose the right path: end of story. Toward the conclusion of *Stagecoach,* Ringo knows that Dallas is highly upset by his decision to continue on with his vengeful mission against Luke Plummer, and yet he goes ahead anyway, without a sign of contemplative hesitation or doubt, as if everything seems to have been predetermined from the start.

In many of the films of Mann, Boetticher, and Daves, on the other hand, attention is drawn to the fact that such choices are indeed the focal points of the respective narratives. We think about these choices *as* self-defining decisions because we are allowed to see characters struggling with their present problems and past bad choices in situations that are moral tests and exercises of autonomy. For example, *Comanche Station* eventually focuses in one crucial scene on the two young men, Frank and Dobie, who bunk under a tree at night and discuss their lives. Dobie naively asks why Ben bosses them around so much, and Frank tells him that Dobie can leave if he wants, since Lane would not stop him. But Frank also admits that he would not go with him if Dobie decides to depart. Frank tells him that it is not personal, but that a man gets used to a thing, just as he has become accustomed to riding with Ben. Frank is a young man whose character has been shaped by the repetition of bad decisions, and he knows it: he sees little reason to change, since he obviously views himself as a creature of habit.

Dobie then professes that he hopes that he "amounts to something," and they consequently discuss what this vague goal really means. Dobie says that Cody is someone who has amounted to something since he "had braid on him"—that is, he had been an army officer in the past. Frank replies that Cody's past military status does not matter now, since he is not in the army anymore. Dobie objects, saying that, according to his father's philosophy of life, a man only has to do *one* thing to prove himself. However, even though he calls his father a "good man," he also admits that his father never did in fact amount to anything, despite his advice. Dobie goes to bed and bids his partner goodnight, but Frank now sits up with his hand on his cheek, pondering these issues of meaning and value.

Cody and his companions continue their journey and eventually camp by a stream. Nancy cries out because she has spotted Frank dead in the stream, having been hit by an Indian arrow, and Dobie rushes into the water to retrieve his body. But Cody pushes them along, saying that they have no time to properly bury Frank (which is what Nancy and Dobie ask for), because if they do so they will all wind up as victims of the Comanche. They quickly depart, and when they eventually come to a rest against a serene backdrop of windswept trees, Cody talks privately with Dobie about Frank. This is a crucial scene in terms of the underlying emphasis on the importance of individual choice. The young man, who obviously misses his companion, observes that all Frank had possessed when he died was a saddle and a shirt, and he notes that this is not much to show for himself. Cody agrees: "Sure ain't."

Dobie adds that Frank's meager property and way of life were not Frank's fault, but Cody questions him on this point. Dobie responds that all Frank knew was the "wild side" of life, and Cody declares matter-of-factly that a man can "cross over" any time he "has a mind to." In many ways this is the crux of the film. Cody, as we learn, is a man who has been driven by the desire to search for his wife, who had been abducted by the Comanche many years before. He has not merely succumbed to the winds of fate, since his tireless searching has been *his* choice, and an entirely personal choice. He lives authentically, even if this decision has made his life a difficult and lonely one.

Here we see a clear emphasis on the ever present possibility of human freedom, no matter the circumstances and hardships. Self-preservation is a necessity, especially when one seeks to exist in a brutal land; but as Cody implies, there must always be a concern with the morality of one's decisions and way of life. Survival may be the primary motivation behind Cody's life choices, but he is certainly not devoid of an ethical sensibility, unlike Lane. He has chosen a life of action, but not simply *any* action. Cody does not excuse Frank from his moral responsibility merely because he had become accustomed to his outlaw existence with Lane. Cody holds the belief that a person's freedom is always possible, most especially in choosing the right judgment or attitude. According to this view, humans are not always able to select the specific ways in which reality impinges on them, and Cody is certainly a man who has experienced the roughness of reality. But humans are always free to choose the ways in which they respond to the world. As Cody implies, Frank had continued to choose the same way of life and had to suffer the consequences, mainly because he refused to renounce his outlaw ways.

Given Boetticher's emphasis on the importance of individuality, human choice, and the possibility of personal self-transformation, we might take issue with certain observations by Kitses and Wollen concerning the "absurdist" nature of the director's basic worldview. It can even be said that, while both scholars have drawn needed attention to this filmmaker and his underlying philosophical concerns, their existential approach to his films sometimes equates existentialism in general with a nihilistic view of reality. For example, Wollen makes the point that the specter of death, nearly always present for Boetticher's various characters, is the absolute limitation of an individual's existence, a limit that ultimately nullifies the meaning and significance of his choices and actions, most especially because the appeal to any collective ideal is absent: "The risk of death is essential to any action in Boetticher's films. It is both the guarantee for the seriousness of the hero's action and the final mockery which makes that action absurd. Meaningful action is both dependent on the risk of death and made meaningless by it."[7] As Wollen sees it, in an ahistorical and contingent world the stark individuality of the characters assures an eventual negation of personal meaning and value when life has reached its absolute end. And Kitses goes so far as to describe the Ranown Westerns as "comedies" in which the "hero" must eventually be viewed as a doomed, helpless, passive victim of cruel fate and a "malignant" world:

> Unsupported by virtue, tradition or the community, Boetticher's characters confront their destiny nakedly. However, we are deceived if we consider them to be in control of it: sustained only by an idea of themselves in the face of a mocking meaninglessness, the characters are helpless, doomed to play out their absurd roles in the tragicomic game of life.[8] . . . Above all, Boetticher's films are comedies, deeply ironic works, but comedies all the same. In contrast with the tragic world of Anthony Mann, Boetticher's small films are bittersweet reflections on the human condition. . . . Typically, the hero is both a victim and a product, an expression of this world; indeed often, it seems that he functions as its tool.[9]

And so Kitses views the Ranown protagonist as a "man beyond all human ties," as a character who is "impotent, never initiating action, ever passively responding." He tells us that "the hero is the very butt of the world, tossed about like a leaf, tragicomically at the mercy of life." He further proclaims, "If half of the Boetticher hero is a sad clown, the other half is a killjoy."[10] And finally, this somber summation: "The moral of Boetticher's films is thus a simple one: everyone loses. Life defeats charm, innocence is blasted. The world is finally a sad and funny place, life is a tough, amusing game that can never be won but must be played. If Boetticher's films can darken to near-tragedy, the pessimism is always held in check by an innate response to the absurdity of it all, the way in which we are forced to take up roles in a farce."[11]

While it is true that Boetticher's Westerns raise the problem of the purpose and significance of the individual's existence in a savage land where death is ever present, it is not so clear that the director (in conjunction with his screenwriter) opts for a nihilistic worldview. If anything, *Comanche Station* offers a form of emotional closure for the hero and the woman he has saved, particularly since the villain has been destroyed, a married couple has been reunited, and a new journey can begin. And while other characters' moral awakenings and struggles for self-knowledge may have gotten them killed rather than having led them to a flourishing life, the deaths of these characters have not taken away the value and dignity that were inherent in their very decisions and actions. If moral value can be a quality inherent in action itself, apart from some external rule or anticipated telos, then death does not rob our choices and deeds of their subjective meaning and merit.

As far as the Boetticher hero goes, this is a man who maintains stoic dignity, has faith in the intrinsic value of his chosen actions, affirms his life in his continued perseverance, and tries to conquer evil when it arises. This quietly heroic westerner is an individual who confronts the world in an active, reasonable, and self-reliant way, not in a helpless or passive manner, and he shares with others (as he does with Dobie in *Comanche Station*) his conviction that an individual, self-transformative choice is always possible, and that a man can "always cross over."

This is a moral lesson, to be sure, but also an existential one, since it involves a view of the very conditions of human nature in which moral values can be formed and ethical commitments forged. Like Cody, Scott's Ben Stride in *Seven Men from Now* vanquishes the villain and works to save the innocent, always remaining true to his own personal code of honor and to his authentically chosen way of life. His trials and tribulations, including the loss of loved ones and the deaths of those around him, are anything but "comic" or "ironic." And while we can agree with Kitses's additional observation that Boetticher's villains, in contrast with Scott's laconic protagonists, tend to be charismatic and fascinating to the viewer, it can hardly be said that, in Boetticher's Westerns, "it is the villain who is our true hero."[12] There is not *that* much moral ambiguity involved in Boetticher's narratives, even if the hero and villain do mirror one another at times. His villains are men, after all, who kill innocent victims and act offensively to endangered women.

The world can appear absurd or indifferent at times, and may indeed *be* so, but this does nothing to diminish or negate the inherent value of one's attempts at heroic decisions and actions, even when life is a Sisyphean chore. Many of the midcentury Westerns teach us such a lesson, and Boetticher's films help to crystallize this existential insight. Whether viewed as sublime or absurd, the natural world frames the westerner's struggles against others, but more important, he struggles with *himself*.

As we can garner from genre-transforming Westerns ranging from *Duel in the Sun* to *Comanche Station*, a good number of midcentury

Westerns—whether we happen to call them "psychological," "existential," "noir," or all three combined—typically abstract the individual westerner from the collective historical context that is emphasized in many of the classical Westerns of the pre–Cold War era. But by doing so, this kind of abstraction does not eliminate or gloss over the brute realities and immediate circumstances with which characters have to contend. If anything, the near-negation of the historical backdrop tends to highlight the concrete "situated-ness" of an individual and to *personalize* his choices and actions in an authenticating manner. Some viewers or scholars may indeed interpret Boetticher's tendency toward historical reductionism as leading to a kind of detached narrative perspective, according to which the westerner becomes little more than an unwitting pawn of fate or a fool in a tragicomic game of life. Yet a contrary viewpoint is not only possible but more convincing. Stripped of historical and social context to a large degree, the westerner realizes himself as a true individual, pursuing or acting upon self-knowledge against the eternal canvas of nature itself.

THE WILD BUNCH

As we have seen in the previous section, Boetticher's Westerns focus on the principle of heroic individuality. His heroes are willing to save innocents who need saving and to take a brave stand against evil when necessary—though always for personal reasons. One later Western of the 1960s that in many ways counters Boetticher's underlying philosophical orientation and serves as a fitting point of contrast is Sam Peckinpah's landmark *The Wild Bunch* (1969). This film prioritizes the value of the group over that of the individual, challenges the very idea of heroism, and concludes with its protagonists' collective destruction.

Throughout the 1960s there was a growing tendency in Hollywood, especially among its younger generation of directors, toward more realistic, less myth-governed movies. Suddenly audiences as well as film critics became interested in "ordinary" characters with everyday problems and flawed lives. As Mark Harris demonstrates in his book *Pictures at a Revolution: Five Movies and the Birth of the New Hollywood*, movies such as *The Graduate* and *Bonnie and Clyde* (both 1967) became immensely influential and popular even though their storylines centered on antiheroes and themes of alienation, violence, and malaise. This growing tendency, as Harris persuasively suggests, was due in part to American audiences' growing dissatisfaction with overly familiar patterns of Hollywood's "Golden Age" filmmaking—a dissatisfaction that led, along with the rise of television, to the subsequent decline of the big studios, the star system, and the reign of the movie moguls. But, as Harris also observes, the movie revolution of the 1960s and early 1970s was also partly occasioned by the rising interest of many younger American filmmakers and screenwriters in the European, primarily French and British, "New Wave" cinemas.[13]

In terms of the Western genre, it is *The Wild Bunch,* whose script the director cowrote, that best exemplifies this tide of departure from traditional Hollywood moviemaking in the later 1960s. Peckinpah's film amplified the type of subtler revisionism that could be found, in very different ways, in Peckinpah's earlier *Ride the High Country* (1962), as well as Ford's *The Man Who Shot Liberty Valance* (1962) and *Cheyenne Autumn* (1964). All four of these movies pay tribute to the "dying" of the Old West in their unique ways, though *The Wild Bunch* is an explosive, action-packed challenge to the genre, while the other three films are melancholy, dialogue-driven ruminations on a fading "culture" of stoic heroes and defeated natives. Other transformative Westerns of the 1960s include Sergio Leone's nihilistic and archetypal "Man with No Name" trilogy starring Clint Eastwood (see chapter 10), as well as Monte Hellman's *Ride in the Whirlwind* (1965) and *The Shooting* (1968), both featuring Jack Nicholson.

The Wild Bunch revolves around a group of outlaws who, despite occasional tensions and disagreements, cling to their long-standing code of unity and honor. They do so in a West that is quickly changing from a primitive land of cunning, resilient "real men" (heroes and outlaws alike) to a growing civilization where gunfighters are synonymous with railroad-paid thugs who are little more than idiots with guns. The very first words uttered by the gang's leader, Pike Bishop (William Holden)—as they arrive in a town for their planned bank heist—are the stern commands "Let's fall in" and "Follow me." These words are meant to express collective action as well as authority and the expectation of loyalty. We are introduced to the outlaws as they ride down the main street of town in unison and are outfitted in the uniforms of a regimented troop of army soldiers. Like the very title of the movie, the men are representative of a group; none is a man out on his own or out for himself. *The Wild Bunch* presents a story in which Bishop's mission to keep his men together and obedient to his command is the only thing that keeps them from becoming less than men, given their primitive conception of manhood. As Bishop proclaims furiously to Tector (Ben

Johnson) after the latter threatens and injures old Freddie Sykes (Ed-mond O'Brien): "We're gonna stick together, like it used to be. When you side with a man, you stay with him. And if you can't do that, you're like some animal. You're finished . . . *we're* finished . . . all of us!"

Interestingly, the "wild bunch" may appear to represent something of a paradox when it comes to the conflict between the individual and the collective. On the one hand, as suggested earlier, the gang is defined by its group identity and group loyalty. On the other hand, some might view these outlaws as "true" individuals, despite their group cohesion, since they reject the rules and laws of a structured society. Are these men to be compared with the scorpions in the symbolic opening credits, crea-tures who struggle against, and eventually are destroyed by, the equally ruthless "society" of swarming red ants? Are we to empathize with the members of this gang, viewing them as heroic individuals who are even-tually sacrificed on the altar of an encroaching industrial civilization? These outlaws dare to be bold adventurers who exercise freedom by maintaining their liberation from society in general. Nonetheless, doubts are soon cast as to how far we can adhere to such a perspective. Are we to celebrate these men as true individuals if it entails our accepting their crimes, viewing their violent actions as somehow "heroic," and forget-ting that their actions involve the destruction of others' lives? Randolph Scott's solitary westerner in Boetticher's films, for example, would easily reject their form of livelihood, as well as their willingness to submit their personalities to the authority of Pike—and all for the sake of *money.*

In addition to such moral tensions, *The Wild Bunch* contains blatant elements of revisionism, but they are intriguingly contrasted with nos-talgic genre references. In terms of plot, one can recall plenty of earlier Westerns about gangs of gunslingers or bands of frontiersmen and their dedication to unifying missions that require teamwork: Vidor's *North-west Passage,* Sturges's *The Magnificent Seven,* or any cavalry movie, for example. Peckinpah also relies on familiar modes of visual styliza-tion and montage as well as a traditional use of the natural landscape to frame the journey of his characters. In addition, there are ample refer-ences to Ford's Westerns in *The Wild Bunch.* Most tellingly, the movie makes use of that director's favorite Christian hymn "Shall We Gather at the River?" (which appears in several of Ford's Westerns, ranging from *Stagecoach* to *The Searchers,* and even appears in his final feature film, *7 Women* of 1965).

In Peckinpah's movie, this hymn is sung by the town's temperance league (also recalling the Ladies' Law and Order League in *Stagecoach*) while they parade down the main street just as the botched bank robbery turns into a blood-flying massacre. The same song is also parodied shortly thereafter by "Crazy" Lee (Bo Hopkins) and his several bank hostages, at his insistence. In addition, *The Wild Bunch* stars Ben Johnson, a regular Western star who became a recurring member of Ford's "Stock Company"; Edmond O'Brien, who was memorable as newspaper editor Dutton Peabody in *The Man Who Shot Liberty Valance;* and of course William Holden, the costar of Ford's *The Horse Soldiers,* who had also performed in earlier Westerns such as Wesley Ruggles's *Arizona* (1940), George Marshall's *Texas* (1941), and Henry Levin's *The Man from Colorado* (1948).

But what makes *The Wild Bunch* a truly transformative Western, despite its traditional visual elements and genre references, is its graphic presentation of violence. Both the foiled bank robbery at the outset and, most especially, the gang's final blood-spattered showdown against the Mexican soldiers at the conclusion are real bloodbaths. And there is also the film's focus on the passing of the Old West in light of the expanding railroad business and new technologies such as machine guns and automobiles. This roving band of outlaws must fight to maintain their ever challenged code of unity and honor amid changing times, and as they rest after having escaped from their failed bank robbery, Pike Bishop declares to his men, "We gotta start thinking beyond our guns. Those days are closing fast."

Despite the world-weary dignity of Pike Bishop and the unwavering loyalty of his right-hand man Dutch Engstrom (Ernest Borgnine), we are more prone to feel the loss of Old West heroism as represented by decent-hearted gunslinger Tom Doniphon in *The Man Who Shot Liberty Valance* than to regret the deaths of these cutthroat criminals. Peckinpah, in fact, does not really summon a sense of mourning when it comes to this dying breed of man, since he emphasizes their frequent ruthlessness and brutality. *The Wild Bunch* merely tells it like it is, which is to say that there are certain types of strong, stoic, dangerous men who eventually face their demise when an era that permitted their existence has passed. The members of the gang are not catalysts of this change, as Doniphon is to some degree; they are, rather, outright enemies of civilization. Despite the fact that these men are exemplars of strength, perseverance, and skill with a gun, their loss is *not* an occasion for audience sympathy. We may want to ride hard and shoot fast like these men in certain escapist moments of our humdrum modern existence, but do we really want to live like them on a regular basis or even tolerate their immoral existence? After all, these are not exactly the type of kindhearted outlaws whom we have met in silent- and classical-era Westerns. Furthermore, they are willing not only to murder innocent civilians ("If they move, *kill* 'em!") but also to steal artillery from their own government's army in order to sell these weapons to the sadistic, unpredictable Mexican general Mapache (Emilio Fernandez).

It is the ambiguity of the band's morality and the theme of the fading away of the Old West, along with Peckinpah's graphic presentation of violence, that makes this a limited but clear example of genre revisionism. The moral ambivalence demonstrated by the film is clear when Dutch, after seeing the arrival of the ruthless Mapache, states matter-of-factly: "'Generalissimo,' hell. He's just another bandit grabbing all he can for himself." Pike Bishop replies laughingly and self-mockingly, "Like some others I could mention?" But despite their obvious vocation, Dutch is the one member of the bunch who not only respects their code of unity but also sees a significant moral difference between their way of doing things and that of the corrupt Mexican army: "We ain't *nothing* like him [Mapache]. We don't *hang* nobody." Is this self-deception, or simply a difference in their method of killing? Or is there a deeper ethical difference in operation here as far as Dutch is concerned? Or, at the end of the day, is this band of outlaws ultimately *amoral* apart from the need to keep their collective operation unified and on the move? The answer is not clear. It is up to us to decide.

Pike, despite his emphasis on an ethos that will ensure the survival of the group *as* a group, seems willing to define the band's ultimate purpose as one of sheer greed, which makes his adherence to their code morally questionable at best when both ends and means are considered. Angel (Jaime Sanchez), their Mexican comrade, asks Pike hypothetically whether Pike would ever sell guns to men who had killed his own family—hence putting into question the rightness of their new mission of stealing guns to sell to Mapache, who is an enemy of Angel's people. The bunch's leader replies, "Ten thousand dollars cuts an awful lot of family ties." Pike appears fully greed-driven when he responds in this way, and therefore so does his old-fashioned principle of gang unity. When Pike later praises his former comrade Deke Thornton (Robert Ryan), who has been granted freedom from a prison sentence in return for hunting down the wild bunch with some other bounty hunters, Dutch scoffs at this praise. Bishop then defends Thornton for at least

FIGURE 46. *From left to right:* Tector Gorch (Ben Johnson), Lyle Gorch (Warren Oates), Pike Bishop (William Holden), and Dutch Engstrom (Ernest Borgnine) march to their certain deaths in the final violent sequence of Sam Peckinpah's *The Wild Bunch* (1969). Courtesy of the Museum of Modern Art.

"sticking to his word"—that is, his promise to the railway owner (Albert Dekker) to bring in the gang, including his former friend Bishop, dead or alive. But Dutch protests that it is not sticking to one's word that counts, but rather "who you give it to." Despite being an outlaw and a killer, Dutch is the one member of the group whose loyalty seems to be defined by more than monetary gain. His obvious personal affection for Pike and his compassion for Angel (after the latter has been abducted by Mapache) are clear evidence of this.

But Dutch's commitment is to a band of ruthless outlaws, therefore bringing into serious question the values in play here—values that are far from those of the traditionally heroic westerner.[14] While one might initially think that Peckinpah celebrates the westerner whose freedom requires liberation from the constraints and impositions of an ordered society and a growing civilization, such an interpretation would be a mistake. We must never forget that these are the brutal killers of innocents—ruthless egoists whose ethos is driven by greed and whose courage should not be admired uncritically. The audience is provoked to ask, "Courage and unity and honor—but for the sake of *what?*"

Once we have answered that question, then the battle that concludes the film must be viewed as utterly nihilistic, despite the fact that the wild bunch is responding vengefully to Mapache's horrifying murder of Angel before their very eyes. Their vengeance against Mapache, knowing that they will surely die, is far from an ennobling final stand. By refusing to question the moral implications of their decision to sell guns to Mapache, and thereby ignoring Angel's protests, these men have reduced themselves to killers who sell killing machines to other killers with no regard for distinctions between killers and victims. If anything, their final stand is merely a reach for retribution that comes too late, given the situation that has resulted from their purely economic alliance with Mapache.

Peckinpah has not merely demythologized the Western gunslinger in this film. He has taken the villainous gangs from traditional Westerns (the Clantons of *Clementine,* Nathan Burdette's men in *Rio Bravo,* Liberty Valance and his accomplices, etc.) and given them a point of view around which an entire narrative is constructed. But transforming villains into protagonists with a perspective does not turn them into heroes, even if it appears this way on the surface of things. The violence is only attractive or heroic if one is already aligned morally and psychologically with those children who appear at the start of the film, during the opening credits: those who take ominous pleasure in watching scorpions succumb to an army of red ants. Are the members of this wild bunch anything more, when all is said and done, than overgrown children enjoying games of death and violence for their own profit and pleasure? Peckinpah's film invites the viewer who finds heroism and entertainment in the actions of these men to ponder a similar question.

BEYOND *THE WILD BUNCH*

Following in the wake of *The Wild Bunch,* there emerged a series of revisionist Westerns that increasingly challenged the parameters of the genre. Admittedly, one can find transformative Westerns throughout the silent and sound eras—for example, *The Wind, Duel in the Sun, The Searchers,* and almost any comedic Western that intentionally subverted genre conventions. As we have seen over the course of the previous two chapters, the rise of the psychological and existential Western began in earnest after World War II and continued through the 1950s and early 1960s. But in the late 1960s, and especially with the combination of reverence and rebelliousness evidenced by Peckinpah, Western film revisionism was in full swing. This, despite the fact that directors such as Burt Kennedy and Andrew McLaglen were still making fairly classical Westerns that continued to be popular throughout the 1970s. These were especially popular with the old guard of moviegoers who relished seeing John Wayne return to his saddle again and again in such films as *True Grit, The Undefeated, Rio Lobo, Chisum, Big Jake, Cahill: United States Marshal,* and *Rooster Cogburn.* While the decade after *The Wild Bunch* was filled with both traditional and genre-challenging Westerns, one can clearly see an intensification of the effort by certain filmmakers and studios to do something novel and more critically minded.

The revisionist Westerns of the late 1960s and the first half of the 1970s tended to follow the trajectory established by Peckinpah in demythologizing the story of the Old West and the figure of the westerner, whether hero or outlaw or both. As noted earlier, one mode of demythologizing, that of parodying or satirizing certain stereotypical elements of the genre, has its seeds in the silent comic Westerns of Douglas Fairbanks and others (see chapter 3). One of the most successful and popular Western comedies in film history is George Roy Hill's *Butch Cassidy and the Sundance Kid* (1969). Released just after *The Wild Bunch,* the movie stars Paul Newman as the witty leader of the Hole in the Wall Gang and Robert Redford as his quick-draw partner, Sundance. As the Old West becomes the New West, a posse pursues their train-robbing gang and the two title characters, along with their beloved Etta Place (Katharine Ross), flee to Bolivia. The movie, written by William Goldman, won four Oscars, and its combination of quirky comedy and frolicking romance, played with great tongue-in-cheek style by the leads against a canvas of familiar Western conventions, made the film a box office smash.

Also in the comic mode of deromanticizing the figure of the westerner is Peckinpah's *The Ballad of Cable Hogue* (1970), starring Jason Robards and Stella Stevens (see also chapter 3). Peckinpah then turned to family drama in a Western setting with his quietly moving drama *Junior Bonner* (1972), with Steve McQueen in the title role. Bonner is a former rodeo star who returns to his hometown, reunites with his parents (Robert Preston and Ida Lupino), and faces challenges involving his family as well as a fast-changing West. In Peckinpah's final Western, *Pat Garrett and Billy the Kid* (1973), aging lawman Garrett (James Coburn) is hired to eliminate his old friend Billy (Kris Kristofferson). The latter film is full of fascinating moments and, though butchered by studio editors against Peckinpah's wishes before its release, the movie was later restored to the director's original cut and vision. This elegiac story of the tragic friendship between the two title characters is filled with death and destruction, and like *The Wild Bunch* it continues Peckinpah's recurring interest in the transition of the Old West into a modern America. A particularly moving scene is the death of Sheriff Baker (Slim Pickens), set against a gorgeous landscape and edited to the haunting rhythm of "Knockin' on Heaven's Door" by Bob Dylan. Dylan not only composed the original music for the movie but also plays a small role as the (appropriately for Dylan) enigmatic Alias.

The year 1970 witnessed the release of two impressive films that dealt empathetically with the relationship between white civilization and Indian peoples. Arthur Penn's *Little Big Man*, scripted by Calder Willingham from the novel by Thomas Berger, depicts in flashback the evolving story of Jack Crabb (Dustin Hoffman), who as a boy was captured and raised by a Cheyenne tribe, and who spends the rest of his life crisscrossing between cultures. Chief Dan George, the Native American actor who later played Lone Watie in Eastwood's *The Outlaw Josey Wales,* was deservedly nominated for a Best Supporting Actor Oscar for his role here as Old Lodge Skins, the Cheyenne chief who helps to raise young Jack.

At the start of the film, Crabb is an allegedly 121-year-old man who agrees to share his biography at the request of a student of oral histories. Crabb recounts various phases of his mesmerizing life: assimilated Cheyenne, gunslinger, apprentice to a snake oil salesman, husband of a white woman abducted by Indians, husband of an Indian woman killed by General Custer's soldiers, and sidekick of Wild Bill Hickok. In addition, he serves at one point as a scout for an increasingly eccentric Custer who leads his men, at Crabb's vengeful urging, into a self-destructive massacre at the Battle of the Little Bighorn. The movie's critique of the American military might be interpreted as an implicit criticism of American involvement in the Vietnam War, given the period in which *Little Big Man* was filmed and released. Penn would return to the revisionist Western a half-dozen years later with his less successful *The Missouri Breaks* (1976), a film that captivates on occasion because of its charismatic teaming of Marlon Brando (in one of his most eccentric performances) and Jack Nicholson (who would later direct and star in his own 1978 parody of the Western genre, *Goin' South*).

The other film of 1970 that explores a white man's immersion in tribal culture is Elliot Silverstein's *A Man Called Horse,* based on a tale by

Dorothy Johnson, who also wrote the story "The Man Who Shot Liberty Valance." The movie stars Richard Harris as an English aristocrat who is abducted by the Sioux, and who, beginning with a brutal initiation ceremony, gradually becomes assimilated. The film was successful enough to warrant two sequels, *The Return of a Man Called Horse* (1976) and *Triumphs of a Man Called Horse* (1982). By presenting the Indian in a far more sympathetic light, *Little Big Man* and *A Man Called Horse* fulfill the trajectory initiated by the early Biograph films about Native American life (see chapter 1). This trajectory was later enriched by such Westerns as Delmer Daves's *Broken Arrow* (1950), Samuel Fuller's *Run of the Arrow* (1957), and Ford's *Cheyenne Autumn* (1964). These movies point forward to Kevin Costner's Oscar-winning exploration of the Native American perspective in *Dances with Wolves* (1990).

Robert Altman's poetic yet nihilistic "anti-Western" *McCabe and Mrs. Miller,* released in 1971, was shot by cinematographer Vilmos Zsigmond in the coldly beautiful Pacific Northwest. The movie is also ornamented with selected songs by Canadian-born bard Leonard Cohen, ballads that offer their own type of icy splendor. The script, cowritten by Altman and based on a novel by Edmund Naughton, centers on the two title characters (played in an effectively understated manner by Warren Beatty and Julie Christie) who establish a joint business venture, a tavern and accompanying whorehouse, in the remote hamlet of Presbyterian Church. The area becomes an object of interest to a mining company, and McCabe becomes the target of the company's hired guns. Altman's film parodies the traditional westerner, presenting McCabe as a fast-talking gambler with no knowledge of gunmanship; he is a coward who takes advantage of his status as an enigmatic stranger by allowing the villagers to continue suspecting that he is an infamous gunslinger. Altman would return to the demythologizing mode of the Western several years later with his *Buffalo Bill and the Indians, or Sitting Bull's History Lesson* (1976), based on a play by Arthur Kopit and starring Paul Newman as the famous showman. The narrative of this movie, in fact, makes the mythical distortion of the Old West's true history its central theme. Altman's picture is a revisionist Western about the very revisionism that was inherent in Buffalo Bill Cody's project of transforming historical reality into a semifictional production that existed for the sake of entertainment and profit.

These Westerns are several of the more significant and influential examples of genre revisionism in the immediate post–*Wild Bunch* era. In many cases, as with *The Wild Bunch,* a Western that could be labeled as revisionist or postclassical was in fact a clever fusion of the traditional and the new—in some cases forming an intriguing dialectic between challenges to genre conventions and tributes to the very conventions being challenged. Furthermore, one cannot fully appreciate the diverse patterns demonstrated by this phase of Western filmmaking without taking into account the career of Clint Eastwood. As we will see in the next chapter, the ways in which Eastwood built on his earlier work with Sergio Leone and Don Siegel reveal a Peckinpah-like mixture of reverence, reaction, and rebellion.

CHAPTER 10

Eastwood and the
American Western

*"High Plains Drifter," "The Outlaw Josey Wales,"
and "Unforgiven"*

I've never pictured myself as the guy on the white horse. . . .
I've always liked heroes that've had some sort of weakness or
problems to overcome besides the problem of the immediate
script. That always keeps it much more interesting than doing
it the conventional way. John Wayne once wrote me a letter
telling me he didn't like *High Plains Drifter*. He said it wasn't
about the people who really pioneered the West. I realized
that there's two different generations, and he wouldn't
understand what I was doing. *High Plains Drifter* was meant
to be a fable; it wasn't meant to show the hours of pioneering
drudgery. It wasn't supposed to be anything about settling
the West.

—Clint Eastwood, interview with Kenneth Turan

Clint Eastwood's diverse acting performances and directing accomplishments in Western films have earned him a solid place high in the
pantheon of such genre artists as Ford, Hawks, Wayne, Cooper, Fonda,
and Stewart. The action-oriented audience long ago fell in love with the
icy but tongue-in-cheek style of Eastwood's grizzled, cigar-chomping
antihero in Sergio Leone's "Dollars" trilogy of the 1960s (*A Fistful of
Dollars, For a Few Dollars More,* and *The Good, the Bad, and the Ugly*).
And many fans appreciated the return of such a character in Eastwood's
own *High Plains Drifter* (1973) and *Pale Rider* (1985). In many ways
this actor's most popular and influential role as urban cop Dirty Harry

is a natural outgrowth of that earlier gunslinger who faces danger with the same cool determination and instinctual spontaneity as, say, an expert jazz musician.[1]

If there are three films that alone would put Eastwood on the map of artists who have excelled in this genre, they are *High Plains Drifter, The Outlaw Josey Wales* (1976), and *Unforgiven* (1992). With these works we see an actor-director who has fused his talents in the service of extending and amplifying, as well as subverting, the essential traditions of the cinematic Western. There are intriguing parallels among these films, and there are also clear differences between Eastwood's more character-oriented, narrative-driven Westerns and the more stylized Westerns in which he plays the anonymous figure emerging inexplicably from the horizon and returning there, leaving dead bodies along the trail. When one considers his Westerns as a whole, especially those that he also directed, we see that his oeuvre provides a fitting consummation of the genre and intriguingly integrates both classical and postclassical elements of the Western's long and varied history.[2]

CAREER OVERVIEW

Eastwood's association with the genre goes back to a point before his work with Leone. After some bit parts in B-films, he kick-started his career by playing cattle drover Rowdy Yates in the long-running television series *Rawhide,* beginning in 1959 and continuing through 1966. While on a brief hiatus from that role, Eastwood moved on to international fame as the "Man with No Name" in Leone's trilogy, beginning with *A Fistful of Dollars* (*Per un pugno di dollari,* 1964).[3] Shortly before becoming a genuine Hollywood superstar in his role as Harry Callahan—beginning with Don Siegel's *Dirty Harry* (1971)—this actor furthered his growing iconic status as a westerner. He performed in such films as *Hang 'Em High* of 1968 (directed by Ted Post, who had worked on the earlier *Rawhide* series) and Siegel's action-comedy *Two Mules for Sister Sara* of 1970, with Shirley MacLaine.

The pre–Dirty Harry Eastwood also starred in a few quasi Westerns that played off the genre in which he had already left a deep boot print. In Siegel's *Coogan's Bluff* (1968), Eastwood plays an Arizona lawman with a very Western way of doing things, sent to New York City to collect a prisoner and to grapple with big-city crime and an urban police system.[4] In *Paint Your Wagon* (1969), directed by Joshua Logan and adapted by Paddy Chayefsky from Alan Jay Lerner's Broadway musical,

Clint undertook what was, in some ways, his most daring role to date: he croons alongside fellow nonsinger Lee Marvin as they play rollicking gold-mining pals in the Old West who share comic adventures as well as a wife. In one of his most intriguing roles, Eastwood starred as John McBurney, a Union soldier recovering from his injuries in an all-female boarding school in the Deep South, in Don Siegel's Civil War–era drama *The Beguiled* (1971).[5]

A year after starring in *Dirty Harry* as a kind of "urban westerner," Eastwood portrayed the title character in *Joe Kidd* (1972), based on an Elmore Leonard–penned script and directed by the reliable John Sturges (*Gunfight at the O.K. Corral, The Magnificent Seven, The Great Escape, Bad Day at Black Rock*). Here Eastwood plays a hired gun who joins temporarily with a posse formed by greedy landowner Frank Harlan (Robert Duvall) to eliminate the Mexican revolutionary leader Luis Chama (John Saxon). Eastwood's character in *Joe Kidd* is as enigmatic at certain points as his previous role in the Leone trilogy, wandering a no-man's-land between various parties in different conflicts. And yet, interestingly, he is given an actual name here and, furthermore, one that helps to form the very title of the movie, as with *Coogan's Bluff* and *Dirty Harry*. So is this the story of a specific individual with a specific name and a given history, or is this the tale of an archetypal stranger, some mythical "good bad man"? Joe Kidd wanders somewhere in between. The question, however, evokes a contrast between two very different conceptions of the westerner: the mysterious, usually unnamed gunslinger who passes through communities like some nomadic spirit, on the one hand, and an identifiable individual who struggles to overcome some concrete life situation, on the other. A tension between these two different kinds of westerner reverberates throughout Eastwood's body of work in the genre.

With the subsequent *High Plains Drifter*, Eastwood began to direct many of the movies in which he starred. He had already directed one non-Western film, the psychological thriller *Play Misty for Me* (1971).[6] In *Drifter* he plays "the Stranger," an almost ethereal gunslinger appearing suddenly in the lakeside town of Lago as an agent of retribution and destruction. Eastwood's character reminds us of Leone's Man with No Name because of his anonymity, seeming amorality, and ruthlessness. The Stranger punishes a corrupt and cowardly town for its faults by demanding that the townspeople turn their community into a symbolic Hades of sorts, and the story's fiery climax echoes the apocalyptic ending of Hart's silent Western *Hell's Hinges* (see chapter 1). Eastwood, in fact, exhibits the same stoic, rough-edged acting style that Hart made famous.

Eastwood then directed and acted in one of his very best Western films, *The Outlaw Josey Wales,* a Civil War–era portrait of a man driven to obsessive vengeance after the murder of his family. The main character departs substantially from Eastwood's earlier incarnations of the no-named stranger, as well as from the title character of his later *Pale Rider.* The latter characters are westerners who nearly transcend the human realm altogether, emerging from and disappearing into a mist of myth and archetype. But Wales is someone who has a definite biography: he is originally a family man, and we know (as with his character in the earlier *Hang 'Em High*) the precise reasons for his current vengefulness. We follow Josey after he has been transformed into an almost robotic creature, driven by a desire for retribution, and witness his eventual restoration as a genuine *person* who falls in love and who cares for his acquired "family." Wales gradually reclaims his own essential humanity in response to the influence of the small community of outcasts he has adopted during his odyssey.

The Outlaw Josey Wales is a kind of precursor to Eastwood's 1992 masterpiece *Unforgiven* in that both films center on rifle-wielding killers who are presented, not in terms of mystery and anonymity, but rather in terms of their character development and ethical motivation. Given such a contrast between the different types of westerner that Eastwood has played, and because the film is an intriguing fusion of classical and postclassical aspects of the Western, it is not surprising that he dedicated (in the final credits) the Oscar-winning *Unforgiven* to both Siegel and Leone, whose cinematic styles and story choices are dissimilar.[7] Siegel tended to favor stories that depict real-life individuals in real-life situations, done in a straightforward no-nonsense manner, while Leone gravitated toward archetype, myth, and stylistic grandeur.

Despite their differences, one similarity between Siegel and Leone is their tendency to veer into dark comedy at times. Eastwood's films are certainly not devoid of levity, and his use of occasional humor recalls the fact that Westerns and comedies have often intersected (see chapter 3). Eastwood's attempts at sporadic comedy in his Westerns often succeed because he is willing to exaggerate or even parody his famously macho persona. For instance, there is a fair degree of cynical wit, helping to balance out the heavy doses of violence, in Leone's "Dollars" trilogy, as when Eastwood's ultracool Blondie plays straight man to Eli Wallach's hysterical Tuco in *The Good, the Bad, and the Ugly (Il buono, il brutto,*

FIGURE 47. Clint Eastwood stars as retired gunfighter and current hog farmer William Munny in Eastwood's Oscar-winning *Unforgiven* (1992). Courtesy of the Museum of Modern Art.

il cattivo, 1966). In *Josey Wales,* Eastwood infuses the movie with subtle humor at times, despite the highly serious theme of revenge and the episodes of brutal warfare. Several of his scenes with Chief Dan George are intentionally comical; Chief Dan's deadpan responses border on the Keatonesque. And despite the movie's frequent funereal somberness, there are also dashes of dark humor in *Unforgiven,* whether in the interplay between Sheriff Little Bill Daggett (Gene Hackman) and Old West–mythologizer W. W. Beauchamp (Saul Rubinek) or in the farewell shot of English Bob (Richard Harris) scolding the entire town of Big Whiskey for being a bunch of "bloody savages."

In terms of outright Western comedy, Eastwood directed and starred in the highly entertaining *Bronco Billy* (1980). This film is a gentle comedy of cowboy manners, playing off the idea of the westerner as a legendary hero for children to admire and enjoy. The title character, a kind of tragicomic descendant of Buffalo Bill Cody, struggles to keep his traveling Wild West show afloat financially while also dealing with humiliation, frustration, friendship, and possible romance. In various ways Eastwood has constructed and deconstructed ideas of the westerner over the decades, sometimes revealing the stark reality behind the legend. In *Bronco Billy* he depicts a small-time businessman attempting to keep the legend alive, despite having a difficult time doing so. Here Eastwood again reveals the vulnerable human being behind his tight-jawed tough-guy image, and the film manages to poke fun at the genre by highlighting its show business side and the artifice of Western myth-making in the contemporary world.

HIGH PLAINS DRIFTER

The persona of the anonymous, ruthless gunfighter that Eastwood had adopted in his earlier "spaghetti" Westerns is amplified in *High Plains Drifter,* the first Western that Eastwood also directed. In his role as tough cop Harry Callahan, he had fashioned a screen image stretching across different films and exemplifying the type of challenge to traditional movie heroism that had blossomed with the more psychological and existentialist Westerns of the 1950s (see chapter 7). However, Eastwood's shaping of his screen persona over the second half of the 1960s and first half of the 1970s did not include the types of hero-deflation or psychologizing that could be found in some of these earlier examples of genre revisionism. Eastwood was still very much the confident gunslinger transcending the boundaries and conventions of "ordinary" society, and the inner lives of his characters were hidden behind a glacial facade. But he was not a hero in the traditional sense, as the actor admitted in more than one interview (see the quote at the beginning of this chapter). Unlike John Wayne and his typical association with America's dominant ideas and values, Eastwood tended toward characters who were *anti*heroes, driven toward revenge and killing for reasons that had little to do with building or defending a growing civilization. And given the cultural climate of the Vietnam and Watergate era, this tendency toward antiheroism fit with Hollywood's growing patterns of cultural critique and tradition-shattering. William Beard nicely summarizes this in his *Persistence of Double Vision: Essays on Clint Eastwood:*

> Eastwood arrived in Hollywood during this wholesale dismantling of prosocial heroism, armed with the knowledge (gained with Leone) of how to present heroic power in the total absence of any kind of social project. Leone's decadent European skepticism totally incinerates all idealist social beliefs and leaves the gunfighting hero—whose constitutional function hitherto has been to enable the good community—stranded in a literal and figurative wasteland with no interest to uphold but his own. The hero's mastery, no

longer connected with a grand ideological project and denuded of classical camouflage, instead takes the form of a mysterious transcendent power. . . . It has been a central feature of Eastwood's persona (and this has surely been important in his cinematic survival through the various culture upheavals over the years of his career) that the project of its heroism has always been accompanied by markers of the implausibility, unnaturalness, and indeed impossibility of its own existence.[8]

High Plains Drifter was released in 1973 and appeared on the crest of a wave of genre-revising Westerns, as discussed in the last section of the previous chapter. Eastwood's movie was a paradigm of the antitraditional Western, with some of the raw violence of Peckinpah, the antiheroism of Altman and Penn, and the nihilism of Leone. Eastwood's more Leone-esque movies, such as *High Plains Drifter,* tend to be highly stylized, where the visual and musical effects, as well as the creative presentations of violence, often trump characterization and dialogue.[9] In his later *Pale Rider,* another avenging angel/demon story that echoes George Stevens's *Shane* (1953), Eastwood plays a mysterious preacher-gunslinger who, as in his earlier *Drifter,* appears when needed and rides away into the desert and mountains when he has completed his task. Such films are, like Leone's, "antipsychological" in the sense that their main characters veer toward archetype, caricature, and even abstraction—and so contrary to the kinds of Westerns made by directors such as Mann and Daves (see chapter 7). In *Drifter* and *Pale Rider,* Eastwood gives us gunslingers who are creatures of enigma and action rather than practitioners of situated introspection.

As seen in previous discussions of films such as Hawks's *Red River* and Ford's *The Searchers,* the style of a Western film includes as one of its integral components the aesthetic relationship between characters and their immediate settings. Eastwood's appreciation for the importance of landscape is certainly on display in *Drifter,* and particularly in his use of the almost surreal terrain around Mono Lake near Yosemite National Park and the California Sierra.[10] The movie takes place in the fictional lakeside township of Lago. The silver-blue expanse of water in the background of many shots may remind one of Brando's similar and original use of a shoreline setting in his *One-Eyed Jacks,* the only film that Brando ever directed. In fact, if one does not look carefully, the viewer may easily think that the body of water behind the town of Lago is a part of the ocean rather than a landlocked lake, and even the production notes on the DVD version of *Drifter* mistakenly refer to its "seaside" setting. Precious few Westerns have this kind of backdrop. As

FIGURE 48. Clint Eastwood as the anonymous stranger who arrives in the lakeside town of Lago in Eastwood's *High Plains Drifter* (1973). Courtesy of the Museum of Modern Art.

director Anthony Mann once observed, it is odd that so many of the classic Westerns are set predominantly in desert regions like Monument Valley, since the West has such a variegated landscape, including the forested and mountainous regions for which Mann had an affinity.[11] Eastwood, like Mann, diversifies the audience's experiences and expectations of Western terrain.

Much of *Drifter* takes place within the confines of Lago, though the surrounding lake and hills are almost always visible, framed between buildings or by the windows of the local hotel, barbershop, and mercantile. Eastwood's emphasis on the natural world that, in the Old West, lies always just beyond the main street of town is even evident in the landscape paintings that hang in the hotel where his nameless character takes a room. And with so many scenes that have as their backdrop shimmering lake-water or olive-green hillside or cloud-spotted sky, the movie does more than merely take advantage of the scenic opportunities of on-location shooting, in the best tradition of the action-filled Western film. The film also gives its audience a sense that the self-centered and morally passive townspeople of Lago have forgotten the world of rugged beauty that lies beyond their small world of material comfort. The landscape here is intriguing, and since this is a fairly dreamlike Western with hints of the supernatural mixed in, it is fitting that the natural scenery appears almost otherworldly. Eastwood once said in an interview about his choice of setting for the film: "I wanted to get an offbeat look to [the film] rather than a conventional Western look. Mono Lake has a weird look to it, a lot of strange colors—never looks the same way twice during the day."[12]

The physical town of Lago, in terms of its buildings and layout, is something akin to a character in the film, as is the case with many other artificially constructed towns in classic Westerns: for example, Lordsburg (*Stagecoach*), Dodge City (*Dodge City*), Tombstone (*My Darling Clementine*), Shinbone (*The Man Who Shot Liberty Valance*), and El Dorado (*El Dorado*). Townships in movies such as *Drifter* play as significant a role as the natural landscape does in other Westerns in shaping the atmosphere in which the characters move and act. And when it comes to the selection and creation of proper settings for his films, Eastwood typically chooses to work with the very best. The town in *High Plains Drifter* was constructed under the experienced art director and set designer Henry Bumstead, who had also worked on *Joe Kidd,* as well as on Mann's 1950 psychological Western *The Furies,* among countless other films.[13] In his biography of Eastwood, Richard Schickel discusses how Bumstead's work for *Drifter* helped to realize Eastwood's intentions: "Bumstead built the village in twenty-eight days, complete with interior sets, and in its rawness, its suggestion of impermanence, it is something of a masterpiece. Reminiscent of silent-film western towns (one thinks of *Hell's Hinges,* the William S. Hart film), its primitiveness says something about the heedless greed of its residents, their lack of rootedness and their lack of interest in building for the future. It—and they—parody the western town in most movies, where neat churches and schools bespeak hopes for more civilized times to come."[14]

But after having exposed us to so much of the memorable landscape around his constructed community of Lago, Eastwood then erases it, so to speak, in the final nighttime sequence. Here the Stranger eliminates the three villains who have come back to town to satisfy their own desire for justice, having been "betrayed" by the townspeople whom they had once guarded. We see only the darkened town itself, painted entirely red and renamed "Hell" at the command of the Stranger. This scene anticipates the rain-soaked, nocturnal finale of *Unforgiven,* where

Munny enacts rage-driven vengeance against Sheriff Daggett. In that scene too we have only meager glimpses of the town itself, without any indication of a surrounding natural world.

Just as *Drifter*'s town and its adjacent lake possess an enigmatic aura, so too does Eastwood's anonymous character. What makes the Stranger most mysterious is the fact that he seems to be connected, without clear explanation, to the former Marshal Jim Duncan of Lago, a man who was whipped to death on the main street while most of the townspeople simply looked on without doing a thing. Even by the end, when the drifter rides out of town past Duncan's visible gravestone, we wonder just who this man is, the very question that forms one of the concluding lines of the film. He is either the ghost of the murdered sheriff, come back to haunt the town that had turned on him—in which case the movie rises to a supernatural level that is echoed by Eastwood's later role as the mystical preacher-gunfighter in *Pale Rider*—or he is the sheriff's brother or friend, also bent on revenge.

Marshal Duncan, as the plot later indicates, was an honest man who had planned to divulge the fact, held secret by the townspeople out of their own economic interest, that the mine on which they depend is located on federal property. The citizens, fearing governmental interference in their profit making, paid three criminals to help enforce the secrecy of this information by punishing, and eventually killing, Marshal Duncan. But unfortunately for the residents of Lago, these hired assassins then lorded it over the town in a tyrannical manner after having murdered the lawman. The citizens responded to this egregious behavior by alerting the regional legal authorities to the trio's crime.

Through its eventual focus on the story of a sheriff who must contend with his own community, *Drifter* makes clear thematic reference to *High Noon* (directed by Fred Zinnemann, 1952) in the same way that the later *Pale Rider* plays off *Shane*.[15] Eastwood has stated in an interview: "The starting point [of *Drifter*] was: 'What would have happened if the sheriff of *High Noon* had been killed? What would have happened *afterwards?*'"[16] As in *High Noon*, three villainous gunslingers are finally released from jail and seek vengeance while a town tensely awaits their arrival. Also as in *High Noon*, the townspeople prefer to depend on the strength and courage of a single man to save them. On the other hand, quite unlike *High Noon*, the citizens' new "savior" is no hero, but just the opposite, a man who would rather see the town destroyed than saved. If anything, he arranges them like targets in a shooting gallery when he advises them to hide in *seemingly* strategic locations and shoot at the three desperados as they approach town. He knows that they will be little more than sitting ducks. Also unlike Zinnemann's classic, where the townspeople did nothing to help their brave sheriff (Gary Cooper), the residents of Lago are forced by the Stranger to prepare for their own self-defense, even if he will finally be the one to flick the whip and pull the trigger.

With *Drifter* we are reminded also of Kurosawa's samurai classic *The Seven Samurai* (1954), as well as his later revisionist samurai film *Yojimbo* (1961). The latter film, in fact, served as the clear basis of Eastwood's first Leone-directed western, *A Fistful of Dollars*.[17] In *The Seven Samurai*, townspeople hire a group of warriors to protect the town from marauding bandits, much as Lago depends on the Stranger in *Drifter*. In *Yojimbo* we see the need for a protective samurai, and the hired warrior (Toshiro Mifune) is, like Eastwood's drifter, a wandering man without a known past—and one who remains cynically neutral even when faced with a conflict that threatens to destroy a community. It is true that the Stranger in *Drifter* does not care for financial gain and even denies at one point that he is a gunfighter, meaning that he does not hire himself out for such purposes. But like Mifune's character in *Yojimbo*, he is apathetic to the welfare of those he is supposed to defend. If anything, the drifter seeks his own revenge against *all* concerned, but in a mysteriously slow and playful fashion.

The reason why the Stranger undertakes a methodical form of vengeance has to do with Marshal Duncan. The supernatural possibility of the drifter being the ghost of the murdered lawman is made all the more probable when he dreams of Marshal Duncan's whipping, an event that only Duncan himself (or those who watched his slaying) could have experienced. As Schickel informs us, it was the director's wish to leave this mystery intact to engage the viewer, though Eastwood "now says the script definitely identified the drifter as the murdered sheriff's sibling."[18] The director's decision to leave the Stranger's identity indeterminate adds effectively to the overall feeling of mystery and ambiguity inherent in the style and landscape of the movie as a whole.[19]

In an intriguing footnote in the history of Hollywood Westerns, John Wayne, who had encouraged Eastwood early on, suggested that the two stars should work together at some point. But Wayne wound up declining when, in the mid-1970s, Eastwood sent Wayne a script that allegedly required more revision. The elder actor used his letter to his younger counterpart as an opportunity to criticize *High Plains Drifter* because its "townspeople . . . did not represent the true spirit of the American pioneer, the spirit that had made America great."[20] Eastwood later reflected on Wayne's letter in an interview and concluded: "I was never John Wayne's heir."[21] He pointed out that Wayne was the westerner who typically played by the rules and lived according to a code of honor, always for the sake of a just cause. Eastwood admitted that his own westerners often did not: "I think the era of standing there going 'You draw first' is over. You don't have much of a chance if you wait for the other guy to draw. You have to try for realism. So, yeah, I used to shoot them in the back all the time."[22]

THE OUTLAW JOSEY WALES

Eastwood's more Siegelesque films, such as *The Outlaw Josey Wales* and *Unforgiven,* are in the Fordian and Hawksian (i.e., classical) mode of stylistic economy, where choices of mise-en-scène and montage become more or less invisible—that is, not pronounced in an exaggerated or self-reflexive manner. The cinematic form here is dictated by the demands of character development and story-governed logic, and this is also true of more recent Eastwood-directed films, such as *Mystic River* (2003), *Million Dollar Baby* (2004), *Flags of Our Fathers* (2006), *Letters from Iwo Jima* (2006), *Changeling* (2008), and *Gran Torino* (2008). Don Siegel's own later Western *The Shootist* (1976), starring John Wayne in his superb career-culminating performance as a semiretired gunslinger dying of cancer, anticipates *Unforgiven* to some degree not merely because of its narrative-driven style but also because of its theme, which is that of a retired killer who must return one last time to his violent ways.[23]

The Outlaw Josey Wales is two hours and fifteen minutes long and moves at a pace accommodating the riders, who wander through forest and canyon, from the Indian territory to the wide open spaces just north of Mexico. Eastwood mocks the very persona that he also partially mythologizes in this visually stunning film, which has the rhythmic patterns of Ford's Westerns, with alternating sequences of action and reflective stasis. *Josey Wales* is one of the finest of Westerns in its thematic and visual use of landscape to illuminate mood, character, and climax.

The film also suggests the oppositions and contradictions within human nature that inform the genre at its most meaningful levels. On the one hand it is a remarkable portrayal of a killer, with its protagonist quick to outdraw and shoot to death a large number of people, either out of spirited vengeance or in cool self-defense. A simple Missouri plowman, Josey Wales becomes a dedicated avenger after he sees his wife and son murdered and his house burned to the ground by marauding Redlegs (Union guerillas). The character of Josey Wales may therefore be compared broadly with revenge-motivated westerners such as the Ringo Kid (John Wayne) in *Stagecoach*, Wyatt Earp (Henry Fonda) in *My Darling Clementine*, Will Lockhart (James Stewart) in *The Man from Laramie*, Ethan Edwards (Wayne again) in *The Searchers*, and Rio (Marlon Brando) in *One-Eyed Jacks*. In addition, Josey can be compared with the William Hart–type hero, stoic and laconic—except for a meaningful dialogue with Ten Bears (Will Sampson), his Indian counterpart—and his humor lean and dry. As Wales moves west, he is seen to be kind and patient while caring for the strays who attach themselves to him: a young mortally wounded rebel, a wise old Cherokee, an experienced squaw, a scrawny dog, and a Kansas mother and her pensive daughter. Most everyone whom Wales eliminates deserves to die for having gone after his family or his fellow rebels or his merry band. The only adversaries as smart as Wales—former rebel Fletcher (John Vernon) and chief warrior Ten Bears—are also the only ones to understand and forgive his actions.

In the first scene of the film, we witness the murder of Josey's wife and son by the Redlegs while he is out plowing his field. He hears horses galloping by and sees black smoke rising above the forest from the direction of his home. He runs to find his house on fire and his wife being assaulted by men on horseback; but before he can react, Josey is struck to the ground and hears his son cry out. One of the Redlegs strikes Wales across the face, leaving a bleeding scar, and the attack is over as suddenly as it began. We then cut to the next day and watch Josey as he buries his wife and child. His son's little arm falls out from under a blanket as Josey drags the corpse to be buried. Grief-stricken, he pushes a wooden cross down into the simple gravesite. We may recall here Ethan Edwards's horror and deep sorrow in *The Searchers* when he returns to his family's destroyed ranch and discovers his beloved Martha's ravaged corpse. Like Wales, Edwards does not waste time in sublimating his sorrow into obsessive revenge, and this is emphasized by his angry interruption of the family's funeral in the hope of catching up with the Comanche as quickly as possible: "Put an amen to it!" (See chapter 8.) We might also remember here Wyatt Earp's similar transformation from grief-stricken mourner to calculated revenge-seeker in Ford's *My Darling Clementine*, though Earp goes about his vengeance in a much quieter, law-abiding way (see chapter 7).

FIGURE 49. In Clint Eastwood's Civil War–era Western *The Outlaw Josey Wales* (1976), the title character, whose wife and son have been brutally killed by Union guerilla fighters, is about to embark on his new life as a gunslinging revenge-seeker. Courtesy of the Museum of Modern Art.

Josey begins practicing with a pistol while preparing for a career of retribution, and he is soon approached by a band of Confederates, including their leader, Fletcher. They say that the Redlegs who committed these killings must be up in Kansas with the Union; Fletcher's own men are going up there to "set things right." Josey agrees to accompany them, and as the credits begin to roll with trumpets blaring and drums beating, we see Josey and the band of men ride quickly through forests and across prairie land, killing Union soldiers along their way. The montage here is rapid and soon fades into gray-and-blue-tinted shots of battle action. The Civil War–era setting reminds us of earlier Westerns such as Raoul Walsh's *Dark Command* (1940), based loosely on the story of Confederate guerilla leader William Quantrill, and Ford's *The Horse Soldiers* (1959), the tale of a Union cavalry unit sent to fight behind enemy lines.

Fletcher eventually tries to persuade the men to surrender to the Union forces so that they can then go home. He tells them that they are the "last of the holdouts," that everyone else has given up, and that he is going to

FIGURE 50. Josey Wales prepares to do battle in his role as revenge-seeker. Courtesy of the Museum of Modern Art.

surrender since he has had enough. He manages to convince everyone except Josey, and when Fletcher tells him that there is nowhere left to run, Josey replies that he "reckons that's true." Fletcher wishes him luck: he recognizes Josey's unconditional determination to seek retribution and see personal justice served. We catch a glimmer of admiration in Fletcher's eyes as he bids Josey farewell.

We then witness Fletcher's men gunned down by Union soldiers after they have been deceptively asked to stand in a row at their surrender and swear a pledge to the United States. Fletcher, standing alongside the Union officers who commanded this, is shocked because he was told that proper Union authorities were supposed to be the ones handling the surrender. It is, however, the Redlegs commander Terrill (Bill McKinney) who coordinates this mass execution, and Fletcher angrily calls him a "butcher." Now that the soldiers have been eliminated, the commanding Union officer, "the Senator" (Frank Schofield), orders Terrill to go after Wales with everything he has got—but Fletcher laughs and sarcastically wishes him luck in catching Wales. Fletcher is offered money to help in hunting down Wales, but the former rebel leader tells the Senator that he has had enough of his money already. We now know that Fletcher

FIGURE 51. Josey Wales (*far right, holding pistols*) squares off against the brutal Redlegs commander, Terrill (Bill McKinney, *center*). Courtesy of the Museum of Modern Art.

had been previously paid by the Union troops to persuade his men to surrender. And so begins a classic tale of revenge and justice in the post–Civil War West, though with several elements that revise the genre in intriguing ways.

Wales's moral character is clear: he is a good man driven to retribution by the evil of others, even if that evil is qualified to some degree by the wartime and postwar situation. Fletcher's morality, however, is questionable, since he has positioned himself between an alliance with the Union officers and feelings of empathy toward Josey. He rejects the Senator's money and expresses anger that he was double-crossed; but we then see him working with the Union men in hunting Wales, having been offered a special commission. Fletcher consents to the assignment, but he prophesizes nonetheless that Josey will be waiting in hell for them. He appears to have eventually surrendered to his doomed mission (and any of the accompanying monetary rewards) after having acquiesced to the Union forces and accepted, however regretfully, the consequences of that decision.

On the other hand, we recognize Josey as heroic from the moment he bravely rides into the Union camp to try to save his fellow Confederates while enacting revenge. Unfortunately he is too late: the Union soldiers have already begun firing on the surrendering Confederates, and Josey escapes, barely, with one man who has survived the massacre: a young soldier named Jamie (Sam Bottoms). His bond with the boy foreshadows our protagonist's eventual rehumanization. From this point on in the movie, Eastwood introduces minor characters in a "vignette" style that echoes Ford's talent for presenting stereotypical characters in a way that makes us *think* we have seen them before, even if we have not.[24]

This is the case when Josey and the boy eventually reach a river and find the ferryman chattering away with a dubious-looking elixir salesman. An old woman in a nearby cabin figures out who Josey is and warns him that Union men had recently stopped by looking for him. After then dealing with two hillbilly bounty hunters, Wales and his young protégé journey on in heavy rain and eventually build a small shelter. Josey goes out to have a look and sees the cavalry camped out by the river; when he returns, he discovers that the boy has died from his wounds. Josey closes Jamie's eyes, puts his body on a horse, and says an overly brief eulogy for him, despite his aversion to burials and blessings after having had to commit his wife and son to the earth not long before. Josey fires a shot and the horse takes off for the cavalry camp, the body of Jamie strapped to the animal. Josey reassures himself that the "blue bellies" will give a better burial than he can. As the Union men go after the horse that has run wildly through camp, Josey passes by unnoticed, journeying deeper into the woods.

Eastwood's film does not shy away from the theme of death, and in anticipation of his *Unforgiven*, it depicts the ugly consequences of violence. This is especially clear given the wartime setting and Josey's persistence in avenging the deaths of his wife and son. The characters' awareness of fate reverberates throughout the film, along with their ever present need for justice and retribution. And perhaps most of all, *Josey Wales* is pervaded by the same sense of tragic loss that informs the greatest of Western stories, ranging from *The Wind* (see chapter 2) and *Red River* (see chapter 6) to *The Searchers* and *The Man Who Shot Liberty Valance* (see chapter 8). It is this sense of loss that typically motivates the hero to act in ways beyond the ordinary, even while making the hero more human by the end, given the lessons learned.

This is a Western that also takes great care in showing us the humanity and nobility behind its Native American faces. In this regard, *Josey Wales* echoes anomalous silent Westerns like Griffith's early "East

Coast" Indian stories, as well as *The Vanishing American* and *Redskin* (see chapter 1), and later "Indian-friendly" Westerns such as Delmer Daves's *Broken Arrow* and Ford's *Cheyenne Autumn*. Wales enters the Indian territory and meets up with Lone Watie, who tells Josey that he has heard of him, and that the white man has been sneaking up on his people (the Cherokee) for years. He tells of how the government broke their promises and treaties and sent the Indians into "the nations." The white man has killed his wife and family, he declares sadly, and we immediately recognize a parallel between the two outcasts. Josey replies that it looks as if *they* cannot trust the white man, and there is an instant bond established, embodied by a clear chemistry between the two actors. Their rapport is wry and solid, and their responses to each other are immediate and comfortable. Lone Watie explains that the whites tried to make his people look "civilized" and told them to "endeavor to persevere." He says that, when the Indians had thought about it long enough, they decided to declare war on the Union. And so there is another parallel suggested here, one between the tribes and the Confederates, both feeling a need to battle the government and its policies. But Josey is now snoring, a comic conclusion to an otherwise somber and moving scene.

The focus on themes of death and loss is echoed by Eastwood's use of natural settings. The narrative plays out carefully against the brilliant landscape, and most of the film is autumnal in mood and in fact. The leaves are turning red in Missouri and blazing yellow as Josey moves west. Nature appears as more or less lifeless, most scenes unfold in daylight, and except for a couple of saloon scenes, all scenes take place outdoors. We also notice that the landscape gets ever more severe as Wales escapes from Missouri into the heat and sun of the southwest. The landscape has a look and feel not unlike certain passages in John Sturges's Westerns: seductively beautiful in places but always rife with danger. It is difficult to see in this landscape, and Wales frequently squints, though his aim is perfect and his quickness on the draw is certain. As John Gourlie and Leonard Engel observe in the introduction to their essay collection *Clint Eastwood, Actor and Director: New Perspectives:* "Wales is a character of greater emotional depth than Eastwood's 'stranger.' The landscape helps portray these depths, for it changes as Wales changes, reflecting his inner states. The film begins with an idyllic, pastoral setting of farmland, then moves to fields filled with blood and killing, then to rain-sodden swamps and lowland, from there to a dry and empty desert, and finally to an Edenic valley, evoking the harmonious landscape of Wales's farm at the beginning of the film."[25]

FIGURE 52. Josey Wales (*center, facing camera*) converses with a Comanche tribe and their leader, Chief Ten Bears (Will Sampson). Courtesy of the Museum of Modern Art.

Wales, once the avenger, eventually becomes a reluctant killer who wants to be left alone, but who cannot escape his many pursuers and opponents. The Union army soldiers are smug and vengeful, self-righteously eager to betray him; the Redlegs are unscrupulous killers, disguised as soldiers for hire; and the rapists and bounty hunters are particularly bloodthirsty in their ugliness and filth. Like other westerners, such as Ethan Edwards, Wales distrusts authority, opting to follow his instincts and act on his own. As the story moves west, however, it is the adopted strays who repeatedly save him. As he leads them to their new homestead, he watches a line of Comanche following alongside him, but the Indians are the only set of men who do not attack. This tribe and its leader, Ten Bears, are (like the Cherokee) more thoughtful than the white men ruling the West after the war. They desire only to live on their land as they always have.

The Outlaw Josey Wales is long like a Howard Hawks Western, and for similar reasons, as the film is concerned more with character development than with action for the sake of action. The various side trips into Indian lands, hostile towns, and canyons help to fill out the portrait of a man in search of regeneration. It is an engaging and often amusing depiction of an emerging community, of hard-luck strangers coming together to start their lives over again: the Cherokee who has lost his homeland, the mother who has lost her son, and even the briefly encountered saloon sitters who lost their town when their nearby mine (along with the liquor and beer) ran out. But it is difficult for Wales, who lost his family and his home, to stop running and killing and stay in one place.

The last scene is bittersweet as he heads back to his strays, riding into the sun, weary and wounded. It is an exceptionally beautiful ending, and quite moving, for Wales is much more than some Dirty Harry on horseback. He is about to cease being a loner and a rebel, unlike Edwards at the end of *The Searchers* (see chapter 8), and more akin to Cole Harden at the end of *The Westerner* (see chapter 5). He wants not only to protect but also to participate in the community he put together. He is another southerner turned westerner, no longer seeking vengeance but instead seeking freedom from his constant task of evading pursuers. And though it is not made absolutely clear in the final shot that Josey is on his way back to his "family" of friendly outcasts, the director certainly intended his audience to hope for such an ending. As Eastwood stated in an interview in regard to a debate with his editor, Ferris Webster: "He [Webster] felt that I should literally show him [Wales] returning to the girl and the group after he has that final talk with the chief. And I said, 'No, you don't need to show him going back. You see him riding off at sunrise and that's enough.' "[26]

UNFORGIVEN

Unforgiven is a movie about violence in the Old West, but it also expresses Eastwood's accumulated appreciation of the natural landscape, an appreciation that he undoubtedly acquired from his personal travels over the years, from his frequent on-location work in Westerns and other films, and from his intimate familiarity with the genre's regular emphasis on the intersections between character and environment. It is likely that Eastwood's reverential use of natural settings has its deepest origins in the many Westerns he watched while growing up. Eastwood made clear the influence of these early viewings in an interview with Kenneth Turan in 1992, around the time of *Unforgiven*'s release:

> When I was a kid there was no television, but you had Westerns on the second half of the bill in theaters a lot. I grew up watching all the John Ford

and Anthony Mann Westerns that came out in the 1940s and 50s, John Wayne in all those cavalry kind of Westerns and Jimmy Stewart. The B-Westerns too, the ones with Randolph Scott. Some of them were good, some were not so good, but we enjoyed them just for the adventure of it all. I grew up through a whole era of them.[27]

Directly following this excerpt in the same interview, Eastwood expresses his interest in another kind of Western, one that has a social conscience but which may be less visually striking in terms of landscape-oriented shots. Such a Western prioritizes its concern with questions of justice and morality. The director told Turan, "One of my favorite films when I was growing up was *The Ox-Bow Incident,* which analyzed mob violence and the power of the mob getting out of control. I saw it again recently and it holds up really well. I don't know how the public feels about those kinds of films, but I just felt it was time to do one again."[28] *The Ox-Bow Incident* (1943), directed by William Wellman, is a morality tale about justice and conscience, but it also revolves around personal awakenings and transformations of character, themes that echo those of certain silent Westerns by Griffith, Hart, and Ford (see chapter 1).

With this in mind, it is easy to see why Eastwood was enthusiastic about David Webb Peoples's script for *Unforgiven* after he read it, since the story is a perfect fusion of Eastwood's long-running interests in the Western film since his earliest experiences of the genre. Just as one cannot appreciate the Westerns of Ford and Mann without absorbing, even if subconsciously, their striking use of the natural landscape, one would be unlikely to choose *The Ox-Bow Incident* as a favorite without some deep interest in how a good story can provoke reflection on the concepts of justice and human nature. William Beard views *Unforgiven* as a later instance of a morally and psychologically complex Western like the ones developed by Anthony Mann in the 1950s, which were echoed and amplified by Ford's revisionist Westerns. According to Beard, these Westerns constitute the "last historical outpost of the antinomic moral and social dualities that organized the genre before the onset of complete alienation, pastiche, and open deconstruction." He concludes that *Unforgiven* is a significant vestige of this earlier phase of the Western, describing the movie "as a peculiar late flowering of the kind of complex western that arose as the famous 'moral clarity' of the genre began to be cast into doubt and the entire system to be undermined."[29]

Unforgiven's screenplay was written by Peoples in 1976 and had been kicking around Hollywood for a good long while. Francis Ford

FIGURE 53. Ex-gunfighter William Munny prepares to come out of retirement, in Eastwood's *Unforgiven* (1992). Courtesy of the Museum of Modern Art.

Coppola had briefly owned the rights to produce the script but had given up on the idea of making the film. Eastwood purchased the screenplay shortly after Coppola dropped it, but he sat on the script for some years. He did this not because his interest faded but because his passion for the story was so strong that he needed ample time to prepare for the film, and perhaps also because he wanted to play the character of Munny when he felt he was the right age to do so.[30] The story concerns a weathered farmer and widower who leaves his children temporarily and goes off to earn a financial reward by avenging a sadistic assault on an innocent young prostitute in the town of Big Whiskey.

Eastwood's emphasis on natural scenery is especially pronounced in the establishing shots in which the town of Big Whiskey is dwarfed by the towering mountains of Alberta, Canada, where most of the movie was made. It is also evident in shots, like the opening one, in which Munny's cabin is silhouetted, along with a tree-crowned hillside, against a gorgeously lit sky. And it is evident in scenes where Munny, his friend and former partner in crime, Ned Logan (Morgan Freeman), and their young new "partner," called the "Schofield Kid" (Jaimz Woolvett), make their way through the sagebrush-spotted wilderness to Big Whiskey, where they will perform the killing and, they hope, collect the resulting financial reward. Edward Buscombe describes the sequence this way: "Ned gives a final look at his wife before riding off. A slow track-in shows her standing impassive as the music swells up. She will never see him again. There follows a lyrical passage, a montage of shots of Will and Ned riding through a field of whispering, golden barley, then across a sunset skyline, a sequence mirrored once Ned and Will have caught up with the Schofield Kid; the beauty of nature appears in contrast to the ugly human acts which are to follow."[31]

Eastwood also uses selective shots of nature, visually elegant and each lasting only a few moments, as scene dividers. These quiet and poetic moments strike the viewer as a fitting contrast to the human-centered scenes of anger and violence that dominate the narrative. They appear at first as gentle grace notes, visual ornaments that add to the aesthetic world of the film beyond the immediate dictates of the narrative.[32] But rather than remaining as merely decorative, such moments are, as Buscombe suggests, ultimately symbolic of a more natural and harmonious world beyond the brutality and artifice of self-centered human beings.

Unforgiven, much like *High Plains Drifter,* winds its way to an ending where the landscape is, in fact, conspicuously absent. Munny's concluding acts of vengeance take place in a night-shrouded, rain-pelted townscape where nothing beyond parts of the main street and the saloon are visible. It is in these scenes that the truly dark side of Munny's character becomes visible, the aspect of his psyche that has been long repressed and that once took the form of a bloodthirsty, and frequently drunken, killer of the guilty and innocent alike (including women and children, as he admits). In these bullet-ridden final scenes, we are thrown into the central message of the movie, a lesson about the terrifying repercussions of violence, even when such acts seem absolutely necessary— whether in self-defense, in the building of civilization, or for the sake of justified retribution. Nature is absent in these shots because we are now summoned to think solely about the negative consequences of our own self-absorbed humanity. In terms of lighting and color, the entire film is consistently muted and drab in tone. But the final sequence depicting Munny's revenge-taking is so soaked in darkness that it may as well have been shot in black and white. Eastwood has remarked about his choice of colors and tones in making *Unforgiven:*

> I remember those high-gloss Technicolor Westerns, those "three-stripers," I saw as a kid. . . . All that light and those saturated colors. I never liked it.

Some of them are called "classics," but they were too artificial and unreal. You had to light things differently in those days, with the "brutes" and everything. [Cinematographer] Jack Green has helped me change that. . . . We asked ourselves, how do you make things look coal-lit and at the same time provide enough light that we can see what's going on? I figured, let's forget that we're shooting in color and think of it in black-and-white terms. We informed the costume designers and the production designers that we wanted muted tones and a "black-and-white" look.[33]

We might also think here of such Westerns as *High Noon* and *Rio Bravo*, where the natural landscape is mostly absent, and especially of Ford's *The Man Who Shot Liberty Valance*, which concentrates most of its concluding scenes in the confines of saloons, newspaper offices, political rally halls, and cramped sections of a main street. Just as it was no doubt the desire of Zinnemann, Ford, and Hawks to narrow the focus of these films to lessons concerning the human condition and the sacrifices that civilization sometimes requires, so it is Eastwood's desire to make primary, in his conclusion of *Unforgiven*, the lessons that humans must learn about themselves. This is why the landscape simply disappears behind rainfall and pitch darkness.

Nonetheless, both *Unforgiven* and *Valance* bid similar farewells to their audiences by returning us ever so briefly to shots of the natural landscape in which the given communities in the narratives have arisen. *Valance* concludes with the shot of a train, a symbol of civilization and progress, taking Ransom and Hallie back East. The train chugs away from us through a wide valley surrounded by hills, the same landscape that we saw at the outset of the movie. *Unforgiven* concludes with a static shot of Munny's tiny cabin silhouetted against a barren hillside and sunlit sky, similar to that of the movie's opening shot, with text emblazoned over the image to suggest that Munny and his children may have finally made it to a life of civilization where, we can hope, the need for violence has been left far behind. And so, after leaving us with messages about the contingencies and dangers that are inherent in the human condition, both films pull us back, so to speak, in order to view the larger natural world that has always been there awaiting us.

Munny is a character who finds himself not only within the actual physical landscape but also within the psychological and moral landscape of his own troubled memories and sense of loss. With his gruff, stoic exterior, he appears as hard as the land itself, but we can see that he is a fragile, aging man who dearly misses his deceased wife and who is not sure how he and his children will sustain themselves. The audience is caught in the strange situation of rooting for Munny, despite our concerns about his morally ambiguous character. There are, of course, the stories about his bloody past, and his mission in Big Whiskey is clearly not a morally redemptive one.[34] And yet we still feel empathy for him, not merely because of our growing dislike of the sadistic sheriff who winds up being his enemy, but also because it is difficult to escape our habituated affinity for Eastwood's many heroic protagonists, no matter how violent they may get.

Munny returns to his old ways purely for the sake of the offered reward. He needs the money to provide a proper life for his children, since his attempts at farming and raising hogs are failing because of his lack of experience, and because of a fever spreading among the animals. He returns to his old ways in order to attain a life beyond the need for violence. Munny's heart is not really in the job of killing the man who attacked and mutilated the prostitute, nor, we might guess, was his heart in many of his past killings. He blames most of those earlier murders on having been drunk out of his mind on a regular basis in those days. But Munny *is* dedicated wholeheartedly to the sober job of killing Sheriff Daggett as retribution for the latter's torture and murder of Ned, and Munny even exhibits visible conviction in killing the saloon and brothel owner for having offered his front porch for the grisly display of Ned's corpse.

There is a parallel here between Munny and Josey Wales, since Josey too had been driven to heartless killing in order to avenge the deaths of loved ones. And before heading to Big Whiskey, Munny recently tried to live the kind of stable farming life that Josey had enjoyed up until the time that his family was slaughtered by the Redlegs. Like Wales, Munny must delve into a dehumanized state of being, at least temporarily, in order to do what he deems necessary, whether for the sake of his children or for revenge. But we get the feeling at the very end of the film that Munny will leave this mode of existence behind since he knows the evils and horrors of such a life.

Unforgiven also prompts reflection on the morality of Little Bill Daggett, a small-town tyrant who acts in the name of "the law" (primitive though this law may be). He appears to believe that he is enacting justice, but he executes his decisions in a slimy and sadistic manner. Eastwood said of the character in an interview, "I think he's a good sort, at least in appearance. He has a certain charm. . . . I believe he thinks he's doing the right thing, just a man who's doing his job."[35] He has also remarked about the character, going beyond the issue of mere appearance: "Little Bill is a sheriff, but he is not really a good guy; he is really

FIGURE 54. William Munny and his friend Ned Logan (Morgan Freeman, *right*) confer about their bounty-hunting expedition. Courtesy of Malpaso Productions/Warner Brothers.

just a killer who happens to have the law on his side. At the same token, Will Munny is also a killer. The only difference between him and Bill is that Little Bill has the rationale of having law enforcement on his side."[36] Actor Gene Hackman has commented about his portrayal of Little Bill: "I tried to make him human and monster at the same time."[37]

Little Bill echoes such villainous but charismatic characters as Judge Roy Bean (Walter Brennan) in Wyler's *The Westerner* and Dad Longworth (Karl Malden) in Brando's *One-Eyed Jacks*.[38] On the one hand, we might simply view Daggett as a killer-turned-sheriff who has risen above the errors of his earlier ways. He now upholds the law, though he enforces it in an excessively violent way to make his point clear to potential lawbreakers. But whatever the code of law in Big Whiskey may be, Daggett's twisted morality is evident in the fact that he barely punishes the men involved in the mutilation of the prostitute. He merely asks that they give several of their horses to the brothel owner (and not right away, at that) in return for his "damaged property": a maimed harlot who has lost her ability to make money because of her permanent scars. Little Bill does not even whip the men, his usual mode of punishment, and Strawberry Alice (Frances Fisher), the brothel's madame, rightly protests against this gross injustice. Little Bill will not listen to her, since in his

FIGURE 55. Sheriff Little Bill Daggett (Gene Hackman, *left*) instructs bounty hunter William Munny on the ways of frontier law. Courtesy of Malpaso Productions/Warner Brothers.

view the men are hardworking fools who simply got "a little carried away." They are not "wicked" in a consistent fashion—not "like whores."

By the conclusion of *Unforgiven,* Munny has unleashed his vengeance against Daggett for what the latter has done to Ned. His acts of retribution are as raw and primitive as Clytemnestra's murder of her own husband in Aeschylus's *The Oresteia.* Munny's revenge is mechanical, nearly inhuman. Eastwood has stated about this scene, referring to his character's relapse into sheer emotion of a demonic nature:

> [Munny has] thrown a switch or something and now a kind of machinery was back in action, a "machinery of violence," I guess you could say. No, it wasn't glamorous. He's back in his mode of mayhem. And he doesn't care. He's his old self again, at least for the moment. He doesn't miss a beat while he loads his rifle and talks to the journalist. Before, he's been very rusty, having trouble getting on his horse, he wasn't shooting very well. He wasn't nailing people with the very first shot (like I would do in my earlier films!). Now, when he goes on this suicidal mission, he's all machine. He not only coldly murders Daggett at point-blank range but shoots some bystanders with no more compunction than someone swatting a fly. Munny has been protesting all the time that he's changed, but maybe he's been protesting too much.[39]

At the end of the film, we learn that Munny may have wound up in the dry goods business in San Francisco, presumably with his children in tow.

FIGURE 56. Gunfighter William Munny prepares to settle accounts at the conclusion of *Unforgiven*. Courtesy of Malpaso Productions/Warner Brothers.

It is only mentioned as a possibility, but we would like to believe it is true, just as we want Josey Wales to return to his "family" at the end of *The Outlaw Josey Wales*. In both films, violence has been required to end violence and to set things right, which is a theme of many traditional Westerns, ranging from *Hell's Hinges* to *The Man Who Shot Liberty Valance*.

Unforgiven reminds us of Henry King's *The Gunfighter* (1950) and Siegel's *The Shootist* because it is a story of a man who desires to hang up his gun for good, but not before one final act of violence becomes necessary. Like these other films, *Unforgiven* has much to say about the reputation that a gunslinger earns and how that man must live, often regrettably, with the consequences of that reputation. Eastwood's film, then, provides another profound lesson about mythmaking and the falsehoods that lie behind the stories that both glorify and haunt men with violent pasts. Its lessons about the deceptions involved in Old West mythologizing, and about the horrifying violence that permeated the reality of the Old West, make *Unforgiven* an exemplar of genre revisionism, even with its classical form of montage and visual stylization. In his biography of Eastwood, Schickel nicely summarizes how this film helps tear down the familiar patterns of the genre:

> *Unforgiven* cuts a narrower, deeper path through the form's conventions. None of its bodies are nameless. All its deaths count for something. . . . On

its way to that conclusion, it casually, almost incidentally, subverts our comfortable expectation of stock western types and situations. This is a movie in which whores turn out not to be golden-hearted, but angry and vengeful; a movie in which a seemingly reasonable lawman turns out to be an ugly sadist who, unlike the reassuring peacekeeper of western lore, is not the source of the community's stability, but of its chaos; a movie in which the celebrity gunfighter, before whose reputation all are supposed to tremble, is revealed to be an empty blowhard, and the seemingly psychotic adolescent, who aspires to similar fame, turns to mush when he actually kills someone. It is finally a movie in which the presumptive hero, lured out of retirement to right a wrong, does not find moral satisfaction in the act, but despair, rage and something very close to madness.[40]

Unforgiven deals in a melancholy manner with the relationship between truth and myth in the ways that Schickel outlines. But rather than arguing for the persistence of legend even while showing us the truth, as we might find in certain Westerns by Ford (*Fort Apache* and *Liberty Valance,* primarily), Eastwood's film reveals the ugly reality behind the mythology of the Old West and leaves it at that. It is Munny's harsh reputation that sends the Schofield Kid looking for him, and that, after twists and turns, eventually gets Ned killed for no good reason. In *Unforgiven* we are not presented with some argument that violence is ultimately necessary in the pioneering and building of a nation. We are instead presented with the brute reality of the violent act and all of its repulsive consequences, with violence begetting more violence. Schickel highlights a crucial exchange between Munny and his young partner:

> "It's a hell of a thing, killing a man," proclaims Munny in one of the film's most profound and reflective scenes. "You take away everything he's got and everything he's ever gonna have."
> "Will, I guess they had it comin'," replies the Schofield Kid.
> Munny: "We've all got it comin', Kid."[41]

Or, as Munny tells the dying Little Bill at the conclusion of the film, right after the sheriff has declared that he does not deserve this particular type of death: "'Deserves' has got nothin' to do with it."

The intersection between the desire for violence and the innate human need for justice, typically in the form of some type of retribution, lies at the heart of the film, but problematically so. The movie relies on certain expectations on the part of its audience, and the viewer's participation in Munny's transformation is at best an uneasy one. Eastwood has said about his intentions in drawing attention to such an intersection, with due reference to audience expectations: "I've done as much as the next person as far as creating mayhem in Westerns, but what I like about *Unforgiven* is that every killing has a repercussion. . . . An incident will trigger decisions, maybe the wrong decisions or the wrong reactions by people, and then there's really no way to stop things. But the public may say, 'Yeah, I get the morality of it, but I like it better when you're just blowing people away.' "[42]

Screenwriter David Webb Peoples is a tad more reluctant about declaring that the film's message is one of antiviolence, preferring instead to say simply that the movie emphasizes the theme of violence, and that violence is indeed "frightening."[43] However, Jim Kitses argues in his analysis of *Unforgiven* that Eastwood's intended critique of violence does not completely succeed in the end, mainly because he strategically appeals to his audience's expected desire to see Munny unleash his final, bloody vengeance against Daggett. If Eastwood in his final sequence depends on a traditional use of violence to satisfy the audience's thirst for the villain's death, then the overall message of the film has been corrupted, according to this interpretation. As Kitses argues:

> It is difficult to understand how the director can hold such views [about the film's treatment of the consequences of violence], given the film he has made. The massacre executed by a Munny of mythic proportions is vastly fulfilling and entertaining, a spectacle that is both "source of humor" and "attraction," effectively blurring the film's argument that violence is the property of an unhinged masculinity. Having Munny become the tool of a lethal and transcendent retribution that culminates the film's action and supposedly resolves its issues in fact implicates the film in the violence it is critiquing. . . . No Brechtian, his [Eastwood's] aesthetic requires the audience to identify with and invest in the action. . . . Ambitious, compelling, but finally flawed, Eastwood's critique of the Western as a genre sustained by masculine codes of violence is itself all too satisfyingly sustained by that same violence.[44]

This criticism of the film is initially persuasive, given the expectation that most viewers will find Munny's brutal vengeance against Daggett satisfying, and that the narrative structure of the movie plays to this expectation. However, upon further reflection, one might ask whether the viewer's patient anticipation of Munny's act of retribution may be the result of her familiarity with the Eastwood persona. If we pay close attention to the final scene, we notice that Munny allows Daggett's men (the ones who do not want to wind up dead) to leave the killing scene, and he shoots an unarmed man (the saloon/brothel owner). He finishes off Daggett, who is lying wounded on the floor, and responds almost mechanically to Beauchamp's questions, as if trivializing the act that has just occurred. Munny then wanders off into the rainy blackness, having regressed into a brutal primitivism that he had once struggled to transcend. It is hardly a scene that glamorizes or celebrates violence, let alone satisfies a viewer's desire for the type of classic Western showdown that resolves issues of justice and retribution. Eastwood concludes his film not with such a showdown but with a pathetic last stand by a man who has lost a beloved friend, and whose only course of action is his return to a way of life that he had sought so desperately to leave behind.

Granted, the typical viewer will find satisfaction in the elimination of Daggett, particularly after the horrible cruelty that Daggett unleashed against an undeserving Ned, and in this Kitses is correct. *Unforgiven* does deliver when it comes to the anticipated extermination of this sadistic sheriff. But it does not deliver "the goods" because of the specific ways Eastwood and his screenwriter have presented this act of primitive justice. Munny is a pitiful figure, not a heroic one, most especially since he has undertaken a morally questionable venture that got his best friend killed—and left his vulnerable children behind, to boot. If we find any genuine heroism in Munny's violent killing of Daggett, given the way this killing is presented, then it is probably *we* who should become the object of criticism, not Eastwood or his film.

With Munny's sweeping and nihilistic declaration that the principle of desert "has got nothin' to do with it," the film ultimately evokes a final question about the concept of justice and the relationship between morality and the law, a question as old as Hammurabi's code and as recent as today's newspaper headlines. The same question emerges in many conscience-themed Westerns. But what lies at the heart of *Unforgiven*, expressed in the very title of the film and throughout its narrative, is the basic truth that, no matter whose justice and whose morality, violence is an ugly thing and gets even uglier. Unless it is somehow transcended, which it all too rarely is.

CHAPTER II

Coda

From "Lonesome Dove" (1989) to "Cowboys and Aliens" (2011)

Film critics and scholars have occasionally and mistakenly predicted the decline or even death of the Western film since the days of silent cinema.[1] There have indeed been brief lulls in the making of Western films, especially when contrasted with such prolific periods as the first half of World War II and the 1950s. The decade of the 1980s, in particular, was graced by a mere handful of significant Westerns: Michael Cimino's *Heaven's Gate* and Walter Hill's *The Long Riders* (both 1980), Eastwood's *Pale Rider* and Lawrence Kasdan's *Silverado* (both 1985), and Simon Wincer's impressive television miniseries *Lonesome Dove* (1989). Nonetheless, Eastwood's work in the genre from the 1960s through to the early 1990s helped to define a singular artistic trajectory within a genre that otherwise experienced a rather unpredictable evolution over the past several decades.

When most film scholars speak of the transition to the postclassical Western, which also includes a move to the postmodern Western, they generally refer to the turn away from the conventional narratives and visual styles that are best evidenced by movies of Hollywood's Golden Age, such as Ford's *Stagecoach* and Wyler's *The Westerner*.[2] As we have seen, the classical or traditional Western film typically portrays heroic protagonists who conquer enemies, vanquish evil, and help to blaze a path through the wilderness so that a law-centered civilization can flourish. These films almost always arrive at happy endings, with little regard for the dead and defeated. They align the values and achievements of their heroes with those of the growing social order and with the dominant national ideology—usually identified with the ideal of Manifest Destiny, a conviction in the inevitable progress of democracy and capitalism. Such a story accords with the general framework of the Western mythos, one that originated with the frontier chronicles and historical novels of the nineteenth century. The cinematic presentations of these plots were usually done with a fair degree of stylistic and narrative economy, driven by the plotline and its focus on the respective heroism and villainy of its main characters.

As we have also witnessed in earlier chapters, the postclassical and revisionist Westerns have their seeds in the noir Westerns of the later 1940s (e.g., *Duel in the Sun, Pursued*) and the more psychological Westerns of the 1950s (e.g., *The Furies, The Naked Spur, Jubal,* and *The Searchers*). Genre-revising Westerns continued through the 1960s (e.g., *The Man Who Shot Liberty Valance, Ride the High Country, The Wild Bunch, Butch Cassidy and the Sundance Kid,* and the films by Sergio Leone) and flowered during the 1970s (e.g., *Little Big Man, McCabe and Mrs. Miller,* and *High Plains Drifter*). However, while such an evolution may be fairly clear in hindsight, the lines of demarcation between the classical and postclassical Westerns are not always so neatly drawn, especially when comparing individual films. Ford's *The Man Who Shot Liberty Valance* and Peckinpah's *Ride the High Country,* for example, are as classical in their visual styles as they are revisionist in their character-oriented narratives, stories that involve hero critique as well as the fading away of the Old West.

The term *postclassical,* when applied to American cinema as a whole, typically refers to the "New Hollywood" era that is generally accepted as beginning with the release of such movies as Mike Nichols's *The Graduate* and Arthur Penn's *Bonnie and Clyde* (both 1967). This transformative period in filmmakers' methods of storytelling and visual presentation echoes earlier variations on and parodies of formulaic plots and styles. The postclassical Western can indeed be understood as a loosely defined and wide-ranging part of the genre that has its roots in the turbulent but fertile soil of the post–World War II period. This category of Western has been enriched over the decades, particularly through forms of revisionism, both subtle and dramatic, ranging from Mann's "neurotic" Westerns and Boetticher's "existential" Westerns to Eastwood's *Unforgiven* and beyond.

The idea of the *postmodern* Western makes it seem at times as though the traditional parameters of the genre have been fully critiqued, rejected, and transcended. In fact, Westerns over the past three decades have been so eclectic, wavering between radical revisionism and revivalist classicism, that it is difficult to speak of an individual postmodern Western per se, since so many of the more significant instances of genre revisionism have integrated classical elements. Since the release of three significant Westerns in the early 1990s—Kevin Costner's *Dances with Wolves* (1990), Eastwood's *Unforgiven* (1992), and Michael Mann's *The Last of the Mohicans* (1992)—there have been attention-worthy returns to the basic traditions of the genre, but also radical as well as subtle departures from those traditions. The more notable examples of revivals and revisions (and fusions thereof) include George Cosmatos's *Tombstone* (1993), Lawrence Kasdan's *Wyatt Earp* (1994), Jim Jarmusch's *Dead Man* (1995), Sam Raimi's *The Quick and the Dead* (1995), Costner's *Open Range* (2003), James Mangold's remake of *3:10 to Yuma* (2007), Andrew Dominik's *The Assassination of Jesse James by the Coward Robert Ford* (2007), Ed Harris's *Appaloosa* (2008), and the Coen brothers' remake of *True Grit* (2010). While none of these Westerns match the cinematic heights of, say, *Red River, The Searchers,* and *The Wild Bunch,* they offer enough adventure and visual splendor to satisfy Western fans who had, by the mid-1990s, begun to hunger for further amplifications of their beloved genre.

Several noteworthy contributions to the American Western over the past few decades have taken the form of television series and miniseries. Wincer's *Lonesome Dove* established a benchmark for any subsequent television Western. Based on an original movie script by Larry McMurtry, one that the writer later turned into an epic novel, *Lonesome Dove* features performances by Tommy Lee Jones as Woodrow F. Call and, most especially, Robert Duvall as Gus McCrae. Call and McRae are two former Texas Rangers who undertake a sprawling cattle drive to Montana. With the type of acting, directing, screenwriting, and landscape photography that can be found in the best works of the genre, the miniseries led to a sequel, Mike Robe's *Return to Lonesome Dove* (1993), and Wincer's "prequel" *Comanche Moon* (2008).

Lonesome Dove remains the zenith of the television Western miniseries, a format ideally suited for the epic adventure-journey narrative. Earlier examples of that format include Burt Kennedy and Daniel Mann's *How the West Was Won* (1977), starring James Arness as frontiersman Zeb Macahan, and Robert Totten's *The Sacketts* (1979), based on Louis L'Amour's third novel in his series of novels about this Western family. *Lonesome Dove*'s exceptional quality was not matched in a television

Western until Walter Hill's majestic *Broken Trail* (2006), also starring Duvall, and the HBO production *Deadwood* (2004–6). The latter series was created by David Milch and stars Ian McShane as Al Swearengen, the diabolical, obscenity-spouting saloon owner and "town boss." Along with such films as Costner's *Dances with Wolves* and Eastwood's *Unforgiven,* these television productions give clear evidence that, while the Western has charted a somewhat chaotic and sporadic course over the past quarter century, the genre is alive and well.

Lonesome Dove also initiated a cycle of performances by Robert Duvall that provide an evolving portrait of the westerner as an older, sagacious, feisty cowpoke who still can handle a gun and drive a herd with the best of them. In the post-Ford, post-Hawks, post-Wayne world, this series of performances by Duvall—along with Eastwood's Westerns and Costner's multiple forays into the genre—contributes to a discernible pattern of artist-oriented genre-exploration in an otherwise eclectic landscape of film and television Westerns. Duvall was of course no stranger to Westerns before taking on the iconic role of cattle puncher Gus McRae. For example, he performed opposite John Wayne as villain Ned Pepper in Henry Hathaway's *True Grit* (1969), as the legendary Jesse James in Philip Kaufman's *The Great Northfield Minnesota Raid* (1972), and as landowner Frank Harlan (who hires Eastwood's title character) in John Sturges's *Joe Kidd* (1972).

But beginning with *Lonesome Dove,* Duvall initiated his most significant engagement in the genre by immersing himself in a fascinating character type that blends the folksy charm of the beloved sidekick played by Walter Brennan with the stoic heroism of a Cooper, Wayne, Stewart, or Fonda. Duvall provides clear echoes of Gus's worldly wise cowboy in his performance as Boss Spearman in Costner's impressive *Open Range* and as Prentice "Prent" Ritter in Hill's miniseries *Broken Trail.* He also starred as Al Sieber, the chief of scouts, in Walter Hill's *Geronimo: An American Legend* (1993). Much as Boetticher's Ranown Westerns are subtle variations on a basic story and character, these performances by Duvall offer nuanced modifications of a recurring persona, not unlike Wayne's enormous contribution to the genre throughout his long career as a repeatedly strong, confident, intelligent westerner.

The achievements of artists like Eastwood, Duvall, and Costner have helped to keep the genre flourishing since the cinematic revolution of the 1960s and 1970s. Their works and performances have revived traditional components of the Western—above all, naturalistic acting, eye-catching landscape photography, an attention to narrative development, and a sustained sense of action and adventure—while also pushing the Western into new terrain. And yet the patterns of genre evolution and transformation that have been noted throughout this book are not so clearly discerned when it comes to the post-1970s Western, and this fact leads us to the idea of a growing postmodern sensibility when it comes to audiences' and filmmakers' current approaches to the Western. We can trace the general moves from the silent Western to the 1930s B-Western and then to the A-Western of the late 1930s and 1940s. And we can show a progression from the post–World War II "super-Western" to the more psychological and existential Westerns of the 1950s, and then to the more revisionist Westerns of the 1960s and 1970s. But the vista becomes hazier after that.

Among obvious returns to more traditional, classical modes (*Lonesome Dove, Open Range, Broken Trail,* and *Appaloosa,* for example), we have seen radical departures from such modes—Jarmusch's *Dead Man,* primarily, following in the tradition of Alejandro Jodorowsky's *El Topo* and Rainer Werner Fassbinder's *Whity,* two campy "cult" Westerns from the early 1970s. But there have also been creative integrations of genre elements in films that cannot strictly be categorized as Westerns: Robert Rodriguez's "mariachi" movies, Paul Thomas Anderson's *There Will Be Blood,* and the Coen brothers' *No Country for Old Men,* for instance. And then there are the fusions of conventional and anticonventional genre elements that resist easy categorization as classical *or* postclassical: *Unforgiven, Tombstone, The Quick and the Dead,* and Walter Hill's *Wild Bill,* for example.

Perhaps the most intriguing and effective illustration of the ways that classical and revisionist aspects of the Western have been combined to create diverse cinematic forms lies in the work of Joel and Ethan Coen. The Coens have specialized in subverting and radicalizing familiar genres in their own eccentric and highly cinematic manner, while also paying tribute to traditional codes and formulas. This is evident in their creative takes on film noir (*Blood Simple* and *The Man Who Wasn't There*), the gangster film (*Miller's Crossing*), the Depression-era screwball comedy (*O Brother, Where Art Thou?*), and the British black comedy (*The Ladykillers*). Other films by the Coens selectively incorporate genre elements while evading categorization altogether (*Raising Arizona, Barton Fink, The Hudsucker Proxy, Fargo, The Big Lebowski, Burn after Reading, A Serious Man*). In terms of their movies that play upon the Western, the Coens have delivered a crime thriller that radically integrates aspects of the genre (*No Country for Old Men*), as well as a revivalist work (their remake of *True Grit*) that downplays the brothers' bent for revisionism and parody.

True Grit exhibits throughout its narrative a dedicated reverence for the classical styling of the Western. This movie is as good as Westerns get in terms of action and adventure, and Jeff Bridges gives the role of Rooster Cogburn (played by John Wayne in the original version) his own unique mix of charm and danger. The Coens' remake is far closer to the dialogue and plotline of the Charles Portis novel than the original, and in many ways their film is more cleverly and dramatically crafted than the version by Henry Hathaway. What makes their adaptation of the story most distinct, however, is the sustained focus on the character of Mattie Ross (Hailee Steinfeld), the self-reliant girl who hires Cogburn to hunt down her father's killer. Here is a young female westerner who, with her consistent inner strength and occasional outer vulnerability, recalls such characters as Lillian Gish's Letty in *The Wind*, Claire Trevor's Dallas in *Stagecoach*, Vera Miles's Hallie in *The Man Who Shot Liberty Valance*, and Julie Christie's Constance in *McCabe and Mrs. Miller*.

But the Coens' *No Country for Old Men* provides the most effective example of a postmodern take on the genre. Primarily a crime and action thriller and a modern meditation on violence and evil, the movie echoes those Westerns that stand on the threshold between the classical and postclassical, especially in the way it focuses on the passing of the Old West and on the fading heroes who made that transition possible. The setting of *No Country* is the "New" West, more specifically that of West Texas along the U.S.-Mexico border circa 1980 (the movie was filmed primarily in New Mexico, with certain scenes shot in Texas). The evil that was embodied by villains in Westerns of the past reaches a new, horrifying dimension in the form of Anton Chigurh (Javier Bardem, who earned an Oscar for Best Supporting Actor for his chilling performance). Chigurh is a psychotic yet methodical killer who is frequently philosophical and who espouses a (not surprisingly) bizarre worldview that zigzags between fatalism and freedom, chance and choice, causation and consequence, destiny and death.

This hit man, sent to retrieve a satchel containing two million dollars in cash from a drug deal gone wrong, obsessively pursues Vietnam War veteran Llewelyn Moss (Josh Brolin), the man who discovered the satchel among littered corpses and near-corpses while hunting pronghorn in the desert. After deciding to keep the money and remain silent, Moss becomes the object of an intense pursuit by Chigurh, who alternates between his two weapons of choice—a slaughterhouse stun gun and a rifle with silencer—as he destroys anyone who gets in his way. Chigurh is a fascinating but also repulsive incarnation of evil situated somewhere between the primal aggression of Robert De Niro's Max Cady in Scorsese's remake of *Cape Fear* (1991) and the self-reflective inhumanity of Anthony Hopkins's Hannibal Lecter in *The Silence of the Lambs* (1991). Chigurh's malevolence reaches almost supernatural dimensions, reminding us also at times of Robert Mitchum's satanic preacher Harry Powell in Charles Laughton's *Night of the Hunter* (1955) and Eastwood's mysterious, revenge-driven "Stranger" in *High Plains Drifter* (1973).

The struggle of Moss for his and his wife's survival against the threat of Chigurh is not precisely a battle between absolute good and absolute evil, as we might find in traditional Westerns such as *High Noon* and *Shane,* since Moss is far from being a knight in shining armor. After all, Moss chooses to keep the fortune he has found and refrains from reporting the crime scene to the police, suggesting perhaps that the remainder of the film is a series of negative consequences through which fate punishes Moss for his bad decision. The hero in the story, if one could call him that, is Sheriff Ed Tom Bell (Tommy Lee Jones), though he is hardly heroic in the traditional sense. He fails to find Chigurh and stop him from killing Moss, seems in no particular hurry at times to attempt to stop him, and laments that he is "overmatched" by the current force of evil facing him.

While Sheriff Bell is indeed the kind of strong, pragmatic, and stoic protagonist who exhibits the authority of experience, and who is initially expected to be able to conquer the villain and save the day, he winds up being more passive and jaded than we would like. Above all, the sheriff looks back to a better and more dignified version of the West, one in which lawmen did not always need to carry a gun (shades of *Destry Rides Again*), where men adhered to a code of honor (or at least a code of humanity, within broad limits), and where one knew what to expect from an enemy. The sheriff recognizes a change in the times and sees around him a West that has gone to the dogs, given the clear disintegration of a common ethos, ranging from a lack of courtesy to a seemingly new brand of evil. Bell declares at one point, "But I think once you quit hearing 'sir' and 'ma'am,' the rest is soon to foller."

No Country's underlying nihilism and the sheriff's inability to comprehend and deal with his current situation make this a postmodern take on the Western, to be sure. It is a playful and cynical response to several of the genre's conventions. The movie is an entirely unique fusion of the Western, crime drama, and psychological thriller, reminding us of the combining of the Western and film noir in such post–World War II films as *Pursued* and *The Furies*. But the narrative of *No Country*, based closely on the novel by Cormac McCarthy, does emphasize the important differences between the cultures of the Old West and New West, particularly when it comes to Sheriff Bell's reflections on the importance of traditional mores and codes of honor in the face of changing times. Above all, the Coen brothers clearly evoke the spirit of Sam Peckinpah's recurring emphasis on the theme of an evolving West, and they pay implicit tribute to his ways of juxtaposing the ugliness of graphic violence with the beauties of the Western landscape.

The evil that Chigurh represents is a force of nature that, in transcending the conventional boundaries of the human condition, lifts the movie's narrative into the realm of the archetypal and the symbolic. It is not simply the evil of the greedy and self-centered gunslingers who obstructed the flourishing of communities and interrupted the progress of civilization. It is, rather, a form of evil that exists for its own sake, connected secondarily with a human mission (money retrieval) that merely provides an occasion for Chigurh's misanthropic destructiveness. As Sheriff Bell confesses at one point to his Uncle Ellis (Barry Corbin) while reminiscing about a more intelligible version of the West, the situation that he now faces is one that defies his very conception of human reality:

I was sheriff of this county when I was twenty-five years old. Hard to believe. My grandfather was a lawman; father too. Me and him was sheriffs at the same time; him up in Plano and me out here. I think he's pretty proud of that. I know I was. Some of the old-time sheriffs never even wore a gun. A lotta folks find that hard to believe—Jim Scarborough'd never carry one (that's the younger Jim). Gaston Boykins wouldn't wear one up in Camanche County. I always liked to hear about the old-timers. Never missed a chance to do so. You can't help but compare yourself against the old-timers. Can't help but wonder how theyd've operated these times. There was this boy I sent to the 'lectric chair in Huntsville Hill here a while back. My arrest and my testimony. He killt a fourteen-year-old girl. Papers said it was a crime of passion but he told me there wasn't any passion to it. Told me that he'd been planning to kill somebody for about as long as he could remember. Said that if they turned him out he'd do it again. Said he knew he was going to hell. "Be there in about fifteen minutes." I don't know what to make of that. I surely don't. The crime you see now, it's hard to even take its measure. It's not that I'm afraid of it. I always knew you had to be willing to die to even do this job. But, I don't want to push my chips forward and go out and meet something I don't understand. A man would have to put his soul at hazard. He'd have to say, "O.K., I'll be part of this world."

The sheriff's uncle, a man who is familiar with the traditional ways of an older West, disagrees with his nephew's verdict, maintaining that this kind of evil has been around for a good long while, and that it must be confronted for what it is, not for what decent lawmen like Bell try to make of it: "Whatcha got ain't nothin new. This country's hard on people, you can't stop what's coming: it ain't all waiting on *you*. That's vanity." But the sheriff does not seem so convinced. He believes that he has something new on his hands, a form of evil that is as chaotic as the times in which he lives. The sheriff is an old-fashioned warrior who has come to recognize the current wasteland for what it is: an amoral abyss that breeds monsters like Chigurh.

The kind of misanthropy and nihilism expressed by *No Country* is echoed by another quasi Western that was also released in 2007, and which intriguingly integrates genre elements within the dark tale of a man's ruthless quest to become an oil baron. *There Will Be Blood* was directed by Paul Thomas Anderson (*Boogie Nights, Magnolia, Punch-Drunk Love*) and based loosely on the novel *Oil!* by Upton Sinclair. It features an Oscar-winning performance by Daniel Day-Lewis as the relentlessly ambitious and egocentric Daniel Plainview. The movie centers on themes of empire building, religion, and violence, and it emphasizes the more sinister side of the story of the Old West's transition to a modern industrial America. The movie also won a well-deserved Academy Award for Robert Elswit's cinematography, which captures stunning images of mostly barren landscape. *There Will Be Blood* was shot chiefly around El Mirage Dry Lake in California's Mojave Desert and around Marfa, a desert town in West Texas that had also served as the filming location for parts of George Stevens's 1956 *Giant* and for selected scenes of *No Country for Old Men*.

Daniel Plainview is an almost demonic exaggeration of the other Western empire-builders we have seen: "Senator" Jackson McCanles in *Duel in the Sun*, Tom Dunson in *Red River*, Colonel Jim Brewton in *Sea of Grass*, T.C. Jeffords in *The Furies*, Jordan Benedict and Jett Rink in *Giant*, and Alec Waggoman in *The Man from Laramie*. As with the epic stories of Dunson and Rink, we witness the process through which Plainview achieves his goal, and through which his character becomes increasingly hardened and hateful. Like *The Furies* and *Giant, There Will Be Blood* does not focus on traditional Western themes of survival amid the wilderness or the conquest of native peoples or a showdown between gunslinging adversaries. However, certain details in addition to its Western setting mark Anderson's movie as a Western: it deals with the expansionist spirit of a growing America, a spirit that sometimes breeds tyranny and violence, and its portrait of the mercilessly self-centered Plainview reminds us of the kind of cruel determination and even megalomania that was sometimes embodied by those who viewed an "empty" territory and its natural resources as theirs for the taking.

This oil prospector, after his empire has been built, descends eventually into isolation and madness. He finally severs a long-standing relationship with his adopted son and enacts a moment of bloodthirsty vengeance against the young preacher-charlatan who had once humiliated Plainview before his church congregation. Plainview's moral and psychological disintegration, along with his later state of self-chosen alienation within a walled fortress of solitude, recalls the similar life course of the title character in Orson Welles's *Citizen Kane* (1941). What makes Plainview especially despicable is that he has managed to sustain and increase his brand of aggressive ambition throughout an entire career and even lifetime. He does not undergo any significant moral transformation but, rather, expresses ever more clearly and violently the inner drive toward wealth and power that had always possessed him. One of the unique characteristics of *There Will Be Blood* is its deliberate pacing, a highly patient and methodical form of montage that produces a meditative rhythm by stretching out shots and scenes in a way that prioritizes reflective stasis over immediate action. This pacing and rhythm makes us increasingly realize that we have had a good long opportunity to experience and reflect upon the character of Plainview, and that he has never taken a respite, no matter how briefly, from his greed-driven pursuit.

No Country for Old Men and *There Will Be Blood* may certainly be categorized as postmodern takes on the elements of a typically tradition-bound genre. The term *postmodern* may be loosely equated with the general idea of postclassical revisionism in describing the genre's turn away from the Hollywood Golden Age Western. But rather than applying that term to specific Western films, we may find it more fitting to think of "the postmodern" as a kind of self-conscious response to a wide-ranging era of Western films, a response that adheres to no fixed or definitive pattern when it comes to either the revival or the rejection of the traditional Western. The philosophical idea of postmodernism derives from a critique of Enlightenment-inspired tendencies to embrace principles of essentialism, universalism, and linear progress. And so, when applied to the Western film, this idea refers to a creative acceptance, on the part of filmmakers and viewers alike, of the old as well as the new, the traditional as well as the antitraditional. We should not attempt to locate the postmodern Western in a particular decade or neatly defined phase of Hollywood moviemaking, or to identify it as a particular form of critiquing or rejecting traditional genre formulas. It is safer to say that the postmodern era of the Western has grown naturally out of the entire development of the postclassical mode—just as the more commonly accepted models of the classical Western (especially A-production works of the late 1930s and early 1940s) grew out of earlier sound-era movies (e.g., Walsh's *The Big Trail*) and, of course, countless silent oaters.

The postmodern phase of the Western revolves around a noncritical openness to this gradual postclassical evolution. With the postmodern spin on the Western, we have entered a period of creative modification of genre elements and of a playful reverence for past developments. And if "revisionism" is to be strictly defined as an intentional critical reaction to the traditional Western—as broad-ranging as the idea of the traditional Western may be—then "the postmodern" may be construed as a move beyond revisionism in a way that incorporates and plays upon the traditional and the revisionist alike. This makes the current phase of Western movie production particularly exciting in its very unpredictability—anything goes.

The Western, then, has entered a cultural landscape where the traditional and antitraditional equally constitute a wide cinematic territory, one in which audience expectations are as eclectic as the times in which we live. "Postrevisionism," if we may call it that, is a free-spirited, playful integration of what came before, and not strictly an outright critique or rejection of it. And in this spirit of contemporary potpourri, it is perhaps fitting that the more interesting and transformative incorporation of Western elements has occurred in those genre-crossing movies that resist being classified *as* Westerns.

Genres are best defined in terms of family resemblances and porous boundaries, not clear lines of demarcation, and the Western is one of the more effective examples of this basic truth. Its original formulas and conventions have been challenged, parodied, and modified since the birth of the comic Western in the silent era. We can expect to see other revivals of the classical Western in the future, especially given the critical and commercial success of the recent remake of *True Grit*. But we can also anticipate further examples of radical genre revising. We enjoy stories that freely traverse space and time and celebrate the thrill of adventure, and it should come as no surprise that the mythos underlying these stories is perpetually open to acts of boundary crossing.

The year 2011, for example, saw the release of Gore Verbinski's animated and comic take on the genre, *Rango,* as well as Jon Favreau's big-budget *Cowboys and Aliens.* The latter film, as its title clearly indicates, is an action-fantasy fusion of the Western and science fiction genres. Starring Daniel Craig and Harrison Ford and set in the Arizona territory of the 1870s, the latter film revolves around a mysterious amnesiac (Craig) who wears a strange mechanical bracelet and arrives in the town of Absolution just in time to contend with the ruthless Colonel Dolarhyde (Ford), not to mention a band of hostile aliens bent on destruction and conquest. The local cowboys, of course, must ride to the rescue, even if Winchesters are not the best weapons to shoot down spaceships; courage, strength, confidence, alliance, and stoic self-reliance are required. *Cowboys and Aliens* shows us that, if nothing else, we have traveled a long and winding trail since the days of the Biograph oaters and the heroics of Cheyenne Harry and Blaze Tracy. On the other hand, and despite its high-tech gloss, Favreau's film loosely recalls some of the earliest silent Westerns, perhaps most especially 1903's *The Great Train Robbery.* That is to say, before creators of Western movies became increasingly interested in more intricate ways of developing character and narrative, their primary goal was simply to astonish audiences with pure action and visual spectacle.

The American Western has evolved in ways that are sometimes clearly delineated and sometimes not. Recent revivals of traditional narratives and conventional visual stylizations have emerged alongside revisionist alterations of genre elements, alterations that play creatively upon the codes of the past while also pointing to the future. While the Western narrative has addressed in mythical terms the story of the transition from wilderness to modern civilization, the history of the filming of this wide-ranging narrative has evolved as much as, and been as self-transformative as, its subject matter. The primitive frontier of the Old West may now even intersect with the "new frontier" of space and our contact with extraterrestrials. Nonetheless, we are continually reminded that the Western's clearest expression of journey, adventure, and expansionism has been the journey, adventure, and expansion of the genre itself.

Notes

INTRODUCTION

1. Wicking and Pattison, "Interview with Anthony Mann (1969)," 201, 202.

2. Turan, "A Fistful of Memories," 249.

3. On the theme of violence in the Western, see Richard Slotkin's essential work *Gunfighter Nation: The Myth of the Frontier in Twentieth-Century America*. This is the third in Slotkin's landmark trilogy on the role of the frontier in American history and culture.

4. Warshow, "Movie Chronicle," 36, 38.

5. Alexandra Keller makes this very distinction in her essay "Historical Discourse and American Identity in Westerns since the Reagan Era." See especially pages 242 and 252.

1. DIVERSE PERSPECTIVES IN SILENT WESTERNS

1. See chapter 1 ("Pioneers") in Silver, *The Western Film*, 12–17.

2. Brodie Smith, *Shooting Cowboys and Indians*.

3. See chapter 2 ("The Eastern Western") in Simmon, *The Invention of the Western Film*, 12–18.

4. *Biograph Bulletins, 1908–1912*, 113.

5. Ibid., 149.

6. Ibid., 113.

7. Prats, *Invisible Natives*, 122. See also 119–120.

8. See chapter 8 ("Pocahontas Meets Custer: *The Invaders*") in Simmon, *The Invention of the Western Film*, 55–78.

9. See Simmon's observations about the self-contradictory nature of the film in *The Invention of the Western Film*, 84–86.

10. See chapter 1 ("Indians to the Rescue") in ibid., 6–11.

11. Buscombe, *Unforgiven,* 45.

12. See chapter 7 ("The Politics of Landscape") in Simmon, *The Invention of the Western Film,* 51–54.

13. See chapter 6 ("Wars on the Plains") in Simmon, *The Invention of the Western Film,* 47–48 and 50.

14. *Biograph Bulletin, 1908–1912,* 465.

15. Prats, *Invisible Natives,* 93–94. See also 100.

16. As Fenin and Everson tell us in their survey *The Western:* "From the very beginning, Hart directed all of his own films, and only very occasionally did another director—Cliff Smith or Charles Swickard—work on his pictures. Even then, the director credit was largely nominal, for Hart's films were made the way he wanted them to be made. . . . Not only did Ince never direct Hart in a single foot of film, but after the first few productions he had little to do even with their supervision, despite the large screen credit he took on each film" (78–79).

17. For the theme of chivalric knighthood and its connection with the theme of love, see Barber, *The Knight and Chivalry,* especially his chapter "The Minnesingers," about an extension of the earlier medieval troubadours. One crucial theme that Barber develops is the connection between passionate love and moral self-transformation.

18. Silver, *The Western Film,* 32. See also Silver's essay "Ford and the Romantic Tradition," 17–33.

19. Bogdanovich, *John Ford,* 40.

20. Ibid., 18.

21. See Gallagher, *John Ford,* 17–19.

22. Ibid., 22.

23. Ibid.

2. NOT AT HOME ON THE RANGE

1. A particularly insightful essay on this film is Tibbets's "Vital Geography: Victor Seastrom's *The Wind,*" 255–261.

2. The most illuminating book expressing the feminist approach to the American Western—and most especially a take on the Western as a response to popular women's fiction in nineteenth-century literature—is of course Jane Tompkins's *West of Everything: The Inner Life of Westerns.* See especially her chapter 2, "Women and the Language of Men," 47–68. Tompkins's book is most effectively read as her own personal response to the genre of the Western, especially in terms of her own writings on nineteenth-century women's popular fiction. An informative essay on the role of the female in the Western film is Pam Cook's "Women in the Western," 293–300. See also Blake Lucas's "Saloon Girls and Ranchers' Daughters," and Gaylyn Studlar's valuable essay "Sacred Duties, Poetic Passions," 43–74.

3. In her analysis of *Riders,* Jane Tompkins notes that "in this orgasmic act of self-destruction, a long-awaited moment of 'wrathful relief' that ends in dust and shrouds, the landscape expresses feelings that are too colossal, too outra-

geous, and too inexplicable for human characters to claim. Wreaking a horrible vengeance on the villain, forcing the hero and heroine to come together, the fall of Balancing Rock commits murder and sexual intercourse at the same time" (introduction to *Riders of the Purple Sage*, xviii). *Riders of the Purple Sage* was filmed several times, including the 1925 version starring Tom Mix and Marion Nixon and directed by Lynn Reynolds, and Charles Haid's 1996 version with Ed Harris.

4. Folsom, *The American Western Novel*, 85.

5. Ibid., 86.

6. Scarborough, *The Wind*, 2–3.

7. Westbrook, "Feminism and the Limits of Genre in *Fistful of Dollars* and *The Outlaw Josey Wales*," 26–27, 28.

8. Not surprisingly, Scarborough's doctoral dissertation at Columbia University is titled *The Supernatural in Modern English Fiction*.

9. Lillian Gish quoted in Sanders, *Lillian Gish*, a documentary film.

10. Sjöström had trained as an actor and theater director in Finland and Sweden after spending part of his childhood in New York. In his thirties he partnered with Mauritz Stiller at the Svenska Bio film company. Both directors came to Hollywood: Sjöström first, in 1923, signing with the Goldwyn Picture Corporation, which the following year merged with Metro Picture Corporation and Louis B. Mayer Pictures to become MGM. Sjöström's fifth Hollywood picture was *The Scarlet Letter* of 1926, followed in 1928 by *The Divine Woman*, starring Greta Garbo and Lars Hanson, and then *The Wind*. Sjöström returned to Sweden, and by 1930 he was making films in Stockholm. His last screen appearance was in *Wild Strawberries*, directed by Ingmar Bergman in 1957.

11. Eder, "Don't Fence Me In," 8.

12. Cowie, *Swedish Cinema*, 28.

13. At MGM, from the mid-1920s through the mid-1930s, Marion was one of the studio's most active and successful scenarists, and she was much relied on by Irving Thalberg. Marion, who had more than three hundred credits, received two Academy Awards, for *The Big House* (1930) and *The Champ* (1931). Her MGM work also included the script for Clarence Brown's *Anna Christie* (1930)—Garbo's first talkie—and her collaboration on scripts for George Cukor's *Dinner at Eight* (1933) and *Camille* (1937).

14. Marion, *Off with Their Heads!* 158–59.

15. Paschall and Weiner, "Nature Conquering or Nature Conquered in *The Wind* (1928)," 54–55.

16. Ibid., 55.

17. See Affron, *Lillian Gish, Her Legend and Her Life*, especially the chapter "The Perils of *The Wind*," 227–234.

18. Gish quoted in Sanders, *Lillian Gish*.

19. Marion, *Off with Their Heads!* 160.

20. Marion, *The Wind*.

21. There are interesting differences between these movies and their literary sources. In the literary resolution for Tom Dunson in Borden Chase's novel *The Chisholm Trail* (1946), he meets his end in the landscape (see chapter 6), as does

Letty Mason in Scarborough's novel. In Alan Le May's *The Searchers,* Debbie's rescuers, Ethan Edwards and Martin Pauley, discover that she does wish to return to the white man's civilization, but the author tacks on an ending that blurs the issue by having the cavalry kill the Comanche and the searchers survive.

22. Ford called *The Searchers* "a kind of psychological epic" (Gallagher, *John Ford,* 333).

23. Scarborough, *The Wind,* 305.

3. "HE WENT THAT-AWAY"

1. Turner, "Cowboys and Comedy," 218, 219–220, 234.

2. Fairbanks, *Laugh and Live,* 72–73, 96–97.

3. Duncan Renaldo starred as the Cisco Kid, and Leo Carillo played his Spanish sidekick, Pancho, in the long-running television series. The character was incarnated in earlier films by such actors as Warner Baxter, Cesar Romero, Gilbert Roland, and Renaldo himself. William R. Dunn portrayed the "Kid" in the 1914 silent *The Caballero's Way,* directed by Webster Cullison; the character was based on one in a story by O. Henry. Clayton Moore starred as the Lone Ranger in the long-running TV series by that name and had played the character in the 1952 film *The Legend of the Lone Ranger.*

4. As reported by Buscombe in his *100 Westerns,* 21.

5. Harvey, *Romantic Comedy in Hollywood,* 258.

6. Van Doren, *The American Novel,* 272.

7. A list of the humiliations in *Ruggles* demonstrates that comedy depends on cruelties, small or large, and this is fundamental to the comic Western. Ruggles learns that he was a stake in a poker game and that, since he has been won by the Flouds, he must go to America. Burnstead is humiliated at having to admit he lost Ruggles. Floud is humiliated at the tailor's and barber's shops. Ruggles is humiliated at the café. Effie is humiliated at the late arrival of the drunken trio to her dinner for important people: "*Je suis mortifee!*" Ruggles is humiliated at being drunk and by admitting his first name to Mrs. Judson, who in turn is humiliated at having her sauce criticized. Effie is humiliated by her husband going to a "beer bust," and because, after reading about Ruggles's triumph in the newspaper, she must now pretend that he is a colonel in the British army. Effie is further humiliated when Floud and Burnstead avoid the dinner by escaping through a window. Ruggles is humiliated when Belknap Jackson fires him, when he learns Lord B. is coming to get him, and when he is subjected to Mrs. Judson's scorn.

8. Turner, "Cowboys and Comedy," 219–220.

9. According to Turner, "To understand why parody works as comedy, it is useful to look at the incongruity theory, one of the major philosophical theories of comedy. Arthur Schopenhauer, one of the most useful proponents of the incongruity theory, describes the comedy of a situation as the tension between the conceived and the perceived, or the expected and the actual" (ibid., 220).

4. LANDSCAPE AND STANDARD-SETTING IN THE 1930S WESTERN

1. Schama, *Landscape and Memory,* 95–96.

2. Carmichael, introduction to *The Landscape of Hollywood Westerns,* 2–3.

3. For the influences of European and American landscape painters on certain Western filmmakers, with a focus on the influence of Frederic Remington's paintings on the cinematic art of John Ford, see Buscombe, "Painting the Legend," 154–168.

4. For a discussion of the intersections among nineteenth-century landscape photography, nineteenth-century landscape painting, and Western cinematic art, see Buscombe, "Inventing Monument Valley," 115–130.

5. Buscombe, *Stagecoach,* 41.

6. Herzog and Cronin, *Herzog on Herzog,* 81.

7. Gallagher, *John Ford,* 509.

8. It must be admitted that there are indeed a few A-Westerns whose directors opted more for studio-shot interiors than rugged real-life exteriors, and these include *Destry Rides Again* (1939) and *The Oxbow Incident* (1943). These latter movies tended to achieve their "A" status because of high-quality direction, screenplay, and performance rather than as a result of any major investment in on-location shooting.

9. McBride, *Searching for John Ford,* 106–107.

10. According to McBride, "Ford, in filming *The Iron Horse,* eagerly responded to the challenge of staging both action scenes and intimate vignettes that offered opportunities for visual poetry reminiscent of the paintings of Frederic Remington and Charles M. Russell. From those Western masters, Ford learned the paradoxical method of capturing the grittiness of frontier life and landscapes in moments of intensely romantic, often statuesque beauty. Both Jack [John] and Francis Ford emulated Remington in their Universal Westerns. [Charles] Russell, who died in 1926, was a frequent guest at Harry Carey's Rancho, where Jack would have had the opportunity to get to know him" (*Searching for John Ford,* 147).

11. Ibid., 448–449. And Edward Buscombe gives clear evidence of the effect of these landscape-centered artistic representations on Western filmmakers like John Ford: "John Ford is on record as having acknowledged Remington's influence. In his interview with Peter Bogdanovich, Ford remarks, 'I like *She Wore a Yellow Ribbon.* I tried to copy the Remington style there—you can't copy him one hundred percent—but at least I tried to get in his color and movement, and I think I succeeded partly' " ("Painting the Legend," 154–157).

12. Stevens, *Conversations with the Great Moviemakers,* 28.

13. Arthur Edeson, director of photography for *The Maltese Falcon* (1941) and *Casablanca* (1942) among countless other films, dating back to the silent era, was Walsh's cinematographer for the seventy-millimeter version of *The Big Trail;* he had also worked previously with Walsh on *Thief of Baghdad* (1924). The cinematographer who handled the photography for the thirty-five-millimeter English-speaking version of *The Big Trail,* and whose long career dates back to the early silent era, was Lucien Andriot.

14. See McBride, *Searching for John Ford,* his biography of Ford, for a discussion of Harry Carey Sr.'s influence on John Wayne (whose real name was Marion Morrison): "Harry Carey's silent Westerns had an enormous impression on a strapping kid whose name was Marion 'Duke' Morrison when he was growing up on a farm in Glendale, California. 'Harry Carey projected a quality that we like to think of in men of the West,' said John Wayne, adding that Ford 'built on his authenticity.' Wayne told actor Harry Carey Jr., 'I watched your dad since I was a kid. I copied Harry Carey. That's where I learned to talk like I do; that's where I learned many of my mannerisms. Watching your father" (102).

See also McBride, quoting Wayne, for Ford's influence on Wayne when the latter worked for Ford as a prop man on silent films: "By then Morrison [Wayne] 'wanted to be a director, and naturally I studied Ford like a hawk. . . . He was the first person who ever made me want to be a person—who gave me a vision of a fully rounded human being" (164).

15. See Cork and Van Eyssen, "The Big Vision: The Grandeur Process," a documentary featurette.

16. Admittedly, *The Big Trail* suffers from several flaws, including embarrassingly dated and stilted humor. In addition, most of the noncomic dialogue in *The Big Trail* is overly theatrical, chiefly because some of the major performers in the film, including Marguerite Churchill and Tyrone Power Sr., had been mainly stage rather than film actors.

17. Simmon, *The Invention of the Western Film,* 138.

18. Ibid., 139.

19. Ibid.

20. Ibid., 122–123.

21. In regard to the widescreen method used, see especially the featurette "The Big Vision: The Grandeur Process" contained in the special edition DVD release from Twentieth Century Fox.

22. See chapter 15 ("Rambling into Surrealism: The B-Western") in Simmon's *The Invention of the Western Film,* especially 160–170.

23. The Sons of the Pioneers recorded songs for John Ford's *Wagon Master* (1950) and *Rio Grande* (1950) and performed the theme song (by Stan Jones) for Ford's *The Searchers.*

24. Buscombe, *Stagecoach,* 10, 12.

25. Fenin and Everson, *The Western,* 203.

26. Gish quoted in Sanders, *Lillian Gish.*

27. An exception is Ford's 1931 war story *Seas Beneath,* set in a village on Spain's Canary Island, in which he eloquently captured a coastal landscape—as did Howard Hawks a year later, off the west coast of Mexico, in *Tiger Shark,* a tale of tuna fishermen.

28. As mentioned earlier in the chapter, Wayne did appear in very minor roles in a few of Ford's late silents and early talkies, including *Hangman's House* (1928), *Men without Women* (1930), and *Salute* (1929).

29. A particularly good essay on Ford's use of Monument Valley in *Stagecoach* is Carmichael's "The Living Presence of Monument Valley in John Ford's *Stagecoach* (1939)," 212–228. See also Hutson's "Sermons in Stone," 93–108.

30. Edward Buscombe states that Ford shot eight Westerns in Monument Valley, including *Stagecoach,* but confesses that he had once mistakenly included *Wagon Master* and *3 Godfathers* in his list of Ford films chiefly shot there when he wrote his *The BFI Companion to the Western.* See "Inventing Monument Valley," 119.

31. McBride, *Searching for John Ford,* 288. McBride also relates here—in a footnote, and citing Carlo Gaberscek's well-documented *Il West di John Ford* (Arti Grafiche Fruilane, 1994)—that both *Wagon Master* and *Rio Grande* were thought by some to have been shot in Monument Valley but had actually been filmed 120 miles from there, near Moab, Utah. See also McCarthy, "John Ford and Monument Valley."

32. Gallagher, *John Ford,* 464–465.

33. Screenwriter Frank Nugent (*Fort Apache, 3 Godfathers, She Wore a Yellow Ribbon, Wagon Master, The Quiet Man, Mister Roberts, The Searchers, The Rising of the Moon, The Last Hurrah, Two Rode Together, Donovan's Reef*) has said, "I'm not sure, but I suspect that when he [Ford] starts thinking about a story, he calmly devotes himself to personal research, gets hold of the music of the period and, generally, comes to his office well provided with a mixture of facts and fancy" (quoted in ibid., 464).

34. Kalinak, *How the West Was Sung,* 64. Kalinak also tells us in regard to the stagecoach theme itself: "My guess is that those few listeners who recognize the tune, or think they do, connect the stagecoach theme to 'Oh Bury Me Not on the Lone Prairie,' an enduring cowboy ballad reproduced in endless school songbooks and folk anthologies. Few listeners, if any, will identify it as 'The Trail to Mexico.' I think the composers of the score were counting on that misrecognition. But whether or not audience members recognize the title, they would respond to the musical cues of westernness infused throughout the song. The loping rhythms and simple harmonies function to connote a sense of western geography without the listener actually knowing the source or even being conscious of the presence of music" (60).

35. Patrick McGee offers an interpretation of *Stagecoach* based on class and gender conflicts in his *From* Shane *to* Kill Bill. See especially 42–45.

36. Kalinak, *How the West Was Sung,* 70.

37. Patrick McGee reads the conclusion of the film in terms of property ownership, which is interesting given his focus on economic themes, family structure, and class conflict. See *From* Shane *to* Kill Bill, 42.

38. For a discussion of the pastoral agrarian ideal as expressed by the final line in *Stagecoach,* see Robert C. Sickels's "Beyond the Blessings of Civilization," 142–152.

39. Buscombe, *Stagecoach,* 81.

40. Bazin, "The Evolution of the Language of Cinema," 29.

41. Bazin, "The Evolution of the Western," 85.

42. Welles quoted in McBride, *Searching for John Ford,* 299–300. The quote by Welles continues: "Every night for more than a month [while preparing *Citizen Kane* in 1940], I would screen [*Stagecoach*] with a different technician from RKO and ask him questions all through the movie."

5. INDIAN-FIGHTING, NATION-BUILDING, AND HOMESTEADING IN THE A-WESTERN

1. Bazin, "The Evolution of the Western," 49.

2. See chapter 15 ("Rambling into Surrealism: The B-Western") in Simmon's *The Invention of the Western Film,* especially 160–170.

3. In his essay "Country Music and the 1939 Western," Peter Stanfield begins by asking why so few A-Westerns were made between 1931 and 1939, and why so many A-Westerns were produced in and just after 1939. An important part of his answer has to do with the effects of the Great Depression as well as the growing specter of world war (23).

4. Glover, "East Goes West," 117–118.

5. See ibid., 114–115.

6. Ibid., 116.

7. For an intriguing examination of the influence of modern painting on King Vidor's aesthetic vision, as well as the influence of Vidor's silent classic *The Big Parade* (1925) on the paintings of Andrew Wyeth, see Gallagher, "How to Share a Hill," *Senses of Cinema,* past issues archive, http://archive.sensesofcinema .com/contents/07/43/king-vidor-andrew-wyeth.html, accessed July 15, 2009. Included in Gallagher's online article are images from *Northwest Passage,* used as evidence to show that the style of illustrations by N.C. Wyeth, father of Andrew Wyeth, had an influence on Vidor's imagery in this film.

8. Glover, "East Goes West," 117, 121.

9. For Vidor's biography and a cogent analysis and appreciation of his films, see Raymond Durgnat's *King Vidor, American.*

10. See Glover, "East Goes West," 117–118.

11. Ibid., 111.

12. Ibid., 121.

13. According to Prats, "The Myth of Conquest is no less *appropriative* than is Conquest itself. . . . And so Conquest's *mythology* presupposes the methodology of historical and cultural appropriation. I am referring to the notion, virtually enjoying the status of a first axiom, that the mythological alterations of historical events—*regardless, and often because, of the resulting distortions*—influence the national character, and that the selfsame alterations, taken as a system, structure, and pattern, become not only the major constituents of American culture but also the presumed methodology that articulates it" (*Invisible Natives,* 3).

14. See Prats's introduction ("Representation and Absence in *Northwest Passage*") to his *Invisible Natives,* 1–20.

15. See Prats, *Invisible Natives,* 19.

16. Prats observes that Konkapot's "Otherness" is expressed most clearly, not by his drunkenness or simplicity, but by his complete dependence on Rogers: he even has to be introduced to Langdon, which is accomplished by Rogers's degrading description of him. See ibid., 16–17.

17. See ibid., 2. Slotkin's trilogy is composed of *Regeneration through Violence: The Mythology of the American Frontier, 1600–1860; The Fatal Environ-*

ment: The Myth of the Frontier in the Age of Industrialization, 1800–1890; and *Gunfighter Nation: The Myth of the Frontier in Twentieth-Century America.*

18. Prats, *Invisible Natives,* 10.

19. Richard Slotkin calls such a person "the man who knows Indians" (*Gunfighter Nation,* 16).

20. See Prats, *Invisible Natives,* 13–14, as well as his chapter 4 ("'Chartered in Two Worlds': The Double Other"), which explores in detail the theme of the white Indian-knowing hero.

21. Fenin and Everson, *The Westerns,* 245–246.

22. According to Glover, "In another reversal, while we are *told* about the savagery of 'the Indians' as Rogers prepares his men on the eve of the attack, we are *shown* the savagery of the Rangers as they silently enter the sleeping village and massacre the men, women, and children" ("East Goes West," 123).

23. McGee, introduction to *From* Shane *to* Kill Bill, xv.

24. Fenin and Everson, *The Western,* 164.

25. Ibid., 163–164.

26. *The Westerner* provides evidence of Toland's brilliance as a cinematographer, with gorgeous desert backdrops poised in perfect tension between light and shadow. Toland had recently won the Oscar for Best Black-and-White Cinematography for his efforts in photographing *Wuthering Heights* for Wyler. Toland shot *The Westerner* in a highly productive year that also witnessed his work on two John Ford classics: *The Grapes of Wrath* and *The Long Voyage Home* (which, like *The Westerner,* were both released in 1940). He was soon to teach Orson Welles the basics of camera technique when they worked together on the landmark *Citizen Kane* (1941).

27. Stanfield, "Country Music and the 1939 Western," 29–30. For more on this period of Western movie production and its relationship with its social and historical context, see Stanfield's important books *Hollywood, Westerns, and the 1930s: The Lost Trail* and *Horse Opera: The Strange History of the 1930s Singing Cowboy.*

28. This connection between these images in the film and Depression-era Dustbowl images is drawn by McGee in the section on *The Westerner* in his book *From* Shane *to* Kill Bill, 52–53.

29. Ibid., 55.

30. Stanfield, "Country Music and the 1939 Western," 29.

6. HOWARD HAWKS AND JOHN WAYNE

1. Early in the film there is a nighttime scene inside the ranch quarters of the cowboys, which look more like part of a convivial saloon than a bunkhouse, when Dunson and Garth sign up the men for the cattle drive to Missouri. Near the end of *Red River* there are two brief interior scenes: in the office of the buyer Melville, and later that night in Garth's hotel room, after Garth signs the contract. On first walking into the office, Garth winces and looks up, saying he is surprised to be under a roof again. The only other interior scenes concern the heroine, Tess Millay, first in her wagon when she asks Cherry and Groot to tell

her all they know about Garth, and then later in her wagon when she offers Dunson dinner. After signing the contract, Garth walks into the final interior scene in his hotel room and finds Millay there to warn him about Dunson.

2. McCarthy, *Howard Hawks,* 417.

3. Ibid., 427.

4. Ibid., 419.

5. Ibid., 411.

6. Springer, "Beyond the River," 119–120. As Springer also tells us, "The film suggests that the men who think they can live without the companionship, guidance, and the help of women who are their equals often are doomed to an obsession with work (read: 'career') that isolates them from a larger community of shared human values to which women provide access" (123–124).

7. The excellent print reissued in 1997 by United Artists is the "book" version. Tag Gallagher notes that it was John Ford who suggested the use of a narrator (*John Ford,* 531).

8. Springer, "Beyond the River," 117.

9. The analogy between America and a "city on a hill" was first made by the Puritan John Winthrop in his 1630 sermon "A Model of Christian Charity," in which he addressed future Massachusetts Bay colonists while aboard the ship *Arbella.* The phrase was later used by President-Elect John F. Kennedy (in his address to the General Court of Massachusetts in January 9, 1961), who explicitly referred to Winthrop and his phrase. The comparison between America and a "shining city" was later used by President Ronald Reagan in his farewell address to the nation (January 11, 1989).

10. Corkin, *Cowboys and Cold Warriors,* 24–25.

11. According to Beard, "Wayne's power sustains the dominant ideology but is also derived from it. In many of his post-war westerns and in the many roles which placed him in the armed services, he is a warrior and an enforcer of order. . . . Wayne's heroic stature is coterminous with his individual mastery, but the individual qualities that allow him to rise above the others are also the expression of a social ideology of individualism: the ideology which holds that the specialness of America lies precisely in its creation of a *society* where individualist values hold the seat of honour" (*Persistence of Double Vision,* 4).

12. Corkin, *Cowboys as Cold Warriors,* 28–29.

13. See McGee, *From* Shane *to* Kill Bill, 82–83.

14. Ibid., 84–85, 89–90.

15. Ibid., 85–86.

16. McCarthy, *Howard Hawks,* 427.

17. Ibid., 410–411.

18. Ibid., 419.

19. Springer, "Beyond the River," 123–124.

20. McCarthy, *Howard Hawks,* 425.

21. See McBride, *Searching for John Ford,* 102.

22. McCarthy, *Howard Hawks,* 616–617.

23. Ibid., 618.

24. Ibid., 621.

25. Ibid., 622.

7. THE POSTWAR PSYCHOLOGICAL WESTERN

Epigraph on page 156: Bazin, "The Evolution of the Western," 51.

1. For a detailed account of John Ford's service as head of the Field Photographic Branch of the Office of Strategic Services, see chapter 10 ("Yes—This Really Happened") in Joseph McBride's biography *Searching for John Ford: A Life,* 335–415. For Ford's own account of his wartime service, see the interviews "Reflections on the Battle of Midway: An Interview with John Ford (August 17, 1943)," 102–110, and Peter Martin's "We Shot D-Day on Omaha Beach: An Interview with John Ford," 111–121, in *John Ford in Focus: Essays on the Filmmaker's Life and Work,* ed. Kevin L. Stoehr and Michael C. Connolly (Jefferson, NC: McFarland, 2008).

2. Scott Simmon focuses on the Hamlet-like delay of action in his fascinating chapters on *My Darling Clementine* (chaps. 18–20) in his book *The Invention of the Western Film: A Cultural History of the Genre's First Half-Century.* See also Simmon, "Concerning the Weary Legs of Wyatt Earp: The Classic Western According to Shakespeare," in *The Western Reader,* ed. Jim Kitses and Gregg Rickman (New York: Limelight, 1998), 149–160. As Kitses states in opposition to the "Hamlet" thesis in interpreting the film: "Is there any hint of the character indulging 'the whips and scorns of time, the law's delay'? The action in fact only occupies a weekend—remarkably, given the sense Ford creates of relationships developing, of characters and the community changing" (*Horizons West,* 59).

3. Gallagher, *John Ford,* 225. This excerpt from Gallagher is also quoted in McGee's *From* Shane *to* Kill Bill, 78–79, where McGee refers to Fonda's Wyatt Earp as a "first sketch of the masculinist Cold Warrior in all of its contradictions" and views the cattle-rustling Clantons as signifying "the threat of fascism" (79).

4. Jim Kitses, "Introduction: *Post-modernism and The Western*" (1998), in *The Western Reader,* ed. Kitses and Rickman (New York: Limelight, 1998), 15–31, 29–30.

5. Kitses, *Horizons West,* 66–69.

6. Ibid., 69.

7. Bogdanovich, *John Ford,* 83, 91.

8. While paying due attention to the psychological dynamics of *Duel in the Sun,* Patrick McGee concentrates on the class, race, and gender conflicts around which the movie often revolves. See *From* Shane *to* Kill Bill, 59–68. He also refers substantially here (see p. 61) to Laura Mulvey's emphasis on the film's gender and sexual dynamics in her book *Visual and Other Pleasures.*

9. Freud expounds upon the dialectical tension between the Eros and Thanatos principles (or instinctual drives) in his later work *Civilization and Its Discontents (Das Unbehagen in der Kultur).*

10. Paul Schrader, "Notes on Film Noir," in *Perspectives on Film Noir,* ed. R. Barton Palmer, 105.

11. See, for example, Raymond Borde and Étienne Chameton's essay "Towards a Definition of Film Noir," in *Film Noir Reader,* ed. Alain Silver and James Ursini, trans. Alain Silver (New York: Limelight, 1996), 25.

12. And a few years later Schnee would go on to win an Academy Award for his screenplay for Vincente Minnelli's noirish Hollywood melodrama *The Bad and the Beautiful* (1952).

13. The choice of the name *Jubal* is an intriguing one. There is a Jubal in the Bible, a descendant of Cain, who has been regarded as an ancestral "father" of musicians, especially those who play the harp, lyre, or flute (see Genesis 4:21). The connection with Cain may have some relevance since Jubal in Daves's film is also a disfavored son, given his later admission of his mother's hatred of him when he was a boy. There is also a Jubal Anderson Early who was a Confederate army general in the Civil War. There is no specific reference to either of these in the movie, however.

14. Interestingly, Borgnine had just won the Oscar for Best Actor for his title role in the film adaptation of Paddy Chayefsky's drama *Marty* (1955), and Steiger had played that role in an earlier television production (1953).

15. A good discussion of *Jubal* that emphasizes its connections with Shakespeare's *Othello* and Freudian psychology is Michael Walker's essay "The Westerns of Delmer Daves."

16. While Freud later in life came to criticize his own earlier overemphasis on the possibility of sexual traumas in the childhoods of most or all of his patients, particularly traumas related to sexual abuse, he nonetheless always maintained his conviction that dramatic personal experiences in people's earlier lives, especially in their youth, can have strong repercussions on their inner lives as adults. Psychoanalysis is, particularly from a Freudian perspective, a process of coming to identify and connect these causes and effects, especially by means of sharing this process of self-learning with another.

17. While various psychological theories might be applied to an analysis of the main characters in such Westerns, perhaps the most fruitful would be Viktor Frankl's idea of "logo-therapy." This is an existentialist and pragmatic approach to the problems of the human personality that emphasizes a person's "will to meaning," the search for an overall goal or purpose in an individual's concrete life. See Frankl's classic work *Man's Search for Meaning,* a revised and expanded version of his earlier book *From Death-Camp to Existentialism.*

18. Bazin, "The Evolution of the Western," 53–54. Bazin's paradigmatic example of the application of this quality is Mann's *The Naked Spur* (see Bazin, 55).

8. JOHN FORD'S LATER MASTERPIECES

1. "Ethan Edwards is uneven, a character not organically conceived, its tone and emphasis (like that of the film itself) faltering and varying from sequence to sequence. . . . The style of *The Searchers* varies continually between the poetic and the farcical, the grand and the mundane, the convinced and the perfunctory. . . . There is a lot of John Ford in *The Searchers,* a lot of his splendid craft and his ambiguous, divided personality; but the sense of harmony, of resolution and of faith which gives his work at its best a special grace is not there" (Anderson, *About John Ford,* 156, 158, 160).

2. Buscombe, *The Searchers,* 68–69.

3. An illuminating essay on Ford's emphasis on landscape and on his specific use of Monument Valley in this film is Dick Hutson's "Sermons in Stone," 93–108.

4. Ford's movie *The Horse Soldiers* (1959), with John Wayne and William Holden, and his "Civil War" segment of the epic *How the West Was Won* (1962) fell outside of this "project" of deglamorizing and demythologizing the story of the Westerner, serving more as war films than as Western films, despite their general narrative contexts and settings.

5. See especially Peter Lehman's essay "Texas 1868/America 1956: *The Searchers*." Lehman states in that essay: "There is a constant tension in the film between Ethan and interior spaces; he does not fit in anywhere" (397). See also Lehman's essays "You Couldn't Hit It on the Nose" and "There's No Way of Knowing."

6. See Paulus, "Ways of Knowing," especially 83–85. For an illuminating analysis of Ford's use of aperture framing and other cinematic framing devices in his silent films, see Paulus, "If You Can Call It an Art . . ."

7. Bogdanovich, *John Ford*, 92–93.

8. The term *strategic opacity* is taken from Greenblatt's *Will in the World*.

9. Buscombe, *The Searchers*, 29. Interestingly, Buscombe interprets Ethan's "savage stabbing" with his knife, right after having discovered and buried Lucy's corpse, as an almost subconscious imitation of the Comanche's rape and murder of his niece. This is certainly likely, though it is also probable that Ethan digs with his knife in the sand, if only for a few moments, because he has just buried Lucy quickly and his mind is still focused on that action. Or, perhaps best interpreted, both actions weigh on Ethan's mind with equal force.

10. Legendary Hollywood producer Darryl F. Zanuck once stated, reflecting on his long career and his association with great filmmakers, that Ford was "the best director in the history of motion pictures" because "his placement of the camera almost had the effect of making even good dialogue unnecessary or secondary" (Gallagher, *John Ford*, 145).

11. Buscombe, *The Searchers*, 21.

12. Kitses, *Horizons West*, 96.

13. Gallagher, "Angels Gambol Where They Will," 272–273.

14. Kitses, *Horizons West*, 99–100.

15. Ibid., 100, 102.

16. Tag Gallagher proposes such an interpretation of Ethan's sudden change of mind when lifting Debbie toward the end of the film: "Does he [Ethan] recall lifting Debbie the night before that massacre? Regardless, he finally *touches* Debbie, grasps the *person* rather than ideas, and all his hate, fury, and insanity is transmuted into love" (*John Ford*, 336).

17. Ibid., 22–23 and 338.

18. Kitses, *Horizons West*, 118, 125.

19. Thomson, *A Biographical Dictionary of Film*, 382.

20. *Liberty Valance* is based on a story by Dorothy M. Johnson published in *Cosmopolitan* in 1949. Johnson, born in 1905, studied at Montana State University, became a magazine editor in New York, and returned to teach at the University of Montana in the 1950s. She wrote short stories, including "The

Man Who Shot Liberty Valance" and "A Man Called Horse" (collected in *Indian Country,* 1953) and novels about Indians and the West; her novels included *The Hanging Tree* (1957) and *Buffalo Woman* (1977). In Johnson's story, the funeral of Bert Barricune (Tom Doniphon in the film) takes place in 1910 in Twotrees. Attending is Senator Ranse Foster, who tells the reporter only the legend, not the truth, by saying Barricune had been a friend of his for more than thirty years. The rest of the story is very much a character study of Foster, a man who comes to hate himself as much as he hates Liberty Valance for humiliating him. When he learns from Barricune who really shot Valance, and why, Ranse decides to live the lie.

21. Pippin, *Hollywood Westerns and American Myth.*

22. According to Joseph McBride, "Ford took the unusual step of writing Bosley Crowther, the lead reviewer of the *Times,* to alert him to the fact that the film was deliberately stylized like a silent Western" (*Searching for John Ford,* 625).

23. Three other Western masterworks by Ford were in color: *3 Godfathers* (1948), *She Wore a Yellow Ribbon* (1949), and *The Searchers* (1956).

24. Bogdanovich, *John Ford,* 74.

25. It has been suggested that *Picketwire* is the Westerner's name for the Purgatoire, a river flowing into the Arkansas River in southeastern Colorado near Comanche territory. South of the Picketwire are the New Mexican and Indian territories that will become, respectively, New Mexico, Arizona, and Oklahoma; south of Indian territory is Texas, a state since 1845. Thus we are given a clue to where *Liberty Valance* takes place.

26. Doniphon will not assume the role and will not leave the West to be a part of the national government, any more than Burt Lancaster's Prince of Salina would leave his beloved Sicily for Turin to take part in governing the new nation of Italy, in *Il Gattopardo (The Leopard),* which was directed by Luchino Visconti and released a year after *Liberty Valance* in 1963. Odd as it may seem, a few notes of comparison between these two stories, both relating to later-nineteenth-century concepts of nationhood, point up the ambivalent attitudes of their hero-observers, characters who assume a melancholic magnificence as each steps to the side of a key moment in history. Each man, rancher or prince, realizes that the expansion of a central government is certain, each is skeptical of his own participation and suggests instead a man who lacks a traditional code of honor, and each values his personal freedom above all else. Each hero-observer has a notion of a symbolic sacred place, whether the territorial West or the Sicilian landscape. All hope of preserving this place, despite the onrush of the new reality, gives way to what seems either a more generous or simply a practical push by each man to effect historical progress. Since both Doniphon and the Prince wish to die where they were born, both will promote upstarts to conduct the new politics of statehood and compromise in the nation's distant headquarters.

27. The following are only four of many possible examples from Ford's body of work: the flowers that Hannah Jessop (Henrietta Crosman) carries to her dead son's grave in France after the war, in *Pilgrimage* (1933); the flowers that Captain Nathan Brittles (John Wayne) waters at the grave of his deceased wife,

in *She Wore a Yellow Ribbon* (1949); the roses that Sean Thornton (Wayne) brings to the home of his beloved Mary Kate (Maureen O'Hara), in *The Quiet Man* (1952); and the fresh flower that Mayor Frank Skeffington (Spencer Tracy) leaves before the portrait of his deceased wife each morning, in *The Last Hurrah* (1958).

28. McBride writes, "Michael Wilmington and I wrote of this scene in our 1974 book on Ford: 'Once the historical process has been given a catalyst, it can't be stopped: that is the tragedy. And the reason Ford "prints the fact" is to ask the public, "*Are* you proud?"'" (*Searching for John Ford*, 634).

29. Folsom, *The American Western Novel*, 31.

30. Perry Miller, *Errand into the Wilderness*, 1–15.

31. Folsom, *The American Western Novel*, 31.

9. THE EXISTENTIAL AND REVISIONIST WESTERN

1. See, for example, Jean-Paul Sartre's lecture "Existentialism Is a Humanism" (*L'existentialisme est un humanisme*). It must be recognized that Sartre's conception of human freedom as unlimited in its subjective nature is dependent on his atheistic worldview.

2. Kitses, *Horizons West*, 175–176.

3. Wollen [as Lee Russell], "Budd Boetticher" (1965), 197.

4. Ibid., 199.

5. There are a few Mann Westerns of the 1950s that gain part of their narrative drive from sociohistorical situations. For example, Mann's *Bend of the River* (1952) revolves around the lives of homesteaders making their way from Missouri to the Oregon territory; and his *Savage Wilderness* (a.k.a. *The Last Frontier*, 1955) centers on the moralities of individuals caught up in the Indian-fighting mission of a remote Oregon army fort.

6. Wollen, "Budd Boetticher," 197.

7. Ibid. He also states on the same page: "For individualism, death is an absolute limit which cannot be transcended; it renders the life which precedes it absurd. How then can there be any meaningful individual action during life? How can individual action have any value, if it cannot have transcendent value because of the absolutely devaluing limit of death? These problems are to be found in Boetticher's films."

8. Kitses, *Horizons West*, 176.

9. Ibid., 177–178.

10. Ibid., 181.

11. Ibid., 184.

12. Ibid., 181.

13. See Harris, *Pictures at a Revolution*.

14. See also Jim Kitses's reflection on the "morality" of Bishop's band of outlaws: "They do what they do because there is nowhere to go. *The Wild Bunch* represents a way of life, a style of action, a technology, with no vision, no values, no goals. The quiet battle cry of the group is, ironically, 'Let's *go*': but we can only ask *where*?" (*Horizons West*, 223)

10. EASTWOOD AND THE AMERICAN WESTERN

Epigraph on page 238: Turan, "A Fistful of Memories," 246.

1. For the influence of jazz on Eastwood, see Schickel, *Clint Eastwood*, chap. 1: "Nothing for Nothing," and especially 29–42.

2. A significant and welcome body of literature has grown around the works and artistry of Eastwood. See Smith, *Clint Eastwood;* Cornell, *Clint Eastwood and Issues of Masculinity;* and Schickel, *Clint*. See also, among other books, the following two essay collections: Knapp, *Directed by Clint Eastwood*, and Beard, *Persistence of Double Vision*. See also Hughes, *Aim for the Heart*, and Bingham, *Acting Male*. Biographies include Schickel's authorized *Clint Eastwood* and Eliot's unauthorized *American Rebel*.

3. As Schickel points out in his Eastwood biography, the label of "The Man with No Name" is actually a misnomer concocted by a marketing person. In all of the scripts for Leone's "Dollars" films, the Eastwood character is named "Joe" (Schickel, *Clint Eastwood*, 139).

4. The basic plot of *Coogan's Bluff* would be echoed loosely by the later TV series *McCloud* (1970–1977) with Dennis Weaver.

5. In his *100 Westerns*, Edward Buscombe tells us about *The Beguiled:* "On one hand, it could be argued that this is not, strictly speaking, a Western at all, but rather an example of Southern Gothic. On the other hand, there is a long tradition of Civil War pictures, such as John Ford's *The Horse Soldiers* (1959), with close connections to the mainstream of the Western genre" (9).

6. Eastwood also directed the *Lolita*-like story *Breezy*, starring William Holden and Kay Lenz. *Breezy* was released in the United States in 1973 several months after *High Plains Drifter* was released.

7. For Eastwood's comments on his dedication of *Unforgiven* to Leone and Siegel, see Kapsis and Coblentz, *Clint Eastwood*, 177 and 192.

8. Beard, *Persistence of Double Vision*, 7–8.

9. As Beard remarks, "The whole of *High Plains Drifter* is visually distinguished, but at the conclusion of the film Eastwood the director creates his first great visual tour-de-force. The wholesale red-painting, and then the burning, of the town results in an astonishing iconic transformation of the town into an almost literally hellish landscape—a gesture of stylization at least as extreme as anything in Leone (and that is saying something)" (ibid., 25).

10. Mono Lake is the actual main site of on-location shooting, and Richard Schickel discusses Eastwood's scouting of this location in his biography *Clint Eastwood* (289).

11. According to Buscombe, "Anthony Mann, famed for his use of mountain scenery, was moved to protest: 'I have never understood why people make almost all Westerns in desert country. John Ford, for example, adores Monument Valley, but Monument Valley, which I know well, is not the whole of the west. In fact the desert represents only a part of the American west" ("Inventing Monument Valley," 119).

12. Thompson and Hunter, "Eastwood Direction," 50. Eastwood also said, "I needed a place that would correspond with the mood and Mono Lake is what I finally found. It's a dead lake. It has some very interesting outcroppings

and the colors almost change moment by moment, so it gave the film an elusive quality" (Gentry, "Director Clint Eastwood," 69). Eastwood is quoted in another interview as saying, "I discovered Mono Lake by chance. . . . I immediately called my art director and had him jump on the first plane. When he arrived, he blurted out, 'You'd think you were on the moon!' I told him, 'It's a weird place, but that's exactly what I want this story to be!' " (Henry, "Interview with Clint Eastwood," 100–101).

13. Bumstead was also to serve as Eastwood's recurring production designer from *Unforgiven* to *Letters from Iwo Jima,* which was released in 2006, the year of Bumstead's death. He had been nominated for an Oscar for Best Art Direction and Set Direction for his design of the town of Big Whiskey in *Unforgiven,* as he had been more than thirty years earlier for his work on Hitchcock's *Vertigo.* And Bumstead had already won two Oscars in the same category for his earlier work on the classics *The Sting* and *To Kill a Mockingbird.*

14. Schickel, *Clint Eastwood,* 289.

15. According to Buscombe, "*Shane*'s classic status means that most makers of Westerns would be familiar with it. But Eastwood seems to have internalized this film to a remarkable extent, since not only *Unforgiven* but *Pale Rider* too exhibits many of the same features" (*Unforgiven,* 33).

16. Henry, "Interview with Clint Eastwood," 99–100. Eastwood states in another interview: "But *High Plains Drifter* was great fun because I liked the irony of it, I liked the irony of doing a stylized version of what happens if the sheriff in *High Noon* is killed, and symbolically comes back as some avenging angel or something—and I think that's far more hip than doing just a straight Western, the straight old conflicts we've all seen" (Frayling, "Eastwood on Eastwood," 134–135).

17. Eastwood has said, "Well, I was kind of curious, so I read it [the script of *A Fistful of Dollars*], and I recognized it right away as *Yojimbo,* a Kurosawa film I had liked a lot" (Cahill, "Clint Eastwood," 121). See also Henry, "Interview with Clint Eastwood," 99; and Turan, "A Fistful of Memories," 248.

18. Schickel, *Clint Eastwood,* 288.

19. Eastwood states, "It was originally written that the Drifter was the brother of the murdered sheriff, but I played it as if it could have been some apparition" (Gentry, "Director Clint Eastwood," 68). See also Henry, "Interview with Clint Eastwood," 100.

20. Schickel, *Clint Eastwood,* 291.

21. Biskind, "Any Which Way He Can," 202.

22. Ibid., 200.

23. For Eastwood's reflections on Siegel's "economic" mode of directing and his influence on Eastwood, see Kapsis and Coblentz, *Clint Eastwood,* 10, 30, 43, 79, 128, 171, 174, 177, 210. For example: "I think I learned more about directing from him [Siegel] than from anybody else" (128).

24. The idea of Ford's "vignette" style is emphasized by Gallagher (see *John Ford,* 466–468).

25. Gourlie and Engel, introduction to *Clint Eastwood,* 1–23.

26. Gentry, "Director Clint Eastwood," 68.

27. Turan, "A Fistful of Memories," 246.

28. Ibid. Eastwood also mentions *The Ox-Bow Incident* as a personal favorite in the interview by Jousse and Nevers, "Interview with Clint Eastwood," 183.

29. Beard, *Persistence of Double Vision*, 54.

30. See Schickel, *Clint Eastwood*, 452–453. See also Béhar, "Portrait of the Gunslinger as a Wise Old Man," 188.

31. Buscombe, *Unforgiven*, 44.

32. See, for example, Joseph McBride's biography of Ford, where the author says that the term *grace note* was used by Ford himself: "By that he [Ford] meant directorial touches, often nonverbal, that reveal character or capture emotion. Such frissons are the cinematic equivalent of the compressed, allusive phrasing of lyric poetry. In his best work, Ford values these seeming digressions above the sometimes laborious necessities of narrative" (*Searching for John Ford*, 175).

33. Tibbets, "The Machinery of Violence," 174.

34. As Beard tells us while emphasizing the immorality of Munny: "But even before the frightening concluding scenes of the film, this Eastwood character has been morally compromised. This is not just a matter of Munny's earlier in-humanness. . . . It is perhaps even more crucially a matter of what can only be described as the criminality of the reformed Munny: the criminality, that is, of engaging in assassination for hire" (*Persistence of Double Vision*, 51, 52).

35. Jousse and Nevers, "Interview with Clint Eastwood," 185.

36. Tibbets, "The Machinery of Violence," 176.

37. Ibid.

38. According to Buscombe, "Yet though one need not look far to find paral-lels to Daggett in contemporary actuality, there are plenty of instances in the Western too of corrupt and sadistic lawmen. One of the most memorable is that played by Karl Malden in Marlon Brando's *One-Eyed Jacks* (1960). Significantly he too, like Daggett, is fond of the whip, generally a cowardly weapon in the Western" (*Unforgiven*, 37).

39. Tibbets, "The Machinery of Violence," 177. Also quoted in Gourlie and Engel, introduction to *Clint Eastwood, Actor and Director*, 10.

40. Schickel, *Clint Eastwood*, 454–455.

41. Quote taken from ibid., 458.

42. Turan, "A Fistful of Memories," 247. Eastwood also remarks that he was trying "to make a statement about violence and the moral issue of it" (Tibbets, "The Machinery of Violence," 177).

43. According to Buscombe, "The writer of the script, David Webb Peoples, is more circumspect, but does try to draw a distinction between *Unforgiven* and earlier films: 'There's certainly no intention on my part to write an anti-violent picture. On the other hand, I think violence is horrifying and I think the reason people think this is an anti-violent picture is that so many other pictures are at least intellectually pro-violence, in other words they suggest if the good guy just beats up the bad guy this will make everything better, and I don't think life's like that, I don't think it's ever as simple as that, I think it's really hard to figure out who the good guy is and who the bad guy is to begin with'" (*Unforgiven*, 73).

44. Kitses, *Horizons West*, 312.

11. CODA

1. See, for example, Hoberman, "How the Western Was Lost." See also Lejeune's article "The Disappearing Cowboy"; Alan Prendergast's article "They Died with Their Boots On"; and the preface to Scott Simmon's *The Invention of the Western Film,* where he states, "The many premature obituaries for the Western film—the first few published in 1911—might warn us off such a pronouncement, but the genre is beginning to feel clinically dead, especially if a living genre requires a critical mass of productions" (xv).

2. For a good discussion of the concept of the posttraditional Western, see Jim Kitses's introduction ("Post-modernism and the Western") to *The Western Reader,* ed. Jim Kitses and Gregg Rickman (New York: Limelight, 1998).

Bibliography

Affron, Charles. *Lillian Gish, Her Legend and Her Life*. Berkeley: University of California Press, 2001.

Aleiss, Angela. *Making the White Man's Indian: Native Americans and Hollywood Movies*. Westport, CT: Praeger, 2005.

Anderson, Lindsay. *About John Ford*. New York: McGraw-Hill, 1981.

Barber, Richard. *The Knight and Chivalry*. New York: Charles Scribner's Sons, 1970.

Bazin, André. "The Evolution of the Language of Cinema." In *What Is Cinema?* Translated by Hugh Gray, 23–40. Berkeley: University of California Press, 1967.

———. "The Evolution of the Western." In *The Western Reader,* edited by Jim Kitses and Gregg Rickman, 49–56. New York: Limelight, 1998.

Beard, William. *Persistence of Double Vision: Essays on Clint Eastwood*. Edmonton, Canada: University of Alberta Press, 2000.

Béhar, Henri. "Portrait of the Gunslinger as a Wise Old Man: Encounter with Clint Eastwood." In *Clint Eastwood: Interviews,* edited by Robert E. Kapsis and Kathie Coblentz, 187–192. Jackson: University Press of Mississippi, 1999. Previously published as "Portrait du flingueur en vieux sage: Rencontre avec Clint Eastwood," *Le Monde,* September 3, 1992, 28.

Bingham, Dennis. *Acting Male: Masculinities in the Films of James Stewart, Jack Nicholson, and Clint Eastwood*. New Brunswick, NJ: Rutgers University Press, 1994.

Biograph Bulletins, 1908–1912. New York: Octagon Books, 1973.

Biskind, Peter. "Any Which Way He Can." In *Clint Eastwood: Interviews,* edited by Robert E. Kapsis and Kathie Coblentz, 193–206. Jackson: University Press of Mississippi, 1999. Previously published in *Premiere* (April 1993): 52–60.

Bogdanovich, Peter. *John Ford: Revised and Enlarged Edition.* 1967. Reprint, Berkeley: University of California Press, 1978.

Borde, Raymond, and Étienne Chameton. "Towards a Definition of Film Noir." In *Film Noir Reader,* edited by Alain Silver and James Ursini, trans. Alain Silver. New York: Limelight, 1996.

Brodie Smith, Andrew. *Shooting Cowboys and Indians: Silent Western Films, American Culture, and the Birth of Hollywood.* Boulder: University Press of Colorado, 2004.

Budd, Michael. "A Home in the Wilderness: Visual Imagery in John Ford's Westerns." In *The Western Reader,* edited by Jim Kitses and Gregg Rickman, 133–148. New York: Limelight, 1998.

Buscombe, Edward. *The BFI Companion to the Western.* London: British Film Institute/André Deutsch, 1988.

———. *"Injuns!": Native Americans in the Movies.* Cornwall, U.K.: Reaktion Books, 2006.

———. "Inventing Monument Valley: Nineteenth-Century Landscape Photography and the Western Film." In *The Western Reader,* edited by Jim Kitses and Gregg Rickman, 115–130. New York: Limelight, 1998.

———. *100 Westerns: BFI Screen Guides.* London: British Film Institute Publishing, 2006.

———. "Painting the Legend: Frederic Remington and the Western." In *John Ford Made Westerns: Filming the Legend in the Sound Era,* edited by Gaylyn Studlar and Matthew Bernstein, 154–168. Bloomington: Indiana University Press, 2001.

———. *The Searchers.* London: British Film Institute Publishing, 2000.

———. *Stagecoach.* London: British Film Institute Publishing, 1993.

———. *Unforgiven.* London: British Film Institute Publishing, 2004.

Cahill, Tim. "Clint Eastwood: The Rolling Stone Interview." In *Clint Eastwood: Interviews,* edited by Robert E. Kapsis and Kathie Coblentz, 117–129. Jackson: University Press of Mississippi, 1999. Previously published in *Rolling Stone,* July 4, 1985, 18–23.

Cameron, Ian, and Douglas Pye, eds. *The Book of Westerns.* New York: Continuum, 1996.

Carmichael, Deborah A., ed. *The Landscape of Hollywood Westerns: Ecocriticism in an American Film Genre.* Salt Lake City: University of Utah Press, 2006.

———. "The Living Presence of Monument Valley in John Ford's *Stagecoach* (1939)." In *The Landscape of Hollywood Westerns: Ecocriticism in an American Film Genre,* edited by Deborah A. Carmichael, 212–228. Salt Lake City: University of Utah Press, 2006.

Chase, Borden. *Red River: Blazing Guns on the Chisholm Trail.* New York: Bantam, 1948.

Cook, Pam. "Women in the Western." In *The BFI Companion to the Western,* edited by Edward Buscombe. London: British Film Institute/André Deutsch, 1988. Reprinted in *The Western Reader,* edited by Jim Kitses and Gregg Rickman, 293–300. New York: Limelight, 1998.

Cork, John, and Lisa Van Eyssen, directors. "The Big Vision: The Grandeur Process." Documentary featurette on Twentieth Century Fox's two-disc special edition of *The Big Trail* (2008).

Corkin, Stanley. *Cowboys as Cold Warriors: The Western and U.S. History.* Philadelphia: Temple University Press, 2004.

Cornell, Drucilla. *Clint Eastwood and Issues of American Masculinity.* New York: Fordham University Press, 2009.

Cowie, Peter. *Swedish Cinema.* London: A. Zwemmer, 1966.

Coyne, Michael. *The Crowded Prairie: American National Identity in the Hollywood Western.* London: I.B. Tauris, 1997.

Cremean, David. "A Fistful of Anarchy: Clint Eastwood's Characters in Sergio Leone's Dollars Trilogy and in His Four 'Own' Westerns." In *Clint Eastwood, Actor and Director: New Perspectives,* edited by Leonard Engel, 49–76. Salt Lake City: University of Utah Press, 2007.

Dibb, Mike. "A Time and a Place: Budd Boetticher and the Western." In *The Book of Westerns,* edited by Ian Cameron and Douglas Pye, 161–166. New York: Continuum, 1996.

Durgnat, Raymond. *King Vidor, American.* Berkeley: University of California Press, 1992.

Eckstein, Arthur M., and Peter Lehman, eds. *The Searchers: Essays and Reflections on John Ford's Classic Western.* Detroit: Wayne State University Press, 2004.

Eder, Richard. "Don't Fence Me In," a review of *Close Range: Wyoming Stories,* by Annie Proulx. *New York Times Book Review,* May 23, 1999, 8.

Eliot, Marc. *American Rebel: The Life of Clint Eastwood.* New York: Three Rivers Press, 2010.

Engel, Leonard, ed. *Clint Eastwood, Actor and Director: New Perspectives.* Salt Lake City: University of Utah Press, 2007.

Erisman, Fred. "Clint Eastwood's Western Films and the Evolving Mythic Hero." In *Clint Eastwood, Actor and Director: New Perspectives,* edited by Leonard Engel, 181–194. Salt Lake City: University of Utah Press, 2007.

Evans, Peter William. "Westward the Women: Feminising the Wilderness." In *The Book of Westerns,* edited by Ian Cameron and Douglas Pye, 206–213. New York: Continuum, 1996.

Fairbanks, Douglas. *Laugh and Live.* New York: Britton Publishing, 1917.

Fenin, George N., and William K. Everson. *The Western: From Silents to the Seventies.* New York: Penguin, 1973.

Folsom, James. *The American Western Novel.* New Haven: College and University Press, 1966.

Frayling, Christopher. "Eastwood on Eastwood." In *Clint Eastwood: Interviews,* edited by Robert E. Kapsis and Kathie Coblentz, 130–136. Jackson: University Press of Mississippi, 1999. Previously published as chapter 6 of *Clint Eastwood,* 61–67 (London: Virgin, 1992).

Gallafent, Edward. "Four Tombstones, 1946–1994." In *The Book of Westerns,* edited by Ian Cameron and Douglas Pye, 302–311. New York: Continuum, 1996.

Gallagher, Tag. "Angels Gambol Where They Will." In *The Western Reader*, edited by Jim Kitses and Gregg Rickman, 269–275. New York: Limelight, 1998.

———. *John Ford: The Man and His Films*. Berkeley: University of California Press, 1986.

Gentry, Ric. "Director Clint Eastwood: Attention to Detail and Involvement for the Audience." In *Clint Eastwood: Interviews,* edited by Robert E. Kapsis and Kathie Coblentz, 62–75. Jackson: University Press of Mississippi, 1999. Previously published in *Millimeter* (December 1980): 127–133.

Glover, Susan Paterson. "East Goes West: The Technicolor Environment of *Northwest Passage* (1940)." In *The Landscape of Hollywood Westerns: Ecocriticism in an American Film Genre,* edited by Deborah A. Carmichael, 111–126. Salt Lake City: University of Utah Press, 2006.

Gourlie, John, and Leonard Engel. Introduction to *Clint Eastwood, Actor and Director: New Perspectives,* edited by Leonard Engel, 1–23. Salt Lake City: University of Utah Press, 2007.

Greenblatt, Stephen. *Will in the World: How Shakespeare Became Shakespeare.* New York: W.W. Norton, 2004.

Grist, Leighton. *"Unforgiven."* In *The Book of Westerns,* edited by Ian Cameron and Douglas Pye, 294–301. New York: Continuum, 1996.

Hall, Sheldon. *"How the West Was Won:* History, Spectacle, and the American Mountains." In *The Book of Westerns,* edited by Ian Cameron and Douglas Pye, 255–261. New York: Continuum, 1996.

Harris, Mark. *Pictures at a Revolution: Five Movies and the Birth of the New Hollywood.* New York: Penguin, 2008.

Harvey, James. *Romantic Comedy in Hollywood: From Lubitsch to Sturges.* New York: Knopf, 1987.

Henry, Michael. "Interview with Clint Eastwood." In *Clint Eastwood: Interviews,* edited by Robert E. Kapsis and Kathie Coblentz, translated from the French by Coblentz, 96–116. Jackson: University Press of Mississippi, 1999. Previously published as "Entretien avec Clint Eastwood," *Positif,* no. 287 (January 1985): 48–57.

Herzog, Werner, and Paul Cronin. *Herzog on Herzog.* Edited by Paul Cronin. New York: Faber and Faber, 2002.

Hoberman, J. "How the Western Was Lost—Tracking the Decline of an American Genre: From Appomattox to Vietnam to Disney World." *Voice* (August 27, 1991): 49–54. A version of this article also appears in *The Western Reader,* edited by Jim Kitses and Gregg Rickman, 85–92 (New York: Limelight, 1998).

Huemann, Joe, and Robin Murray. "Hydraulic Mining Then and Now: The Case of *Pale Rider* (1985)." In *The Landscape of Hollywood Westerns: Ecocriticism in an American Film Genre,* edited by Deborah A. Carmichael, 94–110. Salt Lake City: University of Utah Press, 2006.

Hughes, Howard. *Aim for the Heart: The Films of Clint Eastwood.* London: I.B. Tauris, 2009.

Hutson, Richard. "'One Hang, We All Hang': *High Plains Drifter.*" In *Clint Eastwood, Actor and Director: New Perspectives,* edited by Leonard Engel, 99–118. Salt Lake City: University of Utah Press, 2007.

———. "Sermons in Stone: Monument Valley in *The Searchers.*" In *The Searchers: Essays and Reflections on John Ford's Classic Western*, edited by Arthur M. Eckstein and Peter Lehman, 93–108. Detroit: Wayne State University Press, 2004.

Johnson, Dorothy M. "The Man Who Shot Liberty Valance." In *The Portable Western Reader*, edited by William Kittredge, 180–195. New York: Penguin, 1997.

Jousse, Thierry, and Camille Nevers. "Interview with Clint Eastwood." In *Clint Eastwood: Interviews*, edited by Robert E. Kapsis and Kathie Coblentz, 176–186. Jackson: University Press of Mississippi, 1999. Previously published as "Entretien avec Clint Eastwood," *Cahiers du cinema*, no. 460 (October 1992): 67–71.

Kalinak, Kathryn. *How the West Was Sung: Music in the Westerns of John Ford*. Berkeley: University of California Press, 2007.

Kapsis, Robert E., and Kathie Coblentz, eds. *Clint Eastwood: Interviews*. Jackson: University Press of Mississippi, 1999.

Keller, Alexandra. "Historical Discourse and American Identity in Westerns since the Reagan Era." In *Hollywood's West: The American Frontier in Film, Television, and History*, edited by Peter C. Rollins and John E. O'Connor, 239–260. Lexington: University Press of Kentucky, 2005.

Kitses, Jim. *Horizons West: Directing the Western from John Ford to Clint Eastwood*. New ed. London: British Film Institute Publishing, 2004.

Kitses, Jim, and Gregg Rickman, eds. *The Western Reader*. New York: Limelight, 1998.

Kittredge, William, ed. *The Portable Western Reader*. New York: Penguin, 1997.

Klypchak, Brad. "'All on Accounta Pullin' a Trigger': Violence, the Media, and the Historical Contextualization of Clint Eastwood's *Unforgiven.*" In *Clint Eastwood, Actor and Director: New Perspectives*, edited by Leonard Engel, 157–171. Salt Lake City: University of Utah Press, 2007.

Knapp, Laurence F. *Directed by Clint Eastwood: Eighteen Films Analyzed*. Jefferson, NC: McFarland, 1996.

Lehman, Peter, ed. *Close Viewings: An Anthology of New Film Criticism*. Tallahassee: Florida State University Press, 1990.

———. "Texas 1868/America 1956: *The Searchers.*" In *Close Viewings: An Anthology of New Film Criticism*, edited by Peter Lehman, 387–415. Tallahassee: Florida State University Press, 1990.

———. "There's No Way of Knowing: Analysis of *The Searchers.*" In *Authorship and Narrative in the Cinema*, edited by William Luhr and Peter Lehman, 85–135. New York: Capricorn Books, 1977.

———. "You Couldn't Hit It on the Nose: The Limits of Knowledge in and of *The Searchers.*" In *The Searchers: Essays and Reflections on John Ford's Classic Western*, edited by Arthur M. Eckstein and Peter Lehman, 239–264. Detroit: Wayne State University Press, 2004.

Lejeune, Anthony. "The Disappearing Cowboy: The Rise and Fall of the Western." *National Review* (December 31, 1989): 23–26.

Le May, Alan. *The Searchers*. New York: Harper and Brothers, 1954.

Lucas, Blake. "Saloon Girls and Ranchers' Daughters: The Woman in the Western." In *The Western Reader,* edited by Jim Kitses and Gregg Rickman, 301–320. New York: Limelight, 1998.

Luhr, William, and Peter Lehman, eds. *Authorship and Narrative in the Cinema.* New York: Capricorn Books, 1977.

Maltby, Richard. "A Better Sense of History: John Ford and the Indians." In *The Book of Westerns,* edited by Ian Cameron and Douglas Pye, 34–49. New York: Continuum, 1996.

Marion, Frances. *Off with Their Heads! A Serio-Comic Tale of Hollywood.* New York: Macmillan, 1972.

———. *The Wind,* script versions and related documents. Warner Brothers Archive, University of Southern California Libraries. Dates for documents consulted include scripts dated February 11, 1927, and February 14–27, 1927; "New Ending Sequence," July 20, 1927; "Editing Continuity List," October 22, 1927; and "Final Title List," August 7, 1928.

McBride, Joseph. *Searching for John Ford: A Life.* New York: St. Martin's Press, 2001.

McCarthy, Todd. *Howard Hawks: The Grey Fox of Hollywood.* New York: Grove Press, 1997.

———. "John Ford and Monument Valley," *American Film* (May 1978): 10–16.

McDonough, Kathleen A. "*Wee Willie Winkie* Goes West: The Influence of the British Empire Genre on Ford's Cavalry Trilogy." In *Hollywood's West: The American Frontier in Film, Television, and History,* edited by Peter C. Rollins and John E. O'Connor, 99–114. Lexington: University Press of Kentucky, 2005.

McGee, Patrick. *From* Shane *to* Kill Bill: *Re-thinking the Western.* Malden, MA: Blackwell, 2007.

McVeigh, Stephen. "Subverting *Shane:* Ambiguities in Eastwood's Politics in *Fistful of Dollars, High Plains Drifter,* and *Pale Rider.*" In *Clint Eastwood, Actor and Director: New Perspectives,* edited by Leonard Engel, 129–156. Salt Lake City: University of Utah Press, 2007.

Miller, Perry. *Errand into the Wilderness.* Cambridge, MA: Harvard University Press, 1956.

Palmer, R. Barton. *Perspectives on Film Noir.* New York: G.K. Hall, 1996.

Paschall, Freedonia, and Robert G. Weiner. "Nature Conquering or Nature Conquered in *The Wind* (1928)." In *The Landscape of Hollywood Westerns: Ecocriticism in an American Film Genre,* edited by Deborah A. Carmichael, 51–60. Salt Lake City: University of Utah Press, 2006.

Paulus, Tom. "'If You Can Call It an Art . . .': Pictorial Style in John Ford's Universal Westerns (1917–1918)." In *John Ford in Focus: Essays on the Filmmaker's Life and Work,* edited by Kevin L. Stoehr and Michael C. Connolly, 131–141. Jefferson, NC: McFarland, 2008.

———. "Ways of Knowing: Peter Lehman and *The Searchers.*" In *John Ford in Focus: Essays on the Filmmaker's Life and Work,* edited by Kevin L. Stoehr and Michael C. Connolly, 76–86. Jefferson, NC: McFarland, 2008.

Pippin, Robert B. *Hollywood Westerns and American Myth: The Importance of Howard Hawks and John Ford for Political Philosophy.* New Haven, CT: Yale University Press, 2010.

Prats, Armando José. *Invisible Natives: Myth and Identity in the American Western.* Ithaca, NY: Cornell University Press, 2002.

Prendergast, Alan. "They Died with Their Boots On: The Decline of the Western." *Rocky Mountain Magazine* (March 1982): 37–40.

Pye, Douglas. "The Collapse of Fantasy: Masculinity in the Westerns of Anthony Mann." In *The Book of Westerns,* edited by Ian Cameron and Douglas Pye, 167–173. New York: Continuum, 1996.

———. "Double Vision: Miscegenation and Point of View in *The Searchers.*" In *The Book of Westerns,* edited by Ian Cameron and Douglas Pye, 229–235. New York: Continuum, 1996.

———. "Genre and History: *Fort Apache* and *The Man Who Shot Liberty Valance.*" In *The Book of Westerns,* edited by Ian Cameron and Douglas Pye, 111–122. New York: Continuum, 1996.

Rollins, Peter C., and John E. O'Connor, eds. *Hollywood's West: The American Frontier in Film, Television, and History.* Lexington: University Press of Kentucky, 2005.

Sanders, Terry, director. *Lillian Gish: An Actor's Life for Me.* 1988. Documentary film. American Film Foundation.

Scarborough, Dorothy. *The Supernatural in Modern English Fiction.* New York: G. P. Putnam's Sons, 1917.

———. *The Wind.* Barker Texas History Center Series. New York: Harper, 1925. Reprint, Austin: University of Texas Press, 1979.

Schama, Simon. *Landscape and Memory.* New York: Vintage, 1996.

Schickel, Richard. *Clint: A Retrospective.* New York: Sterling, 2010.

———. *Clint Eastwood: A Biography.* New York: Knopf, 1996.

Sickels, Robert C. "Beyond the Blessings of Civilization: John Ford's *Stagecoach* and the Myth of the Western Frontier." In *John Ford in Focus: Essays on the Filmmaker's Life and Work,* edited by Kevin L. Stoehr and Michael C. Connolly, 142–152. Jefferson, NC: McFarland, 2008.

———. "Landscapes of Failure in John Ford's *Grapes of Wrath* (1939)." In *The Landscape of Hollywood Westerns: Ecocriticism in an American Film Genre,* edited by Deborah A. Carmichael, 61–80. Salt Lake City: University of Utah Press, 2006.

Silver, Charles. "Ford and the Romantic Tradition." In *John Ford in Focus: Essays on the Filmmaker's Life and Work,* edited by Kevin Stoehr and Michael Connolly, 17–34. Jefferson, NC: McFarland, 2008.

———. *The Western Film.* Pyramid Illustrated History of the Movies Series. New York: Pyramid Publications, 1976.

Simmon, Scott. *The Invention of the Western Film: A Cultural History of the Genre's First Half-Century.* Cambridge: Cambridge University Press, 2003.

Slotkin, Richard. *Gunfighter Nation: The Myth of the Frontier in Twentieth-Century America.* Toronto: Atheneum, 1992.

Smith, Paul. *Clint Eastwood: A Cultural Production*. Minneapolis: University of Minnesota Press, 1993.

Springer, John Parris. "Beyond the River: Women and the Role of the Feminine in Howard Hawks's *Red River*." In *Hollywood's West: The American Frontier in Film, Television, and History*, edited by Peter C. Rollins and John E. O'Connor, 115–125. Lexington: University Press of Kentucky, 2005.

Stanfield, Peter. "Country Music and the 1939 Western: From Hillbillies to Cowboys." In *The Book of Westerns*, edited by Ian Cameron and Douglas Pye, 22–33. New York: Continuum, 1996.

———. *Hollywood, Westerns, and the 1930s: The Lost Trail*. Exeter, U.K.: University of Exeter Press, 2001.

———. *Horse Opera: The Strange History of the 1930s Singing Cowboy*. Champaign: University of Illinois Press, 2002.

Stevens, Brad. *"Pat Garrett and Billy the Kid."* In *The Book of Westerns*, edited by Ian Cameron and Douglas Pye, 269–276. New York: Continuum, 1996.

Stevens, George, Jr., ed. *Conversations with the Great Moviemakers of Hollywood's Golden Age at the American Film Institute*. New York: Vintage, 2006.

Stoehr, Kevin L., and Michael C. Connolly, eds. *John Ford in Focus: Essays on the Filmmaker's Life and Work*. Jefferson, NC: McFarland, 2008.

Studlar, Gaylyn. "Sacred Duties, Poetic Passions: John Ford and the Issue of Femininity in the Western." In *John Ford Made Westerns: Filming the Legend in the Sound Era*, edited by Gaylyn Studlar and Matthew Bernstein, 43–74. Bloomington: Indiana University Press, 2001.

Studlar, Gaylyn, and Matthew Bernstein, eds. *John Ford Made Westerns: Filming the Legend in the Sound Era*. Bloomington: Indiana University Press, 2001.

Thompson, Richard, and Tim Hunter. "Eastwood Direction." In *Clint Eastwood: Interviews*, edited by Robert E. Kapsis and Kathie Coblentz, 42–61. Jackson: University Press of Mississippi, 1999. Previously published as "Clint Eastwood, Auteur," *Film Comment* 14, no. 1 (January–February 1978): 24–32.

Thomson, David. *A Biographical Dictionary of Film*. New York: William Morrow, 1981.

Tibbets, John. "Vital Geography: Victor Seastrom's *The Wind*." In *Passport to Hollywood: The Film Immigrants Anthology*, edited by Don Whittemore and Phillip Alan Cecchettini, 255–261. New York: McGraw-Hill, 1976.

Tibbets, John C. "The Machinery of Violence: Clint Eastwood Talks about *Unforgiven*." In *Clint Eastwood, Actor and Director: New Perspectives*, edited by Leonard Engel, 171–180. Salt Lake City: University of Utah Press, 2007.

Tompkins, Jane. " 'Indians': Textualism, Morality, and the Problem of History," *Critical Inquiry* 13 (Autumn 1986), 101–119.

———. Introduction to *Riders of the Purple Sage*, by Zane Grey. New York: Penguin, 1990.

———. *West of Everything: The Inner Life of Westerns*. Oxford: Oxford University Press, 1992.

Turan, Kenneth. "A Fistful of Memories: An Interview with Clint Eastwood." 1992. In *The Western Reader*, edited by Jim Kitses and Gregg Rickman, 245–249. New York: Limelight, 1998.

Turner, Matthew R. "Cowboys and Comedy: The Simultaneous Deconstruction and Reinforcement of Generic Conventions in the Western Parody." In *Hollywood's West: The American Frontier in Film, Television, and History,* edited by Peter C. Rollins and John E. O'Connor, 218–238. Lexington: University Press of Kentucky, 2005.

Van Doren, Carl. *The American Novel, 1789–1939.* New York: Macmillan, 1947.

Walker, Michael. "*Dances with Wolves.*" In *The Book of Westerns,* edited by Ian Cameron and Douglas Pye, 284–293. New York: Continuum, 1996.

———. "The Westerns of Delmer Daves." In *The Book of Westerns,* edited by Ian Cameron and Douglas Pye, 123–160. New York: Continuum, 1996.

Warshow, Robert. "Movie Chronicle: The Westerner." In *The Western Reader,* edited by Jim Kitses and Gregg Rickman, 35–48. New York: Limelight, 1998.

Westbrook, Brett. "Feminism and the Limits of Genre in *A Fistful of Dollars* and *The Outlaw Josey Wales.*" In *Clint Eastwood, Actor and Director: New Perspectives,* edited by Leonard Engel, 24–48. Salt Lake City: University of Utah Press, 2007.

Whittemore, Don, and Phillip Alan Cecchettini, eds. *Passport to Hollywood: The Film Immigrants Anthology.* New York: McGraw-Hill, 1976.

Wicking, Christopher, and Barrie Pattison. "Interview with Anthony Mann." In *The Western Reader,* edited by Jim Kitses and Gregg Rickman, 201–208. New York: Limelight, 1998.

Wollen, Peter [as Lee Russell]. "Budd Boetticher." In *The Western Reader,* edited by Jim Kitses and Gregg Rickman, 195–200. New York: Limelight, 1998.

Wood, Robin. "*Drums along the Mohawk.*" In *The Book of Westerns,* edited by Ian Cameron and Douglas Pye, 174–180. New York: Continuum, 1996.

———. "*Duel in the Sun.*" In *The Book of Westerns,* edited by Ian Cameron and Douglas Pye, 189–195. New York: Continuum, 1996.

———. "'Shall We Gather at the River?': The Late Films of John Ford." In *John Ford Made Westerns: Filming the Legend in the Sound Era,* edited by Gaylyn Studlar and Matthew Bernstein, 23–42. Bloomington: Indiana University Press, 2001.

Woolland, Brian. "Class Frontiers: The View through *Heaven's Gate.*" In *The Book of Westerns,* edited by Ian Cameron and Douglas Pye, 277–283. New York: Continuum, 1996.

Index